WAR AND UNDERDEVELOPMENT

Volume I

War and Underdevelopment

Volume I
The Economic and Social Consequences of Conflict

FRANCES STEWART AND VALPY FITZGERALD
AND ASSOCIATES

OXFORD
UNIVERSITY PRESS

OXFORD
UNIVERSITY PRESS

Great Clarendon Street, Oxford OX2 6DP
Oxford University Press is a department of the University of Oxford.
It furthers the University's objective of excellence in research, scholarship,
and education by publishing worldwide in

Oxford New York

Athens Auckland Bangkok Bogotá Buenos Aires Calcutta
Cape Town Chennai Dar es Salaam Delhi Florence Hong Kong Istanbul
Karachi Kuala Lumpur Madrid Melbourne Mexico City Mumbai
Nairobi Paris São Paulo Shanghai Singapore Taipei Tokyo Toronto Warsaw
and associated companies in Berlin Ibadan

Oxford is a registered trade mark of Oxford University Press
in the UK and certain other countries

Published in the United States
by Oxford University Press Inc., New York

British Library Cataloguing in Publication Data
Data available

Library of Congress Cataloging in Publication Data
Stewart, Frances.
War and underdevelopment / Frances Stewart and Valpy FitzGerald and associates.
p. cm.
Includes bibliographical references and index.
Contents: v. 1. The economic and social costs of conflict—v. 2. Country experiences.
1. War—Economic aspects. 2. Economic development. I. Fitzgerald, Valpy. II. Title.
HC79.D4 S74 2001   338.9—dc21   00-060668

ISBN 0-19-924186-4 (vol. 1, cloth)
ISBN 0-19-924187-2 (vol. 1, pbk)
ISBN 0-19-924188-0 (vol. 2, cloth)
ISBN 0-19-924189-9 (vol. 2, pbk)

1 3 5 7 9 10 8 6 4 2

Typeset by Graphicraft Limited, Hong Kong
Printed in Great Britain
on acid-free paper by
T.J. International Ltd.,
Padstow, Cornwall

PREFACE

This study attempts to address a vital issue of our time to which development economists have devoted far too little attention. When embarking upon this research in 1994 we found very little academic literature or rigorous data, and few scholars focusing on the topic. This enabled us to make a fresh start and gave us the opportunity to build up a new multidisciplinary team of researchers, mostly young scholars completing their doctoral research or assuming their first research posts at Queen Elizabeth. This combination of a new start and a fresh team lead us down unexpected paths and generated an unusual degree of interdisciplinary debate, pulled together by a common sense of the seriousness of the task at hand.

The research programme that is reported on in these volumes was partly funded by the Department for International Development and the Swedish International Development Cooperation Agency. We are grateful for their support, and also the free hand we were given in the development of our own agenda. Valuable editorial assistance was provided by Kate Raworth and Maureen Hadfield. Finally, research at Queen Elizabeth House is greatly facilitated by the efficient and enthusiastic support given by our administrative and library staff—we would particularly like to thank Denise Watt, Wendy Grist, Roger Crawford, Sheila Allcock, and Julia Knight.

The results of the research programme are presented in two related volumes. Volume I is devoted to general analysis of the economics of conflict, derived from analytic and empirical work, while Volume II contains seven in-depth case studies of countries in conflict. The countries studied were Afghanistan, Mozambique, Nicaragua, Sierra Leone, Sri Lanka, Sudan, and Uganda.

EVF and FS

CONTENTS

ABBREVIATIONS AND ACRONYMS

ADB	African Development Bank
BAAG	British Agencies Afghanistan Group
BMS	Breast Milk Substitute
CAFOD	Catholic Fund for Overseas Development
CARE	Cooperative for Assistance and Relief Everywhere (USA)
CONFAID	Conflict-Related Food Aid
DAC	Development Assistance Committee (OECD)
DEVFAID	Development-Related Food Aid
DHA	(UN) Department of Humanitarian Affairs
EC	European Community
ECOMOG	Economic Community of West African States Ceasefire Monitoring Group
EIU	Economist Intelligence Unit
FAO	Food and Agriculture Organization
FEWS	Famine Early Warning System (USAID)
GDP	Gross Domestic Product
GNP	Gross National Product
HIPC	Highly Indebted and Poor Countries
ICRC	International Committee of the Red Cross
IDS	Institute of Development Studies
IFI	International financial institutions
IFPRI	International Food Policy Research Institute
IISS	International Institute for Strategic Studies
IMR	Infant Mortality Rate
LDC	Less-Developed Country
LIC	Low Income Countries
LLDC	Least-Developed Countries
LTTE	Liberation Tamil Tigers of Eelam
NGO	Non-Government Organizations
ODA	Official Development Assistance
OLS	Operation Lifeline Sudan
RUF	Revolutionary United Front
SCA	Swedish Committee for Agriculture
SCF	Save the Children Fund
SIDA	Swedish International Development Authority
SIPRI	Stockholm International Peace Research Institute
SPLA	Sudan People's Liberation Army
UNCERO	United Nations Coordination for Emergency and Relief Operations
UNCTAD	United Nations Conference on Trade and Development
UNDP	United Nations Development Programme

UNHCR	United Nations High Commission for Refugees
UNICEF	United Nations Children's Fund
UNOCHA	United Nations Office for the Coordination of Humanitarian Affairs
UNRISD	United Nations Research Institute for Social Development
UNSYB	United Nations Statistical Yearbook
USAID	United States Agency for International Aid
USCR	United States Committee for Refugees
WIDER	World Institute for Development Economics Research
WFP	World Food Programme
WTO	World Trade Organization

1

Introduction: Assessing the Economic Costs of War

FRANCES STEWART AND VALPY FITZGERALD

> Among the casualties of war may jointly be numbered the diminution of the love
> of truth, by the falsehoods which interest dictates and credibility encourages.
>
> Samuel Johnson, *The Idler*, 11 Nov. 1758

1 War and Underdevelopment

War in general, and civil war in particular, is one of the main causes of human suffering and economic underdevelopment. Yet despite this, economic analysis of developing countries at war is relatively rare.

While the global confrontation between capitalism and communism during the Cold War did not result in nuclear Armageddon, throughout the forty-year period a number of countries in the 'Third World' were at war. Between 1950 and 1990, some fifteen million deaths were caused directly or indirectly by wars of all types in developing countries—including international conflicts, civil war, and government violence against citizens—as Table 1.1 indicates.[1]

With the end of the Cold War, there was a transition towards peace in many of the areas in which conflict had been fuelled by East–West antagonism. But as this antagonism declined from the 1980s onward, new wars erupted which were notably different from the wars by proxy and processes of anti-colonial struggle and national liberation which had characterized developing country wars during the Cold War era. These wars, however, continued to be located almost exclusively in developing countries: from 1989 to 1995, there were between 31 and 54 internationally recorded conflicts in each year, and an average of 15 major wars occurring at any time.

Some older ideological conflicts persisted in a different form, such as that in Afghanistan, while other long-lasting separatist conflicts became stronger, such as in Sri Lanka and Eritrea. The Central American conflicts drew to a close in an uneasy stalemate, but there was a renewed outbreak in Mexico. Ethnic and territorial conflicts which had remained submerged during the Cold War erupted in Eastern Europe—particularly the former Yugoslavia—and the peripheral Russian territories. Last but not least, an alarming number of African countries (including Somalia, Sierra Leone,

---

[1] Includes deaths due to famine induced by war, but not the effect of increases (or less rapid falls than would be otherwise be the case) in rates of infant mortality.

Table 1.1 Wars in the Third World: Estimates of direct and indirect deaths (1,000s)

	1950s	1960s	1970s	1980s	1990–5
Africa	150	2,675	711	2,786	2,060
Asia and the Far East	18	2,084	3,360	1,545	77
Latin America	311	54	136	198	65
Middle East	4	180	87	1,165	239
TOTAL	483	4,893	4,494	5,694	2,441

Sources: Sivard 1991, 1996.

Rwanda, and the Congo) became embroiled in armed conflict, adding to long-running civil wars in Angola and Ethiopia, betraying any optimism arising from the settlements in Uganda, Mozambique, and South Africa.

That war is very costly in terms of the sacrifice of human lives and social and economic development is a truism, of which we are reminded daily by television, radio, and the press. War is universally condemned and that condemnation regularly enshrined in international conventions, which particularly stress the obligation to protect non-combatants. None the less, the precise mechanisms through which these adverse effects occur, and whether they can be offset or prevented, is much less often discussed. While much has been written by historians on the economic costs, and benefits (such as technological and organizational progress), of military activity in industrial countries,[2] modern development economists tend to treat countries at war as subject to exogenous developments which take them outside the normal realms of analysis.[3]

War and its effects were not mentioned by the UNDP in the first *Human Development Report* in 1990 as a cause of failure in human development, despite the fact that the disruptions due to war were a major feature of at least half the worst performers on human development. Seven years later, the 1997 *Human Development Report*, devoted to analysing poverty, again failed to give any in-depth consideration to countries at war. Yet among the ten countries listed with the lowest Human Development Index eight have suffered serious civil wars in recent years—Mozambique, Eritrea, Ethiopia, Rwanda, Sierra Leone, Niger, Mali, and Guinea. In fact half of the fifty countries classified by the UN as 'least developed' have experienced major armed conflict in the last twenty years (UN 1998; see also FitzGerald 2000). Nor does the World Bank's 'Poverty Reduction Strategy' make any reference to countries at war (see World Bank 1998), although countries which have suffered civil war account for eight out of the ten

---

[2] Economists have been less interested in the social distribution of the costs of war, although—as is so frequently the case—Keynes is an exception and regarded this question as a central one in war finance (Keynes 1939, which is extensively discussed in Chapter 2 of this volume).

[3] There are of course exceptions—such as Green (1992) on Southern Africa, FitzGerald (1987) on Nicaragua, Cranna (1994) covering a number of conflict economies—but no coherent body of economic analysis. Recent work on post-war reconstruction in Africa (e.g. Collier and Gunning 1995) refers to wartime conditions but mainly in contrast to peacetime 'normality' rather than as a subject in itself.

countries with the highest infant mortality rates and of those with the lowest per capita incomes.

At best, the Bretton Woods institutions appear to see armed conflicts in or between developing countries as temporary interruptions to an established economic development path, despite the fact that war conditions are a major reason why the adjustment programmes they recommend often fail to work (Mosley and Weeks 1993). In particular, almost no effort has been made to consider what economic policies might be appropriate for both governments and donors during a war which may extend for long periods. For instance, the World Bank programme for Mozambique in the middle of a long war was designed to provide a framework for more effective use of resources 'when the security situation and other exogenous constraints have eased' (Wuyts 1991).

This book attempts to make a start in overcoming this neglect. We believe that this enterprise is justified for at least three reasons: first, because conflict is a major source of poverty and underdevelopment, which is likely to continue since there is no reason to believe that armed conflict in developing countries will cease or even diminish during the coming decades; second, because policies can only be devised to reduce the economic and human costs of conflict if we understand how economies operate during conflict; third, because understanding economic behaviour and motivation during conflict is essential for developing policies to end or reduce war.

1.1   A Typology of Countries at War

In this study we define war as systematic physical violence and killing conducted for political purposes—that is, to gain or sustain political power. This power is essentially reflected in the control of the state, either that constituted within the existing territory or a separate entity. Within this general objective, particular groups also pursue economic objectives: as we shall demonstrate, these latter aims can become a reason for prolonging conflict beyond the point when the achievement of political goals seems feasible.

War, and armed conflict in general, is not a homogeneous phenomenon. Wars vary in magnitude, whether they are inter- or intranational, the nature and extent of foreign intervention and the technology adopted. Our study is only concerned with major armed conflicts[4] as distinct from localized social violence and organized crime which, although they can have enormous human costs, are all too often a characteristic of 'peace' in developing countries. Our concern in this study is with civil wars, most of which involve significant foreign intervention.[5] They are thus distinct from 'traditional' international or inter-state wars, where the power of the state is often increased as a result of war, and nationalism can contribute to greater domestic social trust and cohesion. In contrast, civil wars tend to reduce the control of the state over the national territory and lead to societal disintegration. In the period with which we are concerned the degree and kind of foreign intervention was an important differentiating characteristic among conflicts.

---

[4] Which we have defined as those involving deaths of at least 1,000 per year.
[5] We are not concerned, therefore, with 'classical' inter-state conflicts over frontier disputes or territorial expansion, which has been notably rare in developing countries—Kashmir being one of the exceptions.

During the height of the Cold War, many 'civil wars' were virtually initiated by foreign powers as part of a broader global strategy. Foreign intervention, in the form of financial and military support, determined the course of conflict: Korea, Vietnam, and Afghanistan are examples. These wars were more internally divisive than most international wars because the foreign invaders gained the support of parts of the population and aroused strong opposition of others.

Towards the end of the Cold War, what the major powers described as 'low intensity'[6] wars emerged, locally initiated but with strong foreign logistical, financial, and political support for local opposition groups, for example in Nicaragua, Mozambique, and Angola. Such wars tended to involve bigger internal divisions, since the foreign supporters were responding to (and enhancing) local divisions, and smaller international resource flows than the foreign-initiated ones. In these wars, nationalist and liberation objectives were an important motivation among the local population, while geopolitical considerations motivated the foreign sponsors.

Conflicts also broke out in a number of countries after their liberation struggles. In some, these were initiated by governments, seeking to suppress potential opposition.[7] In others, they were initiated by opposition groups seeking to gain power over the whole territory, or independence for part of it. In practice, the difference between these two types is not always clear—as is illustrated by the cases of Cambodia, El Salvador, Sudan, Guatemala, and Ethiopia. Foreigners still generally played an active role in these conflicts, but in a distinct way—aid was humanitarian rather than military, while military material was supplied by the international market rather than directly by the major powers. Regional intervention—with support for local groups with strong ties with neighbouring countries—is a fairly common feature. Fundamental weakening of social cohesion tends to be a frequent outcome of these wars. Some such conflicts occur in countries with strong governments, which remain powerful and able to raise and dispense resources even after years of conflict (for example, Sri Lanka). But in many cases, the government either starts by being weak or becomes weak as a result of conflict (Somalia is an example).

A weak government may permit conflict to arise, and persist, among rival groups seeking to control resources. One group may take over the state, but since state resources are small and it is difficult for those in power to impose order, it may soon be displaced by rival groups. Examples are Somalia, Afghanistan for some years between the Soviet period and the Taliban victory, and Sierra Leone. The strength of the government is thus an important differentiating characteristic since in the 'weak' government case there is no authority to prevent an anarchical situation with a disruptive effect on economic activity—particularly in the formal sector—while it is especially difficult for the government to maintain revenue and provide basic services.

The military strategy adopted varies across the conflicts and may change as the conflict develops. The prevalent strategy is an important influence on the conflict's economic

---

[6] The term 'low intensity' refers to the decision of the major powers not to commit their own troops rather than any lack of human suffering on the ground: in this sense the concept also includes the Gulf War and the NATO intervention in Kosovo. US military doctrine attributes defeat in the Vietnam War to the unwillingness of the electorate to sacrifice its own children (the 'body bag' syndrome) for national geostrategic objectives.   [7] Halevi (2000) argues that most civil wars are in fact of this nature.

and social consequences. Some wars are mainly confined to one part of the country, while others range over the whole country. Where foreigners are heavily involved, bombing or mining is common, while the military strategy of 'low intensity war' involves the deliberate destruction not only (or even primarily) of the opponent's military capacity but rather of economic and social infrastructure in order to reduce popular support. This deliberate undermining of the means of livelihood of opposing forces clearly increases the human costs of conflict. In contrast, many of the post-liberation, locally initiated conflicts rely on very low-level technology, such as handguns and machetes, which can have devastating effects on human lives, but are less immediately destructive of physical infrastructure.

2   The Economic Analysis of the Human Costs of War

The greater part of the human costs of war does not result directly from battle deaths and injuries, but rather 'indirectly' from the loss of livelihoods caused by the dislocation of economy and society resulting from conflict. In most cases civilian deaths are far greater than military losses, one indication of the proportionate importance of indirect casualties—that is, those casualties not directly due to the physical violence, but which result from lack of access to food and health facilities, which can lead to deaths on a massive scale as well as widespread debilitation. One of the objectives of our research has been to substantiate this important point[8] which has profound policy implications. If we are to understand the causes of these human costs, in the hope of reducing them, it is essential that we attempt to understand the processes that occur during an economy at war—in particular, the ways in which conflict affects economic activity and institutional behaviour at the international, macro- and mesolevels[9] so as to see how this affects people's well-being at the microlevel.

2.1   *The Costs of War as Entitlement Losses (and Gains)*

It might seem that the economic and social costs of war could be divided into two categories—the immediate human costs and the longer term development costs. This division appears attractive as it reflects the discourse of external intervention in conflict situations, which usually separates 'humanitarian assistance' from 'development cooperation'. However, this division is somewhat misleading because human costs, such as worsened nutrition and education, constitute development costs, while development

---

[8] The fact that this point is often overlooked may arise from media presentation of conflict, which tends to stress the drama of battle itself.

[9] We employ the term 'mesolevel' rather than 'sectoral' because the concept embraces not only production sectors as such (e.g. agriculture) but also the fiscal sector, traded versus non-traded sectors, regional markets and so on—all of which have their own institutional structure which mediate between the macroeconomy (national and international) and the microeconomy (i.e. the household or firm). The impact of a macroeconomic shift (e.g. devaluation) on firms and households—and thus on production, distribution, and accumulation—depends on the intervening mesoeconomic behaviour.

costs, such as the destruction of infrastructure or declining exports, are among the causes of human suffering. From the point of view of vulnerable groups, it would seem clearer to start from the notion that the human costs of conflict (other than the immediate deaths and injuries from fighting) arise from the destruction of *entitlements*.

Entitlements consist in the various forms of command over resources that permits people to have access to essential goods and services such as food, water, health services, or education. The term was famously applied by Sen for his analysis of famines (see Sen 1981)—where insufficient (or loss of existing) entitlements prevented vulnerable groups from acquiring adequate supplies of food. This concept of entitlement refers to all forms of legal income from work, assets, and transfers; and differentiates explicitly between *direct* entitlements acquired by subsistence farming, for example, and *market* entitlements, acquired through monetary transactions on the market. Sen concludes, therefore, that entitlement failure can frequently arise from employment loss or from an increase in food prices relative to monetary incomes rather than from a failure of aggregate food availability as such. However, his taxonomy and analysis essentially relate to peacetime, where the rule of law prevails, markets as a whole function properly, and the authorities are unchallenged and are in some sense legitimate.[10] As it stands, therefore, Sen's approach to entitlements is not well suited to the analysis of conflict.

In this study we have found it necessary to distinguish between five distinct types of entitlement: market, direct, public, civic, and extra-legal entitlements.

• *Market* entitlements are monetary entitlements gained from work and the ownership of assets, whose value depends on the returns to work (wages or sales of produce) and assets (rents) on the one hand, and the price of essentials, such as food, on the other.

• *Direct* entitlements refer to goods and services which are produced and consumed on a shared basis by the same household or extended family without a process of exchange as such—sometimes known as subsistence production but also including much of women's work.

• *Public* entitlements are the access to publicly provided goods and services which in theory are secured by virtue of citizenship—although in practice they may be reserved to particular groups. Of particular relevance to human well-being during war are public entitlements to health services, education, water, and sanitation, as well as the public provision of free or subsidized food.

• *Civic* entitlements refer to goods and services provided by a local community or non-governmental organizations, often in response to the collapse of public entitlements or in response to a level of poverty which prevents adequate market entitlements.

• Finally, *extra-legal* entitlements[11] are entitlements acquired by theft or threat of force. These can be an important source of survival during war for individuals or even social groups; although equally their mirror image—the loss of market or direct entitlements through theft—may be an important source of *loss* of entitlements for others, sometimes leading to destitution or death.

---

[10] Essentially those of the Indian subcontinent.
[11] 'Extra-legal' rather than 'illegal' because we are concerned with situations where the rule of law has seriously deteriorated.

The first two of the above five categories are the same as those identified by Sen. The three we have added are particularly important for the analysis of human livelihoods in wartime—and by extension of most 'humanitarian emergencies'. We have added public entitlements because access to publicly provided health and education services, sanitation, and water is an important source of well-being. Their destruction during conflict is one of the major adverse effects of war, leading to rising mortality, especially when people move into crowded camps and infections spread rapidly (see, e.g. de Waal 1989). Civic entitlements can constitute an important compensatory mechanism, as the community and NGOs work to offset the destruction of market and public entitlements, but they too may also fall, constituting a further cost of war, as communities break up and services that are normally taken for granted (such as small loans) no longer occur.[12] Above all, it is impossible to analyse the costs of war without considering *extra-legal* entitlements, since they form such an important dimension of warfare itself in developing countries.[13] This extension of the concept of entitlements is not only essential for analysis of war, but would also be helpful for a deeper understanding of other crisis situations, including both famines and natural disasters, on the one hand, and situations of chronic structural poverty, on the other.

The human costs of war arise from destruction of entitlements: but war also leads to the creation of entitlements for some groups, as will be clear from the studies below. These gains then act to provide an economic motive for prolongation of conflict. Hence the analysis needs to consider both losses and gains in entitlements.

2.2 The Distributional Consequences of War

The analysis of the impact of war needs to differentiate between the effects of conflict on the aggregate supply of goods and services and the impact on the entitlements of vulnerable groups whose basic needs satisfaction is near survival levels. There is a often a presumption that falls in aggregate supply will adversely affect the entitlements of the vulnerable, and conversely that if output is maintained, the vulnerable will be protected. Neither of these presumptions is invariably correct. War is a time of dramatic changes, so that a group may lose drastically even while aggregate output is rising, and in some contexts the apparently vulnerable may be protected despite large output loss. The categories of vulnerable and non-vulnerable can also change, with previously better-off groups being targeted—such as the Dinkas in Sudan, or the Tutsis in Rwanda. The extent of private income gains of small groups of people—capitalist war profiteers at one level, and previously near-destitute who gain jobs as soldiers and incomes through looting at another—induces the gainers to try and perpetuate the war.[14]

Hence it is important to identify the distributional changes during conflict. In a society that is divided by ethnic or territorial divisions, the conventional measure of income distribution in terms of *vertical* inequality is not always appropriate. Changes in vertical distribution are especially important where they indicate that deteriorating

---

[12] See Chapter 5, Vol. II on Sri Lanka. [13] See Chapter 3, this volume.
[14] See Chapter 3, this volume.

distribution is accentuating the negative effects of worsening macroeconomic performance for the poor. None the less, it is rarely the case that vertical conflict as such (e.g.
between rich and poor, or between landlords and landless) has been the main motive
force for armed conflict in developing countries during recent decades.

Descriptions of vertical distribution arrange individuals or households on the basis of
their incomes, expenditure or other measure of well-being such as satisfaction of basic
needs or access to public services. This will tell us little about the relative shares in
entitlements of the particular groups involved in the conflict—in other words *horizontal*
inequality.[15] It is important to assess changing horizontal inequalities, because they
are a potent source of conflict, especially if they occur along a number of dimensions
including political access and control as well as economic entitlements (see Stewart
2000). Persistent or widening horizontal inequalities are likely to fuel conflict, while
peace-making normally requires narrowing of horizontal inequality in both political
and economic dimensions. Hence what happens to horizontal inequality as a consequence of the conflict is of importance for assessing both the human costs of conflict to
different groups and also whether the course of the conflict is enhancing or diminishing
the inequalities which were a contributory cause of the conflict.

While the definition of vertical inequality is relatively simple in principle, identifying the appropriate groups for measuring horizontal inequality presents some fundamental difficulties. This is not just a measurement problem: group differentiation is not
based on objective differences between people, rather it is socially constructed in order
to mobilize people for political purposes. Group construction is thus dynamic and fluid,
changing with circumstances. In some situations, group identification may be widely
recognized: for example, where a conflict has been ongoing for many years or the lines
of differentiation are clearly drawn geographically. In other cases, groups may split
or new groups may emerge in response to the development of the war itself. Indeed,
the identification of groups for the purpose of reducing horizontal inequality may even
change the conflict situation itself by reinforcing distinctions, or creating perceived
political advantages in new alliances and groupings.[16] None the less, because horizontal
inequalities can be so important as a cause of conflict, it is essential to monitor them so
as to be able to design policies which reduce them.

3   The Economy in Wartime

3.1   The Vulnerability of the Economy at War

The economic effects of war are the result of an interaction between a particular type of
war and the economy in which it takes place, which define its 'vulnerability'. Those

---

[15] It is technically possible to have sharp vertical inequality in any dimension without any horizontal
inequality—for example if the average income of all groups were the same and distribution within each group
were highly unequal (with the same inequality within each group). Conversely, it is possible to have considerable inter-group inequality, while overall societal vertical inequality is small because intra-group inequality is
small.   [16]   This is particularly true where foreign aid allocations are in question.

characteristics which seem to be most important are: the average income level and the proportion of the population at or near poverty; the degree of self-subsistence of the population, and especially the poor; the economy's reliance on essential imports; and the flexibility of the production system.

• The *average level of income* of an economy is an important determinant of what proportion of the population is near or below the poverty line—where people are already near the edge of survival a substantial reduction in their entitlements can have devastating consequences in terms of survival.

• A *large agricultural subsistence sector* can help people to protect their living standards during conflict so long as this is not directly destroyed by war. In contrast, heavy dependence of the population on product or labour markets can cause vulnerability where these are undermined by war. Similarly, if people have not had significant access to public entitlements, they will not suffer so much from their loss; it follows that urban populations may suffer more than rural ones. Since high subsistence tends to be associated with low-income economies, this characteristic may act as a moderately protecting feature for low-income economies, despite the fact that many people are near to survival levels of income.

• *Heavy import dependence* for essential commodities, such fuel or food, makes economies especially vulnerable to disruptions in international trade, in the form of conflict-induced loss of export markets or interruptions to normal supply routes. By extension, reliance on particular primary exports produced in war zones also increases vulnerability.

• In contrast, a *'flexible' economy*[17] which can readily switch production to substitute for imports or replace lost exports is clearly less vulnerable. Again, where capacity utilization is low, a potential exists for compensating for destruction of capital by fuller use of the remaining capacity. A flexible industry can also rapidly replace essential facilities in a form that is less vulnerable to attack; flexibility is also often exhibited in the informal sector which is less dependent on specific inputs.[18]

The economic consequences are clearly highly dependent on the nature of the war itself. Most obviously, the duration of the war is an important element. In a long war, reserves will be exhausted, so vulnerability is increased. However, people will have more time to adapt their lifestyles to the war context, and so protect their productivity and living standards. The geographic spread of the war is also important. When confined to one part of the country the war may have only small direct effects on the economy as a whole, thus reducing national vulnerability, although where war expenditures are high in relation to the resources of the state, the indirect social costs can become very large, increasing vulnerability. The extent of foreign involvement in the war is another factor affecting vulnerability, since external support may compensate for lost export earnings.

---

[17] This was a characteristic of the German economy during WW II (US Government 1945). More generally, this kind of flexibility is also a key factor in reducing developing countries' vulnerability to external trade shocks (Killick 1995).   [18] As in the case of Mozambique—see Chapter 3, Vol. II.

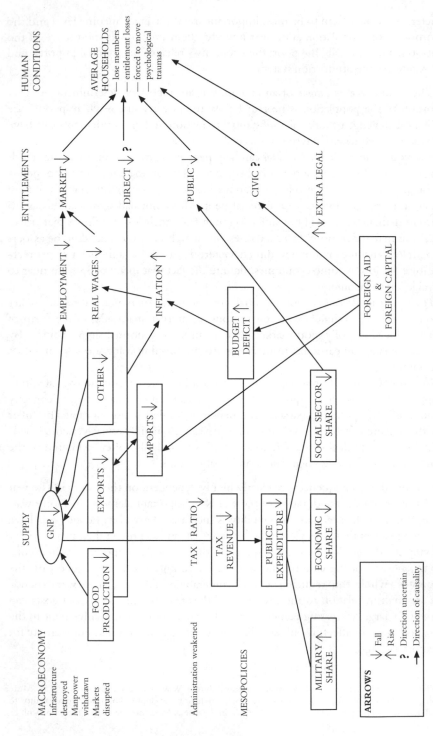

Figure 1.1 A diagrammatic representation tracing the expected human costs of war

3.2 Changes in Economic Behaviour in Wartime

There are complex interactions in an economy resulting from war. Analytically, it is helpful to distinguish between the economic consequences of the direct impact of the conflict on the one hand, and of the compensating behaviour of economic agents in their attempt to moderate or offset the negative impacts of war, on the other. Figure 1.1. provides an overview of the main relationships likely to be affected, with arrows indicating the direction of causality and expected direction of impact.

There are certain direct effects arising from conflict, which cause other effects as they work their way through the economy. These effects include: output loss as people move from their place of work because they join the fighting, are killed, or flee;[19] the destruction of capital (such as large energy plants) through bombing or arson, and consequent loss of output; disruption of transport due to physical destruction; the loss of trust between economic agents, reducing market transactions; the disruption of international markets due to frontier closure or embargoes; and the diversion of scarce foreign exchange from economic and social needs to military uses.

These effects will tend to reduce aggregate levels of output, including exports. Reduced agricultural output, and disrupted internal and international markets are particularly likely to affect exports adversely. Labour markets will be disarticulated as unskilled men of prime working age are particularly hit by violent deaths and military recruitment; while skilled labour is most likely to leave the country. Hence an important indirect effect will be reduced foreign exchange availability for productive inputs leading to a shortage of imported inputs and, consequently, to a further fall in output and exports.

Compensating behaviour which can moderate the negative impact of the effects of war include:

- increased capacity utilization, making up for destruction of capacity, and substituting for imports;
- provision of international credit or 'aid', offsetting loss of foreign exchange;
- the emergence of new forms of social capital compensating for loss of trust in formal transactions—such as enhanced cooperation and trust among members of a group on the same side of the war;
- rapid government or community action to reconstruct facilities destroyed by belligerents.

The ability to take compensating action depends on the vulnerability of the economy, as we have stated above. This in turn depends in part on the nature of the economy and in part on the nature of the war. For example, an economy heavily dependent on the agricultural sector and agricultural exports will be especially badly affected by widespread disruption of agriculture, but may be less badly affected by loss of imported inputs. An inflexible economy with a sizeable industrial sector may suffer little direct loss, but may be particularly vulnerable to foreign exchange loss. However, this would

---

[19] Agriculture is most likely to be affected by movement of people; it can also be seriously affected by mining.

matter less if outside grants or credit were available. An economy with a flexible industrial sector operating at less than full capacity may suffer little, as it will be able to make up for loss of imports by domestic production—the UK in World War II is a classic example.

3.2.1   The macroeconomic consequences

In consequence, the net impact of war on macroeconomic variables is complex but likely to be generally adverse.[20]

• *GDP per capita* is generally likely to be adversely affected (i.e. either to fall or to rise less than it would have done in the absence of conflict), as a result both of direct and indirect effects. How large these direct effects are will depend on the extent to which capacity was fully used prior to the conflict. Indirect effects arise from the knock-on effects of the direct effects; for example, the loss of a power plant not only constitutes a loss in output in itself, but leads other production facilities to close down or operate at lower levels. Reduced finance for (or access to) imports, arising from loss of export earnings, reduced external finance etc., may have a multiplier effect on domestic production (FitzGerald 1987).

• *Domestic savings* are likely to fall in absolute terms, as incomes fall. It is difficult to predict, *a priori*, whether the marginal propensity to save will rise or fall: on the one hand, it might be expected to fall as people attempt to sustain their consumption levels at 'permanent' levels in the face of unexpectedly falling incomes; on the other, precautionary reasons for sustaining savings will increase, and the non-availability of consumption goods may lead to forced savings (di Addario 1997). 'Forced' foreign savings may also arise, through government or private-sector failure to meet interest or amortization due on debt. It seems probable that voluntary *private* lending from abroad would fall with falling confidence; but official foreign lending might either increase or fall, depending on political factors.[21]

• *Investment* is likely to fall in wartime. Private (domestic and foreign) investment will be adversely affected by lesser confidence in the future, lesser trust, and greater costs of transport and communications, raising transaction costs. Local investment is likely to find increasing difficulties in getting access to finance. Foreign investors will be concerned about the safety of their personnel and are likely to perceive a greater foreign exchange risk. Government investment is likely to be negatively affected by reduced revenue, and diversion of expenditure to military uses (see below). Falling investment will affect the growth of GDP adversely.

• *Government revenue* is likely to fall absolutely and as a proportion of GNP as the government finds it more difficult to collect taxes and major sources of revenue (for example, exports) fall away. *Government expenditure* may be restrained by any fall in revenue, although probably not proportionately so that government deficits are likely to rise.

• The logical expectation is that *inflation* is liable to accelerate, as governments resort to deficit financing to finance the conflict and other essential services on the one hand,

----

[20] See also Chapter 2, this volume.   [21] See Chapter 8, this volume.

and public confidence in the currency declines on the other. The price of food is the most important price during wars because that determines the level of food entitlements for non-food producers. While deficit finance can have major inflationary effects on the food price, it is also subject to other influences: one is the effect of falls in supply because of disruptions in production and trade; another is the activities of speculative traders (see Ravallion, 1985); a third influence is government policy towards food subsidies and food distribution (including food aid). Apart from the last, these influences would tend to lead to a rise in the price of food—but against this, severe loss of monetary entitlements may lead to reduced effective demand for food and hence have a moderating effect on the food price.

3.2.2 *Mesolevel consequences*
The adverse macro-effects, with falling real aggregates of expenditure and output, form the background to the meso-changes. Changes are likely to occur in the sectoral distribution of both the private and public sector in response to the conditions of war. War puts new demands on the economy, constrains some opportunities through disrupted markets and raises transaction costs, all of which have implications for sectoral allocation.

• Within the *private sector*, we may expect transaction-intensive activities to fall relative to less transaction-intensive ones (Collier and Gunning 1995). This means that activities involving a higher proportion of sales between agents, those needing a large amount of working capital and those with significant transport requirements are likely to be discouraged. This would imply relatively more subsistence production, reduced formal and increased informal sector activity; proportionately less manufacturing and less long-distance trading domestically and internationally.

• Within *government expenditure*, we may expect increasing resources devoted to military uses, and hence a squeeze on other expenditures including both economic and social. However, although this is the general expectation, the level and distribution of public expenditure will vary according to the nature of the government.

4   Poverty and Development in Wartime

4.1   *The Consequences for Poor Households*

Poor households are critically affected by the changing economic situation, not least because household composition itself is altered by the conflict: adult men join the army, are killed or migrate; women acquire greater responsibilities, often as head of household and chief provider; opportunities for women and younger family members may also open as traditional attitudes are undermined by war.

Both market and public entitlements decline on average in wartime, often disproportionately for poor households. Market entitlements decline as a result of reduced employment and real wages, with the losses in production and rising inflation noted above. These entitlement losses can be dramatic and life-threatening in contexts when food prices escalate—as in the Bengal famine of the 1940s, which Sen attributed to war deficit financing.[22]

Direct entitlements (subsistence production for the family or group) may rise as people retreat from the market, but this can only occur if they have access to land and security conditions do not deteriorate so much that subsistence food production is undermined.[23] Public entitlements to social services (including basic needs such as water) would in general be expected to fall as absolute levels of government expenditure are curtailed and the welfare share within this falls.

Civic entitlements[24] provided by the community or NGOs may rise to offset the fall in other entitlements in contexts where civil society remains effective, but where society itself disintegrates, they too may be sharply reduced. The level of extra-legal entitlements is likely to rise greatly in war—involving substantial gains for some, losses for others.

These entitlement losses then affect the economy itself in a number of ways. Increased household efforts at hoarding and speculation is a form of self-defence which leads to a diversion of goods and capital from consumption and production. The dislocation of small-scale peasant and artisan production leads to a loss of food and export earnings, reducing the supply of key inputs to the rest of the economy and reducing household consumption levels. Finally, the reduced capacity of government and civil society to deliver social services such as health and education leads to declining popular support for these social institutions, and increased reliance on and identity with the extended family and immediate ethnic group.

On average, therefore, the well-being of most households is likely to deteriorate sharply, with falling entitlements of most kinds. Health conditions deteriorate as immunization levels fall, water supplies break down, people are moved and reconcentrated, and resistance levels decline due to poor nutrition (de Waal 1989). There are also negative psychological effects, not only from the traumas of the war itself but also from forced migration and family separation. While for most households, the net effects are likely to be negative, the magnitude of the deterioration depends greatly on household survival strategies, their ingenuity and adaptability.

4.2   Income Distribution

Aggregate indicators of human well-being—for example, mortality rates, nutrition standards, and school enrolment—would be expected to worsen compared with what they would have been in the absence of the war given the changes in entitlements and household composition noted above. This does not mean they necessarily fall in absolute terms, but that improvement is less than in normal times. In addition, distributional changes will occur, and some groups (those favoured by the government or foreign forces, and those with military strength) may gain more than their peacetime prospects while others will lose much more than proportionately to national performance. Indeed

---

[22] Although there was no military activity on the Indian subcontinent, there was a sharp increase in government expenditure on the military.

[23] As occurred in the Luwero triangle in Uganda (see Chapter 9, Vol. II).

[24] See O'Sullivan—Chapter 6, Vol. II.

some individuals can make spectacular fortunes,[25] which in the context of falling average incomes implies that many more households must have suffered disproportionately.

These distributional impacts are critical in two respects. On the one hand, if the poorest are protected against losses, then deterioration in human indicators, including death rates, can be greatly reduced; equally, the worst rises in deaths occur when initially poor groups bear most of the general losses. On the other hand, distributional effects may be important in determining the duration of the conflict. If some groups gain a lot from conflict then they may have an interest in its prolongation, particularly if the gains depend on the war continuing—for example, the gains arise from continued looting, as appears to be the case in Liberia and Sierra Leone. Moreover, since the perception of horizontal inequality is normally an important source of conflict, the effect on this dimension is also a key variable in determining the duration of conflict as discussed above.

In the category of 'vertical distribution' certain groups are likely to do well out of war. Due to shortages of consumer goods, fuels, and foreign exchange, groups with access to these commodities (including not only traders and smugglers but also military leaders, civil servants, and even those working with aid agencies) are likely to make large profits. In contrast, those trying to gain access to these commodities, such as small farmers, formal-sector wage earners, women and children, are likely to suffer from the redistribution implicit in shortages and inflation which undermine their entitlements as discussed above. These in turn can cause vertical income distribution to deteriorate even further. The combination of declining levels of average per capita income and increased dispersion of incomes lead to rapidly rising levels of absolute poverty as well as the emergence of new groups of rich people among traders and military leaders.

'Horizontal' distribution will also change under conflict conditions. Logically, those groups and/or regions likely to gain are those supported by government and/or with strong external support. By extension, those groups and/or regions likely to lose are those attacked by the government or lacking in external support.

4.3   The Development Costs of War

War clearly reduces the potential for future economic growth and social improvements in developing countries, both by destroying installed capital and reducing new investment. By 'capital' we understand not only productive capacity in the form of natural resources,[26] plant and equipment, but also human capital in the form of health and skills, economic and social infrastructure on the one hand, and the less tangible collective assets such as organizational capital (for example, government capacity) and social capital in the form of trust or culture.

The development costs of war are far greater than the destruction associated with natural disasters, for two reasons. First, natural disasters such as floods, hurricanes, and earthquakes tend to destroy housing and transport infrastructure, but have less effect on productive capacity and leave human capital (other than those killed, of course) intact.

---

[25] See Chapter 3 by Keen in this volume.
[26] Even land can be destroyed by war through the sowing of landmines.

Table 1.2 Development costs of war

Category of capital	Destruction of existing stock	Impact on new investment
Productive capital: plant, equipment and buildings	Landmined; factories bombed.	Fall in private productive investment—foreign and local, including farmers' investments. Some new investment in new informal activities; and in arms production.
Economic infrastructure	Transport and communications system, power, irrigation disrupted.	Decline in government expenditure on infrastructure.
Social infrastructure	Schools, hospitals, clinics damaged.	
Human capital	Death, migration especially of skilled; worsened nutrition and health of workforce.	Decline in public entitlements, reduced education in quantity and quality. Reduced private-sector training.
Organizational capital	Government institutions, banks, agricultural extension, science and technology organization weakened.	No resources in formal sector; new informal organizations develop; NGOs take on new activities.
Social capital	Destruction of trust; work ethic; respect for property; community links.	New forms of social capital, through groups that develop links in war; NGO activity.

Second, as organizational and social capital remains intact and natural disasters tend to be of relatively short duration, investment quickly recovers and may even have a positive multiplier effect on the economy as a whole.[27] In marked contrast, war destroys all forms of capital and the uncertainty it causes reduces investment radically. In particular, the destruction of entitlements which occurs during conflict constitutes an important development cost, as worsening levels of human education and nutrition reduce the human resources of an economy. The output losses discussed above will also lead to development costs as they reduce the capacity of the economy to invest, even with an unchanged investment ratio.

As Table 1.2 suggests, the range of capital destruction in wartime is not only broad but also is concentrated on those capacities which are recognized as being critical for sustainable development in poor countries. Civil war is particularly destructive of organizational and social capital. In contrast, industrial societies during international wars may even find that most (or even all) forms of their capital stock are strengthened.

---

[27] The evidence collected by Albala-Bertrand (1993) appears to indicate that this is the case.

Some destruction of physical capital, both plant and machinery and infrastructural capital, usually occurs as a direct outcome of the conflict—including factories, dams and energy plants, schools, hospitals and clinics, roads and railways. The extent depends on the nature of the war. Human capital is also destroyed directly (being killed), and indirectly (fleeing overseas, which is usually especially concentrated among the more educated and skilled). Human resources are also weakened by worsening health and nutrition.

Organizational capital can be severely weakened as a result of the enfeebling of governments often associated with civil war, the worsening infrastructure, and the out-migration of skilled people and foreigners, so that the government administrative machinery becomes less effective, banks may cease to work, etc. But again this depends on the nature of war. In some contexts (normally international wars), government machinery is strengthened by war. In civil wars social capital tends to be destroyed, with trust being weakened, community ties destroyed by fighting or the mass movement of people, and so on.

The destruction of existing capital is likely to be compounded by reductions in new investments, especially with respect to physical and human capital. Governments tend to cut investment as a result of the general reductions in public resources, and the special expenditure demands of war. Capital expenditure on social and economic infrastructure is likely to be most adversely affected during cuts due to war, as it is during cuts due to economic adjustments (Cornia, Jolly, and Stewart 1987; Hicks 1991). Aid agencies may reduce aid generally and investment aid especially, believing that there is little point in building up infrastructure if it is liable to be destroyed, and aid efforts tend to switch away from supporting productive investment towards relief (especially food aid) and military aid. Private investors (foreign and local) reduce their expenditures because of depressed expectations about the economy and profitability and the risks of destruction of their projects. Investment in human capital tends to decline with reduced access to education and health services, while nutritional deprivations affect the growth of children and their long-run productivity.

The situation with respect to organizational and social capital is more complex. Undoubtedly, there tends to be a disintegration of existing forms. But new forms can develop, with, for example, new forms of authority and governance among rebel movements; informal financing mechanisms developing to substitute for the collapsed formal sector; non-government organizations (NGOs), local and foreign, substituting for government, and so on. How far this occurs is likely to depend on the society, the development of the war, and the actions of outside actors. Moreover, these new forms of organizational and social capital may not be so appropriate to peacetime conditions. But they should not be entirely discounted as a new development resource emerging, to a varying extent, in some conflict–ridden societies.

5 The Approach in this Study

Our approach in this study is multidisciplinary: political and sociological analysis is essential for understanding motivations and behaviour of economic agents during

conflict, while the economic mechanisms formed or distorted under conflict conditions in turn affect motivation and behaviour. In this complex canvas, in which human
reactions and economic behaviour vary substantially according to the economic, social,
and cultural conditions of the society in question, generalization is difficult. Some
might argue that wars are so 'abnormal' that no generalization is possible. Yet our work
suggests some generalization is possible—if only because wars are all too 'normal'—
although conclusions depend critically on the nature of the economy, the level of
development, the role, strength, and objectives of the government, as well as the nature
of the conflict. It is necessary to collect a great deal more information on conflict
societies before one can be confident about results; yet our work suggests some generalization is possible.

The differing conditions in war-affected countries, in terms of the nature of conflict
and of the economies in which they occur, make it impossible to make precise predictions about the probable consequences. The outcome of conflict, as of natural disasters,
is a combination of the immediate consequences of the conflict and the reactions to
these direct effects. Humans are very ingenious, and while it is fairly straightforward to
predict the immediate consequences, the reactions to conflict can be large, unexpected,
and even have positive effects, as has been shown in the realm of natural disasters (see
Albala-Bertrand 1993).

However, our earlier discussion suggests that, broadly, the following scenario
seems likely to occur compared with what might have been expected in the absence of
conflict. At the macroeconomic level falling GDP per capita, reduced export earnings
and probably lower imports (unless aid increases), a lower investment ratio and savings
ratio (unless consumption is restricted by rationing), reduced government revenue and
expenditure, higher budget deficits, and accelerating inflation. At the mesoeconomic
level, a switch in government expenditure from economic and social to the military
would be expected; while supply would switch from tradables to non-tradables, from
marketed output to subsistence production, and from the formal to the informal sectors.
At the microeconomic level, average levels of entitlements of all kinds are likely to
decline, sometimes with catastrophic consequences for human survival. There can also
be sharp changes in both vertical and horizontal entitlement distribution.

In this two-volume study we aim to explore how far these broad predictions are
validated by further analytic and empirical work. This volume is devoted to general
analysis, derived from such work. The second volume, on which we draw heavily in
this volume, contains seven in-depth studies of countries in conflict. This volume opens
with two chapters which present an analytical focus on the economic, social, and political aspects of developing countries under conflict conditions. Chapter 2 examines the
main economic changes taking place under wartime conditions, developing a perspective derived from Keynes's analysis of the British economy during World War II in order
to integrate financial and poverty considerations. Establishing 'who pays for the war'
permits a fresh approach to the distributive consequences of war and thus the best means
of alleviating economic deprivation. In Chapter 3, David Keen starts from a historical
overview of those groups who gain from war and those that lose from it, as a means
of looking at the dynamics of continued conflict, then applying these notions to the

African experience. He demonstrates that civil wars in developing countries are rather more rational than are generally thought.

These analytical foundations are followed by two chapters providing some empirical investigation of developing country economies during war. Chapter 4 provides a comprehensive statistical overview of some 16 conflict economies over the past 25 years, as a means of assessing the validity of the changes predicted in this chapter. Chapter 5 summarizes the results of the country case studies presented in Volume 2, which cover the conflicts in Afghanistan, Mozambique, Nicaragua, Sierra Leone, Sri Lanka, Sudan, and Uganda applying the methodology set out in this chapter. These case studies explore and contrast the social and economic effects of war in some detail, and also permit a comparison of policy initiatives by governments and donors in conflict economies.

The next three chapters of the book address key 'cross-cutting' issues which are widely regarded by both donors and policymakers as central to reducing the costs of conflict, but which can be misread if treated in isolation from the wider economic and social framework. In Chapter 6, Eric Greitens examines the experience of children during conflict, and the measures taken to enable them to survive not only the physical but also the psychological effects of war, where the effects of prolonged conflict may be felt for generations to come. Chapter 7 takes up the issue of food aid, which is a major form of donor intervention in response to what appears to be the immediate priority in wartime—but which may have negative consequences for the economy and even prolong conflict. Chapter 8 analyses the relationship between poor economies and world markets and considers whether it exacerbates or ameliorates conflict. These three chapters make a strong case for re-examining the way in which the international economic institutions handle these situations if the human cost of war is to be reduced.

Finally, in Chapter 9 we draw together the threads of the argument set out in this introduction in the light of the materials presented in the intervening chapters. The interactions between conflict and economic behaviour, in a variety of circumstances, are summarized, and the implications for policies are drawn.

In this book we hope to make a contribution to the understanding of the interactions between conflict and economic behaviour in a range of circumstances, and to suggest policies—sensitive to this variation—which would contribute to reducing suffering and economic losses during conflict, and to bringing conflict to an end. Our policy propositions are presented in the concluding chapter. However, it should be borne in mind that policymaking cannot be treated as an objective exercise in welfare maximization. All policymakers are subject to political constraints and conditioned by their own objectives. This is especially true in developing economies subject to civil war, where the government is one of the most important actors in the war and the retention of state and economic power predominates in policy construction—just as the objective of acquiring such power dominates the behaviour of opposing groups. Moreover, international actors (aid donors in particular) have their own political and economic objectives, including strategies of strategic containment and economic expansion. Hence, policy recommendations need to understand these forces of political economy as well as economic behaviour—in other words, how economic behaviour affects the politics of war as well as how war affects the economy.

   The ultimate aim of policy recommendations in wartime should clearly be to bring the conflict to an end, not in the sense of one side 'winning' but rather that of addressing the root causes of conflict and establishing a cohesive society with a sustainable economy. This clearly is the most complete solution to eliminating the costs of conflict. Designing policies with the objective of bringing conflict to an end requires an understanding of the economies of countries in conflict, which lead to its continuation and condition the reconstruction process. The current policy focus on 'peacemaking', based on political agreements between warring parties and 'reconstruction' initiatives based on a return to a previous 'peacetime' economy which no longer exists, we believe to be fundamentally misguided. Equally, we would suggest that to argue that deprivation should not be alleviated during wartime because this might prolong the conflict by, for instance, maintaining political support for the incumbent government is highly dangerous if not immoral. The poor are rarely responsible for state policies or in any position to change them, while there are many more effective ways of placing pressure on governments violating international law.

2

Paying for the War: Economic Policy in Poor Countries Under Conflict Conditions

VALPY FITZGERALD

1 Introduction

Over half of the low-income countries have been seriously affected by armed conflict since 1960. In such countries, the human cost of conflict has not been due principally to direct violence—even when civilian casualties from undisciplined troops, deliberate terror and widespread mining are included. Rather, as Chapter 1 suggests, it is the hunger, forced migration, and collapse of public services arising from the wider effects of protracted conflict on the economic and administrative structure of the country as a whole which lead to the greater part of misery and death.

An important component of these indirect costs of conflict arises from the extreme macroeconomic disequilibria which tend to emerge in wartime—expressed in the form of hyperinflation, falling real wages, and widespread shortages of basic goods and services. On the one hand, rebel[1] troops may deliberately target production facilities and key infrastructure in order to weaken the economy, while military mobilization and refugee movements further reduce the supply capacity of the economy. On the other hand, government attempts to mobilize resources in order to supply its troops, and to ration foreign exchange in order to support public-sector activities, tend to generate excess demand pressures.

Macroeconomic policy in wartime is thus concerned with containing (rather than eliminating) these disequilibria so as to reduce human suffering, particularly in poor countries where a large proportion of the population is near or below the poverty line. In particular, the pressure of declining supply and rising demand may well result in declining consumption by poor households—who are in a real sense 'paying for the war' in Keynes's phrase.

The characterization of a 'conflict economy' is addressed in Section 2 of this chapter, which distinguishes 'war shocks' from other shocks familiar from modern development macroeconomics, and outlines the main fiscal and external-sector disequilibria that tend to emerge in wartime. Section 3 turns to the way in which civil society—firms and households—respond to the shocks and uncertainties of war, and what the

---

[1] I do not presume that the 'government' is more deserving of support or advice than the 'rebels'. However, as this chapter is about macroeconomic conditions and policy formation in conflict economies, for which governments are held responsible, it seems logical to look at the problem from this point of view.

consequences are for the macroeconomic behaviour. Macroeconomic policy in low-income countries affected by armed conflict is discussed in Section 4. Governments try to increase administrative control over the economy in wartime, but this can easily break down where the modern sector is import-intensive and the informal sector responds rapidly to demand imbalances; however, orthodox stabilization policies also have serious welfare costs under these circumstances.

In consequence, Section 5 sets out the basis for an alternative approach to macroeconomic stabilization which takes into account explicitly the disequilibrium nature of the low-income economy in conflict. It is inspired by Keynes's insight into the distributive effects of wartime consumption constraints and inflation, and the need to prepare for post-war reconstruction; and also has implications for the design of aid programmes. Section 6 concludes with the policy implications of the analysis presented in this chapter.

2   War and the Low-Income Economy

2.1   Defining the Conflict Economy

Conflict economies in the developing world are in a very different position from industrial powers engaged in traditional inter-state conflicts.[2] In industrial countries wars often involve technological advance as industrial capacity is used more intensively and forced modernization is undertaken, while the living standards of the poor can actually improve due to full employment and the extension of entitlements to social services and food supplies as part of the process of national mobilization under centralized government direction (see Milward 1979).

In common with other poor economies,[3] most low-income countries experiencing conflict are dependent on primary exports with a considerable small-scale sector of peasant farmers typically producing food for domestic sale and 'informal' urban traders and artisans, also producing for domestic demand. They are vulnerable economies, commonly exposed to recurrent 'exogenous shocks' in the form of sudden changes in the world market for their export products (reflected in large fluctuations in import capacity) and devastating natural disasters in the form of floods, droughts, and epidemics. The extreme poverty of a large proportion of households makes them particularly vulnerable to economic instability, while the limited human and financial resources of the state make it very difficult for government to protect these social groups effectively.

In addition, a war economy has particular features which, superimposed on these structural characteristics, tend to worsen the economic disequilibria and increase the vulnerability of the poor. The wartime situation tends to affect the whole economy,

---

[2] Pre-modern wars in Europe and Asia were limited in their scope because of the danger of disarticulating agricultural economies: troops would return home (with or without permission) at harvest time.

[3] Which means that in terms of available statistical indicators such as growth rates the variance within the universe of poor economies is such that it is very difficult to distinguish statistically those which have experienced armed conflicts (FitzGerald, forthcoming).

rather than a single sector (such as exports in the case of a trade shock) or a single region (in the case of a natural disaster). A fall in export prices creates a new status quo to which producers then adjust, but war creates a widespread and prolonged sense of uncertainty which in turn leads to considerable changes in household location, labour use, and portfolio choices. Although considerable destruction can take place which might seem to be similar to the effect of a natural disaster,[4] there is a much wider effect on both trade networks and markets for labour and credit.

Conflict economies—and wars tend to go on for many years in poor countries—thus experience intrinsic disequilibrium. First, the material requirements of the military effort[5] require large resource reallocation on non-market criteria, which must logically be achieved by administrative direction; although this should of course attempt to minimize (but cannot eliminate) distortions in the rest of the economy. Second, the effect of conflict on the balance of payments is bound to be considerable, and some degree of administrative allocation of imports and external funds (for example, aid) to national priorities is inevitable—as it is in industrial countries under wartime conditions. Macroeconomic analysis under these circumstances should logically take these disequilibria into account explicitly—rather than just treating them as 'distortions'—if there is to be any possibility of designing stabilization policies which reduce the effects of conflict on the economy as a whole and thus on human hardship.

2.2   The Fiscal Constraint

Upward pressure on public expenditure during wartime is inevitable, due both to the demands of military activity and the need to replace damaged or destroyed facilities. Although some budgetary reallocation is possible as non-priority activities are reduced, the most probable cutbacks will tend to occur in public investment and thus long-term development capacity. Moreover, there may exist strong pressure to reduce expenditure on social programmes with long-term benefits such as education, in favour of more immediate needs such as preventive health.

Budget allocations in nominal terms will not translate into real resource allocation in a disequilibrium situation. Higher rates of inflation will inevitably reduce the real value of the resources allocated to social services, especially affecting the ability to acquire material inputs on the local market, with implications for both current operations and the maintenance of existing capacity. What is more, declining real wages in the public sector may well reduce the efficiency of civil servants and encourage them to seek other income-earning opportunities—ranging from second jobs to petty corruption—while some may leave the country. Even if the value of social expenditure is maintained in constant price terms, the reallocation of scarce resources—particularly skilled labour

---

[4] Indeed, natural disasters appear to have a positive effect of output because of the subsequent reconstruction effort, while destruction is usually largely confined to housing rather than production facilities as such (Albala-Bertrand 1993).

[5] Although arms may be provided from abroad, the troops need food, fuel, uniforms, construction materials, etc, which all represent a drain on scarce domestic resources.

and foreign exchange—towards other priorities can severely constrain the real supply of social services. This is likely to have a disproportionate effect on poor households who cannot replace these public services by private purchases (for example, of medicines) on the parallel market.

Conflict conditions tend to reduce the revenue base for the government, as economic output and taxable profits in the modern sector fall, and large areas of informal activity become effectively impossible to tax. However, there is a greater incentive to exploit the remaining tax base more effectively, particularly activities that are relatively easy to control administratively such as non-essential imports, bottled drinks, cigarettes, and gasoline. The net result may be for taxes as a proportion of national income ('tax pressure') to rise or fall, depending on net outcome of the two trends; but the shift away from income taxation towards excise taxes on consumption will presumably have a negative effect on distribution and thus poverty.

Deficit finance is likely to rise with upward pressures on expenditure and downward pressures on revenue. The form of deficit finance in wartime LDCs is also a central determinant of macroeconomic policy and ultimately of the redistribution of resources within society in order to support the military effort and adjust for wartime destruction—in other words, 'how to pay for the war'. It is limited in effect to three sources: first, foreign borrowing or grant aid; second, forced credit from existing banking resources; and third, increased monetary emission by the central bank. We can assume that this will also be the government's order of preference. However, the first source is limited to and constrained by aid donors, because commercial borrowing opportunities are extremely limited, and is thus determined by exogenous geopolitical considerations. The second source also meets limits in terms both of the depth of the banking system (which is itself adversely affected by the war) and the requirements of production sectors for credit. Monetary emission—with inevitable inflationary effects when the economy is externally constrained[6]—remains the default option. This has disproportionate effects on poor households with money incomes from wages or self-employment, although the retreat into subsistence agriculture can act as a buffer.

The government is thus faced with a problem of how to accommodate increased military expenditure with increases in taxation or borrowing on the one hand, and reductions in social expenditure on the other. This problem is no different in essence from that faced by peacetime governments, except that the relative priority (that is, weight in the government's objective function) given to military expenditure is higher; while the political disutility of taxation, and to an even greater extent borrowing, presumably declines. In particular, an increased weight given to military expenditure will inevitably increase total expenditure, which will both enlarge the fiscal deficit and reduce social expenditure.[7]

---

[6] In terms of the simple monetary identity ($Mv = PT$), there is not only an increasing supply of money (M) but also a reduction in real transactions (T) due to war damage and the dislocation of markets, and a rise in the velocity of circulation (v) due to currency substitution and uncertainty, the combination of which must therefore be accompanied by a rise in prices (P).   [7] See Appendix.

2.3 The External Constraint

Conflict conditions necessarily reduce the growth of export income and may also reduce its absolute level. This happens for a number of reasons: the direct destruction of export capacity; lack of production inputs and transport systems; and reduced producer profitability due to increased costs and reduced productivity. These factors reduce the quality as well as the quantity of exports, and thus prices received fall too. In addition, the geopolitical context of the conflict may interrupt external transport and trade links, closing markets and increasing freight costs.

Most poor countries, and the conflict economies in particular, are heavily dependent on external finance to sustain import requirements. Borrowing from international commercial banks (beyond a small amount of pre-export finance) and direct foreign investment are not likely to be significant in view of the degree of country risk involved. In consequence, external finance is only available from international financial institutions and bilateral aid agencies. From neither of these two sources are the flows determined by a purely economic calculus: both the balance of payments support and humanitarian assistance typically received by conflict economies are aimed at the maintenance of household consumption levels and essential government activities rather than capital formation or longer-term development objectives.[8]

The non-grant element of such external assistance leads to the build-up of considerable debt levels, the servicing of which becomes very difficult when export income is falling and the proportion of imports considered to be 'essential' is rising. Under these conditions, a considerable part of new borrowing in fact represents the accumulation of arrears in debt service. Import levels under these circumstances are determined by the sum of exports and net external finance. A considerable proportion is determined by military requirements, and a large share of 'civilian' imports will be predetermined as part of import support schemes—that is, tied to programmed supplies of food, medicines, etc. decided by the donors. Although there may be some degree of fungibility, the amount of uncommitted foreign exchange available to the authorities is likely to be small. In consequence, the elasticity of imports with respect to the official exchange rate is extremely low.

However, the scarcity of foreign exchange is likely to create a parallel market, fed not only by leakages from official institutions and aid agencies, but also by family remittances from overseas and by export smuggling in order to finance non-official imports. There thus emerges a dual price structure reflecting the parallel exchange rate, which then feeds back into reduced profitability for exporters selling through state marketing boards at the official rates, and further diversion of foreign exchange from the official channels. The existence of this is not merely due to a misguided exchange rate policy or excess money supply. Rather, in any war economy there is bound to exist a mismatch between market demand for imports and the socially desirable allocation of scarce foreign exchange, so that a dual market is likely to emerge in any case.[9]

---

[8] See Chapter 8, this volume. [9] As was the case of the UK during WW II, of course.

3 Private-Sector Response to Wartime Conditions

3.1 Domestic Economic Activity, Income Distribution, and Civil Society

Domestic production levels in wartime depend to a great extent upon the macroeconomic factors discussed in the previous section. The direct and indirect military destruction vary from one case to another, but the overall level of activity—particularly in the 'modern' sector of the economy—is strongly affected by the amount of imports available. Within these constraints, the way in which the fiscal deficit is financed and the way in which foreign exchange is allocated has crucial effects on economic variables such as the availability of credit, the rate of inflation, food supplies, and real wages, and thus on incentives to production—particularly among small-scale producers—as well as on individual well-being.

However, the way in which the economy responds depends upon the changes in the behaviour of households and firms (in other words, the 'private' sector) that occur in conflict economies, in response to the shocks and uncertainties of war. Extensive losses of human, physical, and financial assets, combined with major alterations in expectations severely affect expenditure and portfolio decisions, and feed into currency substitution and hoarding as well as widespread poverty. The disarticulation of markets for essential products, foreign exchange and labour has profound consequences—mainly through parallel markets—for relative prices, levels of production, the tax base, and the propagation of inflation. The distribution of income can rapidly deteriorate as those few with access to state or foreign resources take advantage of the quasi-rents generated by wartime shortages and the majority slide towards or even below the poverty line.

3.2 The Response of Firms to Conflict Conditions

The category 'firms' in poor economies is highly heterogeneous. It includes a relatively small number of subsidiaries of multinational corporations, state-owned enterprises, and domestic private companies in the 'modern' sector on the one hand, and a mass of peasant farmers, artisan workshops, and petty traders in the 'informal' sector on the other. The direct effect of war as such on production is likely to be greater among the latter group if fighting is widespread in rural areas where assets are stolen and producers forced to migrate. Modern firms are usually located in less exposed areas, and can often organize some form of security protection, although they are more vulnerable to disruption by power shortages and the deterioration of transport infrastructure. Informal firms—particularly in rural areas—are more vulnerable to asset theft and forced relocation, suffer more from the breakdown of established commercial networks, and have less financial assets to help them survive temporary difficulties.

The indirect impact of the macroeconomic disequilibria discussed above on production levels is different from direct destruction. Severe foreign exchange shortages affect modern firms disproportionately because they rely to a great extent on imported inputs, so that a process of forced import substitution takes place—from which informal firms are in a particularly good position to benefit, particularly in urban areas. More widely, a shift from traded to non-traded activities is likely to take place (Collier and Gunning 1995). The inflation and credit shortage generated by the fiscal deficit have a differential impact on firms. On the one hand, it creates large nominal profits for modern manufacturing firms producing for the domestic market (unless price controls are imposed) and for urban traders with access to scarce goods. On the other, it reduces profitability in modern export firms and, if the internal terms of trade deteriorate, for peasant producers. Primary exports and food supplies tend to move out of official channels and towards smuggling and parallel markets in order to recover profit margins.

From the macroeconomic point of view, the investment behaviour of firms is of central importance in determining both short-term demand and long-term growth. Within the category of firms, however, the response is heterogeneous. Multinational affiliates and domestic companies are unlikely to increase capacity at all due to uncertainty and the existence of other less risky uses for their funds. State-owned firms are always willing to replace losses or increase capacity (FitzGerald 1993, ch. 8) but are constrained by access to investable funds, particularly foreign exchange. In consequence, their investment depends on the availability of concessional foreign finance from bilateral donors and development banks. In the informal sector outside the zones of active conflict (peasant farmers, transport firms, urban construction, and so on) it is usually the case that considerable small-scale investment demand exists. However, in those economies where small firms rely on bank credit (e.g. for export production) investment may be restricted by the lack of funds as financial resources are diverted to the state; while in others essential investment goods such as cattle, barbed wire, or cement may be lacking.

In the modern sector, therefore, fixed investment decisions are largely independent of macroeconomic policy, although this is not the case in the informal sector. Fixed capital formation is not the only investment choice open to firms. Generally, uncertainty leads to a portfolio shift from fixed to financial assets because real fixed assets are vulnerable to damage during a war (Collier and Gunning 1995). Further, there is substitution out of domestic currency denominated financial assets into foreign currency (often in cash) or capital flight, and out of immobile physical assets into mobile ones (Brück 1996). In other words, there is a substantive increase in liquidity preference. In the case of conflict economies, moreover, firms' investment response to the destruction of productive capacity is very different from that to other types of external shocks: it will necessarily be less than that resulting from a negative trade shock; while private investment actually rises after natural disasters.[10]

However, the existence of chronic macroeconomic disequilibria and specific supply shortages generates a series of quasi-rents which are in effect attractive investment opportunities for those with access to scarce resources. In particular, investment in foreign exchange as part of import/export operations in the parallel market, in transport equipment in order to supply urban markets, or in construction materials in order to build informal housing are all very attractive options open to the new groups of

---

[10] See Appendix.

entrepreneurs which emerge under conditions of social and administrative breakdown. In sum, investment is likely to fall in conflict economies and its composition to shift away from production.

3.3   The Response of Households to Conflict

The consumption and savings behaviour of households is the other main underpinning of macroeconomic behaviour. In wartime, there is the added uncertainty of death or mutilation from soldiers or minefields, as well as entitlement failure from loss of employment and reduced income, the dislocation of markets, and the breakdown of social mechanisms (whether family or state) for securing the access of the vulnerable to nutrition.

In the standard life-cycle model, increased uncertainty about future income should lead to higher savings rates (Gersovitz 1983). However, this model assumes an ability to choose consumption in each period (that is, access to goods and credit markets) which is unrealistic—especially under the conditions we are discussing. In addition, it does not allow for the effect of uncertainty about lifespan on household behaviour, which would increase consumption in wartime. In fact, when household survival is threatened current consumption improves health and thus the chance of surviving until the next harvest or at least until a safe haven is reached.[11]

However, the tendency for household consumption demand to rise under these circumstances is met by restricted supplies of consumer goods, which can be further aggravated by the desire to increase household inventories of consumer goods ('hoarding') when future access to them is uncertain. This can lead to 'forced saving' (undesired accumulation of cash balances) or, more probably, inflation in consumer prices on parallel markets.

Under inflationary circumstances real wages tend to fall and become de facto a means of containing the real budget deficit because it depresses the real wages of public-sector employees. Seasonal labour in agriculture and casual labour in the towns are also affected negatively. Nominal revenues from informal (non-traded) sector activities rise but only households with access to quasi-rents from scaroe commodities gain substantially. Peasant farmers may receive higher prices, but lower production and the high prices of rural producer goods (that is, deteriorating internal terms of trade) often mean falling real incomes. In the urban informal sector, low barriers to entry mean that swelling numbers of street traders 'share' a given level of real demand, reducing per capita income. The distribution of real household income is thus likely to deteriorate under wartime conditions unless specific entitlement systems such as rationing are introduced.

However, rationing systems are very difficult to administer fairly unless civil society is itself robust, cohesive, and well organized. In practice, they tend to be limited to

---

[11] If the probability of non-survival is endogenized by making health a function of consumption, then even if incomes are stochastic (which sharply raises savings rates in the standard life-cycle model) it pays households to spend additional money in order to build health capital—as opposed to accumulation of financial assets—when uncertainty increases (Glomm and Palumbo 1993).

urban areas or modern-sector employees. To the extent that the fiscal deficit is effect-ively met through macroeconomic adjustment in the form of inflation and a forced decline in household consumption levels—as opposed to taxation or external finance —then it is the poor, who have less access to informal quasi-rents and fall outside the official welfare net, who are mainly 'paying for the war'.

A key aspect of household response to macroeconomic stress is the reallocation of its own labour power. Labour markets themselves are critically affected by conflict condi-tions. On the one hand, established employment patterns (including migrant labour flows) break down due to the dislocation of war as the modern sector lays off workers, leading to potential unemployment. On the other hand, the military (of both sides) is recruiting young men and the informal sector offers new employment opportunities —particularly in urban petty commerce which requires minimal capital. Household survival thus requires 'portfolio reallocation' of its labour resources: not only to maximize money income but also to ensure entitlements at an acceptable level of phys-ical security. This may well require some members to continue in the public sector or join the armed forces, while others engage in risky high-gain activities ranging from theft to prostitution.

Thus both consumption/saving behaviour and labour market participation change radically under wartime conditions. Whether aggregate household (that is, private) consumption rises or falls depends on three factors: first, the impact on the level of national income, according to the extent of war damage and import capacity; second, the prior claims on national resources made by government expenditure and firms' investment decisions; and third, the supply of essential consumer goods (especially food) and social services (especially health). The change in the distribution of real house-hold incomes around the mean depends on the internal terms of trade, real wage and employment trends, and access to scarce resources.

4 Macroeconomic Policy in Poor Economies Under Conflict

4.1 The National Government

The structural characteristics of the wartime economy and the changes in the economic behaviour of civil society discussed in the previous two sections both place severe limits on macroeconomic policy and mean that the effects of any particular instrument are different from what would be expected in peacetime. Policy objectives will also change.

The immediate policy of the government is presumably to remain in power, and therefore to mobilize sufficient resources to make this possible. The other—closely connected—objective is to retain and strengthen popular support by sustaining essen-tial consumption levels and providing basic welfare services. In macroeconomic terms, stabilization policy to contain inflation and balance of payments problems is the most that can be expected, with most development goals being postponed to post-war reconstruction.

As we have seen, the ability to increase tax revenue is limited by the tax base, but governments can and do raise excise duties on certain consumer goods, increase vigilance over dutiable imports through the main border crossings and ports, and collect more revenue from formal-sector firms. Curiously there appears to be considerable resistance in most cases to higher gasoline taxes and electricity tariffs (both of which are mainly consumed by the better off and easy to administer) for fear of the inflationary consequences. None the less, there is an intrinsic limit to the tax pressure which can be applied without exceeding the administrative capacity of the government or driving firms into parallel markets.

The first alternative to deficit finance is foreign aid. From the point of view of a government under extreme pressure this is inevitably seen as a 'free resource' without regard to eventual repayment requirements in an uncertain future—when either the war will have been lost, or the economy will recover and debt-service ratios would be acceptable. As debt repayments become due and the conflict continues, new loans are used to service existing debt and the net inflow is still regarded effectively as current fiscal income. This pattern of behaviour is strengthened by the aid agencies' practice of allowing counterpart funds from import support schemes to be used for budgetary purposes. The government therefore has little concern for the problem of long-term external debt solvency in the formal sense.[12] In consequence, the level of foreign borrowing (or if available, grant aid) is set not by the domestic government but by the lenders, on a set of different criteria—so an additional objective of government policy is to prevent donors from withdrawing their support.

The second source of deficit finance is the banking system. The deposit base is likely to be reduced by the direct effects of the war on firms and richer households, and the indirect consequences of the portfolio reallocation discussed in the previous section. However, the accumulation of unspent cash balances by state enterprises and small producers may counteract this, to some extent, if inflation remains low. The government borrows from the central bank, which raises reserve requirements on the commercial banks, or the banks are obliged to subscribe to treasury bonds at low interest rates and unclear redemption dates. Banks tend to prefer their larger customers (particularly state enterprises and foreign firms) so that medium-size producers—particularly farmers—and households are crowded out of the credit market by the fiscal deficit, being forced to reduce their activity level.

If this level of bank borrowing becomes unsustainable, the central bank is authorized to monetize the deficit. Unless there is a marked increase in the demand for money or a fall in the velocity of circulation—neither of which is at all likely—this policy has a marked inflationary effect in view of binding supply constraints. In fact we would expect currency substitution to take place, and the velocity of circulation to rise, due to uncertainty, which increases the inflationary effect of any level of monetization. In consequence, wartime inflation cannot really be regarded as a 'policy error' as such, but rather as the consequence of a conflict between state and civil society, and within civil society, as to who is to pay for the war.

---

[12] In the sense that the discounted sum of future budget deficits and surpluses equals or exceeds the present debt.

In order to ameliorate the social consequences of this macroeconomic disequilibrium, governments under conflict conditions invariably attempt to increase their administrative control over the economy. However, this control can easily break down in an economy where bureaucratic capacity is limited, the modern sector is very import-intensive and the informal sector responds to price controls by reducing supply or establishing parallel markets. Efforts to protect urban consumers by rationing, food price controls, and state marketing monopolies also turn the terms of trade against the peasantry (Saith 1985). The maintenance of a fixed official exchange rate in order to avoid imported cost inflation reduces export profitability and stimulates a parallel market in foreign exchange due to excess demand. Eventually these 'black market' activities have to be tolerated, but the lack of central control and emerging inequalities undermine both of the government's strategic objectives.

4.2   The Aid Agencies

Under conflict conditions, aid agencies come to play a major part in the economy, through import support programmes, humanitarian projects, and by the local expenditures of their own personnel. Their own operational policies can thus play a crucial role—albeit unwittingly—in the way the macroeconomy works in practice. Import support programmes for poor countries are not mainly intended to raise investment or government expenditure, but rather to allow existing productive capacity to be used more effectively (raising employment and incomes) and where possible to sustain nutrition, health, and other essential services for the population (White 1992).

In a conflict economy, where large development projects are difficult to implement, import support becomes the main form of resource inflows and frequently accounts for the greater part of the import bill. Programme aid in effect becomes commodity aid, which in turn is mainly food aid—although fuel supply from non-DAC donors can be significant. From the point of view of the donor, import support has several advantages. It is not limited by absorptive capacity, existing processing plants can be used, disbursement is rapid and uses existing administrative structures, and the countervalue from the sale of goods can be used to support specified social expenditures. Moreover, import support can be initiated or suspended quite quickly, which makes it an ideal instrument for policy conditionality. Imports under these schemes can be allocated administratively, but donors often prefer an auction system where possible in order to minimize corruption. However, a workable auction system needs an efficient banking system to administer the licences and a transparent private sector, neither of which may obtain in wartime.

The macroeconomic impact of aid in general and import support schemes in particular depends upon demand displacement in the short run, and the supply response in the long run. As in a peacetime economy, aid will reduce domestic saving in a conflict economy and lead to an overvalued exchange rate; but if the aid resources are used to increase supply, then incomes will rise, savings increase and exports recover (Bhaduri and Skarstein 1996). However, in a war economy the positive supply response is small or non-existent so the productive effect of aid is likely to be limited. None the less, by reducing the need for monetization of the fiscal deficit, aid can and does reduce inflation and thus the burden on the most vulnerable households. Moreover, the possible disincentives to agricultural production in a peacetime economy are derived from the price effects as food aid pushes out the domestic supply curve, lowering the domestic price of agricultural output (Maxwell and Singer 1979).[13] In wartime, however, supply problems are likely to maintain strong domestic demand for food relative to supply, so that the constraint is likely to be the lack of inputs. If the government uses the revenue to reduce the fiscal deficit, the effect can actually be deflationary (Roemer 1989).

4.3   International Financial Institutions

Aid agencies tend to leave the macroeconomic policy dialogue to the international financial institutions (IFIs). However, their analysis of the problems of underdevelopment and poverty does not include war as a characteristic feature—as pointed out in Chapter 1. The main concern of the IFIs in situations of extreme macroeconomic stress is to implement a short-term stabilization programme, defined in terms of devaluation of the nominal exchange rate, a sharp reduction in the growth of the money supply and credit creation, positive real interest rates and a reduction of government expenditure and thus the budget deficit. The aim of this standard programme is to reduce inflation, restore currency convertibility, and renew debt service. However, the application of this type of monetary adjustment to an economy with the type of structural constraints, private-sector behaviour and budgetary burdens we have discussed can have effects quite contrary to policymakers' expectations.

Large nominal devaluations, to be effective, require considerable price elasticity of import demand and export supply on the one hand, and a sharp downward adjustment of household consumption on the other (the 'income effect'). However, as we have seen, when imports are largely debt-financed or administratively allocated, the devaluation will be passed through entirely to domestic prices. Export profitability will increase of course, but as supply is constrained by the lack of investment and imported inputs, export volume may not rise at all. In other words, the real exchange rate is not really available as a policy variable.

The main macroeconomic consequence of nominal devaluation is thus to reduce domestic demand. The fiscal impact of devaluation depends on the foreign-exchange composition of revenue and expenditure: only in the case of a very heavily aid-dependent government would devaluation reduce the budget deficit; however, even if nominal budgets are incompletely adjusted, to the extent that public-sector imports are covered by aid, then increased counterpart funds cover the difference. Private-sector real demand will only fall if firms reduce investment or households reduce consumption; among the latter—as we have seen—the impact of inflation is not often evenly distributed, with poor wage earners being particularly vulnerable.

---

[13] See also Chapter 7 in this volume for an analysis of the distributional effects of food aid.

Real reductions in government expenditure under Bretton Woods stabilization programmes tend to be spread across the whole budget, and in effect take the form of investment cuts and real wage reductions for civil servants, with the consequences discussed above. However, reduced government credit requirements, combined with a lower overall credit ceiling, can reduce inflation considerably. The problem is that the credit reductions and high nominal interest rates harm production—particularly that of small producers who are the banks' least preferred clients—and thus may reduce food supply just when it should be increased. Rising real interest rates do not increase bank deposits due to the degree of exchange risk, while the increased profitability of exporters cannot be immediately translated into growth, employment, and import capacity.

There is no doubt that price stability, fiscal solvency, and a manageable balance of payments are desirable objectives; the problem is the social and economic cost of taking the view that wartime macroeconomic imbalances are essentially monetary in nature when private and public-sector behaviour is so different from that in peacetime. The effect of this view is to ensure that the poor continue 'paying for the war'.

In the case of wartime poor economies, an orthodox structural adjustment package is thus likely to have damaging results for vulnerable groups. Import liberalization would undermine the supply of essential goods and services and stimulate capital flight; privatization would be impossible or merely involve the enrichment of senior government officials; and real devaluation involves the distributional problems discussed above—compounded by structural fiscal deficits unless public investment and many social services are abandoned. Farm-price deregulation does not increase peasant output unless there are improved credit conditions and an adequate supply of rural producer goods. Above all, private investment would not increase sufficiently to restore growth and employment in view of the degree of uncertainty about future profits or even asset ownership.

5   An Alternative Approach to Stabilization in Conflict Conditions

5.1   Keynes on Paying for the War

Our critique of the macroeconomic policies of domestic governments and international financial institutions in conflict conditions implies a need for an alternative stabilization policy. In general terms, an appropriate policy design should combine three elements: first, the basic requirements of any stabilization programme—that is, containing inflation and the balance of payments while stimulating production; second, the protection of the most vulnerable groups in society—or at least that the poor should not get poorer; and third, laying the foundations for economic recovery and thus confidence among all parties of the likelihood of a sustainable peace.

Keynes addressed this problem early in World War II, and returned to the theme at various points during the following four years.[14] He started from the position that

[14] See Keynes (1939; 1978), especially pp. 41–51 ff.

the UK economy would be working at full capacity during the war, with enormous mandatory demands on supply from the requirements of the military. He also took for granted that exchange controls would be imposed on both current and capital accounts so that imports could be restricted to essential supplies and to prevent capital flight. Keynes identified a double problem. During the war there would be full employment (and thus wage goods demand) at a time when the supply of consumer goods would of necessity be reduced in order to make room for military production. Once hostilities ceased, there would be collapse in demand as military expenditure ceased, and large-scale unemployment would return.[15]

Keynes regarded this dilemma not only as an economic issue, but also as a political one—wartime shortages would cause hardship among the working classes, and a post-war slump would breed popular discontent. He critically examined the four conventional policy options for dealing with the mismatch between rising demand and falling civilian supply. First, there was the possibility of comprehensive rationing, which he felt was not administratively feasible and would lead to extensive black-marketeering. Second, the adoption of anti-profiteering measures in order to prevent prices being raised excessively, but this he felt also to be administratively unfeasible and liable to depress production by legitimate enterprise. Both these measures, moreover, would only suppress latent inflation rather than eliminate it. The third alternative was to allow inflation to reduce real wages and thus the demand for consumer goods, and to use the increased money demand to finance government borrowing from the Bank of England.[16] Fourth, indirect taxes could be raised to absorb excess demand, which would also allow the budget to be balanced. Keynes argued, however, that these last two options were highly undesirable because they would in effect force workers to finance the war and would be widely seen as inequitable at a time when national unity was required.[17]

Keynes, in contrast, proposed a quite different solution. Obligatory savings schemes for workers were to be established through the post office, which would in effect leave them with lower real wages during the war but would also allow them to build up considerable financial assets. This would have two advantages during hostilities: on the one hand, demand for consumer goods could be kept down to the level of supply; and on the other, workers would feel that they were being treated equitably. Further financial requirements would be met by a progressive income tax, which would have similar social benefits. Once victory was achieved, the workers could draw down their savings accounts and in adjusting to their desired income/wealth ratio, would stimulate consumption demand and thus sustain employment and investment in the post-war years.[18]

---

[15] He was concerned, of course, to avoid a repetition of the slump that had occurred after WW I.

[16] 'We all know, of course, that the alternative is inflation. And we also know that the political arguments in favour of inflation are almost overwhelming. No one has to take the responsibility for inflation, not even the Chancellor of the Exchequer' (ibid. 76).

[17] And presumably reduce labour productivity as well, on an 'efficiency wages' argument.

[18] In the event, the British government adopted a combination of rationing, anti-profiteering measures, and indirect taxation; and the Conservatives lost the first post-war election by a large margin.

5.2   An Alternative Approach for Low-Income Economies

The UK was a highly organized and industrialized economy, where direct war damage was relatively slight and the financial system was sufficiently robust to make Keynes's proposition feasible. It might seem, therefore, that poor countries could not apply such a model. None the less, there are profound insights in Keynes's proposal which do seem to be relevant to our problem: the need to adjust household consumption to available supplies of consumer goods, to maintain production incentives, and to avoid increasing poverty on the one hand; and the desirability of distributing the economic cost of war equitably and providing for post-war reconstruction on the other. An equivalent scheme for low-income wartime economies would emphasize food supply and real asset accumulation by small producers.

The key determinant of real living standards of the urban poor is the marketed supply of food, and that of the rural peasantry is the real terms of trade received for this food supply. Average real urban wages are determined by effective per capita food supply whatever its nominal price level (as long as market entitlements are maintained), but for farmers to provide this surplus, they must receive in exchange essential production inputs—seeds, tools, fertilizer, and so on. As we have seen it is this material exchange that breaks down in wartime: while high nominal prices may well be available in parallel markets, they have no real value to the producer. In consequence, the first element of an alternative stabilization programme would be to divert import support programmes towards the supply of agricultural producer goods and appropriate rural consumption goods. In this way, aggregate output can be raised within the foreign-exchange constraint and food-price inflation kept under control—two essential conditions for improving the income distribution in poor economies.[19]

The equivalent to the Keynesian saving programmes for industrial workers in wartime would be some parallel form of asset accumulation appropriate for a rural economy dominated by small producers. The logical equivalent would be the opportunity to obtain land (and the simple capital goods required to work it) and housing. This could take the form of an extensive land-reform programme, supported by international aid for agricultural implements and building materials. This would absorb the excess money balances of the households involved, sustain production during wartime, and provide the basis for small-scale accumulation as the motor of post-war reconstruction. The inevitably lower levels of consumption during wartime would be more tolerable if accompanied by the prospect of rising living standards in peacetime, and would provide a powerful incentive for peace-building itself. An approach of this kind would thus be consistent with tight fiscal measures in order to prevent excess monetization and thus prevent growing income inequality arising from excess demand and supply dislocation.

5.3   Complementary Fiscal and Aid Policies

Direct taxation is notoriously difficult to administer in poor economies, if only because an efficient system requires a high proportion of income to take the form of registered

---

[19]   A point made forcefully by Kalecki—see FitzGerald, 1993.

transactions. The nearest equivalent in our case would be duties on luxury goods—including gasoline, electricity, cigarettes, and bottled drinks, and above all imported non-essentials. The containment of expenditure at the macroeconomic level clearly requires the limitation of nominal budgets. Within these allocations, it would clearly be better to maintain priority activities (such as preventive health and road transport) with adequately paid personnel and sufficient domestic and imported inputs—albeit at the cost of closing down other activities for the duration of the war—than to allow services to deteriorate 'across the board' through lack of skilled personnel, working equipment, and specific inputs. In effect, the monetary budget actually authorized should correspond to the planned use of these real resources. Import support programmes should be constructed by donors in order to support those programmes which are designed to reach vulnerable groups and provide essential services for the population as a whole.

Counterpart funds should always be used in the first instance to reduce the fiscal deficit rather than to increase government expenditure, so that the need for monetary emission can be reduced to a minimum. The reduction of inflation to an acceptable level must be a central objective of any stabilization policy, not only because the poor with few market entitlements are often most vulnerable to rising prices, but also because the required control over the macroeconomy is easily lost thereby. This would also make the real internal terms of trade improvement discussed above easier to achieve and thus stimulate food production and improve income distribution.

However, monetary control will only be effective if—as Keynes pointed out—the underlying macroeconomic imbalances are kept within reasonable limits by non-monetary means. In a dependent economy, budgetary balance and an adequate supply of wage-goods is not sufficient, however. The foreign exchange balance must also be maintained. This requires a realistic official foreign-exchange rate that renders exports profitable and discourages smuggling; as well as officially supervised overseas marketing in order to reduce capital flight. Last but not least, this approach would require external support in the form of suspension of debt service during periods of conflict—conditional upon the implementation of a poverty-oriented stabilization programme.[20]

6   Conclusions

In sum, the main welfare loss from armed conflict in poor countries is not the destruction and battlefield deaths, but rather the consequence of economic breakdown, forced migration and administrative collapse; in consequence, appropriate macroeconomic stabilization has an important part to play in reducing these human costs as far as possible. The chronic fiscal and external constraints on macroeconomic equilibrium in low-income countries are made worse in wartime by the requirements of resource mobilization for the military effort and the negative impact of the war on output and exports; stabilization policy must thus aim to contain these imbalances and stimulate domestic production.

---

[20]   This point is taken up again in Chapter 8 in this volume.

However, the behaviour of the private sector—both firms and households—changes fundamentally during conflict, due to changes in expectations, increased uncertainty, survival strategies and resource constraints; these changes, which render wars quite different from natural disasters, imply that stabilization policy will have unexpected consequences. Thus although government policy under wartime conditions tends to focus on resource mobilization and exercising direct control over key economic activities, this often aggravates macroeconomic imbalances. Aid agencies focus on import support programmes and humanitarian relief, without taking into account the macroeconomic consequences of their actions; the application of standard Fund and Bank programmes can easily worsen the problem.

An alternative stabilization programme can be designed, inspired by Keynes's ideas in *Paying for the War*, which seeks to improve exchange relationships with small producers as underpinning the living standards of the poor, and the provision of suitable means of petty accumulation; it would also be necessary to redesign fiscal and aid policies in this direction.

However, the design of any alternative stabilization programme designed to help the poor in conflict must confront the problem of the political economy of such initiatives. Wars have economic winners as well as economic losers. New and powerful groups emerge to take advantage of the quasi-rents generated by shortages and macroeconomic imbalances, and their interests in a continuation of the situation can combine with those of the military in prosecuting the war until final victory and the bureaucracy in maintaining control over economic activity. The position of aid donors may thus be crucial if poor households are not to end up paying for the war.

APPENDIX

The Fiscal Balance

Consider a developing country government welfare function of the type defined by Heller (1975). This is defined in terms of parameters—weights (a, b) and elasticities (α, β)—for military expenditure (G_m) and social expenditure (G_s) on the one hand, and taxation (T) and budget deficits (Z) on the other. This gives the government maximand (U) as:

$$U = a_1 G_m^{\alpha_1} + a_2 G_s^{\alpha_2} - b_1 T^{\beta_1} - b_2 Z^{\beta_2} \qquad \alpha < 1, \beta > 1$$

There is thus a declining marginal utility (i.e. political benefits) of expenditure and rising marginal disutility (i.e. political costs) of revenue subject to the budget identity:

$$G_m + G_s = T + Z$$

For given levels of taxation (T) and military expenditure (G_m), the policy process leads to an optimal fiscal deficit $(Z^\star)$ and social expenditure $(G_s^\star)$ such that:

$$Z^\star = G_m - T + \frac{b_2 \beta_2}{a_2 \alpha_2} Z^{\frac{\beta_2 - 1}{\alpha_2 - 1}}; \quad G_s^\star = T - G_m - \frac{a_2 \alpha_2}{b_2 \beta_2} G_s^{\frac{\alpha_2 - 1}{\beta_2 - 1}}$$

In wartime the utility of military expenditure (a_1) obviously rises, which not only increases military expenditure itself but (from the solution above) also increases the optimal fiscal deficit $(Z^\star)$ and reduces optimal social expenditure $(G_s^\star)$. However, if the disutility of borrowing (b_2) declines as the government's time horizon contracts, then for a given level of military expenditure not only will the deficit rise but so will social expenditure.

The Investment Decision

Generally, a firm's investment depends upon the difference between its existing capital stock (K) and its desired capital stock $(K^\star)$, the latter depending on expected profitability, market size and so on. The speed (λ) at which the firm adjusts its capital stock from the existing to the desired level is determined on the one hand by the availability and cost of funds, and on the other by uncertainty about the future because of the difficulty of reversing fixed investment decisions once undertaken (Dixit and Pindyck 1994). Thus investment (I) is given by:

$$I = \lambda(K^\star - K)$$

In wartime, the existing capital stock (K) is reduced by deliberate destruction and inadequate maintenance, but the desired capital stock $(K^\star)$ is also reduced by the prospect of continued wartime restrictions—except perhaps in import-substitution activities. The speed of adjustment (λ) is also reduced by financial constraints and increased uncertainty. In consequence the level of investment (I) is very low indeed. The reaction to a natural disaster is very different, even though the destruction of existing capacity (K) might be equivalent. This is because the desired capacity $(K^\star)$ is similar to what it was previously, while the adjustment speed (λ) actually rises because of government reconstruction efforts and increased foreign aid. As a result, private investment rates after natural disasters tend to rise sharply (Albala-Bertrand 1994). Finally, a negative external trade shock will depress investment much less than wartime destruction—even if the immediate effect on export revenues is equivalent—because even though desired capital stock falls $(K^\star)$ the speed of adjustment (λ) remains unchanged.

Table 2A.1 Private investment response to trade shocks, natural disasters, and wars

	Trade shock	Natural disaster	Wartime
Speed of adjustment (λ)	=	+	–
Desired capital stock $(k^\star)$	–	=	–
Existing capital stock (k)	=	–	–
Level of realized investment (I)	–	++	– –

Note: =, no change; –, decline; – –, strong decline; ++, strong increase.

3

The Political Economy of War

DAVID KEEN

1 Introduction: Understanding 'War'

The industrialized countries have experienced a period of relative peace since World War II, and, particularly in the 1980s, this was reflected in the common assertion that nuclear weapons had 'kept the peace'. The experience in poorer countries has been very different, however. Indeed, we have seen a steady rise in the number of wars in the world—rising around fivefold from 1960 to the 1990s (Gantzel 1994, cited in Duffield 1994b).

This chapter is intended to point up new ways of thinking about war and possible directions for research derived from a review of the existing literature. What follows provides only a very partial literature review. The literature on civil wars alone is a huge one. For example, some 50,000 books have been published on the US Civil War. This review looks particularly at the economic causes and consequences of war. It deals primarily with civil wars, while keeping one eye on inter-state wars. This distinction is unlikely in any case to be hard and fast. Civil conflicts frequently have an important international dimension. Moreover, many inter-state wars have their origins in civil wars.

The chapter focuses particularly on the indirect costs of war, rather than on the direct costs (in terms of human casualties) that are frequently emphasized. These indirect costs are discussed in Section 2. It is suggested, in addition, that significant economic benefits may arise from war. These benefits may be intended or unintended. In so far as intended benefits arise from war, it is reasonable to talk about the functions of war as well as its causes. The benefits or functions of war are discussed in Section 3.

Following work by Stewart (1993), the analysis suggests dangers in the common [*key theme.*] view that development interventions should be put 'on hold' for the duration of a conflict. It also suggests limitations in the common assumption that peace will come when warring parties 'come to their senses' and recognize the irrationality of war.

2 The Nature of War

To some extent, the study of war has been characterized by a kind of mental block. Sometimes war appears as a kind of 'black box', an important phenomenon which we somehow think we understand but avoid analysing in any detail. Part of the problem, of course, is that wars are not easy to study 'up close'.

War also presents particular difficulties for economists within the classical tradition. Markets are unlikely to work smoothly in wartime, and many of the usual tools for analysis are of dubious value. The concept of 'market forces' may itself be rather unhelpful in explaining how a particular economy works during wartime. Not only are markets likely to be severely disrupted and disintegrated, but the concept of market forces omits the importance of outright theft and the key role of violence in shaping the way that particular markets work (see, Keen 1994*b*, for example on 'forced markets'). Taking the example of theft, let us suppose that person A hits person B over the head and takes B's food. This can be seen as an economic (as well as a political) process. After all, it involves the transfer of wealth from A to B, and it is likely to have important economic causes and implications. But how is one to describe this incident in the language of classical economics?

War and violence have been largely marginalized from the study of famine, with Drèze and Sen contributing to this shortcoming with their assertion that:

> It would be, particularly, a mistake to relate the causation of famines to violations of legality . . . the millions that die in a famine typically die in an astonishingly 'legal' and 'orderly' way. (Drèze and Sen 1989: 22)

Similar omissions can be found in thinking about development. Stewart (1993) makes the important point (on which, more later) that the World Bank and the International Monetary Fund have failed to design policies that take full account of the realities of war.

Two of the most common (and contrasting) models of war both tend to 'elbow out' political and economic analysis. One model depicts war as essentially chaotic. According to this model, war is a largely incomprehensible eruption of violence. 'Normal life' comes abruptly to an end, while 'anarchy' or 'mindless violence' prevails. The conflict may end when people 'come to their senses'. The model (which might better be called a confession of bafflement) has been applied particularly to civil wars; much of the media coverage of war and related famine in Somalia, for example, followed this line.

Portraying violence as somehow 'irrational' is actually part of a long and often honourable philosophical tradition. Spinoza saw violence as arising when reason gave way to passion, producing violence among a species whose self-interest lay in cooperation. A similar line can be found in Bertrand Russell, who was shocked by what he saw as the 'war fever' in the run up to World War I, and who saw war as stemming from impulse rather than from the calculation of advantages (Russell 1961). Particularly in the nineteenth and early twentieth centuries, liberal thinkers often emphasized that foreign conquests did not pay, with peace and free trade seen as objectively in the interests of all states (Marwick *et al.* 1990: 37).

More recently, Scheff (1994)—in an argument quite close to Spinoza's in important respects—has argued that since people are always better off negotiating on topics of dispute, it is inevitably emotion that tips them into war (just as it is emotion rather than self-interest that tips people into interpersonal violence in the domestic sphere).[1]

---

[1] Scheff (1994) attaches importance to the acknowledgement of shame and guilt, and the use of psychological insights in the design of war–crime trials and the reconciliation process.

The argument that war is 'irrational' tends to be bolstered when we focus exclusively on the costs of war. One could make an enormous list of the 'bad economic consequences' of war (as well as the purely human consequences), and in many ways this endeavour would supplement the habitual emphasis placed by television on the visible devastation caused by war and on the plight of civilians 'caught in the crossfire'. When such a task was completed, one might be left mystified as to how an event so manifestly catastrophic for so many sections of society could be allowed, and indeed made, to happen. The implication would appear to be that war, as Spinoza implied, was a case of 'sheer madness'? It would follow that we should leave the attempt to understand it to the psychologists and psychiatrists, dismissing the assortment of sociologists, economists, and political scientists who might claim to throw light on the causes of war.

Whilst not denying that the discipline of psychology, for example, is likely to have an important role in explaining violence,[2] nevertheless the portrayal of violence as purely 'irrational' tends to minimize the role (and even the apparent need) for any serious political or economic analysis. By contrast, this chapter takes seriously the possibility that violence and war may have important functions, that they may be in some sense 'rational'. (The use of this word is not intended to imply moral approval, although those who portray violence as 'irrational' sometimes gain a degree of plausibility from the common association made between 'irrational' and 'immoral'). It is also emphasized— and this will be an important part of our approach—that war does not necessarily lead to a complete cessation of 'normal life', a complete 'breakdown' in the economic and political system. Rather, it is likely to modify and distort ways of living (and ways of making a living) that are already in place. Moreover, many people may continue to enjoy some form of physical protection. In other words, economic and political processes will continue to operate in wartime. These processes will affect—and will in turn be affected by—the course of the war. The modification of old systems is likely to be supplemented by the creation of new ones. These (mutating) systems are susceptible, at least in theory, to investigation.

The task of reviving the analysis of war from a political economic perspective is all the more urgent since it would appear that the portrayal of war as chaos and 'sheer madness' plays a part in paralysing international responses. For one thing, the portrayal of war as chaos suggests that 'nothing can be done'. Sometimes, this may serve as a convenient excuse for international inaction. As Bradbury comments in his study of conflict and international response in Somalia, 'The situation in Somalia is "complex". Such a description is often used as an excuse by people who do not want to understand' (1993: 2). The weak international response to the early stages of the Rwandan genocide reflected, in part, a perception that Rwanda was afflicted by 'mindless violence' stemming from 'age-old ethnic hatreds'. This perception was linked to certain quasi-racist assumptions about tribalism in Africa. But even the most 'liberal' instincts may shape our perceptions of war in dangerous ways. Most notably, in the rush to show up war as

---

[2] One of the most fruitful lines of inquiry may be an investigation of the relationship between violence and ideas about masculinity (see, for example, Theweleit 1987). The role of gender in warmaking and peacemaking is an important area of enquiry.

an unmitigated evil, we may miss important information about the functions of wars, why they are made to happen, and what can be done to bring them to an end or even to prevent them.

The portrayal of war as chaos may make it harder even to engage mentally with news of distant lands. In a sympathetic description of the position of the television viewer, German writer Hans Magnus Enzensberger notes that:

We are expected to remember the names of gangsters before we can pronounce them, and to concern ourselves with Islamic sects, African militias and Cambodian factions whose motives are and will remain a complete mystery to us.   (Enzensberger 1994: 60)

The elements of rationality and even 'order' that may be present within a situation of war are put in a new light by work that to some extent blurs the distinction between 'peace' and 'war'. Bradbury (1993), for example, observes that a degree of low-level warfare in Somalia is to some extent 'normal'. This suggests the possibility that a degree of violence serves some kind of function in Somalia society, even in 'peacetime'. It also raises the interesting question of whether we should regard war or peace as normal. Rather than always asking 'What are the causes of war?', we might also ask 'What are the causes of peace?'. It may also be worthwhile asking 'What is it that imposes limits on warfare and what is it that causes violence to escalate?'.

Both Enzensberger (1994) and Kaplan (1994) have recently noted important points of similarity between gang 'warfare' in industrialized countries and the kinds of factional warfare taking place in many poorer countries. While some societies are undoubtedly much more violent than others, this kind of work calls into question the assumption that societies can be neatly divided into those that are 'at war' (and chaotic) and those 'at peace' (and orderly).

In contrast to the view of war as chaos, a second model of war is the bureaucratic model. This also tends to 'elbow out' political and economic analysis in important respects. According to this model, war is declared and the processes of violence follow more or less automatically with violence largely restricted to the competing military forces.[3] This model is applied particularly, though not exclusively, to inter-state wars. To a large extent, this is the study of war as a series of battles: one analyses war as one might analyse a 'wargame', discussing tactics, the movement of troops, the victors, and the defeated.

A brief look at the literature on World War I reveals a plethora of books on the war's causes, with political and economic analysis playing a considerable role. Then there are studies of the war itself, and this, by and large, is the sphere of the military historians. Finally, we find studies of the 'consequences of World War I', at which point the political and economic analysts typically rejoin the endeavour. In other words, we have a three-stage model (causes/war/consequences), in which the analysis of the war itself is strangely devoid of political and economic content.

Indeed, the political and economic literature on such wars reveals a concern with why war was declared and what the consequences of the war were—as if one were

---

[3] The supposedly automatic nature of this process is implied by the common use of the phrase 'military machine'.

asking why a car had been pushed towards a steep downward incline and what the eventual destructive consequences were. The danger is that political and economic processes accompanying war somehow get lost. When applied to something like World War I, the deficiencies of the bureaucratic model of warfare are to some extent disguised. The pattern of violence was to a large extent shaped by bureaucratic hierarchies; resources were mobilized by the state through normal legal channels; and the bulk of the casualties were military.

In the case of civil war, the deficiencies of the bureaucratic model seem more glaring. In particular, in civil wars it becomes much more obvious that war is shaped by—and in turn shapes—political and economic processes already at work within a society. A particular configuration of causes dictates not simply that a war takes place, but also the type of war it is. And similarly, the complex pattern of consequences will follow not simply from the fact that 'there was a war', but from the particular type of war it was.

In civil wars, it is also likely to be particularly evident that the unfolding of war over time will depend on the evolving relationship between war and society (for example the way that the war affects and is affected by the changing interests of civilians and soldiers). As wars evolve, the consequences of an early stage in a war may become the causes of later developments. Thus—particularly in the case of civil wars—unless we study the political and economic processes taking place during war itself, we are likely to be blind not only to the nature of war but also to the reasons why it evolves as it does.

This means treating wars as processes particular to a given context, while still entertaining the possibility that certain wars may resemble each other in important respects. War may take many different forms. Faced with a varied set of processes displaying various degrees and types of violence, it would be dangerous to assume that we are talking about the same thing, just because we call them all 'war'.

A comparison with disease makes the point in another way. In order to understand, a disease we cannot confine our attention to the causes of the disease (germs, lifestyle, and so on) and the consequences (loss of capacities and so forth), important though these areas of enquiry undoubtedly are. We must first study the disease itself, looking for laws that seem to govern its development and evolution. Further, we must be prepared to study individual diseases without assuming that all diseases are the same. (At the same time, our insight will be limited if we assume that each individual's disease is an entirely unique occurrence.)

It is, of course, legitimate to ask about the 'causes of war' and the 'consequences of war'. These are questions of self-evident importance. However, we should be aware that these very formulations run the risk of implying that 'war' is somehow an entity that can be separated from its 'causes' and 'consequences'. They run the risk, in other words, of seducing the reader with the three-stage model (causes/war/consequences). Yet it would be a mistake to think that the causes of war or the consequences of war can somehow be studied without looking at the nature (and the varied, often local, functions) of war. The same is also true of the study of famine (Rangasami 1985; Keen 1994*a*).

What exactly is this thing called 'war' to which everything seems to lead and from which everything seems to follow? Political and economic analysts need to study the particular patterns and functions of violence in given societies and not simply the 'overall causes' and 'overall consequences' of some supposedly self-explanatory (and ultimately opaque) event called 'war'.

Michel Foucault (1988) made a similar point when he commented on the imprisonment of dissidents in the former Soviet Union. In opposition to those on the Left who wished to 'explain it away', Foucault suggested that a proper investigation of 'the Gulag question' involved:

> refusing to restrict one's questioning to the level of causes. If one begins by asking for the 'cause' of the Gulag (Russia's retarded development, the transformation of the party into a bureaucracy, the specific economic difficulties of the USSR), one makes the Gulag appear as a sort of disease or abscess, an infection, degeneration or involution. This is to think of the Gulag only negatively, as an obstacle to be removed, a dysfunctioning to be rectified—a maternity illness of the country which is painfully giving birth to socialism. The Gulag question has to be posed in positive terms. The problem of causes must not be dissociated from that of function: what use is the Gulag, what functions does it assure, in what strategies is it integrated?

Even from a purely philosophical point of view, it is difficult to see how the study of any phenomenon can be separated from the study of its causes and consequences. One may look, for example, at the causes of a natural phenomenon such as the wind (warm air rising and so on). One may look at the consequences of wind (for example, falling leaves). But what is this 'wind'? Perhaps it is not a 'thing' at all, but rather the name we attach to the process by which a particular set of causes turns into a particular, predictable set of consequences.

Mention has been made of the need to study particular patterns and functions of violence in particular societies. Different types of war are likely to lead to different types of costs and to serve different types of functions. A key variable may be the degree to which violence is controlled along bureaucratic hierarchies.[4] Although we often think that we know what war is, it is instructive to compare 'war' with other related phenomena, notably 'genocide', 'rebellion' and 'counterrevolution', 'banditry', and 'crime'. When does one of these become another?

Is it possible to have a revolution (as opposed to a political coup) without some form of mass mobilization and war? And if so, is it possible that war is here serving some 'legitimate', even desirable, functions? 'War' may be partly generated by (and may in turn reinforce) political and economic inequalities which predate the war. It may be a response to suffering as well as a cause of it.

At the same time, war may serve a counter-revolutionary or repressive function. For example, militias may be armed to protect particular exploitative patterns of trade and development against groups who violently oppose this exploitation (as has been the case with mining interests in Liberia, for example, and with oil and agricultural interests in Sudan).

In Sudan, war has not been simply an irrational phenomenon. Rather, it has served as an expression of economic and political discontent (rebellion), a means of suppressing

---

[4] In medieval Europe, warfare could 'spread from top to bottom after an initial decision by official authorities, who endeavoured to direct, monopolize, organize and terminate it' or it could 'rise from below'. The latter form of warfare threatened the state's authority, and encouraged repeated prohibitions on the bearing of arms (Contamine 1980: 242–3).

discontent (counter-revolution), a means of wiping out or severely weakening particular ethnic groups (something close to genocide) and a means of economic enrichment (banditry, crime, trading in 'forced markets'). Moreover, the aim has not been simply to 'win the war' but also to make money under the cover of war (in a context where certain ethnic groups are deemed 'fair game'). Some have accused Sudanese governments of attempting to weaken their own army (by engaging it in a long, unwinnable war in the south) whilst building alternative sources of political support (in the form of government-supported militias). The use of wars to distract potentially rebellious troops is an historical phenomenon of long standing. Again, it will be important to avoid the assumption that we know what 'war' is and that we only need to list its 'causes' and 'consequences'.

If it is often difficult to distinguish precisely between war and other related phenomena, the question of definitions may also be a profoundly political one. In Rwanda, a tendency to describe the conflict as 'civil war' whilst avoiding the term 'genocide' played a part in weakening international responses to the crisis, particularly during the crucial early weeks of the genocide (African Rights 1994). In contexts where there has been armed resistance to alien rule, the ruling government has often portrayed the resisters as no more than criminals. Conversely, revolutionary groups may portray every criminal act as somehow a contribution to the struggle. Such ideological battles are likely to add to the difficulty of distinguishing crime and rebellion (Tilly 1982). Perhaps it is precisely on the boundaries between 'war' and related phenomena not normally classed as war that one may hope to gain the freshest insights into the nature of war.

So how are we to define 'war'? This is very difficult. One possible definition might be 'the sustained infliction of violence between two or more organized groups'.[5] One of the challenges of war studies is that this word 'organized' begins to look increasingly out of place, particularly as banditry plays an apparently increasing role in modern conflicts.

3   The Costs of War

The costs of warfare have rarely been studied systematically, and those studies that have addressed the costs have often simply drawn up a 'list' of these costs—without either establishing clear analytical categories or analysing the likely impact of these costs on the future direction of conflict. Among the useful studies of the economic costs of war are Mysliwiec's (1988) study of Kampuchea/Cambodia and Drèze and Gazdar's (1992) study of Iraq, while Hanlon (1991) has described the negative impact on human welfare of warfare and structural adjustment programmes in Mozambique. In both the Cambodia and Iraq cases, the damage done by war has been aggravated by international isolation and sanctions. Drèze and Gazdar suggest that the very severe economic and welfare consequences of the UN/Iraq Gulf War (including the effect of international sanctions) have been more severe than the suffering arising directly from the war. Drèze

---

[5] One might object that football hooligans fit this description while hardly engaging in what most people understand to be 'war'. Perhaps the answer—and the appeal—is that hooligans mimic war, though their activities do not fully merit the description of 'sustained infliction of violence'.

and Gazdar's is a relatively sophisticated case study, but even they do not say much about the amount of economic damage and human suffering attributable specifically to the war and the amount attributable to sanctions.

The following section suggests some ways of categorizing the costs of war, before considering a number of relatively neglected topics: warfare as a drain on resources; deliberate attempts to increase the costs of war; deliberate attempts to reduce the costs of war; and the impact of the costs of war on the prospects for peace or further war.

It should be borne in mind that analysis of the total costs of war will need to take account of any benefits that may also arise from war. The latter are discussed in Section 3.

3.1 Some Analytical Categories

A first step in systematically assessing the costs of war is to decide on the appropriate analytical categories. One useful distinction, highlighted by Stewart (1993), is between the direct and indirect costs of war, in other words between the direct effects of violence (killing, wounding) and the indirect effects on human welfare of war-induced changes in economic, social, and political life. Stewart notes that there has been little systematic analysis of the economic impact of war, and of the human costs arising from economic developments associated with war. One could add that there has sometimes been an attempt by governments and the media (either more or less systematic) to cover up these costs. The present paper focuses on the indirect costs of conflict.

Within the category of indirect costs, one can distinguish between long-term and short-term costs. Some of the costs of war may be to a large extent 'hidden', only becoming fully evident at a later stage. The psychological damage to children may be one example. On the other hand, it is possible that some of the costs of war may later translate into benefits, for example if widespread destruction (as in Germany and Japan during World War II) prompts a major restructuring of the economy along more 'modern' lines.

Another way of analysing indirect costs is to employ the entitlement perspective outlined by Sen (1981) and elaborated by Stewart (1985), and Drèze and Sen (1989), and discussed in Chapter 1 of this book.

Stewart (1993: 375) has noted that,

Many of the indirect deaths during war are due to entitlement failures, especially entitlements for food (from subsistence or the market) and health services (provided by the state).

In wartime, especially, it is important to move beyond the 'legal' entitlement perspective to 'non-entitlements' or 'extra-legal entitlements', that is commodities or money secured by means that lie outside the existing legal framework. There is likely to be a 'grey area' between economic activities that are clearly legal and economic activities that are clearly illegal. Looking at extra-legal entitlements in addition to entitlements is likely to involve looking at the way that certain activities can shift between the categories of 'illegal', 'quasi-legal' and 'legal'. Groups who possess something close to a monopoly of the means of force in a given geographical area may define an activity as legal (either explicitly or implicitly) which was previously considered—and perhaps is still considered by the national government—to be illegal. For example, 'robbery' can become 'taxation' by a local warlord or by a rebel administration. Where illegal economic activities are widely practised, it may be that the state (or some elements of the state) are shielding the practitioners from prosecution (perhaps in return for a 'pay-off'). The 'informal' economy may be widely tolerated. Those who conduct raids on a rebellious section of the population may be granted effective immunity from prosecution.[6] Given the importance of extra-legal activities in many poor countries (and also in many rich ones), it is unlikely that one can capture the essentials of their economies with an approach that focuses exclusively on legal means of obtaining commodities.

A consideration of 'extra-legal entitlements' would include income from: raiding, protection rackets (for example, charging money to spare people's lives or to spare or protect their property, charging money to protect relief), diversion of relief, charging people for moving from one area to another, official corruption and the use of public funds for private purposes, the use of force to 'skew' markets in particular ways (for example, through raiding, intimidation in the market place, blocking relief, forced labour or slavery), ejecting people from productive or mineral-rich land. The strategies of the different warring parties will need to be distinguished. Such an investigation would be closely linked with an examination of the functions of war (see Section 3.2).

Economic strategies adopted during wartime can be divided into:

1. Economic strategies that are exploitative (by which I mean strategies that create suffering among others and that are predicated on the infliction of violence). These strategies may be legal or illegal. Such strategies can include raiding and protection rackets.

2. Economic strategies that are not directly exploitative but that are damaging to long-term production, for example, stripping the environment, selling off assets, consuming seed, leaving productive land (perhaps for relief distributions in urban areas), investing in activities of limited usefulness (for example, smuggling) rather than putting money into production, 'legitimate' trade or savings; directing public policy towards attracting external aid rather than developing the domestic economy. Again, these activities may be legal or illegal.

3. Economic strategies that contribute to public welfare (for example, labour or investment in farming; in herding; in industrial production; in trading activities; in saving . . .). Once again, these activities may be legal or illegal. It is important to investigate to what extent a poor security environment tends to encourage strategies that detract from public welfare and to discourage strategies that enhance public welfare.

Another way of looking at the costs of war is to examine different indicators of human well-being, such as health (and ill-health) indicators, nutrition, and psychological damage. One can also look at the differential impact of war by gender, including indicators of well-being and changing gender roles.

---

[6] The lack of legal redress by groups considered 'fair game' in the context of civil war has been an important cause of famine in Sudan, for example.

It is useful to distinguish between war's effect on capital and on investment. War causes destruction of existing capital and reduces investment by government, aid agencies, and domestic and foreign capitalists. Destruction of existing capital may include destruction of physical production and infrastructure (such as transport, irrigation, power, and factories), social infrastructure (such as schools and clinics), human capital (death, migration, knowledge), institutions (extensions, banks, marketing links, science and technical institutions), and social/cultural capital (trust, work ethic, and respect for property) (Stewart 1993: 363).

Another way of dividing up the costs of war is to look at its impact on: labour (for example, death, migration, restrictions on movement); capital; and markets (for example, restrictions on movement, changes in demand).

3.2   War as a Drain on Resources

Although most people often think of outright destruction when they think of the costs of war, a major source of the costs of war is likely to arise from the resources required for warmaking. The damage done when war takes resources from other activities has been stressed by Shindo (1985) among others, although (as will be noted in more detail in Section 3 on the 'benefits of war') some writers, notably Benoit (1978), have argued that war leads to the efficient mobilization of previously underutilized resources. However, Shindo pointed to important mechanisms by which military spending could create poverty and ultimately famine. But, the connections were stated rather than proven and the use of statistical data was not very precise.

An analysis of the drain of resources that may occur as a result of military spending was conducted by Moon (1991). Whilst conceding that military spending can sometimes be a stimulus for growth, Moon (p. 162) notes that whatever economic growth may occur through military spending may actually be paid for by increased inequality and a reduction in the provision of basic needs for the poor.

To the extent that wars are not paid for by increased debt, by increased taxation, or by diversion of funds from other sectors, they may simply be paid for through the illegal and forcible appropriation of resources. Armies may steal provisions, a practice of long standing. Among the Franks—the German tribes who settled in what is now northern France and the Rhineland during the fourth century—soldiers were expected to bring their own rations; when these ran out and foraging proved difficult, pillaging, even of friendly territory, was a regular and predictable result (Norman 1971: 23). Centuries later, pillage remained a key source of finance for armies in seventeenth-century France. Sometimes, army commanders were able to secure resources not only from the Crown (which sought to build a strong national army) but also from ordinary people (who could be robbed) (Tilly 1982). Such profiteering within the military can only magnify the diversion of resources into the military (either through taxation, pillage, or both). Private militias in modern civil wars like that in Sudan have sometimes relied on looting for some or all of their pay. When armed men ask unarmed villagers for supplies, the borderlines between 'requesting', taxing, and looting may be very indistinct. Even armies possessing some degree of discipline often emerge from discreet regional or ethnic military organizations which may exhibit a fluctuating degree of loyalty to central command. Where flows of pay and food are for some reason interrupted, discipline is likely to suffer and raiding civilians may become common. This pattern has been observable among the rebel Sudan People's Liberation Army forces in Sudan.[7]

In so far as states are unable to afford the full cost of provisioning their military forces, they are likely, in effect, to license a degree of pillage. Governments lacking resources may, in effect, delegate to particular armed groups the right to inflict violence on others. Those subjected to this violence are likely to be marginal and/or rebellious groups lacking political muscle within their own societies. Those carrying out the violence may also be rebellious groups (as were the Baggara in Sudan, whose militias attacked the Dinka to the south). Giving such groups a licence to attack and exploit others may be one way of controlling them, and forestalling rebellion—particularly in the context of scarce economic resources. Certainly, this dynamic could be observed in Sudan (Keen 1994b). One of the questions to bear in mind when investigating the type of civil war being fought will be the degree to which violence follows rigid bureaucratic lines of command, and the degree to which it is 'decentralized' and 'privatized'.

Recruiting for military forces may severely disrupt agricultural production by taking labour away. Intriguingly (though this is probably the exception), it may be the conflict which bends and adapts to the demands of agricultural production, rather than the other way round. Among the Franks, military campaigning was generally limited to the three months between seed-time and harvest-time, due to the demands of agricultural life (Norman 1971: 23). In England, Alfred the Great appears to have had half his army cultivating at home, while the other half performed their military duties. This allowed long campaigns that could continue even after the 'serving-half' of the army had consumed its provisions. By contrast, the competing Danish armies had no such relief and could be worn down by keeping them constantly on the move (Norman 1971: 85). Anecdotal evidence from northern Ethiopia/Eritrea suggests that in recent times conflict has sometimes intensified during droughts, partly because the competing demands of agricultural labour have been reduced.

An assessment of the costs of the 'military economy' should include assessments of the possible diversion and appropriation of resources as well as the possible beneficial mobilization of resources. This would involve examining the processes by which military entities get hold of money, fighters, transport, food, and other resources. It would also mean looking at the costs arising from conflicts engendered by this process of creating a military force.

3.3   Deliberately Increasing the Costs of War

It is important to examine the unfortunate side effects that wars may have on civilians 'caught in the crossfire' of conflict (either literally, or indirectly through the economic damage inflicted by war). However, we should not assume that damage to civilians is unintended. It is particularly important to assess such intentions when we come to

---

[7] Personal communication from Douglas Johnson.

consider possible interventions to reduce the costs (and duration and intensity) of conflict.

Analyses that (explicitly or implicitly) portray civilian costs as unintended have an affinity with what we have called the bureaucratic model of war, which imagines two tightly controlled armies fighting out their battles, with civilians unable fully to escape the 'collateral damage' from such conflicts. However, we should also consider the possibility that warring parties may deliberately target civilians as part of their military strategy.

Contamine points out that during wars in medieval Europe, some strategists favoured withdrawing foodstuffs (including livestock) from contested frontier areas, so that an invading force would not find sustenance when it came to lay siege to fortified positions (Contamine, 1980: 220). It is not difficult to see that the results may have been disastrous for civilian populations in these areas. Contamine also notes the importance for Edward III's English forces of destroying the economic resources of Philip of Valois of France during the Hundred Years War (p. 222).

The deliberate targeting of civilians has been notable in many contemporary African conflicts (see, for example, Africa Watch 1991). One of the main aims of parties in contemporary civil wars is to secure control over civilian populations, thereby gaining critical legitimacy and resources, while hoping to undermine the legitimacy and resources of one's opponents. One of the most effective ways to control civilian populations is to destroy their economy and to force their migration into areas where they can be closely observed and supervised (and perhaps fed). Such destruction and mass migration is not so much the unfortunate by-product of conflict, as an intended consequence of conflict.

International governments and other international actors may in some circumstances be interested in increasing or prolonging the costs of civil conflict. Quite apart from civil wars in which international governments were directly involved, one could point to the United States' reluctance to back anything resembling reconstruction for the Vietnamese-backed regime in Cambodia in the 1980s (Shawcross 1984: 247). The lack of a major effort to rehabilitate the economy in Iraqi Kurdistan can be interpreted as an attempt to appease Iran and—more especially, Turkey—by keeping the Kurds weak (Keen 1993). Hanlon (1991) has suggested that international donors have intentionally undermined the Mozambican state with a view to increasing the potential for the penetration of Western capital. In effect, he suggests, the donors were assisting Renamo in its battle against the Mozambican state.

3.4   Deliberately Reducing the Costs of War

If attempts have sometimes been made deliberately to increase the costs imposed on civilians by conflicts, the reverse is also true. Many attempts have been made to limit the costs of conflict for civilians. Some of these attempts have recently taken the form of economic interventions, something that will be discussed in Section 3. Other attempts (many of them of long standing) have taken the form of legal and/or moral codes which seek to constrain fighting within certain parameters and to secure some protection for prisoners. The most important contemporary example is the Geneva Convention, which stipulates that particular kinds of military action are contrary to international law.

A primary aim of the Geneva Convention is to provide some form of protection to civilians caught up in conflict.[8]

Modern laws of war are a modification, elaboration, and institutionalization of often very old ideas about chivalry and 'civilized warfare'. The very idea of 'civilized warfare' may seem in many ways a bizarre one (and this perhaps reflects the common conception of war as a complete break from normal life). Yet moral codes have at various times had a real impact on patterns of war. Whilst noting that actual warfare in medieval Europe often diverged significantly from the ideal, Contamine (1980: 238) notes that the ideal of medieval warfare 'was to fight with and against recognized troops, under a recognized authority in a limited, familiar and customary geographical region'. One is struck by certain similarities between this ideal and the logistics of sport, which is perhaps the most extreme (and therefore the safest) example of limited warfare.

Echoes of sporting encounters were also present at the battle of Turnham Green, which took place in 1642 during the English Civil War. Some 12,000 Royalists were pitted against 24,000 Parliamentarians. The latter brought a vast crowd of wives and families waiting on the sidelines, and the crowd made loud noises when any movement was seen among the Royalist troops (which included cavalry looking for an opportunity to charge). In the evening, after the Royalists withdrew without fighting, many Parliamentarian women brought their husbands' dinners onto the field (Russell 1971: 354).

The scene at Turnham Green gives some idea of how conflict may sometimes be constrained, but we should be wary of generalizing from this. The English Civil War was often a very brutal one, and seven years after Turnham Green, in 1649, Cromwell's troops were to demonstrate a contempt for civilian lives in Ireland that illustrates the other extreme in warfare. Faced with the prospect of an Irish alliance with Charles II, Cromwell carried out a series of massacres to subdue the Irish. Then, once Cromwell had returned to England, the English Commissary, General Henry Ireton, adopted a deliberate policy of crop burning and starvation, which was responsible for the majority of an estimated 600,000 deaths out of a total Irish population of 1,400,000 (Russell 1971: 385–6). Russell suggests that most Englishmen agreed with Cromwell that the Irish were 'barbarous wretches' not entitled to the protection of the rules of civilized warfare (p. 385).

The depiction of a particular population as somehow less than fully human has repeatedly played a part in military campaigns characterized by widespread brutality. The pattern is observable not just in seventeenth-century Ireland, but in twentieth-century Sudan and on Germany's Eastern front during World War II where unimaginable casualties were inflicted on Jews and Russians in particular.[9] In so far as violence deprives people of the culture, livelihoods and even the physical appearance that we associate with human beings, it may facilitate further violence. (Just as dehumanizing language facilitates slavery, so also slavery itself is likely to contribute to a dehumanizing

---

[8] The Geneva Convention and the Swiss-based Red Cross seek to bolster civilians' status as 'neutral' and deserving of special protection, rather in the same way that Switzerland has attempted to secure protection from its status as 'neutral' in international politics.   [9] This brutality is considered in Bartov (1985).

ideology—as legitimizing ideologies are sought and as slaves are deprived of the kind of life that makes them seem fully human.)

Discipline within armies may vary widely. In Rwanda, even in the face of genocide against the Tutsis (and some Hutu) in 1994, the mostly Tutsi Rwandan Patriotic Front tended to maintain remarkable discipline. The Scots' army fighting for Parliamentarians punished irreverent speech against the King as high treason (Russell 1971: 356). Regular pay may be a particularly important factor in instilling discipline in an army. Russell notes that in the English Civil War the Parliamentarians' New Model Army probably owed its fighting prowess more to regular pay than religious enthusiasm. When not paid, it mutinied like other armies (p. 359). It may also be significant that the brutality in Ireland followed major interruptions in pay.

3.5   *The Costs of War: An Impetus for Peace, or Further War?*

The costs of war (direct and indirect) may provide a powerful impetus for peace. They may also sometimes encourage further conflict. It is important to try to assess the precise relationship between the various costs of a war and the war's future course.

As wars proceed, many people are likely to become increasingly disillusioned with violence. Sheer physical tiredness may be widespread. Armies may begin to run out of the resources they need to fight. Armies may lose the populations (through migration, death, or both) that they need to sustain them. Raiders may find there is nothing left to raid. Businessmen see trade disrupted. Farmers see their fields untended.

The list of the costs of war is likely to be a long one, and the incentives for peace correspondingly powerful. However, wars often continue for a long time, despite these powerful incentives for peace. One interesting line of enquiry is to ask, first, on which groups the costs of war primarily fall, and, second, what is the relationship of these groups to the structures of political power that determine patterns of conflict? Conversely, one can ask which groups are relatively immune from the costs of war (direct and indirect), and what is the relationship of these groups to the structures of political power? If we combine this kind of analysis with an examination of the functions of conflict (see Section 3.2), we may have a powerful tool for understanding why wars persist and why they come to an end.

The pursuit of a solution to a war can be compared with the pursuit of a solution to a particular public health issue (or any other 'social evil'). The energy with which a solution is pursued is likely to depend on the perceived distribution of costs. Thus, for example, money available for the fight against AIDS will depend to some extent on whether the disease is seen as confined to a particular (often stigmatized) group (for example, gays, drug-users, Africans), or whether the anticipated costs are seen as affecting a broader (or more powerful) sector of the population.

Questions about the relative immunity of particular groups and particular geographical areas from the costs of war are consonant with our point that war is not necessarily a complete break from political and economic processes preceding a war. Indeed, it is quite possible to visit a country at war and see very few signs that a war is actually going on. This has been true of large parts of northern Sudan during the civil war there.

In the case of Sudan, the degree to which the civil war has been confined to the south appears to be an important variable in determining changing patterns of conflict. At times when the war has threatened to encroach militarily on the north (notably in 1987), the government has been able to instil a kind of 'war fever' which facilitates a determined military drive against the rebels in the south. On the other hand, when the costs of war (especially the economic costs) began to take a heavy toll on the capital, Khartoum (particularly by 1988–9), this seemed to provide a powerful (though ulti-mately unsuccessful) impetus for peace. More generally, the degree to which the phys-ical costs of war are borne by senior military personnel as well as common soldiers is likely to affect the senior staff's enthusiasm for continued conflict.

Degrees of enthusiasm for inter-state wars can also be related to the anticipated costs. The enthusiasm of the United States for war with Grenada and Iraq can be contrasted with its reluctance to engage in intercontinental ballistic nuclear combat with the former Soviet Union. Particularly in the 1980s, European anxieties about nuclear warfare owed something to a strain of military thought in the USA which sought to limit any nuclear conflict to the 'European theatre', thereby protecting the USA from the costs (at least in theory).

The impact of costs on future conflict will be affected by the question of blame: it could plausibly be argued, for example, that Saddam Hussein's willingness to undertake military initiatives which impose predictable costs on his Sunni civilian population (through bombing and sanctions in particular) reflects a belief that he will be able to blame Western governments for these costs, and will to some extent escape blame himself.

The distribution of costs is likely to be relevant when examining low-intensity conflicts associated with endemic crime. Schemes to tackle the root causes of conflict in Los Angeles received a boost from riots that spread the costs of conflict into new, better-connected areas of the city. In New York, violence against women — which had received relatively little media attention so long as it was seen as largely confined to the poorest, non-white sections of the city—was given massive media attention when a white woman was raped in downtown Central Park.

Whether or not the costs of war feed into peace, it is unfortunately the case that the costs of a war may actively feed into further war. For one thing, the process of recruit-ing, provisioning and equipping a military force may create new types of conflict within a given society. This reflects the fact that resources for wars have, ultimately, to be raised from civilians, who may object. In his study of conflict in seventeenth-century France, Tilly puts this well when he says that 'War is a form of contention that creates new forms of contention' (Tilly 1982: 28). When Vendée peasants revolted against the French Revolution in 1793, the most important reason was probably the revolutionary government's attempt to enforce conscription for the army in 1793 (Cobban 1965: 214, 224). (However, conscription created an army of some 650,000 for the Committee of Public Safety in Paris—far larger than any armies that could be brought against it (Cobban, p. 229), and this helped ensure the defeat of the Vendée revolt.)

The economic costs of war (of funding the war, and of destruction) may drain re-sources from the state, which may then become unable to offer physical protection to its people. This might encourage crime and organized banditry. It may also encourage people to turn to private militias or warlords in search of protection. The origins of feudalism lay partly in a breakdown in state protection and a search for alternative protection from warlords.[10]

Economic disruption and destruction during a war may also encourage young men in particular to turn to, and cling to, military options in pursuit of an income. In Iraq, the destruction of much of Kurdish agriculture by Baghdad since 1974 helped to provide recruits for the government's military and security forces, which were then turned against the Kurds. Continuing economic scarcity in northern Iraq has made it difficult to achieve a lasting disbandment of the Kurdish militias that fought against Saddam Hussein's forces in 1991 (al-Khafaji 1994: 22; Keen 1993).

A similar dynamic can be found in English history. As the English Civil War drew to a close, Parliament was anxious to disband an army it did not trust (Russell 1971: 361). However, the army was owed significant arrears of pay. A combination of rapid inflation and high unemployment made the prospect of being disbanded unattractive, particularly if arrears were still owing. In April 1647, Parliament offered six weeks' arrears and proposed to send those not disbanded to suppress the continuing revolt in Ireland (while purging the officers) (Russell 1971: 378–9). With Parliament pressing for elections as well as disbandment, it was eventually the army that persuaded Cromwell to dissolve a weakened English Parliament (Russell 1971: 386).

In general, economic scarcity may lead to increasing conflict over resources. This is evident not only in the current fighting between Kurdish factions in northern Iraq but also in the fighting between rival rebel factions in southern Sudan. Within the language of 'economic strategies' outlined above, we can say that a shortage of lucrative economic strategies of a kind that promote public welfare may lead people to adopt economic strategies (including violence) that are damaging to public welfare.

A state's ability and desire to wage war on one section of its population may depend on its demand for the labour of that group. Some types of conflict may enhance the ability to exploit labour. For example, in Sudan conflict forced many southern Sudanese to work for low or non-existent wages on government- and merchant-controlled farms in northern Sudan. In Germany and Poland, the forcible concentration of Jewish people in ghettos and camps facilitated the exploitation of their labour. Together with the appropriation of property, these are some of the functions of conflict. However, certain types of conflict may weaken people so severely that it becomes difficult or impossible to exploit them. This in itself may impose certain limits on conflict. (The point can be compared with Marx's argument that 'capitalism', whilst determined to exploit the proletariat, nevertheless had an interest in providing sufficient rewards to keep the proletariat alive). However, where, for example, the labour of a particular group is deemed dispensable, this may open the way for extermination. It has been

---

[10] In his study of 'The Medieval Soldier', Norman (1971) locates the origins of feudalism in the fact that dukes and counts were looking for retainers (and they for protection) in the course of the conflicts between the descendants of Merovingian kings, conflicts precipitated by the death of each king. The Merovingian kingdom was seen as akin to a piece of property, to be divided between the sons, rather than as a state (Davis 1970: 111).

argued that, in view of the economic functions of concentration camps and ghettos, it was the capture of large amounts of alternative 'labour' on Germany's Eastern front that paved the way for the extermination (rather than 'merely' the hyper-exploitation) of the Jews.

4 Benefits of War

Although the costs of war are frequently very great, we should not ignore the possibility that war may also confer benefits. Particularly where a country, group, or individual is relatively immune to the costs of war, it is possible that the benefits (for that country, group, or individual) may exceed the costs.

Again, as when assessing costs, one can divide benefits into: long-term and short-term. One can also consider: labour, capital, and markets. The latter are frequently stimulated by war (as well as frequently disrupted). Benefits from what I have called 'forced markets' may also be significant. As when assessing costs, it will be important to distinguish between different types of war. This is likely to affect the type, intensity, and distribution of benefits.

Within the possible benefits of war, one can distinguish between those that are an intended consequence of war (and by implication, a contributory cause of war) and those that are unintended. One can also distinguish between benefits accruing to a relatively narrow section of the population and those accruing to a relatively large section. One might hypothesize that those benefits that both accrue to a narrow section of society and are an intended consequence of war are also likely to be a significant cause of war. In contrast those benefits that accrue to a broader section of society and are an incidental consequence of war are unlikely to have played a role in causing war, though they may play some part in perpetuating it.

Where benefits appear to have been intended and appear to have played a part in the causation of war, they can be described as part of the function of war. In so far as war has functions for powerful groups within society, any attempt to prevent, reduce, or stop a war will need to take these functions into account. Benefits accruing incidentally to broad sections of society may arise in two main ways. First, war may provide a direct and significant stimulus to economic activity. Second, war may alter the balance of political power within a society in ways that contribute to welfare.

As noted, war may confer some economic benefits if it leads to the utilization of previously underutilized capacity. Advancing an essentially Keynesian position, Benoit argued that capacity utilization in poor countries was often low and military spending could be expected to move the economy closer to full employment of resources. Military recruitment could have this affect in the context of unemployed labour in poor countries. As noted, demand for military spending could also make growth-inducing expansionary monetary and fiscal policies more palatable and could lead to tax increases, which might be expected to shift resources away from consumption (especially luxury import consumption) and toward greater domestic investment. Military training, Moon noted (1991: 165), could also have a 'modernization effect' on the economy.

War may stimulate changes in prices which lead to increases in particular kinds of production. Production of weaponry is the most obvious example (though the benefits of such production are more likely to accrue to industrialized countries from which the bulk of weaponry comes). Production of food may sometimes be stimulated by the increase in food prices that frequently accompanies war. In so far as war leads to a reduction in imports into a country, it may encourage increases in production. 'Import-substitution industrialization' during sanctions against Rhodesia might be one example.

War may improve the state's treatment of certain groups. This may be particularly likely where a group has been neglected by the state but is now considered necessary to the war effort. Particular social groups may be to some extent empowered by war, and systems of rationing may improve the entitlements of broad sections of the population. Marwick has observed that the living standards of the British working class actually rose during World War I. Britain was helped by experiencing no invasion or physical devastation, as well as by its navy, merchant fleet, and overseas possessions, which together helped Britain to secure imports (in contrast to Germany and Austria-Hungary, which were effectively blockaded) (Marwick *et al.* 1990: 105). War may also provide an impetus to health and educational reforms as governments may perceive that an ill-educated, unhealthy workforce is unlikely to be successful in battle. Some historians have attributed French educational reforms in the late nineteenth century to France's critical self-examination in the wake of the country's defeat by Prussia in 1871.

Marwick also suggests that World War I helped improve the position of women in Britain. Although he acknowledges that overall levels of women's employment dropped to pre-war levels once the war had finished, he stresses the permanent gains in some professional spheres and a more intangible but still important increase in 'assertiveness' (Marwick *et al.* 1990: 106). It is possible that the war merely accelerated processes that were already under way. In the case of France, McMillan has argued that World War I did not do much for the position of women.

Even during civil wars, it is possible that the treatment of some groups will improve —as government and rebel groups attempt to win the 'hearts and minds' of civilians.[11] Radical rebel movements may consider progressive social and economic practices within areas of their control to be both desirable in themselves and a vital way of winning and maintaining civilian support. The rebel movement in Eritrea provides one example of this approach.

War may serve as an engine of radicalism in another way—when government repression propels a previously 'moderate' or 'apolitical' population into adopting a radical political agenda. Some rebel strategies may even be designed to provoke this repression, and thereby engineer a new radicalism.

Finally, war may help to undermine the legitimacy and/or economic power of groups that traditionally exercise power within a given society. This may be a powerful

---

[11] The Guatemalan government, advised by the USA, adopted a number of schemes to win the 'hearts and minds' of civilians displaced from areas associated with the rebels. However, the overall benefits were extremely doubtful, as this was part of the government's strategy of depopulating rebel areas (Barry 1987).

engine of social change.[12] The importance of World War I in precipitating the Russian revolution has been noted by many historians: the Tsar's regime suffered from war-induced economic disruption and a major loss of prestige as a result of military defeat.

Wherever violence has taken place, we might expect a loss of prestige on the part of who have made some claim to provide protection against that violence, whether these claims are made in the role of national leader, warlord, tribal elder, husband, or parent. Mark Chingono (1994) has noted how the recent civil war in Mozambique saw a collapse in what he calls the economic basis of patriarchy in the countryside, something that has tended to reduce the ability of fathers to control the marriage patterns of their daughters and to reduce men's decision-making powers more generally.

Of course, the two stated categories of broader, unintended benefits—boosting the economy and changing the political balance—are not entirely distinct. For one thing, war may change the distribution of political power by stimulating the economy. Moreover, as Chingono has argued, war may stimulate the economy by changing the distribution of political power. The latter phenomenon is considered briefly here. One of the effects of war may be a partial (or perhaps a near total) breakdown of the authority of the state in particular geographical areas. While the consequences of this are frequently negative (see, for example, Hanlon 1991; Stewart 1993), Chingono points out that a diminution in state authority may also open the way for certain benefits. Perhaps most importantly, a decline in the state's ability to control economic life may encourage an expansion in the informal economy. Many analysts have suggested that economic progress in poor countries depends to some extent on a reduction in state interference. In some circumstances, war could be seen as creating a kind of enforced privatization (or at least partial privatization) of economic life, something that may bring benefits as well as costs. Chingono points out that anyone examining recent official statistics on the Mozambican economy would be left wondering how it was that people have been able to survive at all. (It might be helpful to view official statistics not so much as an indicator of what is going on in a war-torn economy as an index of the government's ability to control that economy). While not denying the real economic and human costs of the war, Chingono suggests that the informal economy has flourished in Mozambique—a critical factor in the welfare of Mozambicans. Chingono emphasizes that the advantages of the war have been unevenly distributed: some have gained, and some have lost.

Where warlords or 'mafia-type' bosses have secured their own geographical domains (in which they can at least partially monopolize trade, revenue collection, and the means of violence), there may be certain benefits that accrue to large sections of the population, arising principally from a degree of security that may operate in these areas. This may apply even in industrialized countries. Some analysts have suggested, for example, that one of the reasons for the very high crime rate in Washington, DC is that

[12] In France, the French knighthood lost legitimacy in the course of the violent fourteenth century as a result of its inability to protect ordinary people from the murdering and pillaging of the English and, later, their own mercenary bands. This, and the disgrace of the nobility at Poitiers, led to a meeting of the Estates in Paris in 1357, attempts to subordinate nobles to local authorities, and the creation of 3,000 men-at-arms to be paid by the estates and not the Crown (Norman 1971: 253–4).

this city—in contrast to, say, Chicago, has no single, powerful 'mafia' to organize underground economic activities, but rather a proliferation of mafias, all of them prepared to use violence to stake out their 'turf'.

A breakdown into 'warlordism' may sometimes be a kind of 'turning back', a return to a time when feudal or clan-based relationships were dominant. As Bradbury (1993) has noted in relation to Somalia, the reascendancy of clan politics there, while it has encouraged particular patterns of conflict, offers the prospect of reviving traditional patterns of conflict resolution. Clan politics does not necessarily mean anarchy; indeed, one of the reasons why clan politics has revived so strongly in Somalia is that it serves important functions for a variety of groups.

Morale may be an important factor in determining the degree of benefits that arise from war.[13] A country (or rebel movement) that sees itself as fighting a just cause may be able to 'pull together' and maintain or even improve its economic and welfare performance.

One possible hypothesis is that populations in developed countries may do quite well from war (provided it does not involve large-scale physical destruction in that country or loss of life), while populations in poor countries (where war may be fought more directly at the expense of civilian populations) may do badly.

Many possible causes of war have been highlighted in the literature, and these often appear to have little to do with economics. For example, some wars have been attributed to purely political and diplomatic rivalries, some to religious rivalries, some to ethnic hatreds, and some to largely psychological factors such as a desire for glory or revenge.[14] However, economic motives for war may also be significant, and we should not ignore the possibility that all of these apparently 'non-economic' causes may actually have an important economic component. For example, a 'political', 'ethnic', or 'religious' struggle may reflect underlying conflicts over resources,[15] whilst psychological factors such as anger may reflect underlying economic deprivation.[16] Or motives may be more purely economic, such as a desire for loot.

It is reasonable to surmise that unless war had significant functions—offering the prospect of significant practical (rather than simply psychological) benefits to groups in a position of political power—it would be unlikely to occur or to persist. Moreover, even where peace is economically preferable to war for a particular group, it may be that this group will nevertheless find ways of manipulating war and the 'war economy' in order to 'make the best of a bad job'. This is another element of possible 'rationality' in

---

[13] Nick Lea, personal communication.

[14] On some psychological motives for war, see Scheff (1994).

[15] See, for example, Keen (1994b) on economic motives underlying allegedly religious conflict in Sudan. During the Crusades, religious motives mixed with economic ones. Many sought the glory of God and remission for their sins, and the crusaders' courage was fuelled by a feeling that God was on their side. The prospect of loot was also important, however, and the Pope played on economic ambitions quite openly in his appeal for assistance. The Crusades had a particular attraction for the landless and younger sons (Norman 1971: 168–9).

[16] In his study of the civil war in Mozambique, Chingono (1994) has pointed to the need to understand the particular role of youth, both as perpetrators and victims of violence. He suggests young men's role in generating violence cannot properly be comprehended without looking at economic factors such as unemployment.

war, a rationality we are likely to miss when we look only at causes and consequences but not at the nature of war or its relationship with economic and political processes. Instead of simply condemning violence as an 'irrational', it is more helpful to try to understand why it occurs. This includes investigating the possibility that conflict is a response to complicated (but ultimately comprehensible) economic and political pressures.[17]

Violence during wartime may serve important economic functions for particular groups. It may also help to provide the resources for warfare itself. In practice, it may be difficult to distinguish between actions that are designed to reap economic benefits per se and actions designed to provide resources for the prosecution of war. In so far as acts of violence result in the transfer of economic resources, the victims of this transfer may later become perpetrators of economically motivated violence. It is important to understand the complicated interaction between violence and deprivation, and the way each may feed into the other.

Those benefiting economically from violence may often be relatively immune from its costs. This can help to explain patterns of conflict, including the persistence of conflict. Officers benefiting from the war economy may sometimes be in a position to avoid serving on the 'front line'. Merchants may reap large profits from dangerous trade in wartime, and yet not undertake the trips themselves. It may be relatively easy for those with money to avoid the potential costs of fighting and trading.

Where economic relationships and 'the market' are relatively unencumbered by any 'traditional' emphasis on 'fairness' or on the importance of preserving 'social order', young and relatively uneducated people will be at a considerable disadvantage. Young people often lack the skills of their elders, and it takes time and money to inculcate these skills. In a completely 'free' market (that is, one where people are also free to use violence), the young do, however, have an important 'comparative advantage', namely their physical strength and agility. This creates opportunities for gaining access to commodities by force. Where weaponry is plentiful and cheap, young people may have relatively little difficulty in supplementing natural physical advantages with weaponry.

The economic functions of violence may be of particular importance in a context of economic scarcity (often itself engendered by violence). In contexts as diverse as seventeenth-century England and twentieth-century Sudan and Iraq, as noted in Section 2, economic crisis has tended to encourage important sections of society to adopt (or cling to) armed force, at least partly as a means of making a living.

It should not be assumed that conflict makes economic and social life impossible. For example, even where 'warlords' control large areas of territory, economic transactions will still operate. Violence will influence the sale and distribution of goods and labour. It will tend to direct economic activity along certain lines. But it is unlikely to bring economic activity to an end. The threat of violence may also create a kind of 'bubble' of security in which particular kinds of economic activity can take place. Wartime transactions may be exploitative, with the bulk of benefits going to an elite that is capable of wielding the means of violence. But this may also be true in peacetime.

---

[17] A good example of this approach is Bradbury's (1993) analysis of conflict and negotiation in Somalia.

Warlords may threaten violence and at the same time offer a degree of protection to those who conform. Certainly, this may threaten the interests and writ of the state. But it represents, in one sense, a rebirth of the state at a new level. Warlords are likely to seek taxes to maintain this new 'state'.

The possibility that violence may bring economic benefits should not surprise us, since this is likely to be true in peacetime as well as in wartime. An obvious example is the phenomenon of crime, which may sometimes be organized and may even be organized along ethnic lines. So far from making economic and social life impossible, violence may even in some sense underpin normal economic and social practices. For example, given a particular set of property rights, the convention that I own what you produce on my field is ultimately underpinned by violence, since I can prosecute you (and ultimately have you detained) for 'stealing' such produce. Moreover, there would be little point in my working to acquire property if the state did not threaten penalties (and ultimately, violence) against those who would steal this property from me. Although we are aware that normal life is underpinned by a set of laws, we often forget that these laws ultimately depend on the threat of violence. In fact, one of the achievements of Western capitalist democracies is to disguise this threat of violence by engineering considerable consent to the law.

Whilst violence has been presented (quite reasonably) as a threat to family life, some feminists have argued that the threat of 'other men's violence' may sometimes allow the creation of domestic units in which men offer 'protection' but not much else. Thus, a particular (perhaps even 'traditional') pattern of labour and a particular distribution of goods within the home may be underpinned by male violence both inside and outside that home. On a global level, both capitalist and Communist economic systems have been bolstered by state violence and legitimated by the threat (real or imagined) of violence by a foreign state.

The point here is not to insist that all societies and economic systems, whether at peace or war, are somehow 'equally violent'. That would be ridiculous. The point, rather, is to suggest that violence affects economic and social transactions at all times, whether in peace or war. We would be well advised to try to understand how it affects these transactions, rather than assuming violence is banished during peace and that it somehow 'replaces' economic and social processes in wartime.

Some groups may use violence to gain access to resources, which in turn permit an expansion of violence (and perhaps a further increase in available resources, and so on). For example, in Somalia, the ability of a particular clan to gain control of critical ports and roads has sometimes allowed an expansion of revenue and military muscle, permitting a further expansion in geographical territory controlled. The dynamics of imperial expansion may be a useful point of comparison. In conflicts where mercenary fighters have been significant, the link between economic resources and the ability to gain territory may be particularly strong.

Below, some of the possible economic functions of violence in wartime are considered. All except the 'wages' category centre on achieving some kind of change in the distribution of economic resources through the use or threat of violence. Under each heading (again, except for the 'wages' category), there may be defensive violence. Just as some people may resort to violence in order to facilitate a transfer of economic resources to themselves, others may see violence (or at least a resort to arms) as a way of protecting themselves from such forced transfers. In other words, military defence may serve an economic, as well as a more purely physical or political, function. In practice, it may not always be easy to distinguish defence from attack. One distinction in analysing the economic functions of warfare is between those groups who actively manipulate violence (who may be motivated by 'greed') and those who are ready to be manipulated into carrying out violence (who may be motivated by 'need'). This distinction is unlikely to be clear-cut.

Wages and pillage

An important economic function of warfare (and of preparing for warfare) are the economic benefits accruing to armed personnel in the form of wages or salaries. One way of looking at war is to see it as the pursuit of livelihoods by armed individuals. Another (related) economic function of warfare is pillage. The fruits of pillage have sometimes been used to supplement wages and salaries (see, for example, Tilly 1982).

Contamine notes that medieval conflicts were 'fought primarily for immediate material profit' (Contamine 1980: 219). Medieval conflicts were characterized by widespread pillage, a large number of sieges and a tendency to avoid pitched battles (Contamine). By the fourteenth century, Norman notes, the main wars were fought almost entirely by mercenaries, with contracts tending to replace homage as fighting for gain emerged at the expense of the chivalric ideal (Norman, 1971, pp. 256–7). During the Hundred Years War between England and France, English military commanders signed complex contracts with the English royal authorities, contracts that stipulated conditions regarding 'the advantages of war', including loot, captured lands, and castles (Norman, p. 252).

Banditry

Marginalized sections of the population may be particularly likely to turn to organized banditry. For example, Contamine (1980: 243–4) notes that, in France at the end of the twelfth and thirteenth centuries, marginalized regions provided a high proportion of the mercenaries breaking away from the King's control and refusing to disband. These regions were Provence, the Pyrenean mountains, and the already over-populated provinces of Brabant, Flanders, and Hainault. Contamine (p. 244) observes that these were:

regions of poor soils, uplands or lands where men were already feeling too constricted, but also regions on the periphery of the kingdom of France. The sources agree in seeing the routers (brigands) both as poor men, even uprooted by their miserable condition, and as men excluded from the normal ranks of society.

A contemporary example of economically marginalized peoples turning to banditry is provided by elements of the Baggara in Sudan.

Given the importance of pillage in warfare, the boundaries between war and crime may be quite indistinct. The importance of pillage in encouraging pogroms against the Jews should not be underestimated (Tuchman 1989; Browning 1995). The distinction between war and crime can be further blurred when criminals are a prime target of recruiting drives. An important recruiting technique during the Hundred Years War, for example, was to grant remission to outlaws in return for military service (Contamine, p. 239).

In warfare, one or both sides may be unable to control (or pay, which is closely related) its own fighters. This is likely to encourage raiding of civilians to meet the needs of the fighters. The functions of war (for those carrying out the violence) may diverge from the military to the economic. If this happens, warfare may come to resemble a virus which mutates, making it much more difficult for outsiders to tackle the virus (particularly if they do not understand the nature of this mutation).[18]

Protection money

Another possible economic function of warfare is securing 'protection money' from those who are 'spared' from having violence (or confinement) inflicted upon them. This technique, which is used in a modified form by all states seeking to extract resources from their citizens in peace or war, may also be used, in wartime or peacetime, by a variety of warlords or mafia-type bosses offering some combination of violence and protection with a view to extracting money from those who fear for their safety. The contracts between English commanders and English royal authorities during the Hundred Years war laid down conditions not only for the distribution of loot and land, but also for the ransom obtained for prisoners (Norman, p. 252).

Although often occurring in 'peacetime', the use of state terror for economic purposes has been a significant and under-recognized phenomenon. For example, guards in prisons inflicting torture have sometimes allowed prisoners to escape when relatives have offered sufficient payment (see, for example, Keen 1993). The lure of 'protection money' creates a powerful incentive for junior officials, soldiers, and private militiamen to both inflict violence and selectively withhold violence. Understanding conflict should involve an understanding of individuals' economic incentives for inflicting (or withholding) violence. These incentives may help secure recruits for state repression, but at the same time they may in some ways limit the state's ability to dictate patterns of violence.

The extraction of protection money creates a complicated relationship between wealth and vulnerability to violence. On the one hand, those with money may be particularly likely to be targeted for threatened violence. On the other hand, those with money will be better equipped to purchase immunity to such violence.

Control of trade

A fourth economic function of warfare is the (monopolistic) control of trade. Warlords' attempts to monopolize the means of violence within particular geographical areas may

---

[18] Similarly, a war that is primarily about the struggle of ideologies and classes may 'mutate' into a regional war. One of the difficulties faced by the so-called Rump Parliament in England in the period 1648–53 was that the struggle between King and Parliament was broadening into a struggle between England and the rest of the British isles for regional supremacy. The Scots and Irish were still holding out for Charles II (Russell 1971: 385).

be designed not only to secure protection money but also to monopolize trading profits. This is part of the phenomenon of 'forced markets'. As Chingono has noted in relation to smuggling on the Mozambique–Zimbabwe border, government officials (in this case border guards) may cooperate with illegal and profitable trading operations. To the extent that official permission for trading is required, the opportunities for traders to secure a monopolistic position may be particularly great. Meanwhile, officials can benefit from a partial breach of the rules they are charged with enforcing. They may even create rules 'on the spot' in order to benefit from allowing them to be breached. This is the rationale behind many of the 'roadblocks' to be found in some African countries.

Lenin and Hilferding observed that international wars may result from the pursuit of exclusive geographical domains where nations can engage in monopolistic trading. One can hypothesize that a similar process may sometimes occur in civil wars. Lenin also stressed that falling rates of profit were a key impetus for war. Again, this may sometimes be true in civil wars. In Sudan, in both the nineteenth century and the 1980s, falling rates of profit helped encourage both merchants and soldiers to resort to the use of force in order—at least in part—to establish a more profitable and monopolistic form of trading (Keen 1994*b*).

Exploitation of labour

A fifth function of conflict is that it may facilitate the exploitation of labour. Threatening violence against an individual or group may be used to force the individual or group to work cheaply or for free. Of course, this has been the basis of slavery through the ages. Such violence may not necessarily lead to the more obvious forms of conflict, since the imbalance of power between slaver and enslaved may be so great that the enslaved simply capitulate. Violence or conflict may facilitate labour exploitation more indirectly. For one thing, people migrating out of an area of conflict are likely to be vulnerable to the exploitation of their labour and perhaps even to forms of slavery. This was certainly the case in Sudan in 1987–8 (Keen 1994*b*). Secondly, conflict may create a climate of ideas that is conducive to the exploitation of 'enemy groups', that is to say groups (often ethnic groups) that have been deemed to be 'fair game' in the context of a particular conflict. In Sudan, the ties (real and imagined) between the Dinka and rebel groups helped to create a high degree of official tolerance for abuses against the Dinka, and this was true under British rule as well as more recently in the 1980s and 1990s (Keen 1994*b*).

The relationship between conflict, genocide, and economic processes during the Jewish holocaust is more complicated than we are often led to believe. It seems unlikely that the pattern of violence during the World War II can be fully understood without looking at attempts to exploit and expropriate the Jews (as well as the drive to genocide). To the extent that Jews were envied for their alleged wealth, this was not simply a 'psychological root' of genocide; it was also a practical incentive to deprive them of their jobs and property (which was often the first stage in a genocidal process) (see, for example, Browning 1995). In addition to the economic pay-offs to rural and urban looters from violence against Polish Jews, such violence also helped to create the concentration of Jews inside the ghettoes which in turn allowed the hyper-exploitation of their labour. Many leading Nazis (particularly during the early years of the war, when alternative Soviet labour had not yet been secured) saw Jewish labour as a vitally important resource in the war effort.

Control of land

A sixth possible economic function of conflict is the prospect of controlling land. Conflict may lead to the partial or near total depopulation of tracts of land, allowing new groups to stake a claim to land, water, and mineral resources under the land. These were some of the important economic benefits promised (and to some extent delivered) by warfare and related famine in Sudan in the late 1980s. The prospect of gaining access to scarce natural resources like land and water appears to have been an important factor in encouraging various factions within Somalia and northern Iraq to cooperate with acts of military repression—sponsored by Said Barre and Saddam Hussein respectively— against neighbouring factions and clans (see, Keen 1993).

Relief supplies

A seventh possible economic function of conflict is control of relief supplies that conflict often conjures up. In some circumstances, the prospect of appropriating relief appears to have encouraged raiding, since raiding can create predictable suffering and a predictable 'windfall' of aid (Keen and Wilson 1994). In Mozambique, Chingono (1994) reports, aid channelled through the Mozambican government has often ended up in the market under the control of 'economic warlords'.

Control of state resources

An eighth possible economic function of conflict is the prospect of gaining, or retaining, control of state resources.[19] Here, warfare (though not violence) is likely to be initiated by rebel groups (perhaps rebelling against forced economic transfers in peacetime), with government/elites responding with a kind of defensive violence.[20] Such defensive violence may greatly exceed the rebellious violence in its ferocity (particularly where those carrying it out are at least partially motivated by a desire for loot). In extreme cases, defensive violence may take the form of genocide, as recently in Rwanda (African Rights 1994). Gaining control of state resources does not necessarily require gaining control of the capital city. It may include rebel groups and/or warlords gaining control of local taxation.

Sometimes it may be governments, rather than rebels, that initiate warfare—with a view to strengthening their hold on state resources. This may take the form of initiating an 'internal war' on a troublesome population, perhaps as a distraction from social grievances. Or it may take the form of a 'foreign war', which again may divert attention from social injustices. Machiavelli, who regarded all dynamic 'healthy' polities as

---

[19] Useful discussions of insurgency and counter-insurgency strategies have been conducted by Callwell (1990) and Snow (1993), among others.

[20] For example, Chinese peasants were stirred into rebellions in the early twentieth century when they were forced to grow cash crops to provide revenue for local warlords and for the Chinese government (Thaxton 1982).

conflict-ridden, saw foreign war (and the organization of the state for war) as a neces-sary source of unity and authority within the state (Marwick *et al.* 1990: 37). The same dynamic has been noticed (but condemned) by many liberal commentators, who have also portrayed war as a distraction from domestic problems and have suggested it may be provoked with that in mind (ibid.).

Wars may also serve a function for the state by physically occupying (and substantially rewarding) potentially rebellious troops or ethnic groups, whose frustrations might otherwise be turned against the state. The Sudan government has been accused of trying to weaken its own army by involving it in a long war of attrition in the south, whilst attempting to build an alternative power-base through the Baggara militias. Successive governments—and especially the 1986–9 government of Sadiq el Mahdi—have attempted to turn the frustrations of economically marginalized Baggara herders in the west against southern groups. In the early nineteenth century, the conquest of Nilotic Sudan by Mohamed Ali's Turko-Egyptian regime offered a means of distract-ing his Albanian troops from the insubordination to which they were prone (Holt and Daly 1988: 48). In the Ottoman Empire during the late nineteenth century, the Ottoman government armed Kurdish militias and gave them a 'licence to raid'. This appears to have served a somewhat similar function in appeasing the Kurds, while at the same time offering a way of suppressing dissent (in this case, among the Armenians) (van Bruinessen 1992: 185–6).

As noted, a scarcity of state resources may make the manipulation of ethnic con-flict a particularly attractive strategy for elites seeking to hold onto power. This strategy is likely to be cheaper than raising a large conscript army. It may also help to reduce international criticism (as the international community is 'mesmerized' by apparently 'mindless', 'tribal' violence). The function of conflict in distracting (and provisioning) potentially rebellious soldiers and ethnic groups is one reason why wars can be difficult to bring to an end.

5 International Functions

Even civil wars may have important functions for governments and groups outside the country at war. This is reflected in the involvement (directly or indirectly) of for-eign powers in civil wars. For international actors, some of the functions of conflict may again be economic. In some circumstances international governments and other international actors may be interested in increasing or prolonging the costs of war.

Particular patterns of civil conflict may help international governments to secure, or maintain, a distribution of political and economic power that underpins profitable international trading. These patterns of conflict may serve important 'geopolitical' aims, which may or may not be separable from economic considerations. Moreover, the sale of arms by international governments and traders is likely to be boosted by conflict and by the preparation for conflict.

In some circumstances, we have seen an initial application of violence (often in 'peacetime') by a national government, which has provoked a rebellion, which in turn has provoked international involvement designed to allow the infliction of a degree of violence sufficient to defeat the rebels. This model is of some relevance in Central America, for example.

6 Conclusions

It is important to think about policy interventions that might make civil wars first, less likely and secondly, less devastating to human welfare when they do occur. In order to think about these tasks with some degree of clarity, we need carefully to analyse both the costs and the benefits of warfare. Analysis of the costs should include consideration not just of the direct costs (wounding and killing of people) but also of the indirect costs (notably, the impact of war on the economy and social services). Minimizing human suffering in wartime is likely to depend on minimizing these indirect costs.

Understanding the benefits conferred by warfare will be critical in understanding why wars occur and how they might, conceivably, be made less likely. This may involve the facilitation of livelihoods that provide an alternative to economically motivated violence. Understanding the benefits conferred by warfare will also be important in facilitating economic and welfare interventions that take account of the vested interest that a variety of local groups (including governments) may have in the promotion of human suffering and in the complex systems of profiteering that typically accompany civil wars.

4

Internal Wars in Developing Countries: An Empirical Overview of Economic and Social Consequences

FRANCES STEWART, CINDY HUANG, AND MICHAEL WANG

1 Introduction

The aim of this chapter is to present an empirical overview of some of the economic and social costs of civil conflict in the last 25 years. Attention is focused on internal conflict (inappropriately named 'civil') because it has been much more prevalent among poor countries in recent years, and tends to have different effects, often more disruptive for the economic and social system, than international conflicts.[1] In many cases, it is difficult to draw a clear dividing line between internal and international conflict, since foreign countries can take a strong role in internal conflicts (for example, in Korea, Vietnam, or Mozambique). We shall define as 'internal' any conflict where there are major groups on different sides within a nation, even though other nations may also be active participants.

The next section of the chapter identifies the incidence, regional location, and severity of internal conflict, focusing on the recent past, but putting this into the context of the history of the last 200 years. The third section briefly points to expectations about the nature, direction, and magnitude of the effects of civil war, at macro, meso, and household level, based on the analysis in Chapter 1. Section 4 reviews some empirical evidence of how major economic and social variables changed in the countries worst affected by conflict in the 1970s and 1980s. However, actual developments may not be indicative of the effects due to conflict, since many other changes were occurring simultaneously (for example, the debt crisis and falling commodity prices) which affected what happened. Some attempt is made to allow for the counterfactual, by comparing performance in major variables in a conflict country with that of developments in the region as a whole. Section 5 presents some conclusions.

2 The Incidence of Violent Conflict

The first issue to be dealt with is that of definition. Violent conflict occurs in all societies at all times: how does one differentiate what is commonly called 'crime' from 'civil

[1] International wars can stimulate economic growth by increasing capacity utilization and activity rates and stimulating technological change. As, for example, in World War II in Britain.

war'? Two criteria are used: one is that the conflict challenges the government's authority, aiming to overthrow or change the regime, whereas crime, per se, is not directed towards political change. This challenge to government authority is usually organized. The second criterion is one of magnitude: only conflicts involving more than 1,000 deaths a year will be considered.[2] Such deaths may be the direct outcome of the conflict (that is, due to bullets, bombs, mines, and so on), or indirectly caused as a result of some of the economic and social consequences of violence, notably deaths from famines that arise because of conflict. The latter data (for indirectly caused deaths) are necessarily more speculative than the former. Moreover, they do not include all indirect deaths—but only those most obviously associated with conflict. For example, they do not include higher rates of infant mortality that may be associated with conflict. For the years before 1960, we have access only to data for direct battle deaths. When we come to an assessment of economic and social consequences our investigations relate to countries that have lost 0.5 per cent or more of their 1995 population over the 25 years between 1970 and 1995, including both direct and indirect deaths as estimated by Sivard (1996). The reason is that smaller conflicts may not have visible consequences in the country-wide data which will be used. Once effects of the large conflicts have been identified, subsequent research may explore whether similar effects are to be found among countries experiencing smaller disturbances.

An investigation into international and civil conflicts from 1816 found there were 54 international conflicts from 1816 to 1960, with battle deaths of more than 1,000 per nation-year, of which in 11 more than 0.5 per cent of the current population of at least one of the nations involved died. Over the same period there were 71 civil conflicts with more than 1,000 battle deaths per year, of which 9 conflicts caused the deaths of over 0.5 per cent of the population, a further 5 the deaths of between 0.25 and 0.15 per cent of the population and 8 the deaths of between 0.1 and 0.25 per cent.[3] Regionally, the conflicts were widely distributed, as shown in the distribution of conflicts (with over 20,000 deaths) shown in Table 4.1. In contrast to post-1960 conflicts, no major African civil conflicts were recorded, although a number were excluded from the database on the grounds that the countries concerned were not recognized states. There were more conflicts in Latin America than in the post-1960 era, while there were a number of conflicts in China and Europe, and a major conflict in USA, areas which do not feature in the 1960–95 count of major civil conflicts (see Table 4.2).

During the nineteenth century there were large fluctuations in the number of ongoing civil conflicts with deaths of more than 1,000 a year, but no trend. In the twentieth century, there were increases in the total number of such wars from 1948, but not in conflicts per nation as the number of nations also rose. The 1940s holocaust saw the peak in deaths from civil conflict for all recorded time. Apart from that period, battle deaths from civil conflicts peaked in the decade 1860–70.

---

[2] This is the cut-off point used by Wallensteen in his work (see Wallensteen and Sollenberg 1997).

[3] Data from Small and Singer 1982. The data set excludes what are described as 'massacres', as well as conflicts with less than 1,000 deaths. This leads to some extremely strange exclusions including the holocaust, which is not an event referred to in the list of conflicts that are known to be excluded; and the Muslim/Hindu massacres during Indian partition, which are noted among the 'excluded' conflicts.

Table 4.1 Deaths from conflicts, 1816–1960

Regions/Countries	Deaths:		Years
	100,000 +	20,000 – 99,999	
Asia			
China	350,025	—	1860–88
		75,000	1929–30
	200,000		1930–5
	1,000,000		1946–50
Indonesia		30,000	1956–60
Europe			
USSR	502,225		1917–20
Spain	658,300		1936–9
Greece	160,135		1944–5
Portugal		20,100	1829–34
Spain		32,650	1834–40
France		20,000	1871
Germany and occupied territories	6,000,000 (approx.)		1940–5
North America			
USA	650,000	—	1861–65
Latin America			
			1899–1903
Colombia	100,000	—	1949–62
		—	1910–20
	300,000	—	1859–63
Mexico	250,000		
Venezuela		20,000	

Note: A number of conflicts are excluded from the Small and Singer data base either because of a lack of data or because less than 1,000 p.a. were killed, or because the conflict was defined as a 'massacre' rather than a civil conflict. These exclusions explain the absence of conflicts in Africa in this table.

Source: Small and Singer 1982.

From 1960 to 1995, Africa, with one-third of the total had by far the greatest number of conflicts in which more than 1,000 died per year of war (Table 4.3). Although the African incidence is less than in other regions when expressed as a proportion of the countries in each region, the number of deaths in Africa (direct and indirect) are the highest as a proportion of the population, at 1.5 per cent of the 1995 population, while deaths as a proportion of the 1995 population were 0.5 per cent in the Middle East, 0.3 per cent in Asia, and 0.1 per cent in Latin America (Table 4.3). (If India and China are excluded, however, the Asian incidence is comparable to that of Africa). Low-income countries had a higher incidence of wars—59 per cent of the countries, compared to 33 per cent among lower-middle-income countries and 11 per cent

Table 4.2   War deaths 1960–1995 by region and country

Regions/Countries	No. of countries	No. of countries with wars	% of countries with wars	Deaths (1,000s)	
				Mean	Total
AFRICA	46	21	46	418	8,774
Mozambique					*1,080*
Nigeria					*2,011*
Sudan					*2,000*
(Other)				*(205)*	*(3,683)*
FAR EAST	16	8	50	612	4,892
Cambodia					*1,221*
Vietnam					*2,394*
(Other)				*(213)*	*(1,277)*
SOUTH ASIA	6	5	83	538	2,691
Afghanistan					*1,550*
Bangladesh					*1,000*
(Other)				*(47)*	*(141)*
MIDDLE EAST	15	9	60	139	1,252
Iran					*588*
(Other)				*(83)*	*(669)*
LATIN AMERICA	24	13	54	37	479
OCEANIA	4	0	0	0	0
NORTH AMERICA	2	0	0	0	0
EUROPE	47	11	23	39	425
Bosnia					*263*
(Other)				*(16)*	*(162)*
TOTAL	160	67	42	299	18,513

Note: Sample includes 160 countries surveyed by Sivard; FSU countries are counted individually.
Source: Sivard 1996.

among upper-middle-income. The incidence of deaths was also higher for low-income (0.5 per cent) than lower-middle-income countries (0.3 per cent) and much lower among upper-middle-income countries (0.01 per cent) and developed countries (0.02 per cent) from 1960 to 1995. The very high incidence of wars among low-income countries almost certainly reflects a two-way causality, with low-income predisposing to conflict, and itself being a probable outcome of conflict.[4]

As shown in Table 4.4, since 1950 there has been a definite rise in the numbers of conflicts, both large and small, with the total increasing from 8 to 27, in the 1950–4 to

---

[4] See Auvinen and Nafziger (1999) for a statistical analysis of the association between low average per capita income and propensity to conflict.

Table 4.3 The incidence of conflict by region, 1960–1995

Region	No. of countries in conflict	No. of countries in region	% of countries in conflict	Deaths from wars, 1960–95, (1,000s)	% of population in region who died in conflict
Africa	21	46	46	8,774	1.50
Asia	13	22	59	7,583	0.30
Middle East★	9	15	60	1,252	0.50
Latin America	13	24	54	479	0.10
Europe	11	47	23	425	0.10
Low-income	38	64	59	15,000	0.50
Lower-middle income	22	66	33	3,000	0.30
Upper-middle income	4	35	11	600	0.01
High-income	3	45	7	200	0.02
TOTAL	67	210	32	18,513	0.30

★ Includes Iran and Iraq international conflict.
Sources: Sivard 1996; World Bank 1996.

1990–5 periods, with large conflicts (over 100,000 deaths) rising from 3 to 8. The change is entirely accounted for by the rise of conflicts in Africa, from 2 small conflicts to 10 large and 1 small one. The number of independent nations, of course, grew massively over the 40 years, whereas during the colonial era, potential conflicts and/or information about them were frequently suppressed. In Africa, with nearly half the countries affected, and with many showing signs of heavy social and economic costs, conflict has emerged as a major obstacle to development.

Table 4.5 records the 25 worst affected countries from 1970 to 1995, including 1 international war (Iran/Iraq), with the remainder being internal, though frequently with strong intervention from outside. These 25 countries constituted the preliminary sample for the empirical analysis in the chapter. However, in practice lack of data forced us to focus mainly on the countries in Africa and Latin America.

3 Expectations about the Economic and Social Consequences of Civil Conflict

Expectations about the adverse effects of conflict on economic development and human welfare were analysed in Chapter 1. Here we briefly summarize the main conclusions there, as a background to the statistical findings.

First, the effects of conflict depend in part on its nature and duration, and the conditions (income levels, structure, external dependency, flexibility) in the economy concerned. Consequently, we should expect variation in outcomes according to these

Table 4.4 Incidence of wars of varying severity by region, 1950–1995

Regions	1950–4			1955–9			1960–4			1965–9			1970–4			1975–9			1980–4			1985–90			1990–5		
	a	b	c	a	b	c	a	b	c	a	b	c	a	b	c	a	b	c	a	b	c	a	b	c	a	b	c
Far East	5	2	2	2	1	—	2	1	1	3	2	2	3	2	1	3	2	1	2	1	—	2	—	—	2	—	—
Latin America	1	1	1	1	1	1	1	1	—	1	1	—	1	1	—	1	1	—	4	1	—	5	1	—	4	1	1
Africa	2	—	—	4	2	—	6	3	—	5	2	2	6	2	2	6	3	3	7	4	4	8	6	6	11	6	4
Middle East	—	—	—	1	—	—	1	1	—	3	1	—	1	—	—	1	1	—	1	1	1	2	1	1	3	1	1
South Asia	—	—	—	—	—	—	—	—	—	—	—	—	1	—	—	1	1	—	2	1	1	3	1	1	3	1	—
Europe	—	—	—	—	—	—	—	—	—	—	—	—	—	—	—	—	—	—	—	—	—	—	—	—	6	1	—
TOTAL	8	3	3	8	4	1	10	6	2	12	6	4	12	5	3	12	7	4	16	8	6	20	9	8	27	9	5

a: Wars in which 1,000 or more died each year.
b: Wars in which 100,000 or more died in total.
c: Wars in which 300,000 or more died in total.

Source: Sivard 1996.

features. There are reasons to expect that the more-developed countries, with more flexible economies, will suffer lower costs than the more undeveloped economies, dependent on a single export commodity. More long-lasting and geographically pervasive conflicts can be expected to have more acute effects than shorter or regionally based ones. Further, the human damage will depend on how much and how effective compensatory action is; such action includes that of governments, aid donors, communities, and households.

Bearing in mind that initial conditions and the nature of war help to determine economic consequences, the analysis in Chapter 1 suggested the following general directions of change in economic variables that are likely to result from civil conflict:

- First at macrolevel, a fall in GDP per capita, as a result both of direct and indirect effects. Particular indirect effects may occur via falling foreign exchange availability for imports and labour migration.
- Second, gross investment (domestic and foreign) is likely to fall with rising uncertainty. Domestic savings may either rise (in a precautionary reaction) or fall as people seek to maintain consumption standards. 'Forced' savings may rise because of lack of consumption goods.
- Third, both government revenue and government expenditure are likely to fall with weaker government and a diminished tax base, but a rise in deficit financing seems probable as governments seek to spend on military as well as other items. A rise in inflation would be expected as the budget deficit increases.

At the mesolevel, it seems probable that there will be a rise in non-traded activities at the expense of traded, as transactions costs (including trust and transport costs) rise: that is, a rise in services and subsistence agriculture and a fall in industry and marketed agriculture. The share of government expenditure going to defence is presumed to increase, depressing the share allocated to the social sectors. At the level of households, a general loss in entitlements can be expected with rising unemployment and worsening economic opportunities generally, as well as rising inflation and lessened public expenditure, leading to worsening human indicators.

However, as noted above, while all these negative effects are to be expected, as well as the heavy development costs detailed in Chapter 1, compensatory action taken by various agents can help reduce these costs. Moreover, for some groups, war may actually increase their economic opportunities.

4 The Consequences of Conflict: An Empirical Survey

In this section we attempt to see how far such predicted changes in fact occurred in the 25 countries identified as being worst affected by conflict in Table 4.5. Lack of data for a number of countries at war means that much of the evidence covers a subset of the countries. This chapter aims to explore whether the (partial) data for the countries taken as a group point firmly in a particular direction, not to identify precise consequences in particular countries, which is the subject of Volume II, and considered in summary in Chapter 5 here.

Table 4.5 Twenty-five major conflicts: Countries where over 0.5 per cent
of the population died, 1970–1995

Country	Deaths			Notes
	1,000s	% 1995 pop.	% civilian	
Afghanistan	1,550	7.1	65	USSR intervention in civil war (78–92); fighting between factions (91–5)
Angola	750	7.6	—	Civil war (75–95)
Bangladesh	1,000	0.8	50	India intervention; famine and massacre (71)
Bosnia and Herzegovina	263	8.0	—	Civil war; massacres (92–5)
Burundi	280	5.3	—	Hutus vs. government; massacres (72), Tutsi massacred Hutu civilians (88–95)
Cambodia	1,221	12.2	69	NV and US interventions in civil war (70–5); Pol Pot, famine and massacre (75–8); Vietnam vs. Cambodia (78–88)
Croatia	25	0.5	—	Civil war (91–2)
Cyprus	5	0.7	60	National Guard; Turkish invasion (74)
El Salvador	75	1.4	67	Democratic Salvadoran Front vs. government (79–91)
Ethiopia	614	1.1	84	Eritrean revolt and famine (74–92); Cuba and Somalia intervened (76–83)
Guatemala	140	1.3	71	Government massacred Indians; US intervention (66–95)
Iran	588	0.9	20	Islam vs Shah; dissidents (78–89); Iraq vs. Iran (80–8)
Iraq*	400–600	3.0	10	Iran vs. Iraq (80–8); Kurd civilians killed by army (88); Kurds, Shiites rebel (91–2); Kurdish factional fighting (94–5).
Kuwait	200	12.0	50	Iraq invades Kuwait; UN and US intervention (90–1)
Lebanon	163	4.9	71	Syria intervention in civil war (75–6); Israel invaded Lebanon (82–90)
Liberia	155	6.7	—	Reprisal for coup attempt (85–8); rebels vs. rebels vs. government (90–5)
Mozambique	1,050	6.2	95	Famine worsened by civil war (81–90)
Nicaragua	80	1.9	50	Sandinistas vs. Somoza (78–9); Contras vs. Sandinistas (81–8)
Rwanda	502	8.4	—	Tutsi vs. Hutus (92); ethnic massacres (94–5)
Sierra Leone	30	0.7	—	Civil war (91–5)
Somalia	355	5.6	99	Civil war (88–95)
Sudan	1,500	4.8	97	Civil war, south vs. government (84–95)
Tajikistan	50	0.9	—	Communists vs. Islam (92–5)
Uganda	611	3.1	98	Idi Amin massacres (71–8); Tanzania vs. Amin; Libya intervention (78–9); Army vs. people; massacres (81–7)
Vietnam	1,000*	1.4	49	US and South Vietnam vs. North Vietnam (65–75); China vs. Vietnam (79); China vs. Viet border (87)

* Estimates uncertain.

Sources: Sivard (1996) and WDI-CD ROM, 1997.

There are two main reasons why it is difficult to identify the consequences of civil conflict empirically. The first is that there is generally a lack of reliable data during conflict, itself partly a reflection of a weakening in the collection and processing of data, as bureaucracies are undermined and their focus diverted to conflict-related issues. In addition, the tendency for the official economy to decline relative to the informal and subsistence economy means that available indicators, normally mainly concerned with the formal economy, fail to capture a large and growing segment of activity.

The second reason is that even when the basic facts are established, this does not mean that what happened can be attributed solely to conflict as other developments, such as changing international terms of trade, are usually taking place simultaneously. It is necessary to try and establish a 'counterfactual'. Moreover, it is even more difficult than normal to make reasonable estimates of the counterfactual for three reasons: first, pre-conflict relationships that might be used to model the economy may break down (see Di Addario 1997); second, the data deficiencies during conflict make modelling the economy almost impossible; and third, comparisons with developments in similar but not war-affected countries may not be legitimate because, often, the differences in the initial economic conditions gave rise to the conflict.

This chapter adopts three approaches to this difficult issue. The first is to explore the direction of change in the major variables identified above as likely to be affected by conflict. This simply records what happened and does not deal with the counterfactual. The second approach is to compare the behaviour of the variables during the conflict with previous performance; if everything else is unchanged, the change provides an indicator of the effects of conflict. The third approach is to compare each conflict country's ranking according to various indicators within its region before and during the conflict. This approach takes the counterfactual position to be the behaviour of the rest of the region.

Taking the conclusions of all three approaches together provides, we believe, a good indication of the direction of the effects, but none of the methods, of course, can get round the problem of deficiencies in data. Further, assuming the behaviour of the rest of the region represents the counterfactual, a calculation of the difference between actual behaviour of a variable in a conflict-ridden country and the change in the variable on average in the region (excluding war-affected countries) provides a rough estimate of the magnitude of the effect.

4.1 Macro-changes

The findings with respect to macro-variables are summarized in Tables 4.6 and 4.7. These tables first show whether there was positive or negative performance during the conflict, and for comparison, whether change in the region as a whole was positive or negative. Second, they show whether a country's performance improved or worsened in the conflict compared to the pre-conflict situation, and third, how a country's ranking in the region altered.

Each of the indicators suggests that the GDP per capita growth rate was reduced by the conflict in every country except one; 15 of the 16 countries had falling GDP per

Table 4.6   Selected macro-effects of conflict: GDP, food production,
exports, imports, and debt

Regions	No. of countries during conflict years: Increase (+ve)/ Decrease (−ve)		Change in regional average		No. of countries during conflict years		Regional ranking	
	+ve	−ve	1965–80	1980–95	Improving	Worse	Improving	Worse
GDP per capita change, constant prices								
TOTAL	1	15	+ve	+ve	2	10	1	12
Latin America	1	2	+ve	−ve	0	2	0	2
Sub-Saharan Africa	0	9	+ve	−ve	2	4	1	6
Asia	0	1	+ve	+ve	na	na	0	1
Middle East	0	2	+ve	−ve	0	3	0	2
Europe	0	1	+ve	−ve	0	1	0	1
Food production per capita change								
TOTAL	4	13		+ve	1	13	2	14
Latin America	0	3		+ve	0	3	0	3
Sub-Saharan Africa	1	6		−ve	1	5	1	5
Asia	1	2		+ve	0	1	0	3
Middle East	2	2		+ve	0	4	1	3
Export growth per annum (value US$)								
TOTAL	6	12	+ve	+ve	0	17	3	14
Latin America	1	2	+ve	+ve	0	3	0	3
Sub-Saharan Africa	4	6	−ve	+ve	0	9	2	8
Asia	0	1	+ve	+ve	0	1	na	na
Middle East	1	3	−ve	−ve	0	4	1	3
Import growth per annum (value US$)								
TOTAL	12	6	+ve	+ve	3; 1nc	13	9	7
Latin America	2	1	+ve	+ve	1nc	2	1	1
Sub-Saharan Africa	8	2	−ve	+ve	3	6	6	3
Asia	1	0	+ve	+ve	0	1	0	1
Middle East	1	3	+ve	+ve	0	4	2	2
External debt as % of GDP								
TOTAL	8	0		na	0	8	2; 2nc	4
Latin America	2	0		na	0	2	1; 1nc	0
Sub-Saharan Africa	6	0		na	0	6	1; 1nc	4

Notes: War years defined as in Table 4.5; nc = no change, defined as occurring where ranking changes are no greater than one; na = not available.

Source: World Bank, *World Development Indicators*.

capita during the conflict. Iraq suffered an annual decline in GDP per capita of nearly 15 per cent during the war, Sierra Leone of nearly 6 per cent, and Nicaragua of more than 7 per cent. Sharp declines also occurred in Bangladesh, Iran, Rwanda, and Tajiskistan. The one country which managed some growth in per capita income during the conflict was Guatemala, where the conflict was mainly confined to one part of the country. The 1980s were, in general, a bad decade for economic growth in Africa and Latin America, but in 12 out of 13 countries where we can rank countries within their region before and during the conflict, the ranks worsened. In Africa, there was an average drop in rank among war countries of 5 places.

Data for food production per capita (see Figure 4.1) show a clear negative impact for almost all countries. There were falls during the conflict years in all affected countries,

Table 4.7 Selected macro-effects of conflict: Savings, investment, and inflation 1965–1990

Region	No. higher compared with pre-conflict	No. lower compared with pre-conflict	Regional average: Increase (+ve)/ Decrease (–ve)	Ranking change: no. higher	Ranking change: no. lower
Gross domestic savings (as % GDP)					
TOTAL	2; 2nc	10	+ve	2	11
Latin America	1	2	nc	0	2
Sub-Saharan Africa	1; 2nc	5	+ve	2	6
Middle East	0	2	na	0	2
Asia	0	1	na	0	1
Gross domestic investment (as % GDP)					
TOTAL	4	10	+ve	1; [2 nc]	10
Latin America	1	2	–ve	0	2
Sub-Saharan Africa	2	6	+ve	[2 nc]	6
Middle East	1	1	na	1	1
Asia	0	1	+ve	0	1
Government revenue (as % GDP)					
TOTAL	2; 1nc	3	+ve	3	3
Latin America	1; 1nc	0	+ve	1	1
Sub-Saharan Africa	1	2	na	2	1
Middle East	0	1	na	0	1
Government revenue (as % GDP)					
TOTAL	8; 2nc	4	na	3; 1nc	2
Latin America	1; 1nc	1	+ve	1	0
Sub-Saharan Africa	7	2	na	1	1
Middle East	1nc	1	na	1	1
Budget surplus deficit (as % GDP)					
TOTAL	0	7	na	1	4
Latin America	0	2	na	0	2
Sub-Saharan Africa	0	4	na	1	1
Middle East	0	1	na	0	1
Inflation: Consumer price change (%) Improving (lower) Worsening (higher)					
TOTAL	2	12	na	3; 3nc	6
Latin America	0	3	na	1; 1nc	1
Sub-Saharan Africa	2	4	na	2; 1nc	3
Middle East	0	3	na	1nc	2
Europe	0	2	na	0	0

Notes: nc = no change, defined as occurring where there is a change of 1% or less, or a ranking change of one or less; na = not available.

Source: World Bank, *World Development Indicators* 1997.

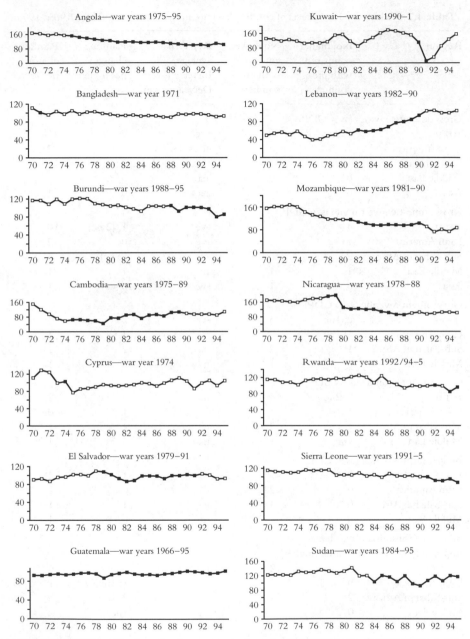

Figure 4.1   Food production per capita in war-affected countries (1990 = 100)

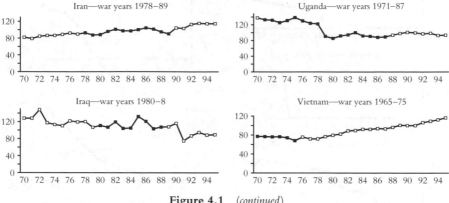

Figure 4.1 (*continued*)

although Iran and Lebanon suffered only temporary and relatively slight declines. The worst falls appear to have taken place in Kuwait, Bangladesh, Rwanda, Sierra Leone, and Burundi. There was also a severe drop in regional ranking with 14 out of 16 countries showing a worsening performance. The food production indicator is particularly valuable, because in principle at least, it should encompass non-marketed production. Moreover, food availability is a key element in determining human welfare, and indeed survival, especially as foreign exchange problems will diminish the capacity to import food—although food aid may offset some of the decline, as it did in Mozambique (see Chapter 7). The near-universal, and often large, declines in food production confirm the negative impact on GDP per capita, since food production accounts for a large proportion of GDP in most low-income countries. Moreover, food shortages can, of course, involve very heavy human costs. In general, food production as a share of GDP increases during conflicts.[5]

The US$ value of exports fell during the wars in almost two-thirds of the countries, although 7 countries achieved a rise. Both Angola (exporting minerals) and Iran (oil) achieved high rates of growth of exports, and Guatemala experienced an annual rise of over 9 per cent in export value during its long war. But in Guatemala there was a marked deceleration of export growth in the 1970s and 1980s compared with the 1960s, when the conflict was less severe. Sharp falls in exports were experienced by Sierra Leone (−16 per cent a year), Somalia (−7 per cent a year) and Nicaragua (−7 per cent a year). Export performance was weaker than pre-war in every case, and rankings worsened in 14 out of 17 countries. In Latin America country rankings in export performance within the region fell in every case, as they did in 8 out of 10 of the African examples, confirming that reduced growth in export revenues is an effect of conflict. Sharp and prolonged falls were experienced in Sierra Leone and Afghanistan. Imports, however, were *not proportionately* affected, rising in absolute terms in one-third of the cases, and in ranking in two-thirds in Africa. Countries which managed to increase

---

[5] As indicated by the data for the change in agricultural share of GDP.

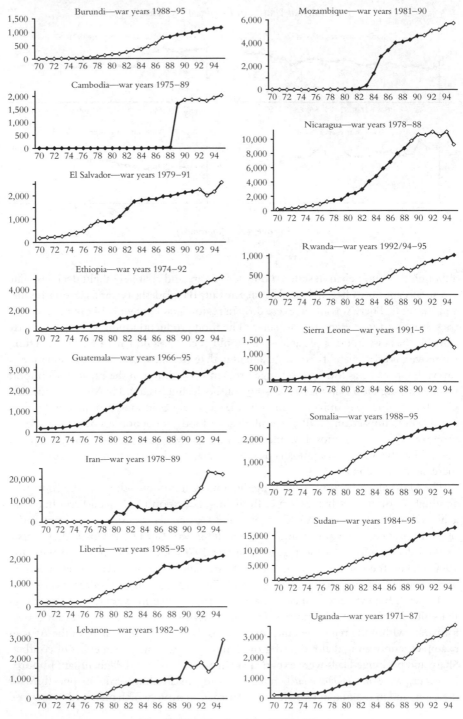

Figure 4.2 Foreign debt (US$ million)

imports significantly despite falling export revenues included Ethiopia where imports rose on average in US$ values by 10.2 per cent a year, while exports rose by less than 0.5 per cent a year. There was a similar divergence in Afghanistan, Mozambique, and Somalia where imports grew while exports fell. The relative insulation of imports can be explained by aid and rising foreign debt (see Figure 4.2). Foreign debt rose as a percentage of GDP in every war country, and debt accumulation tended to be greater in war countries, as indicated by the rankings.

In Section 3 we argued that the effect on the savings propensity was ambiguous, although we would expect a negative effect on investment. In this sample, however, the gross domestic savings ratio fell in most cases; there was a quite dramatic fall in many cases—El Salvador, Ethiopia, Mozambique, Lebanon, Nicaragua, and Uganda—the ratio at least halving and sometimes becoming negative. The regional ranking worsened in 6 out of the 8 African countries for which there are data, and in both El Salvador and Nicaragua. Guatemala was again the exception with a rising savings ratio. However, this does not tell us much about private savings behaviour for a number of reasons: first, as the gross savings ratio includes both public and private savings, private savings as a proportion of GDP could have increased, to be offset by rising government dissaving; second, given the lack of consumption goods, savings may have been 'forced'; and third, savings may have taken the form of capital flight.

Contrary to expectations, the negative effects appeared less marked for the investment ratio, which rose in 4 cases and fell in 10; and where it fell, it did so by much less than the fall in savings. But the ranking position typically worsened. Plotting the course of absolute levels of investment, shown in Figure 4.3, shows significant falls in most cases. The rise in the investment ratio in about a third of the cases is surprising, indicating a greater resilience than expected, perhaps in response to war damage and new economic opportunities offered by the war.

Government revenue as a proportion of GDP did not invariably fall in conflict countries: in those countries where data are available, it fell in 3 cases, rose in 2 and showed no significant change in 1. This indicator showed the biggest divergence in behaviour. For example, in Nicaragua and Ethiopia the revenue ratio rose sharply, while in Uganda and Iran it fell dramatically. There are indications of similar divergence among the countries lacking systematic data—with a large fall in revenue in Somalia, Cambodia, and Afghanistan, but sustained revenue collection in Mozambique, Angola, and Vietnam. Budget deficits, however, increased in every country for which data were available. Massive deficits developed in Mozambique, Nicaragua, and Somalia—of more than 15 per cent of GDP. But others, such as Uganda and El Salvador, ran small deficits of less than 5 per cent of GDP. Government expenditure mostly rose as a proportion of GDP. But in some countries it fell dramatically—in Uganda and probably also Somalia, Cambodia, and Afghanistan. These were countries where tax collection capability was severely weakened. Falling GDP per capita meant that only the countries with very large increases in their expenditure ratios were able to sustain real levels of government expenditure per head—Nicaragua and Ethiopia. Elsewhere, and especially where the effects of falling GDP per head were compounded by falling expenditure ratios, there were large falls in government expenditure per head.

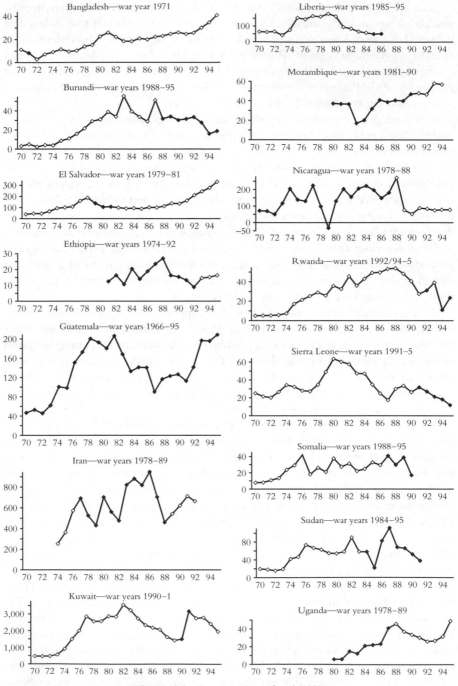

Figure 4.3 Investment per head (US$)

Source: World Bank (1997).

The inflation rate generally rose, as predicted. In Burundi and Liberia, however, consumer prices apparently fell, although there is only limited data for Liberia. The inflation rate reached alarming levels (over 1,000 per cent) in Nicaragua; rates of over 40 per cent a year were recorded in Mozambique, Uganda, Somalia, and Sudan. Most of the African countries in conflict experienced inflation rates considerably above the regional norm, but in Latin America, with the notable exception of Nicaragua, the inflation rates were moderate, well below regional averages. The impact on inflation may be a key variable determining market entitlements, especially in the short run, with sharp increases potentially having very damaging effects on well-being and even survival.

4.2 Meso-changes

4.2.1 Sectoral changes

It is difficult to capture sectoral change accurately because data are normally based on formal sector performance, and make only a crude allowance for the informal sector. Given this limitation we can detect some general changes in the conflict-affected countries in the predicted direction. For the most part there was a decline in the proportion of output accounted for by industrial activity in African countries: it declined significantly in 4 African countries (Uganda, Mozambique, Somalia, and Liberia), remained unchanged in Ethiopia, and rose in the Sudan. Among the Latin American countries, it fell slightly in El Salvador and rose, also by a small amount, in Nicaragua. In parallel, the proportion of GDP accounted for by agriculture rose in most of those countries where the industrial proportion fell. For example, in Mozambique industry fell from 24 to 18.5 per cent of GDP and agriculture rose from 47 to 55 per cent. In most countries, the proportion of output accounted for by services also rose, Uganda being the exception. The changes are probably greater than appear, given the burgeoning of the informal and subsistence sectors, which were almost certainly underestimated in the statistics. Chingono recorded a large rise in informal sector activity in Mozambique (Chingono, Chapter 4, Vol. II), while Green (1981) documented informal sector development in Uganda, which anecdotal evidence suggests occurred during all the conflicts (see also Duffield 1992).

These sectoral changes are in the opposite direction to the changes for the regions as a whole: in sub-Saharan Africa and Latin America there was a large rise in the share of industry from 1965 to 1990, and a fall in the share of agriculture, the service share increasing slightly.

The sectoral changes in conflict countries are consistent with the predictions of what might be expected following a breakdown in trust associated with conflict. They may also be due to a shortage of foreign exchange to finance imported inputs, which are used more intensively in industry than agriculture or services.

4.2.2 Government expenditure patterns

It is not possible to generalize about the consequences of conflict for government expenditure patterns, partly because of limited data, and partly because countries followed different paths. The classic predicted syndrome is of rising military expenditure

Table 4.8 Changes in patterns of government expenditure during conflict

Country	War years[a]	Military		Education		Health		Economic services		Capital expenditure	
		Start[b]	End[b]	Start[b]	End[b]	Start[b]	End[b]	Start[b]	End[b]	Start[b]	End[b]
Angola	1975–95	31.3	64.2	11.4	5.9	2.2	3.1	na	na	na	na
Burundi	1988–95	11.0	19.6	8.6	11.2	2.4	6.8	na	na	na	na
Ethiopia	1974–92	20.4	30.4	14.4[d]	10.6[d]	5.7[d]	3.6[d]	20.3	23.5	17.2	16.3
Liberia	1985–95	8.0	10.2	16.5[d]	11.6[d]	7.1[d]	5.4[d]	26.0	11.0	16.7	12.7
Mozambique	1981–90	28.3	33.2	17.8	17.0	7.3	12.1	na	na	na	na
Sierra Leone	1991–5	6.2	16.3	14.9[d]	13.3[d]	9.1[d]	9.6[d]	24.6	9.0	20.1	32.0
Somalia	1988–95	6.7	20.6	3.0	1.1	3.0	2.5	na	na	na	na
Sudan	1984–95	13.6	11.0	18.8	16.6	0.9	1.7	23.5	na	na	na
Uganda	1971–87	9.2	57.3	15.3[d]	11.8[d]	5.3[d]	2.5[d]	17.3	14.8	14.2	11.6
El Salvador	1979–91	12.0	40.8	19.8[d]	12.8[d]	9.0[d]	7.3[d]	21.0	19.1	16.3	9.6
Guatemala	1966–95	11.0	36.7	19.4[d]	19.5[d]	9.5[d]	9.9[d]	23.8	16.0	33.2	25.9
Nicaragua	1978–88	17.2	71.3	18.9	7.9	2.2	14.0	39.1	12.0	23.8	14.1
Afghanistan	1978–95	1.9[c]	8.7[c]	2.0[c]	1.8[c]	na	1.6[c]	na	na	na	na
Vietnam	1965–75	12.9[c]	20.9[c]	na	na	na	na	na	na	na	na
Iran	1979–89	24.7	na	17.4	22.8	3.6[d]	7.1[d]	36.6	13.8	33.1	17.3
Iraq	1980–8	25.2	na	12.0	14.0	4.0	3.0	na	na	na	na
Lebanon	1982–90	4.3[c]	12.0[c]	na	4.8[c]	na	na	na	na	na	na

[a] 1995 is the final year for this data (if wars are ongoing they are deemed to end in 1995).
[b] Nearest date available.
[c] Share of GDP.
[d] *World Development Reports*.

Sources: Calculations based on issues of SIPRI for military expenditure; HDR for education and health (unless indicated); WDR and IMF Government Finance Statistics for economic services.

Table 4.9 Military expenditure as % of GDP

Country	War years	Military expenditure at:		
		Start of conflict or nearest year	Peak of conflict	1996 or latest year
Angola	1975–95	14.0 (1979)	36.8 (1994)	4.8 (1995)★★
Burundi	1988–95	3.2	4.9 (1996)	4.9
Ethiopia	1974–92	2.8	10.7 (1989)	1.8
Liberia	1985–95	2.3	3.5 (1990)★★	2.5 (1994)★★
Mozambique	1981–90	7	12.1 (1984)	3.4
Sierra Leone	1991–5	0.8 (1989)	2.6 (1993)	1.8
Somalia	1988–95	1.8 (1987)	7.5 (1989)	3.0 (1990)★★
Sudan	1984–95	2.9	3.2 (1989)	1.6
Uganda	1971–87	2.0 (1970)	5.9 (1985)	3.8
El Salvador	1979–91	1.8	4.9 (1986)	0.9
Guatemala	1966–95	1.1	3.3 (1985)	0.8
Nicaragua	1978–88	3.1	34.2 (1987)	1.6
Iran	1978–89	10.6	36.0 (1985)★★	2.5
Iraq	1980–8	6.3	29.1 (1984)	23.0 (1988)
Lebanon	1982–90	4.3	12.0 (1983)	6.3
Afghanistan	1978–95	1.9	8.7 (1985)★★	na
Cambodia	1970–89	5.6 (1969)	na	4.7
Vietnam	1965–75	12.3 (1964)★	20.9 (1972)	4.0 (1994)

★ South Vietnam.
★★ HDR, various issues.
Source: SIPRI Yearbook, various issues unless indicated.

financed by squeezing social and economic expenditures, thereby accentuating the social and economic costs of conflict. But this pattern rarely occurred. In fact, Table 4.8 shows only El Salvador, Liberia and Uganda followed this pattern consistently with a reduction in the shares of each of the social and economic sectors in government expenditure, and a rise in the military share, while there were drops in the shares of health and education in Somalia, but no data for the economic sectors.

As expected the share of military expenditure in GDP and in government expenditure rose in every case (apart from Sudan) as shown in Tables 4.8 and 4.9. The extent of the rise varied considerably. According to the Swedish Institute for Peace Research Institute (SIPRI) data, military expenditure rose to well over 30 per cent of GDP in Angola, Iran, and Nicaragua, and nearly 30 per cent in Iraq. But in Burundi, the Sudan, Sierra Leone, El Salvador, Liberia, and Guatemala it remained below 5 per cent of GDP, and in Uganda it reached 5.9 per cent of GDP at its peak (for the years for which data are available). The experience of Ethiopia, Mozambique, Vietnam, and Lebanon was between these two extremes, rising to 10 to 20 per cent of GDP. None the less, the war years saw a considerable increase in military expenditure as a proportion of GDP in most countries, including the more moderate spenders: expenditure more than doubled as a proportion of GDP in Ethiopia, Sierra Leone, Somalia, Uganda, El Salvador, Guatemala, Afghanistan, and Lebanon.

We should note that these data are for official expenditure on the military. Non-governmental groups also brought arms—so that the total resources devoted to the war effort were considerably greater than that indicated for official spending. Assuming rebel groups spent just one-quarter of what the government spent, the proportion of GDP going to the military would amount to over 40 per cent of GDP in Angola, Nicaragua, and Iran at the peak of their military spending.

In some of the countries where military expenditure increased sharply as a share of GDP, the share of health and education in GDP fell (for example, Ethiopia and Uganda), but in other cases government expenditure on health and education also increased as a percentage of GDP—Mozambique and Nicaragua.

The share of investment in total government expenditure and the share devoted to economic services fell in all but one country (Table 4.8). For example, in El Salvador the investment share fell from 16.3 per cent (pre-conflict) to under 10 per cent (post-conflict). Expenditure on economic services contracted as well, in almost all cases, pointing to a medium-term development cost. A similar fall in investment and in expenditure on economic services occurred in general among non-conflict countries, with the cutbacks in government expenditure associated with adjustment policies in Africa and Latin America.[6] As noted by Stewart (1995, ch. 3) the falls in the share of health and education were paralleled by falls among adjusting countries in general in the 1980s. The rise in military expenditure as a share of government expenditure, however, contrasts with developments elsewhere, where the military share fell over these years.

What matters for social and economic development, of course, are the absolute changes. On the one hand, the rise in the share of government expenditure in GDP, which occurred in the majority of cases, protected social and economic expenditures, but on the other, GDP itself was falling, as recorded above. The net effect varied as indicated in Table 4.9. This table shows the changes in social expenditure (defined as health and education expenditure) per head and its determinants calculated in the following way:

$$\text{Social expenditure per head, } s = y.E/Y.S/E,$$

where y is income per head, E/Y is total government expenditure as a proportion of national income (termed the expenditure ratio), S/E is the share of total government expenditure going to social (namely, health and education) expenditure (termed the social allocation ratio). Hence a change in s may occur due to a change in income per head, in the expenditure ratio or in the social allocation ratio. During conflict, it might be expected that each of these elements would decline. Table 4.10 estimates the change

[6] A comprehensive analysis of countries whose overall government expenditure fell in any year between 1970 and 1984 indicates that when government expenditure was cut, capital expenditure was cut more severely than current (Hicks 1991). See also Pinstrup-Andersen, Jaramillo, and Stewart (1987).

Table 4.10 Factors underlying changing expenditure on social and economic services

Country	War years	% annual change in GNP per capita (1987US$)		Expenditure ratio (government expenditure as share of GDP)		Social allocation ratio (education and health expenditure as % government expenditure)		Economic allocation ratio (economic expenditure as % government expenditure)		Estimated % change in level of social expenditure per capita over war[e]	Estimated % change in level of economic expenditure per capita over war[e]
		% change	Years	Start[b]	End[b]	Start[b]	End[b]	Start[b]	End[b]		
Angola	1975–95	-4.7	85–95	45	57	13.6	9.0	na	na	-49	na
Burundi	1988–95	-3.6	88–95	29	25	11.0	18.0	na	na	+9	na
Ethiopia	1974–92	-1.3[a]	72–89	14[c]	18	20.1	14.2	20.3	23.5	-29	13
Liberia	1985–95	-3.9	85–7	29[d]	34[d]	23.6	17.0	26.0	11.0	-41	-66
Mozambique	1981–90	+2.7	83–90	25[d]	34[d]	25.1	29.1	na	na	+118	na
Sierra Leone	1991–5	-5.1	91–5	13	16	24.0	22.9	24.6	9.0	-3	-65
Somalia	1988–95	-3.6	88–90	27[d](88)	36[d](89)	6.0	3.6	na	na	-37	na
Sudan	1984–95	-0.15	84–92	21[d]	29[d]	19.7	18.3	23.5	na	+24	na
Uganda	1971–87	-0.2[a]	72–87	22[c]	10[c]	20.6	14.3	17.3	14.8	-68	-61
El Salvador	1979–91	-2.2	79–81	15	12	28.8	20.1	21.0	19.1	-56	-44
Guatemala	1966–95	-0.1	72–95	10	9	28.9	29.4	23.8	16.0	-10	-43
Nicaragua	1978–88	-7.8	78–88	18	48	21.1	20.9	39.1	12.0	+34	-59
Iran	1978–89	-4.1	78–88	43[f]	18[g]	21.0	29.9	36.3	13.8	-63	-88
Iraq	1980–8	-13.4	80–8	25	26	16.0	17.0	na	na	-22	na

[a] Estimated based on World Bank, *World Tables* (1994) at current $, translated into 1987 using US GDP deflator from IMF *World Economic Outlook* (May 1994).
[b] Nearest date to start and end.
[c] *World Development Report*.
[d] World Bank, *African Development Indicators*.
[e] Calculated assuming GNP per capita growth at same rate as shown in column (2) over whole war period, and expenditure and social allocation ratios shown represent changes over the whole period.
[f] Economic and Social Commission for Western Asia (ESCWA), *Survey of Economic and Social Developments in the ESCWA Region* (1995).
[g] *United Nations Statistical Yearbook* (1995).

Sources: Unless indicated GNP per capita and expenditure ratio from WDI-CD ROM, 1998; social and economic allocation ratios from Table 4.8; US GDP deflator from IMF *World Economic Outlook*.

in each and also the resulting changes in social expenditure per head. The magnitudes for total government and social expenditure should be treated with extreme caution, as in many cases data were not available for the precise war years, and both growth rates and changes in the expenditure patterns have been assumed to apply to the war period as whole, while relative prices have been assumed to remain unchanged. Nevertheless, the estimates give a rough idea of the changes that occurred.

Income per capita declined in every country except one.[7] But the picture was more mixed with respect to the other variables. As already noted, the expenditure ratio in fact increased in the majority of countries in conflict, against expectations, while the social allocation ratio also increased or remained the same in over a third of the cases, also against expectations.

Putting these trends together the net effect on social expenditure per head was a significant increase (over 20 per cent) in 3 countries (Mozambique, Nicaragua, and Sudan), relatively unchanged spending in 3 others (Burundi, Guatemala, Sierra Leone), and a decrease in 8 (Angola, Ethiopia, Liberia, Somalia, Uganda, El Salvador, Iran, and Iraq). The increase in social expenditure was secured mostly through a large increase in the share of Gross National Product (GNP) going to government expenditure; in Mozambique and Nicaragua but not Sudan, a significant rise in the social allocation ratio also contributed. Despite a fall in both the expenditure ratio and GNP per capita, Burundi managed to sustain a small rise in social spending per head by increasing the share of government expenditure going to the social sectors.

The decline in GNP per capita invariably contributed to the fall in social expenditure per capita. In some countries, this was compounded by a fall in both the expenditure and social allocation ratios (Uganda and El Salvador); and in many countries by a fall in either the social allocation ratio (Sierra Leone, Ethiopia, for example) or the expenditure ratio (Iran). The worst fall in social expenditure per head, according to these calculations, occurred in Uganda (with a fall of nearly 70 per cent) where all factors were adverse and the conflict was prolonged; other severe falls were in Iran, Iraq, El Salvador, Liberia, and Angola (all over 40 per cent). In Iraq, the fall in income was responsible, as allocation ratios remained unchanged. In Iran the drop in income and a very sharp fall in the expenditure ratio was responsible. In Angola it was a combination of falling GNP per capita and a fall in the share of government expenditure going to the social sector. Although the actual percentage fall was a little less in Ethiopia (at 30 per cent) and Somalia (37 per cent), these countries had low levels of social expenditure even before the war so that the reductions resulted in extremely low levels of expenditure —for example, in Somalia, per capita expenditure on education and health in 1990 is estimated at US$1.40 in 1987; in Ethiopia it was just US$3.30 and in Uganda, with the worst fall during conflict, it was US$3.20 in 1985. In contrast, in Iran after the cuts, the level of per capita expenditure was estimated at US$139.[8]

---

[7] The calculations here use GNP per capita, not GDP per capita and are therefore a little different from those used earlier.

[8] In Liberia, data shows that both education and health expenditure fell as a proportion of GDP, although government expenditure as a whole was maintained. Data are lacking for GDP per capita growth, though it seems safe to assume that this was falling. In Afghanistan, in the post-Soviet period, the government has lost control of much of the country (Marsden and Samman, Chapter 2, Vol. II), as it has in Somalia. General devastation of all aspects of economic and social life were recorded for Cambodia in 1990 (see UNICEF 1990).

Expenditure on economic services fell in absolute terms in almost every case, with falling allocation of government expenditure to the economic sector. The overall situation with respect to social and economic expenditure is probably worse than that shown in Table 4.10 because countries where evidence is lacking—Cambodia and Afghanistan—are known to have had a very poor performance, with weakening governments, falling revenue, and reduced ability to provide social services. Moreover, even though governments may have sustained or increased levels of social expenditure per head, the distribution was often deliberately biased against war-affected areas. This is shown most clearly in the Sudan where services worsened in the South while improving in the North (see Chapter 3, Vol. II). It should be noted that these estimates do not take into account relative price changes. Price changes in the social sectors may move differently from GDP as a whole, and a correct appraisal of 'real' availability of social services should incorporate relative price changes (see Collier and Gunning 1998). In general one might expect falling wage costs relative to GDP during conflict which could be offset by rising prices of other inputs, such as drugs.

Taken as a whole, this information contains an important finding: governments can sustain social expenditure during conflict, even in the face of falling per capita income and rising military expenditures. The most effective way of doing so seems to be by increasing government expenditure as a whole. The simple model of military expenditure squeezing out social expenditure frequently does not apply.

The large differences in behaviour among countries with respect to these variables underlines the importance of government policies. At times of conflict, expenditure on the social sectors, especially health and support for food security, becomes of even greater importance for human well-being. Many of the 'indirect' deaths were due to malnutrition combined with disease, which would have been preventable with effective health services and sufficient food. The worst case, from this perspective, was Uganda, where revenue collection collapsed and government expenditures could not be sustained. This was not a policy decision, of course, but a reflection of the debilitating nature of the conflict on the government machinery. It was paralleled in other conflicts—for example, Ethiopia, and, probably Afghanistan, but the data are lacking. In the case of El Salvador the decline in social expenditures can be attributed to policy decisions, since the large fall in the social allocation ratio, from nearly 30 per cent to 20 per cent, accentuated a moderate decline in government expenditure per head.

4.2.3 Effects on human conditions

The insecurity, migration, and deaths that were the direct outcomes of the fighting, obviously, had adverse effects on human well-being in all conflicts. The indirect effects caused by changing entitlements varied. As far as market entitlements are concerned, the fall in GDP per person which occurred in almost all the conflicts, had negative effects for many people, although in the majority of cases, consumption levels were somewhat protected by a rise in consumption as a proportion of GDP. None the less, in Mozambique, Uganda, Nicaragua, and Iran and for a period in Guatemala total real consumption fell, with sharp falls in consumption per head. Only El Salvador sustained growth in consumption. The situation with respect to public entitlements was rather better in many countries, as discussed above and shown in Table 4.10, with falls in average public expenditure on health and education per head in Uganda, Mozambique, and El Salvador, but increases elsewhere where we have data. It seems likely that the non-data countries experienced a worsening situation on public entitlements.

It is possible to build a fuller picture of the household situation, extending to more countries, by looking at specific basic needs goods and services availability (Table 4.11). Calorie availability per person fell in almost all the African and Asian cases, but rose in two-thirds of the cases in Latin America and the Middle East. It is noteworthy that, in general, the richer countries were better able to protect their calorie consumption, as might be expected. Indeed, in Guatemala, Iran, and Lebanon where calorie consumption started at adequate levels, it improved during the conflict, while in some poor countries deficiencies became acute, attaining, on average, only 70 per cent of requirements in Mozambique, Ethiopia, and Afghanistan for some years according to some international estimates, adopting FAO standards of requirements. Angola, Burundi, Ethiopia, Liberia, Mozambique, Sierra Leone, Somalia, and at times Uganda all showed average calorie availability well below 2,000 calories per head during the conflicts.

There was also a worsening situation with respect to doctor availability, proportionately more acute among the countries with worse initial ratios: in Mozambique the ratio of population to doctors was 36,900 in 1981 and had risen to 50,000 by 1990. There was a marked deterioration as well in Uganda and Cambodia, countries with fairly poor initial ratios. Countries in quite a good situation initially, such as Guatemala and El Salvador, continued to improve; in El Salvador the ratio of 3,220 in 1980 fell to 1,560 in 1990.

The changes in primary school enrolments were mixed. Enrolment fell in Angola, Mozambique, and Sierra Leone between the beginning and end of the conflict; and improved significantly in Burundi, Guatemala, Afghanistan, Cambodia, and Uganda, taking the war years as a whole. However, during the most severe years of the war, the case study evidence (see Chapter 5, this volume and Volume II) suggests that the situation in Afghanistan and Uganda deteriorated—and it is certain that enrolment fell in other countries, such as Cambodia, in the middle of the war.

It is clear that the deterioration in these indicators during conflict, though not universal among war countries, was worse than occurred among similar countries not at war for the majority of war-affected countries. The data refer to each country as a whole. Undoubtedly some groups within any economy avoided the negative effects altogether and flourished, while others were able to protect their standards relatively— for example by retreating into subsistence activities. In some cases (see Utting 1987; and Drèze and Gazdar 1991), the distributional effects were mitigated by government policies: for example, in both Nicaragua and Iraq there were strongly redistributive food-rationing policies, in each case apparently providing relative protection for poorer regions and/or groups. Collapsed governments were unable to pursue such policies, while other governments, for example in Guatemala and Sudan, did not want to.

The Infant Mortality Rate (IMR) is a sensitive indicator of human well-being. While there are strong forces making for improvements in these rates over time, including rising levels of female education and higher levels of immunization, these forces were overturned at the peak of the conflict in most countries—13 of the 16 countries showed

Table 4.11 The availability of basic-needs goods and services during conflict

Country	War years	Primary school enrolment (% gross)		Daily calories per head		Population per doctor ('000)	
		At start of war (or latest year)	At end of war (or latest year)	At start of war (or latest year)	At end of war (or latest year)	At start of war (or latest year)	At end of war (or latest year)
Angola	1975–95	174 (1980)	88 (1991)	2,071 (1970)[a]	1,904 (1995)[a]	13.15 (1965)	14.29 (1990)[c]
Burundi	1988–95	52 (1985)	70 (1992)	2,025 (1980)	1,741 (1995)[a]	21.1 (1984)[c]	16.67 (1993)[c]
Ethiopia	1974–92	16 (1970)	23 (1992)	1,711 (1970)	1,610 (1992)	84.85 (1976)	25.0 (1993)
Liberia	1985–95	35 (1986)[b]	na	2,398 (1980)	1,640 (1992)	9.2 (1984)	9.34 (1990)[c]
Mozambique	1981–90	99 (1980)	67 (1990)	1,953 (1980)	1,680 (1992)	36.9 (1981)	50.0 (1990)[c]
Sierra Leone	1991–5	50 (1990)	48 (1991)[b]	1,895 (1990)	1,694 (1992)	14.29 (1990)[c]	na
Somalia	1988–95	25 (1985)[b]	na	1,788 (1980)	1,499 (1992)	16.08 (1984)	14.29 (1990)[c]
Sudan	1984–95	50 (1985)	54 (1995)[c]	2,244 (1980)	2,310 (1995)[a]	10.1 (1984)[c]	11.11 (1990)
Uganda	1971–87	38 (1970)	76 (1987)[b]	2,294 (1970)[a]	2,159 (1992)	9.21 (1970)	25.0 (1990)[c]
El Salvador	1979–91	79 (1979)	79 (1991)	1,827 (1970)[a]	2,663 (1992)	3.22 (1980)	1.56 (1990)[c]
Guatemala	1966–95	50 (1965)	84 (1995)	2,100 (1970)[a]	2,298 (1995)[a]	3.83 (1965)	2.27 (1990)[c]
Nicaragua	1978–88	84 (1978)	101 (1990)	2,411 (1970)[a]	2,297 (1990)	1.59 (1977)	1.67 (1990)[c]
Iran	1978–89	101 (1977)	110 (1990)	2,005 (1970)	2,647 (1990)	2.56 (1977)	3.14 (1990)
Iraq	1980–8	113 (1980)	111 (1990)	2,260 (1970)	2,121 (1992)	1.8 (1980)	1.81 (1990)[c]
Lebanon	1982–90	111 (1980)	118 (1991)	2,743 (1980)[a]	3,317 (1992)	0.51 (1981)	0.67 (1990)[c]
Afghanistan	1978–95	29 (1978)	49 (1995)	2,082 (1970)	1,523 (1992)	28.7 (1977)	6.43 (1990)[c]
Cambodia	1970–89	30 (1970)	118 (1990)	2,715 (1970)	2,215 (1990)	22.41 (1965)	25.0 (1990)[c]
Vietnam	1965–75	na	119 (1975)	2,328 (1970)	2,053 (1980)	5.34 (1976)	5.62 (1977)

[a] UNDP, *Human Development Report* (various editions).
[b] World Bank, *World Tables* (1988, 1994, 1995).
[c] UNDP, *Human Development Report* (1998).

Sources: Unless indicated, *World Development Indicators*, CD-ROM, 1998 for enrolment rates; FAO *Production Yearbook* (1994) for calories; *World Development Report* (various issues) for doctors.

Table 4.12   Infant mortality rates (IMR) in countries at war

Countries with deteriorating IMR

	1965	IMR (Year)	IMR (Year)	IMR (Year)	1994	War years
Angola	193	152 (1981)	169 (1987)	170 (1992–4)	170	1975–90
Ethiopia	166	145 (1981)	154 (1987)		161	1974–90
Liberia	180	127 (1985)	87 (1987)	146 (1992)	144	1985–90
Mozambique	172	113 (1980)	141 (1987)	167 (1992)	161	1965–75; 1981–90
Somalia	166	145 (1981)	152 (1985)	126 (1990)	125	1988–90
Sudan	161	97 (1977)	112 (1985)		94	1963–72; 1984–95
Uganda	122	96 (1981)	116 (1981)	111 (1992–4)	111	1971–87
Lebanon	68	40 (1981)	44 (1985)		32 (92)	1982–90
Iran	150	105 (1981)	112 (1984)		40	1979–88
Guatemala	114	59 (1987)	62 (1990)		51	1966–95
Afghanistan	223	215 (1965)	237 (1978)		165	1975–89
Cambodia	135	145 (1985)	117 (1990)	135 (1994)	135	1970–89
Vietnam	89	97 (1981)			35	1965–75

Countries with improving IMR

	1965	1981	1987	1990	1994	
Iraq	121	76	73	na	33	1980–8
El Salvador	120	75	59	53	42	1979–91
Nicaragua	123	88	62	55	49	1978–88
Low-income	127	95	76	69	64[a]	—
Mid-income	104	81	56	48	39[a]	—
Sub-Saharan Africa	167		115	107	93[a]	—
Latin America	94		56		43[a]	—

[a] 1993.
[b] 1992.
[c] For the Middle East mid-income countries average, and for Asian countries, low-income averages.
[d] Assuming the difference between the actual and potential IMR increased steadily from 1965 to 1994.

Sources: UNICEF, *State of the World's Children*; World Bank, *World Development Reports*.

increasing IMRs at some point during the 1965–94 period; only Iraq, El Salvador, and Nicaragua improved their rates throughout (Table 4.12). The worst affected were the low-income countries, whose high initial rates showed little improvement over a 20-year period, and none at all in the case of Cambodia. All the African countries did worse than the average for the region (which includes their own performance). The performance of Cambodia and Afghanistan was also much worse than low-income countries generally.

4.2.4 Gender differences during conflict

Casual observations about the gender aspects of war tend to be somewhat schizophrenic. On the one hand, it is suggested that women bear a particularly heavy burden as they take on new responsibilities for supporting the family in the absence of men; adopt the burden of protecting children in difficult circumstances; and are often the victims of mass rape, while it is men and boys who do most of the direct fighting. On the other hand, sometimes new opportunities open up for women, when men are absent. A full picture of the gender differences associated with war would require detailed ethnographic research. It is probable that the effects, like others, would vary according to the nature of the war, and the role of women in the economy and society. Here, we present just a brief statistical overview of some education, health, and economic changes in war-affected countries. This gives a mixed picture with girls faring better than boys on education (as might be expected given that they are less likely to be out of school fighting), but with a worse record on mortality. Changing economic occupations do not seem to be systematically different in war years than non-war years, according to the limited evidence.

As far as education is concerned, girls' primary enrolment improved relative to boys during the war years in 14 out of the 18 war-affected countries (as it did in 13 out of 15 of the same countries in non-war years) (Table 4.13). A similar performance occurred in secondary education. There was an absolute worsening in enrolment among both boys and girls in war years in Angola, Burundi, Iraq, Mozambique, and Somalia, but apart from Iraq this was more marked among boys than girls. In Iran, boys' enrolment worsened and girls' improved. As regards secondary education, this worsening performance was less sharp for girls than boys, and in Nicaragua and Iraq, girls' secondary enrolments improved while boys' worsened. Data for illiteracy show that for the most part, girls progressed relative to boys, during war, and this progress was greater in war years than non-war years.

Evidence on mortality shows that women definitely fared worse than men, albeit with considerable differences among countries (Table 4.14). As might be expected mortality performance was worse in war years than non-war years for most war-affected countries. Less expected, is that the change in female mortality was worse than male mortality during war for 15 out of 19 countries. Where there was an absolute worsening in mortality rates, it was nearly always worse among women than men. This lends support to the view that the indirect impact of war on mortality via health service collapse, famine, and so on, is more important than the direct impact of fighting. In many countries, women suffered exclusively and badly from lack of health services during pregnancy and childbirth.

As far as economic activity is concerned, women were more likely than men to remain in agriculture during war, and much less likely to go into industry, but this was not systematically different in these countries in war years as compared with non-war years (Table 4.15). This limited evidence does not suggest a big opening of improved opportunities for women during wartime, as occurred in industrialized countries during World Wars I and II. This is confirmed by the Mozambique study of the informal sector (Chapter 4, Vol. II) which shows continued gender differentiation in job opportunities, in favour of men.

Table 4.13   Change in female school enrolment during wars

Country	Primary enrolment		Change in secondary enrolment	
	Female enrolment during war compared to non-war	Female enrolment during war compared to male enrolment during war	Female enrolment during war compared to non-war	Female enrolment during war compared to male enrolment during war
Afghanistan	++	+	++	+
Angola	−−	+	−−	−
Burundi	−−	+	−	+
Cambodia	++	−	++	++
El Salvador	−	+	−	−
Ethiopia	−−	+	+	+
Guatemala	na	+	na	+
Iran	−	+	−−	+
Iraq	−−	−	−−	+
Lebanon	+	+	−	+
Liberia	+	+	−	+
Mozambique	−−	+	++	+
Nicaragua	−	+	−−	+
Rwanda	++	−	+	−
Sierra Leone	−	−	−	+
Somalia	−−	+	−−	+
Sudan	−	+	−−	+
Uganda	++	+	++	+

−− = much worse
−   = worse
++ = much better
+   = better

Source: Calculated from data on www.unesco.org.

4.3   Summary Measures of the Costs of War

Two summary measures of the costs of war are presented below. One is an aggregate estimate of the economic costs, defined as the loss in output calculated by estimating how output would have grown if it had done so at the average rate of growth for the region (excluding countries at war) for the war period for each country, and presenting the results as the cumulated sum of the annual losses expressed as a share of 1965 GDP. The other is an estimate of the human costs of war, based on the number of infants that would have been alive if the country had improved its IMR at the rate of the region (again excluding countries at war) over the war period. Clearly these estimates are very crude: for one reason the time period adopted is fairly arbitrary. The 'war-affected period' is defined for the purpose of these calculations as including the year immediately preceding the war and 5 years following it, since it seems probable that economic and social performance over these years would also be affected by the war. The justification for the choice of years is that the effects of war extend well beyond the actual war period, especially affecting post-war growth, but also having a deleterious effect on the pre-war situation, when war is anticipated or starts on a small scale.

Table 4.14   Female mortality during war

Country	Change in female mortality during war compared to non-war	Change in female mortality during war compared to change in male mortality during war
Afghanistan	−−	−
Angola	++	−
Burundi	−−	−
Cambodia	−	−
El Salvador	−−	−−
Ethiopia	+	+
Guatemala	−	+
Iran	+	−
Iraq	−	+
Lebanon	−	−
Liberia	−−	−
Mozambique	−	−
Nicaragua	−	−
Rwanda	−−	−
Sierra Leone	+	−−
Somalia	−	−
Sudan	++	−
Uganda	−−	+
Vietnam	+	−

−− = much worse
− = worse
++ − much better
+ = better

Sources: World Bank (1999), *World Development Indicators*; (1998/9) *African Development Indicators*, CD-Rom.

Using the methodology described, output losses are shown in Table 4.16 and Figure 4.4. Thirteen of the 14 countries had growth rates lower than the non-war regional average, Guatemala being the exception. The worst output loss was in Iraq, with an annual loss in the growth rate of 16 per cent compared to the regional average, over a 13-year period: this adds up to an astounding loss of output equivalent to 50 times 1995 GDP; very large losses were also sustained by Nicaragua, with an annual average reduction in growth of 5 per cent over a 17-year period, and Iran with an annual loss in growth of over 4 per cent for 17 years, cumulating to more than 1,000 per cent of 1995 GDP. Output losses of over a 100 per cent of 1995 GDP were experienced by El Salvador, Ethiopia, Liberia, and Mozambique. The calculations for Angola, Liberia, Somalia, and Uganda were based on limited data, which were available only for the very beginning and end of their conflicts, and so may underestimate costs. Burundi showed a net improvement in GDP because it grew slightly faster than the regional average in

Table 4.15 Change in distribution of economic activity during war and non-war years by gender

Country	Change in female reallocation out of agriculture during war compared to:		Change in female reallocation into industry during war compared to:	
	Non-war	Male during war	Non-war	Male during war
Angola	+	−	+	−
Burundi	+	−	−	−
Ethiopia	−	−	+	no change
Liberia	−	+	−	+
Mozambique	no change	no change	no change	−
Rwanda	+	−	+	−
Sierra Leone	−	+	−	−
Somalia	+	+	−	−
Sudan	+	−	−	−
Uganda	−	+	−	−

+ = faster
− = slower

Source: UNECA, *1994 African Socio-Economic Indicators*, Table 8.

Table 4.16 Estimates of cumulative GDP loss

Country	War-affected years[a]	Average annual regional growth in war years (%)[bc]	Average annual country growth in war-affected years (%)[cd]	Net difference = annual average loss in growth (%)	No. of years affected by war	Estimated cumulative GDP gain/loss as a ratio of 1995 GDP[d]
Angola	1974–95	3.24	0.37	−2.86	22	−1.48
Burundi	1987–95	2.47	0.68	−1.78	9	+0.006
Ethiopia	1973–95	3.25	1.42	−1.82	23	−3.95
Liberia	1984–95	2.77	−1.41	−4.18	12	−1.56
Mozambique	1980–95	2.7	2.14	−0.57	16	−2.83
Sierra Leone	1990–5	2.1	−3.93	−6.03	6	−1.47
Somalia	1987–95	2.47	0.69	−1.78	9	−0.29
Sudan	1983–95	2.62	1.82	−0.8	13	−1.72
Uganda	1970–90	3.84	2.96	−0.88	21	−0.5
El Salvador	1978–95	2.64	0.99	−1.66	18	−5.67
Guatemala	1965–95	3.27	3.45	0.19	31	+0.006
Nicaragua	1977–93	2.77	−2.34	−5.11	17	−13.5
Iran	1977–93	4.53	0.28	−4.25	17	−10.99
Iraq	1979–91	4.16	−12.01	−16.17	13	−48.06

  [a] War-affected years include year preceding start of war and the 5 years following end of war. In case of conflicts which have finished recently, i.e. within the last 10 years, the year for which data is most readily available is taken as the endpoint of war, even though that may not be the end-of-war + 5 year.
  [b] Average for region excluding war-affected countries. For Guatemala, regional and country growth are for the period 1971–95.
  [c] Annual average growth rate in war-affected years is for period 1986–95 in Angola; 1984–95 in Ethiopia; 1984–7 in Liberia; 1981–95 in Mozambique; 1987–90 in Somalia; 1983–94 in Sudan; 1984–93 in Uganda; 1971–95 in Guatemala.
  [d] Cumulative loss estimated based on average annual loss for 1986–95, Angola; 1984–7, Liberia; 1987–90, Somalia; and 1984–93, Uganda.

Source: World Bank (1999), *World Development Indicators*.

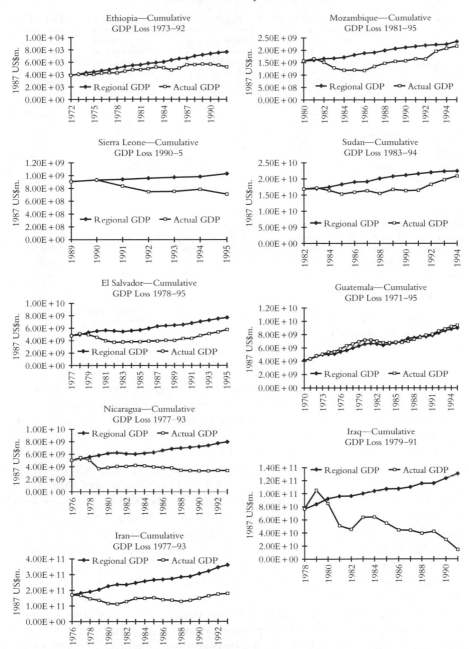

Figure 4.4 Estimated loss of GDP due to war

Source: World Bank (1997).

Table 4.17   Estimates of additional infant deaths due to increases in IMR associated with war

Country	War-affected years	No. years affected by war	Average change in regional IMR during war years, %	Average change in country IMR during war years, %	Net difference, %	Additional infant deaths associated with increase in IMR due to war (% 1995 population)	Numbers of additional infant deaths over war period
Angola	1974–95	22	−6.44	−5	1.44	0.73	80,300
Burundi	1987–95	9	−6.53	−5.56	0.97	0.13	7,800
Ethiopia	1973–95	23	−6.78	−4.31	2.47	1.57	879,200
Liberia	1984–95	12	−6.3	4.01	10.31	1.76	36,900
Mozambique	1980–95	16	−6.26	−6.67	−0.41	Improvement	na
Sierra Leone	1990–5	6	−6.53	−1.48	5.06	0.57	22,800
Somalia	1987–95	9	−6.53	−3.5	3.03	0.31	29,760
Sudan	1983–95	13	−6.3	−4.9	1.4	0.22	59,400
Uganda	1970–90	21	−6.78	−1.58	5.2	2.03	385,700
El Salvador	1978–95	18	−11.68	−15.18	−3.5	Improvement	na
Guatemala	1965–95	31	−10.8	−11.07	−0.26	Improvement	na
Nicaragua	1977–93	17	−12.47	−11.77	0.7	0.53	21,200
Iran	1977–93	17	−17.1	−16.17	0.93	0.37	236,800
Iraq	1979–95	15	−17.1	12.14	29.24	1.5	300,000
Lebanon	1981–95	15	−14.71	−7.78	6.93	0.35	14,000
Cambodia	1970–94	25	−8.44	−3.25	5.19	3.18	318,000
Vietnam	1970–82	13	−6.95	−14.95	−8	Improvement	na

Source: World Bank (1999), *World Development Indicators*.

the first 6 years of conflict, but much slower in the last 3, giving it positive real gains in aggregate, even though the average growth rate was below the regional average. The estimates emphasize the obvious point that the aggregate cumulative costs tends to be higher for long-lasting wars than for short ones.

Estimates for the additional infant mortality incurred in conflict countries in 1995 and cumulatively over the war period, using the methodology described above, are given in Table 4.17 and illustrated in Figure 4.5. In 13 of 16 countries, IMR either worsened taking the period as a whole (for example, in Liberia and Iraq) or improved by less than the non-war countries in the region. However, in Mozambique, where the initial level of IMR was very high, El Salvador, Guatemala, and Vietnam the IMR fell faster than in the non-war countries. The greatest costs in terms of additional infant deaths as a proportion of the 1995 population were borne by Cambodia, where extra infant deaths over the period as a whole amounted to over 3 per cent of the 1995 population, which is about a quarter of the estimated deaths during the conflict—shown in Table 4.5, which excludes these additional infant deaths. Uganda's extra infant deaths amounted to 2 per cent of the 1995 population or two-thirds of deaths estimated to be due to the conflicts. Ethiopia, Liberia, and Iraq also show large (over 1 per cent of the 1995 population) additional infant deaths. In Ethiopia these exceeded the numbers of deaths attributed to conflict as shown in Table 4.5. In terms of absolute numbers, the Ethiopian war cost the most lost infant lives—at nearly 880,000. Other very large losses (over 300,000) occurred in Uganda, Cambodia, and Iraq.

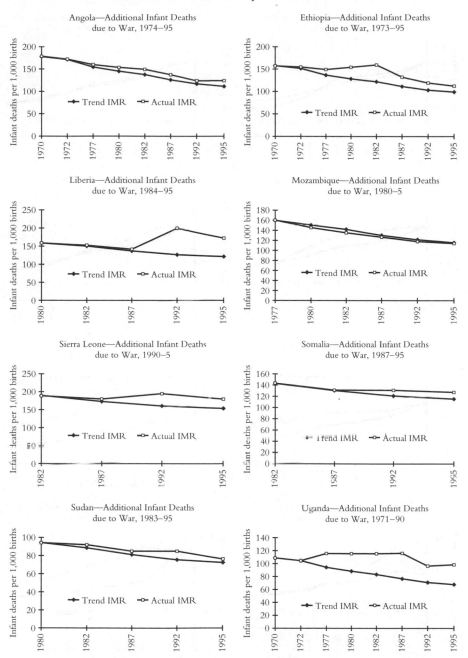

Figure 4.5   Estimated loss of infant lives due to war

Source: UNICEF (various editions).

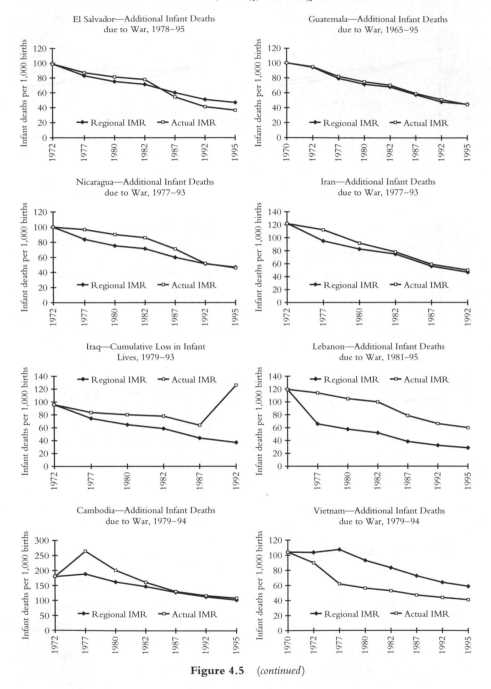

Figure 4.5   *(continued)*

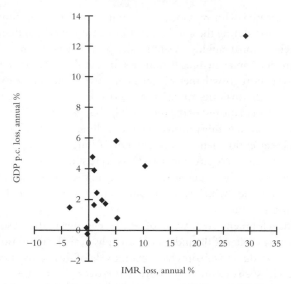

Figure 4.6   Relationship between GDP loss and IMR loss

Comparing GDP loss with extra infant deaths over the war period (see scatter diagram, Figure 4.6) suggests some correlation, but also considerable variations in the relationship; some countries, notably Nicaragua, suffered much higher loss in GDP per capita than additional infant deaths. Mozambique and El Salvador managed to improve their IMR while suffering a GDP loss, in contrast to Uganda where a very small loss in GDP per capita for the war period as a whole was associated with a considerable loss in infant lives. Iraq sustained much the largest loss in both GDP and infant lives, while Guatemala suffered no loss in either GDP or infant lives. The countries with governments committed to social objectives even during war—Mozambique, Nicaragua, and El Salvador—thus appear to have managed to protect health entitlements and infant mortality, relative to GDP, while countries which put little store on this—Somalia, Liberia, and Uganda—did particularly poorly on IMR relative to GDP.

5   Conclusions

An empirical investigation of the economic and social consequences of major civil war is inevitably beset by data deficiencies—one of the adverse consequences of conflict. There is also, unavoidably, the problem of identifying what would have happened in the absence of conflict. None the less, our survey permits some important conclusions. Two stand out.

First, there is clear evidence of large economic and social costs over and above the direct battle deaths. The economic costs are shown in falls in GDP, food production, and exports. Ten out of twelve countries in conflict showed worsening performance on

GDP growth compared with previous years, with 15 out of 16 countries showing falling output per head during the conflict, and almost all for which there is evidence, a worsening in their regional ranking. A similar sharp adverse performance was shown in food production per capita in most countries in conflict. Another typical adverse change was falling export growth (negative in nearly two-thirds of the cases), in contrast to rising imports in the majority of cases; in two-thirds of the countries in conflict, imports rose faster than in the rest of the region. The budget deficit increased in all cases, and in all but two economies inflation accelerated. Falling output per head was reflected in worsening market entitlements, with generally falling consumption per head and food availability per capita. Negative social effects were shown by a severe deterioration in calorie and doctor availability per head, especially in the poorest countries and by the impact on infant mortality, which rose for some part of the war period, against general trends, in 13 of the 16 countries.

Longer-run development costs were of two types. First, the destruction and/or migration of existing capital of all kinds, including physical plant, infrastructure, human and social capital. No direct estimates have been made of this destruction here, but the loss of output can be seen as a proxy measure. Moreover, additions to the capital stock did not occur, or were less than they would have been without conflict, as shown by reduced levels of investment, both public and private, reduced allocation of government expenditures to economic services, and lower school enrolments compared to what might have happened, as indicated by regional performance among non-conflict countries.

The second finding is the divergent behaviour among conflict-affected countries, with some countries better able to protect themselves from various economic and social costs than others. The crude estimates for GDP loss in Table 4.16 indicate that some countries experienced modest losses (for example, Sudan) and Guatemala actually did better than the regional average, while in other countries GDP losses were extremely large (especially Iraq, Sierra Leone, Nicaragua, Liberia, and Iran) both annually and cumulatively because of the long period of war. Another example of divergence was in exports: in some countries, such as Angola, exports continued to grow while in others, such as Afghanistan, they fell, sometimes quite dramatically. Imports also showed divergent behaviour, rising in most countries, quite rapidly in some, for example, Somalia, part-financed by foreign debt, and falling in others (such as, Iraq and Sierra Leone). The investment ratio (though not the absolute level of investment) also rose in one-third of the countries and fell in others, although the savings ratio almost invariably fell, indicating a rise in foreign savings. Against expectations, government revenue rose as a proportion of GDP in about half the countries, but fell quite dramatically in some (for example, Uganda); government expenditure as a percentage of GDP rose in some countries—sometimes by a large amount (as in Nicaragua) while it fell in other countries where revenue collapsed, but invariably the budget deficit got larger. Even though the military share of government expenditure invariably rose, 3 countries also increased the share going to health and education significantly, and a further 3 showed no change. This meant that expenditure on health and education per head actually rose in Mozambique, Nicaragua, Sudan, and Burundi during the conflict, despite falling

GDP per capita and rising military expenditure. The protection of public entitlements contributed to the reduction of potential social costs. As shown in Table 4.17, in 4 countries the IMR was lower in 1995 than if the non-war regional average improvement had been achieved. In some of these, notably Vietnam and Mozambique, government policies were committed to bringing about social improvements.

The differing costs of conflict are the product of the nature of the conflict and of government structures and capacity, which are themselves affected by the conflict. The highest costs were incurred where the conflict was pervasive geographically and the government severely undermined, to the extent of being unable to collect taxes or provide services. This seems to have been the case in Uganda in the 1980s and in Somalia and Afghanistan. Negative effects on social capital are also likely to be greatest in this context. In contrast, the Nicaraguan government was able to sustain social progress, although heavy economic costs were incurred. At the other extreme are the international conflicts, where most of the battle is localized and government authority may be strengthened by the conflict, as in Iran and Iraq. Quasi-governmental structures, with ability to tax and deliver services, can also protect people from the worst effects. In this sample while effective governments were able to sustain public entitlements, they could not prevent the negative impact on economic entitlements. Here people's own capacity to find alternative occupations was important in helping to sustain livelihoods —in particular through subsistence agriculture and the informal sector. The extent of these activities cannot be recorded here because of a dearth of statistics, but other evidence emphasizes their importance. The fact that the effects on human indicators were relatively moderate is a reflection of human resilience in severely adverse circumstances.

5

An Overview of the Case Studies

VALPY FITZGERALD, FRANCES STEWART, AND MICHAEL WANG

1 Introduction

The aggregate statistical evidence presented in the previous chapter allowed us to identify a number of 'stylized' facts regarding the nature and magnitude of the costs inflicted by conflict. But to understand exactly how various economic and political processes condition the costs of war, and how economies actually operate under conflict, in-depth studies at the country level are essential. The seven country cases presented in Volume II represent such an attempt to canvass the divergent experiences of war-affected countries, in order to elucidate more clearly the complex two-way interaction between warfare and its consequences. The purpose of this chapter is to provide an overview of those studies, and to draw some tentative conclusions based on their findings in the light of the hypotheses put forward earlier.

The countries studied vary widely in terms of geography as well as initial economic conditions. They include 4 countries in Africa—Mozambique, Sudan, Sierra Leone, and Uganda; 2 in Asia—Afghanistan and Sri Lanka; and 1 in Latin America—Nicaragua. While almost all possessed extremely low levels of GDP per capita and a dominant agricultural sector at the start of conflict, they differed in the degree to which their economies depended on external trade. Some countries relied heavily on subsistence agriculture (for example, Afghanistan, Mozambique, Sudan), with up to 80 per cent of the population engaging in such activities in some cases, while others relied more on world markets for exports of primary commodities (and sometimes manufactured goods), as well as imports of consumer goods (for example, Sierra Leone, Nicaragua). Another difference was the degree of state involvement in the economy. For example, Sri Lanka began to dismantle its interventionist planning system at the start of its conflict in favour of a more laissez-faire, market-style economy, while Sudan, Nicaragua and Mozambique continued to pursue import substitution policies and, in the latter two cases, socialist planning methods.

In addition, the countries differed in the nature of their conflict, despite the fact that all suffered internal—as opposed to international—wars. Following the typology set forward in Chapter 1, the case studies can be classified as:

1. wars with strong foreign intervention (Afghanistan, Mozambique, Nicaragua);
2. locally initiated conflicts (Uganda, Sudan, Sri Lanka); and
3. anarchical situations which degenerated into conflict (Sierra Leone),

with the proviso that there exists great diversity even within a particular grouping. As we will discuss below, the nature of the war pursued, including its duration and magnitude, coupled with the economic conditions prevailing at the start of conflict, substantially affected the human costs generated by warfare. We begin by summarizing the individual experiences with war for each of the country studies; secondly, we present some comparative data on country performance at macro-, meso-, and micro-levels; and finally, we discuss the factors explaining the considerable variation in the costs of war in this sample of countries.

2   Country Summaries

2.1   *Afghanistan*

Afghanistan's war was marked by pervasive foreign intervention, the near collapse of government institutions and massive migration from the country. For nearly twenty years, foreign financial and military support helped prolong the struggle and exacerbate internal divisions. The war led to the virtual disintegration of the state and collapse of public services. Despite extensive NGO action to provide civic entitlements, the war in Afghanistan inflicted severe economic and human costs. Marsden and Samman investigate the costs of conflict, using Nepal, a country possessing similar peacetime socioeconomic circumstances, as a counterfactual.

The Afghan civil war originally had its roots in part in an ideological divide between those elements of the populace espousing traditional customs and others seeking modernization. However, Afghanistan became a focal point for Cold War politics, owing to its geographical position, near the Soviet Union and the Persian Gulf. The Soviet Union invaded Afghanistan in 1979 when it became concerned that the socialist government then in power could no longer protect its considerable political and economic interests.

The Soviet presence intensified local divisions, provoking conservative Islamic parties, namely, the Shi'a Mujahedin, to initiate a military campaign to overthrow the socialist regime in Kabul and expel the Russians; it also prompted other foreign powers to deepen their involvement. Both Pakistan and the United States provided financial aid and military supplies to the Mujahedin, which gained control over most of the country between 1986 and 1989, following the withdrawal of Soviet troops. Soon afterwards, however, Mujahedin authority was successfully challenged by the Taliban, a more radical Islamic group, who had gained command over 90 per cent of the country at the time of writing. Geopolitical stratagems continued to provide an obstacle to a resolution to the conflict, as different coalitions of foreign powers resolved to support the Taliban (Pakistan, the United States, and Saudi Arabia) or their northern Mujahedin opponents (India, Russia, and Iran).

Even before the war, comprehensive and reliable statistics in Afghanistan were limited, and with the onset of conflict, they became even more so. As a result, it is difficult to come to reliable conclusions about the impact of the conflict on the economy.

Nevertheless, by piecing together fragmentary evidence the authors find some clear trends regarding the effects of war.

In line with the theoretical predictions outlined in Chapter 1, all the main macro-indicators were adversely affected. GDP declined by nearly half between 1980 and 1994, contracting at an annual rate of 7.4 per cent between 1990 and 1994 alone. The conflict also had large negative effects on savings and investment; the available data suggest there was very little private investment due to insecurity, while, public investment dropped by more than half between 1978/9 and 1984/5, partly as a result of increased military expenditure. Prices rose roughly a thousandfold over the 1980s due to infla-tionary deficit financing and supply disruptions, with correspondingly adverse effects on the price of food. Foreign debt also increased dramatically over the course of the war, growing from US$1.2 billion in 1980 to US$5.1 billion in 1990. With a simultaneous fall in foreign assistance, the government further aggravated inflationary pressures by turning to domestic bank borrowing to finance the budget deficit.

The dramatic decrease in GDP over the war period was due both to the direct effects of conflict and the indirect repercussions generated as the direct effects worked through the economy. The destruction of economic assets from fighting and landmines was particularly disruptive to the agricultural sector which accounted for the largest share of GDP and nearly 90 per cent of exports before the conflict. Between 1978/9 and 1990/1, agricultural production fell by an estimated 15 per cent, and per capita grain production by 50 per cent, with adverse consequences for both foreign exchange earnings and market entitlements. Transport and trade routes were also severely dis-rupted by the destruction of road networks. Output in the energy sector fell nearly 90 per cent in the late 1980s as a result of damage to natural gas fields. Moreover, the huge displacement of people, totalling more than 5 million refugees and 3 million internal displacees, seriously reduced the availability of labour.

There were knock-on effects from the direct destruction and consequent declines in output on other parts of the economy; for example, the drop in exports, the result of the physical destruction to agricultural and natural gas production just noted, reduced the availability of foreign exchange, and hence the supplies of imported productive inputs.

While the aggregate indicators indicate a large negative macro-impact of war, official statistics probably fail to account fully for informal activities. Moreover, given the con-text of global recession and economic restructuring in which the civil war took place, it is likely that Afghanistan's economic performance would have worsened regardless of conflict. None the less, comparison with Nepal suggests a strong decline in national income attributable to conflict. Between 1980 and 1994, Nepal's GDP increased nearly 65 per cent, contrasting with the large fall in Afghanistan over the same period.

At the mesolevel, Afghanistan's wartime sectoral distribution of public spending also conformed to theoretical predictions. The absence of a robust central administration and, at times, a central government at all, seriously impeded public-sector spending. Social expenditure, which was traditionally low, diminished further over the course of the war owing to the virtual collapse of formal tax collection and increased military spending. Coupled with the erosion of the government's administrative capacity, there was minimal government provision of agricultural, health, educational, and sanitation services. In Kabul, for example, 8 of the city's 14 hospitals ceased to function between 1980 and 1993. A 1991 study found two-thirds of the schools had been damaged or destroyed, while many others were forced to close following the Taliban takeover. Comparing the mesolevel changes in Afghanistan to those in Nepal, where defence spending remained at 1 per cent of GDP throughout the period and the share devoted to health and education increased steadily, further underlines the squeeze on social expenditure induced by war.

Although little data exist on changes in the private sector, the collapse of the formal banking sector, coupled with the shift to informal activities in services industries and the destruction of transport infrastructure, suggests a shift by private agents to less transaction-intensive activities involving less manufacturing and long-distance trading.

As result of the decline in both public and market entitlements, household-level indicators worsened over the course of the war. With hyperinflation affecting many staple food items and a decrease in food production, daily per capita calorie consumption fell from 2,186 in 1980 to 1,573 in 1992. Consequently, malnutrition increased from affecting 15 to 20 per cent of children under 5 during the 1980s, to over 50 per cent in a 1994 study. Similarly, with the decline in sanitation and health services, the incidence of communicable diseases rose dramatically. Leishmaniasis, for instance, rose from 14,000 cases in 1995 to 300,000 in 1998. Cholera, tuberculosis, polio, and acute respiratory infections remained at epidemic levels in 1998.

Yet, given the dramatic deterioration of public entitlements and the macroeconomic environment, in some respects household welfare decreased less than might have been expected. Although there was widespread malnutrition, there was not extensive starvation of the kind experienced in Sudan. Moreover, some demographic and health-related indices actually improved over the course of the conflict. Apart from maternal mortality, it appears that the health and literacy situation in Afghanistan was not markedly worse than Nepal, despite the negative effects of war on public spending. Indeed, World Bank estimates show higher literacy rates in Afghanistan than in Nepal in the mid-1990s, as well as a greater rate of improvement between 1990 and 1995.

In the Afghan case, NGOs were particularly important in explaining why the decline in public and market entitlements did not produce more devastating social costs. In the absence of public entitlements, humanitarian agencies helped to fill the gap in provision, being especially active in providing access to education and health facilities. One study estimates that 70 per cent of the health-care system was entirely dependent on external assistance. UN agencies and NGOs engaged in relief services and also carried out important preventive efforts, for example, through immunization programmes. NGOs were more constrained in supporting services heavily dependent on public infrastructure, such as water and sanitation facilities. The sizeable humanitarian assistance, however, may have distorted power relations at the local level, allowing commanders to buy the support of the populace.

People's own actions also helped to prevent household entitlements from deteriorating disastrously. While warfare disrupted formal production in the agricultural sector, producers retreated into subsistence farming, or turned to cultivating poppies for heroin production. In the poorest areas, more than 65 per cent of arable land was planted with poppies. Indeed, by 1996, poppies became Afghanistan's major export, accounting for over 40 per cent of the world's poppy production. People also turned to a variety of informal activities, including street trade, the sale of scrap metal stripped from inoperative factories to Pakistan; non-legal entitlements in the form of smuggling activities were also important, furnishing scarce goods while allowing some groups to profit considerably.

One of the most important coping strategies was migration to neighbouring countries. During the war, more than 5 million people, nearly one-third of the population fled to Pakistan (3.3 million) or Iran (2.25 million). Contrary to usual expectations, becoming a refugee did not entail a drastic reduction in welfare. For the most part, the conditions in refugee camps were no worse, and possibly better, than those in Afghanistan. For example, refugees in Iran were accorded free access to health and education facilities, and provided with subsidies on food and other staples on the same bases as Iranian citizens. For those in Pakistan, the host government provided them with tents, a regular food ration, and basic health and education services. Many also benefited from skills and training and income-generation projects. The escape to other countries thus provided an important means of protecting household welfare.

There was a wide disparity in the impact of war between and within groups. For example, the better off were most able to flee overseas, while the most vulnerable sectors of the population were more constrained. Suffering also differed between urban and rural areas. It appears that urban groups, traditionally more privileged as the result of a strong urban bias in government provision, were particularly hard hit by conflict. The most destitute of urban households were those headed by widows and the elderly or disabled. Women were particularly badly affected by the Taliban take-over in 1992. Since then, women have been barred from education and employment, and their access to health care has been severely limited.

The conflict in Afghanistan also inflicted long-term development costs through its destruction of many forms of capital. The war took a large toll on human resources through fatalities, and through the mass exodus of the educated and skilled, the large majority of whom have yet to return. Moreover, the debilitation of the education sector reduced human-capital formation. There was also a collapse of governmental administrative capacity as well as worsened physical infrastructure. Human, institutional, and cultural capital, vital for economic growth and social development, sustained particularly heavy costs from the insecurity bred by the type of warfare pursued,—that is, the indiscriminate use of violence against civilians and the extensive deployment of landmines—notably weakening the prospects for Afghanistan's future development.

2.2   *Mozambique*

Except for a brief period of relative stability shortly after independence in 1974, Mozambique experienced almost continuous civil war for nearly twenty years. The Renamo rebel force, with the logistical and military support of South Africa, waged a low-intensity conflict aimed at destabilizing the government in Maputo. Tactics of sabotage and terrorism against civilians were adopted, as was the deliberate destruction of physical capital and food production. The undermining of agriculture proved especially damaging, as more than 80 per cent of the population worked in agriculture prior to the war. The rebels' war aims fluctuated between maximizing control over territory and simply maximizing destruction, while the extent of the authority of the central government also varied. Unsurprisingly, the conflict in Mozambique proved extraordinarily destructive in terms both of human costs—with nearly a million deaths, and many more displaced—and economic destruction. By 1986, real GDP was below 60 per cent of its level in 1980.

Despite the centrality of conflict to Mozambique's recent economic history, there has been little effort to explore the economics of its war in a systematic manner. Brück attempts to remedy this, analysing the macroeconomic channels that operate in a war economy to identify the effects of conflict on Mozambique's economic development.

Starting from the assumption that war can be modelled as a shock to the economy, and operating under standard neoclassical assumptions of maximization, substitutability, and choice, Brück first explores how one might expect different economic agents —that is, households, firms, and governments—to alter their behaviour in conflict conditions. He focuses on a few key economic relationships, including individual agents' objective functions, the household budget constraint, the production function, the investment equation, and the government's objective function and budget restraint. Next he explores how key economic variables might respond to war shocks, with particular attention given to the effects of uncertainty on increasing transactions costs and reducing investment. He then models these relationships into a two-period, overlapping-generations model, in order to generate a set of hypotheses concerning the probable effects of war on the economy.

Based on this model, Brück concludes that war will reduce output, long term growth, consumption and welfare, and increase government debt, as a result both of direct effects, arising from the physical destruction of capital and increased government deficit finance, as well as indirect effects stemming from increased uncertainty and higher transaction costs. The extent of these changes depends on the nature of war, with unstable, inconsistent conflicts having the largest impact on uncertainty and transactions costs.

Although data deficiencies in Mozambique make it difficult to conduct analyses with much confidence, most of the available evidence supports his theoretical predictions. There was massive destruction of capital during the civil war, with nearly 40 per cent of all immobile capital either completely destroyed, or eroded beyond use, implying an annual rate of war-related capital reduction of almost 4 per cent. Capital inputs that were highly visible, immobile, and specific were most affected. Export agriculture, for example, suffered more damage than the subsistence sector, while in general, the formal, tradable sectors proved more vulnerable than informal, non-tradable activities. There was a large toll on human capital as well, as schools and hospitals were destroyed, and families displaced and psychologically traumatized. Investment plummeted, with foreign direct investment during the conflict years only a fraction of its value in the post-war period.

Transaction efficiency also decreased as a result of the war shock. Domestic marketing activities fell drastically, with the net number of commercial structures such as warehouses, shops, and trading posts decreasing by approximately 30 per cent during the 1982–8 period. This was accompanied by an increase in transport and distribution costs, particularly affecting export agriculture. There were high levels of uncertainty throughout the war, with adverse consequences for social organization, the reallocation of capital, and transactions efficiency, although the degree of uncertainty appeared to fluctuate over the war years as the central government's legitimacy waned following independence, then gradually increased over time.

Public finance also suffered; the real value of tax receipts fell by half during the 1980s, recovering only slightly from 1985 with the implementation of adjustment programmes. Fiscal deficits increased each year from the start of the civil war, more than doubling from 1980 to 1984. Military expenditure increased, then levelled off, while public investment expenditure decreased significantly as a proportion of GDP during most of the 1980s.

As predicted by the dynamic model, the destruction in capital, the increase in uncertainty, the rise in transactions costs, and increased fiscal deficit led to falling output in the medium term and reduced growth in the longer term. During the early and mid-1980s, output declined by 30 to 40 per cent, but started to increase in the late 1980s, due in part to economic reforms and heavy inflows of aid, despite the continuous destruction of capital. There was a consequent deterioration in welfare, with a worsening in most social indicators such as mortality and literacy rates.

The only hypothesis of Brück's not supported by the evidence from Mozambique concerned consumption patterns. Contrary to the model's predictions, the savings ratio fell, with the level of private consumption falling by less than the drop in output. This implies either that consumers were operating according to some sort of permanent income hypothesis, or that among individuals close to subsistence saving behaviour is determined by an immediate concern for survival.

Two important conclusions emerge from Brück's analysis. First, even if the one-off destruction of capital stock is restored to pre-war levels following conflict in Mozambique, growth may not recover due to the persistence of increased levels of uncertainty and transaction inefficiency, which draws attention to the importance of 'abstract' forms of capital, sometimes defined as 'social capital'. As a result, war may undermine the capacity of an economy to sustain development in the long term. This result may explain the absence of a strong peace-dividend in post-war Mozambique.

Second, aid resources can potentially play a crucial role in reducing the long-term development costs (as well as the immediate welfare costs) of war, by helping to protect civil administrative institutions and sectors that are particularly important in determining regression in technology. This, in turn, would help minimize the transaction inefficiency and uncertainty associated with war, and thereby reduce long-term damage to economic growth. In this sense, pursuing policies that reduce the immediate costs of conflict also serve to promote sustainable development in the medium to long term.

Although Brück's analysis makes it clear that war in Mozambique proved extremely destructive at the macrolevel, it may have also had a constructive effect. In Chapter 4,

Volume II, Chingono examines the 'grass-roots' economy which developed as people responded to the destruction of employment opportunities occasioned by war, illustrating the positive economic changes conflict may generate.

As violence deprived people in the countryside of their previous means of subsistence (agriculture) and drove them from their homes, they sought new ways to survive in the cities to which they moved. Given the virtual collapse of state enterprises and the scarcity of formal-sector employment, most became 'barefoot entrepreneurs', creating a burgeoning informal economy. Chingono documents this process in Manica Province in south-west Mozambique, where an estimated 250,000 out of 635,000 people were displaced. Of these, 100,000 moved to Chimoio city (previous population 50,000), which contained several distinct grass-roots markets.

The informal activities that Chingono describes arising in the war economy of Chimoio city are noteworthy for their scope and diversity. Some involved production including peri-urban agriculture and horticulture, pottery, handicrafts, metalworking, and food production/processing; others, the transport of passengers and goods through the war zone; most, however, centred around petty trade in second-hand clothing, basic consumer goods (for example, soap, tinned fish, oil), and rural products (for example, sugar cane, cassava, wild fruit).

An important characteristic of these activities was their stratification according to gender and class. The more lucrative activities, such as trade in second-hand clothing and manufactured commodities, were largely the domain of men, while women and more recent arrivals to the region were relegated to the trade in basic consumer goods and agricultural products, which were less profitable. Children also participated in the war economy, forming the lowest rung of the economic hierarchy, working for themselves or to supplement family income, producing simple products such as kerosene lamps and ashtrays, or just trading.

The grass-roots economy involved considerable differentiation in income. Some groups, especially those with connections to and opportunities arising from the formal sector not merely survived, but actually became quite rich. For example, most of the entrepreneurs in the lucrative trade in second-hand clothes possessed ties with commercial bureaucrats who had easy access to clothes donated by aid agencies. On the other hand, those with little capital and no connections barely secured subsistence.

Many of those engaged in illegal activities made huge profits from bypassing the restrictions enforced by conflict. For example, smugglers of goods in short supply profited handsomely by bringing in bread, beer, and sugar from Zimbabwe and selling them at profits of over 200 per cent. Other lucrative illicit pursuits included money changing; poaching game, and trafficking in precious materials and arms; and trading in abducted labour. It is important to note, though, that these activities entailed considerable risk from both formal channels (capture by police) as well as informal ones (bandits and pirates), and that some made fortunes from these activities, while others only a bare subsistence.

The distinction between the formal and informal sectors was sometimes blurred, as were the precise economic roles undertaken. For example, low-level bureaucrats from the formal sector also participated in the grass-roots economy, owning some of the most successful enterprises in the market place. Similarly, drivers employed by the formal sector used their vehicles to transport goods and people for the grass-roots economy. In other instances, people straddled several economic roles. A single worker, for example, could simultaneously be a labourer (working to produce agricultural products), employer (employing children to sell the produce), and trader (selling manufactured goods purchased from the savings generated by the sale of agricultural goods). These diverse relationships illustrate the complexity of the economic logic enforced by the exigencies of war. Although similar developments can be observed in some peacetime economies, particularly in economic crisis and where regulations abound, the shortages and regulations of a war economy created greater opportunities and a population desperate to exploit them.

Chingono concludes that, on balance, civil conflict played a constructive economic role in Mozambique not only by conferring large profits on particular groups, but also by creating a new class of entrepreneurs, and unleashing an entrenched 'entrepreneurial ethic' which benefited the economy as a whole. In forcing former subsistence farmers to engage in new survival strategies, it encouraged new forms of economic organization. This, in turn, may have accelerated the transformation of productive relations in Mozambique from traditional pre-capitalist to capitalist ones.

One conclusion that contradicts Brück is that the war may have had a beneficial effect on society's organizational capacity by fostering new forms of social capital and relations. The use of family bonds, kinship relationships and ethnic connections played a crucial role in helping to establish the grass-roots economy. Contrary, to traditional analyses, the war in Mozambique led to the generation of new economic opportunities, accelerating the process of social change, which helped to offset some of the negative impact of war both on individuals and the economy as a whole and may also have provided a basis for post-war reconstruction.

2.3   Nicaragua

As is evident from most of the country cases, wartime distortions almost inevitably produce extreme macroeconomic disequilibria, with negative effects on production, distribution, and welfare. In some cases, these costs are made worse by misguided policies on the part of both national governments and aid agencies, based on concepts of structural adjustment and humanitarian relief designed for use in peacetime.

FitzGerald and Grigsby examine the impact of such inappropriate strategies on Nicaragua's wartime economy under the Sandanista regime (1979–87). Contrary to conventional conceptions of civil war as an exogenous shock to the economy, they argue that incoherent economic policies represented a prime cause of the conflict in Nicaragua, and also exacerbated wartime macroeconomic distortions. A central proposition of FitzGerald and Grigsby is that an economy experiencing war has particular structural and behavioural characteristics that must be specifically allowed for when designing macroeconomic policy. Because of the failure to adapt policies to the war situation, attempts to stabilize the economy from policy-generated disequilibria had serious welfare consequences.

Prior to the revolution that brought the Sandanistas to power, the Somoza government adopted a policy of agrarian modernization that favoured capital-intensive agricultural exports at the expense of domestic food production and peasant farming. Grain prices received by peasant farmers were reduced, worsening the already regressive income distribution. Economic opportunities became increasingly scarce for rural groups, resulting in horizontal economic inequalities that led to armed insurrection. The peasant-supported uprising, led by the Sandanistan Liberation Front displaced the Somoza regime in 1979, in a civil war which was costly both in terms of immediate lives and income lost, and also the longer-term effects of disarticulated internal and external commercial networks.

The Sandanistas adopted Kaleckian-style policies aimed at taxing luxury goods to support the provision of basic needs, in reaction to the capitalist model of industrial development pursued under Somoza. This involved supporting agricultural production to ensure basic food security, and increasing social provision to include free access to primary education, health, and housing for the entire population. In addition, the state increased its economic role, taking properties confiscated from Somoza and his allies into state control, and introduced price controls and subsidies. It was the Sandanista's hope that through this state-led basic-needs strategy, all groups would be guaranteed a share of economic recovery.

Not all groups benefited equally from such reforms, however, and once again, horizontal inequalities developed into conflict. State intervention in domestic markets and foreign trade adversely affected large and medium agricultural producers and manufacturers, while the failure of the Sandanistas to redistribute confiscated land to the peasants, and the displacement of traditional rural–urban trading networks by state channels, angered the peasantry. In addition, indigenous groups were forced to relocate and integrate with Hispanic populations along the coast, to allow large state corporations access to their resource-rich territory. As a result, these groups, frustrated by the considerable policy-induced horizontal inequality, formed the backbone of the Contra rebellion of 1981 which was strongly supported by the United States with finance and logistical resources. The rebels' strategy was one of low-intensity conflict, aimed at political delegitimization of the government and the promotion of economic chaos. This strategy led to heavy economic costs.

Macroeconomic imbalances had already arisen as a result of the basic-needs policy—due to an increase in domestic demand without a corresponding increase in industrial or agricultural output. This disequilibrium was worsened by the war, as a result of the destruction of productive inputs, particularly in the export agricultural sector. As the economy was largely dependent upon agro-exports, this proved especially devastating for both national income and foreign-exchange earnings. The decline in output for the economy as a whole was heavy, with cumulative losses over the 1980–90 period estimated at some US$2 billion. Over the years of most intense conflict (1987–9), the cumulative total economic damages were approximately equivalent to one year's GDP.

Other macro-indicators were also eroded by the effects of the civil war. The government resorted to expanding the money supply, with the need to finance increasing fiscal deficits as a result of ambitious state-led basic needs and investment projects together with increased military spending, driving the annual inflation rate to an average of 70 per cent during 1983–4. There was also a significant accumulation of debt arising from the large balance of payments deficits.

Indirect macro-effects of conflict were also large. Estimates suggest they were more than double the direct effects, when adding together the effects of the US trade embargo, the cessation of loans from international financial agencies, and the 'multiplier' effect of lost foreign exchange upon domestic production.

To combat these macroeconomic imbalances, the Sandanista undertook a stabilization programme that included exchange-rate devaluation, credit ceilings, higher nominal interest rates, and the elimination of subsidies. The inconsistent application of the adjustment package, however, failed to restrain domestic demand as some parts were carried out with a time lag. The fiscal deficit rose to 18 per cent of GDP, financed mostly by monetary emissions, which drove inflation to 200 per cent. Rather than ameliorating the macro-imbalances, the government's implementation of stabilization policies made them worse, failing to stimulate production, and undermining the distributional objectives of the reforms through inflation.

The meso-effects of war did not conform to the predicted war behaviour. While public spending in the military sector did increase, doubling to 18 per cent of GDP in 1987 and absorbing half of the government budget, expenditures on the social sectors *also rose* during the war, although there were sharply reduced subsidies from 1984.

The basic-needs strategy of the government meant that, despite the large number of war casualties, effects on households were comparatively mild. Most social indicators, including literacy, infant mortality, school enrolment, and life expectancy, improved up to 1987. Moreover, the distribution of income and assets among households also improved over the course of the conflict as the government, aware that rural discontent fuelled Contra resistance, attempted to ameliorate the position of peasant groups. Starting in the mid-1980s, government policy stressed food production over exports, while reducing urban consumption subsidies and improving rural terms of trade. The government also modified its agrarian policies in an attempt to recover political support from the peasantry, substantially increasing land redistribution and improving rural marketing networks, as well as the provision of inputs for rural producers. However, this attempt to improve the agricultural situation proved too late to stem the effects of the previous emphasis on state-led export agriculture. A major cause of the economic collapse at the end of 1987 was the extended neglect of the peasantry.

Import support programmes and external credits provided by aid agencies also contributed to the economic crisis by allowing the government to disguise some of the worst effects of macroeconomic disequilibrium and to postpone tackling the underlying economic problems. The ready supply of international credit enabled the Sandanistas to continue importing goods, including food, at the expense of the development of exports and domestic food production and thereby worsened the macroeconomic imbalance.

The long-term development costs have also taken their toll on the post-war reconstruction effort, as there was destruction of both physical and abstract capital. The private sector experienced a high degree of uncertainty during the war period, partly due to the low-intensity, guerrilla-style combat tactics used by the rebels. This affected the level of private investment; large and medium-sized firms investing very little over the war and post-war decades, confining their activities to financial and commercial operations which promised rapid gains and high liquidity; and multinationals undertook only minimal investments. Perhaps even more negative has been the erosion of trust between social actors and the break-up of families which contributed to a marked decline in the effectiveness of Nicaraguan institutions. There was little institutional recovery during the 1990s and its absence remains a serious obstacle to the resumption of economic development.

The Nicaraguan case offers some important lessons for countries attempting reform programmes in a conflict situation. Government policy can exacerbate the chronic fiscal and external constraints during wartime by marginalizing small producers through its direct control over key economic activities and its focus on resource mobilization for the war effort. Unless carefully designed, import support programmes and humanitarian relief provided by aid agencies can add to this effect. Although a stabilization programme becomes necessary to prevent the ill effects of such macroeconomic imbalances, which can engender further conflict, the application of standard Fund and Bank programmes can easily worsen the economic situation of a conflict society. What is needed, instead, is an alternative stabilization programme which takes into account the special structural and behavioural features of a war economy, and seeks to improve exchange relationships with small producers in order to underpin to the living standards of the poor and to create a 'peace asset'.

2.4   Sierra Leone

The civil war in Sierra Leone has involved considerable costs for the economy. During 1985–94, GNP per head is estimated to have declined, at an average rate of 1.9 per cent, in real terms. Coupled with high rates of inflation, which averaged 86 per cent annually during 1985–92 and 25 per cent per year in 1993–5, market entitlements deteriorated substantially. Tactics on both sides involved indiscriminate violence against civilians, causing major disruption and displacement of Sierra Leonean society. By 1995, nearly 900,000 civilians had been displaced, and nearly 300,000 killed.

The decline in the Sierra Leone economy cannot be solely attributed to the effects of war. Before the conflict a pattern of economic development based on elite exploitation of Sierra Leone's considerable mineral wealth, combined with widespread corruption, rendered the country one of the world's poorest. During the 1970s and 1980s, President Stevens distributed state resources among key sectors of society to secure political support, creating a highly centralized system of patronage that produced private monopolies in various industries through the preferential allocation of import/export licences and foreign exchange.

Increasingly, economic activity fell outside official control. Diamond production, in particular, was controlled by a small group of Lebanese traders, who were presidential allies. As a result, a high proportion of diamonds was smuggled out of Sierra Leone without passing through government hands, such that by 1989, on the eve of civil war, official diamond exports plunged to just US$2 million from US$150 million in 1970 (Ministry of Mines, quoted in Reno 2000). Indeed, officials estimated that by the mid-1980s, 70 per cent of all exports left the country through clandestine channels (Reno, p. 7), leading to a decline in internal state revenues from 1977/8 to 1985/6 of over 80 per cent.

The inequitable nature of the peacetime political economy generated the conditions for civil war. The system of patronage among politicians and their cronies created deep resentment among those excluded from this system of profit and power. When the conflict in Liberia spilled over the border in March 1991, a small band of armed men, reportedly sponsored by Charles Taylor in retaliation for Sierra Leone's role as an air base for ECOMOG forces (the Economic Community of West African States Ceasefire Monitoring Group), moved in, calling themselves the Revolutionary United Front (RUF).

The RUF's purported war aims were to seek political changes at the national level and, particularly, to act against government corruption. But once the war started a new economic logic took over. In the context of severely constrained economic and educational opportunities generated by decades of underdevelopment and corruption, the RUF provided a vehicle for a wide variety of Sierra Leonean groups to make money. For the rebels, the incursion allowed previously marginalized groups, particularly youths with little opportunity for formal-sector employment, to benefit economically from looting goods and cash from the civilian population. In addition, the rebellion provided a means for such people to participate in trading networks that had previously been the tightly controlled domain of Freetown elites, in particular, the illegal trade in diamond production. The diamond-rich district of Kono became a major focus of rebel activity.

The study illustrates the various functions that war can serve for particular groups orchestrating or carrying out the violence. Keen contends that the civil war in Sierra Leone represents neither a descent into chaotic warfare, nor a contest which the parties involved are trying to 'win'. Rather, he emphasizes that perpetuating war has served the individual goals of rebel forces and government authorities alike, leading to the creation of a powerful war economy based on the well-organized and rational exploitation of civilians and material resources. The process of violence in Sierra Leone has proved crucial for the economic well-being of particular groups. Government soldiers, mostly poorly paid with little training, saw the civil war as a vehicle for self-enrichment, particularly as some felt excluded from the wartime profits enjoyed by their superiors. The war exercised a psychological function as well in that it provided those with few opportunities and low status in society a sense of purpose and empowerment.

With both sides gaining from the civil war, a perverse logic to the violence ensued in which the warring factions took actions that seem calculated to perpetuate conflict. Government soldiers, realizing their presence in resource-rich areas depended on continued violence, appear sometimes to have backed the rebels, as well as selling arms and munitions to groups they were supposedly fighting. Such tactics allowed for the evacuation of civilians from resource-rich territories by depicting the rebel incursion as a credible threat and, in so doing, facilitated military control over those areas. Significantly, the number of outright battles between properly armed troops in the war was very small, largely restricted to diamond-rich areas. The great majority of violent acts were against unarmed civilians.

Humanitarian agencies, for their part, have framed the conflict as a 'rebel war' or 'food emergency'. The concentration of aid resources in Freetown—itself largely the result of insecurity—has constituted an important additional benefit from violence for those elements of the government able to 'cream off' a substantial share, and has also helped to disguise the macroeconomic costs of conflict, and the devastation of the economy outside the capital.

Keen concludes that there may be little chance of engineering a lasting peace in Sierra Leone if the underlying economic and psychological functions of war are not properly understood. The analysis underlines the inadequacy of conventional models of war, based on the notion that both sides are seeking to triumph, for understanding the Sierra Leone conflict. He argues that war is not exogenous to the economic system but, rather, a development of the various economic and political processes taking place during peacetime. Simply aiming to secure an end to the violence without addressing the nature of the peacetime political economy that generated conflict in the first place, including the limited economic opportunities available to young people, may doom the viability of peacemaking schemes.

2.5   Sri Lanka

The mechanisms linking war and economic change have traditionally pointed to the destructive nature of conflict. Sri Lanka, however, provides a compelling counter-example to conventional thinking about warfare, as it has experienced neither a reduction in growth nor a severe breakdown in welfare. Admittedly, the conflict in Sri Lanka has been limited in geographic scope, with the majority of fighting confined to the north-east. Still, the limited spread of violence does not explain why growth actually *increased* during the war period.

O'Sullivan (Chapter 6, Volume II) seeks to account for Sri Lanka's success in maintaining robust growth and household entitlements in the context of warfare, drawing attention to the effects of public policy and alternative societal structures in mitigating the costs of conflict. A complex network of official and quasi-official providers emerged which directly supported market, public, and civic entitlements during the war, and also reduced the uncertainty which is the source of damaging indirect economic effects. The study shows that the opportunities for constructive policymaking during wartime are greater than commonly thought.

At the outset of the civil war, the Sri Lankan economy possessed a relatively high level of human development despite its low GNP per capita, a result attributable to the government's long tradition of supporting public entitlements in the health and education sectors. Although the majority of the population worked in agriculture, Sri Lanka also possessed a quite well-developed manufacturing sector, which grew from less than 6 per cent of GDP in 1958, to over 15 per cent in the 1980s. A series of structural adjustment programmes beginning in the late 1970s reduced exchange controls, liberalized imports, established a unified exchange rate, and abolished price controls and rationing. Such changes led to a more flexible production sector, which helped Sri Lanka to avoid heavy macroeconomic costs of conflict.

The fruits of economic diversification, however, were not evenly distributed among ethnic groups. The Sinhalese majority discriminated against the Sri Lankan Tamils, with respect to educational and employment opportunities, as well as political access. Such horizontal inequalities between the two groups provided a potent source of conflict, and violence erupted between the Liberation Tamil Tigers of Eelam (LTTE) and government forces in 1983. In the course of the civil war, the LTTE gained control of the northern and some parts of the eastern provinces, creating a de facto state in those regions. Significantly, most violence remained confined to those districts. Although the conflict is still ongoing, O'Sullivan limits her examination to the situation in the north-east up until November 1995, that is, before the LTTE's control of the northern district of Jaffna was successfully challenged.

Contrary to expectations, the protracted civil conflict produced very limited macroeconomic dislocation. In fact, rather than contracting during the period of conflict, the Sri Lankan economy actually grew, on average, faster than in the pre-war period. Moreover, the performance of Sri Lanka compares favourably with other developing countries not at war, as does its GNP per capita, which is more than double the South Asian average. Foreign-exchange earnings, too, were largely maintained, although fiscal deficits did rise throughout the 1980s and 1990s, generating a corresponding, albeit moderate, rise in inflation.

The immediate explanation for the limited macro-impact of the war lies with the restricted geographic area subject to direct combat. The bulk of economic activity centred outside the war zone, with only those sectors to which the northern and eastern provinces made the greatest contribution registering losses—for example, fishing, non-export rice cultivation, and chemical production. For the most part, productive assets were evenly distributed across the island such that production, particularly in the export sectors, was only disrupted to a minor extent, helping to maintain foreign-exchange earnings. As noted above, the flexibility of the economy also played a key role in promoting growth. In particular, a dynamic manufacturing sector—especially textiles—did not appear to be affected by war conditions.

A strong government also helped reduce the insecurity and uncertainty accompanying armed conflict. Instead of being undermined, as in many countries suffering conflict, Sri Lanka's institutional capacity appears to have increased, with an increase in presidential powers. The government was thus able to implement economic reform programmes despite the civil conflict, albeit partially at the expense of the institutions of liberal democracy. The influence of strong government policies and institutions helped to sustain investor confidence and also worked to reduce transaction costs, facilitating the growth of the most dynamic sectors of the economy. In fact, those sectors normally deemed less vulnerable to the influences to war, such as agriculture, accounted for a smaller proportion of GDP after a decade of conflict than before the war period, while the more transaction-intensive manufacturing exports grew.

Consonant with these macro-trends, for the most part, the increase in poverty and deterioration in entitlements usually associated with war did not ensue in Sri Lanka. In the areas outside the war region (the south-west), there was a *decrease* in the incidence of poverty, as well as in its depth and severity, from 1985/6 to 1990/1. Human indicators outside the north-east fared favourably in comparison not only to other countries at war, but also to other non-conflict Asian countries.

O'Sullivan attributes such counterintuitive trends to the key role exercised by public policy. The government preserved market entitlements to a large degree through its promotion of labour-intensive manufacturing as well as government cash transfers that increased consumption among rural populations. The state's continued commitment to universal provision of health and education services also preserved public entitlements throughout the period of turbulence.

The story inside the war zone, however, was different. Data for the war-affected north-eastern region, although harder to verify, suggest a rise in infant mortality, a decline in immunization coverage, and a drop in educational attainment throughout the period of civil conflict. Human indicators for the eastern province suffered similar effects.

Yet the effect of war on entitlements in the north-east still proved comparatively mild. The trend in some indicators actually improved over the course of the war; and even the worst case estimates for human indicators in the war-affected areas, such as infant mortality, still compare favourably to other countries at war as well as other developing countries, although it should be noted that Sri Lanka's social performance was very good to begin with.

The limited damage to household welfare in the war zone was largely due to the emergence of a complex network of official and quasi-official providers. Market entitlements, for example, were supported by the employment of large numbers in government jobs, as well as the guarantee of a ready supply of basic foods and commodities to the north-east. Throughout the war period, the government continued to provide a steady proportion of expenditure to education and health in rebel-held areas, actions intended to counter the LTTE's claim that the government was at war with the Tamil people and not simply the rebel insurgency.

In the north-east, alternative societal structures developed to complement government initiatives. The LTTE, for example, also became an important source of employment, not only for armed combatants, but to many others in 'non-military' positions. It ensured that the wartime supply of goods was distributed progressively favouring poor and vulnerable groups, and worked to 'normalize' life in the Northern province by providing its own institutions—for example, fully functioning judicial and police systems—that stabilized social interactions and discouraged opportunistic behaviour. Local and international NGOs also worked to sustain welfare, providing civic entitlements, by contributing to immunization programmes, as well as providing some other additional essential services ranging from maternal health care to financial services. Informal family networks also worked to support entitlements through intra-household transfers, including foreign remittances.

Households in the war zone themselves exhibited considerable adaptability and ingenuity in exploiting new opportunities created by conflict. While the war reduced conventional employment opportunities in the north-east, new ones emerged in the informal economy. These included the high profits possible from exploiting the shortages generated by the blockade of the Jaffna district, the provision of alternative modes of transport as conventional ones ceased because of fuel shortages, taking commissions for waiting in queues, or charging fees for typing letters to the government demanding compensation. As in Mozambique, the range of such coping mechanisms attests to the fact that the economic opportunities generated during war may be greater than is commonly supposed.

There was great disparity in the costs sustained between the two war-affected regions in Sri Lanka and the effectiveness of alternative societal structures. In the east, NGOs and quasi-official providers were more limited in both scale and effectiveness, with the majority of their efforts confined to relief rather than the rehabilitation and development programmes adopted in the north. This was partly due to the fact that the east has historically had a lower literacy rate and a more pronounced patron–client political culture. But the greatest impediment to the growth of alternative social providers in the east was the way the war was fought. The massacres, round-ups, and disappearances that characterized the conflict led to a breakdown in trust. This destruction of social capital prevented the development of strong civic institutions and, in particular, alternative social networks to help people cope with the hardships of war. In contrast, there was much less disruption of social capital in the north, where warfare took the form of a blockade rather than direct combat, while LTTE initiatives aimed at introducing law and order into the region also made the environment more secure. Hence, civic institutions were able to function much more effectively in the north.

The Sri Lanka case contains important insights. The first lesson is that government actions can exercise an effective role in maintaining household entitlements during the course of conflict. Second, alternative social structures can be useful in mitigating the social costs of warfare. Third, there is a need to bolster institutions during conflict, be they governmental or quasi-governmental, to reduce the potentially harmful effects of uncertainty on the economy. However, the possibilities here depend critically on the nature of the war as the contrast between the two war-affected areas in Sri Lanka indicates.

2.6 Sudan

The civil war in Sudan has been characterized alternatively as a religious conflict, pitting Christian separatists against Islamic fundamentalists, or as ethnic rivalry between Arab elites and Nilotic groups. While ethnic and religious tensions contributed to the outbreak of conflict, economic motives also help to explain the recent violence in Sudan.

In his case study, Keen highlights the material motives behind the Sudanese civil war, focusing on the political economy of the Bahr-el-Ghazal and southern Kordofan regions between 1968 and 1988. He argues that war represents the culmination of long-standing conflicts over resources (such as land, cattle, labour, and oil) and, more important, a means for certain groups to maximize the benefits of economic transactions through the exercise of force. As such, the participants involved did not pursue victory as their sole or even most important objective but, instead, sought to manipulate violence in ways that would achieve their economic goals. Far from the irrational process that it is commonly portrayed, Keen attempts to show that conflict in Sudan proved to be 'rational' for those groups that sought to maximize their economic gains through violence.

Much of the civil strife in Sudan was shaped by the peacetime political economy. Since the early 1800s, northern Arab interests have continually exploited the non-Muslim peoples of the south, plundering their material and manpower resources, and effectively denying them means of representation within the state. The situation improved slightly under colonial rule, with the British granting the south a modicum of protection, but the pattern of excluding southerners from educational and economic opportunities continued. Moreover, British officials exploited traditional ethnic rivalries to exert their control over rebellious southern territories, employing local Baggara Arabs in punitive expeditions against various Dinka groups.

This pattern of uneven development persisted in the post-independence era, as southern groups were further marginalized economically through the loss of agricultural land, and politically through the reduction of southern representation in the military and government. Frustrations erupted into Sudan's first civil war in 1955, which lasted until the 1972 Addis Ababa agreement established regional autonomy for the three southern provinces.

The accord, however, did little to improve the highly inequitable political economy that existed prior to conflict. Increasingly, the prosperity of significant northern groups came to depend upon greater exploitation of resources in the south. Three developments, in particular, inflamed the peacetime struggle over resources. First, the expansion of mechanized agriculture led to the amalgamation of unregistered land into large state-owned mechanized farms, depriving small landholders in the fertile plains of the south-east of their property, and blocking traditional southern livestock grazing routes. Second, because southerners generally lacked the capital, agents, and family ties necessary to transport their livestock to markets, Arab merchants reaped huge profits from purchasing cattle cheaply from towns in southern Kordofan for sale at several times the purchase price in northern markets. This created a powerful interest among northern commercial elites in maintaining their oligopolistic position, and preventing southerners from entering this trade. Third, large deposits of oil were discovered in the south in 1978. The government sought control over these reserves, gradually transferring southern Sudanese troops north (the immediate spark for the second civil war in 1983) and northern troops south, notably to the oil-rich Bentiu area.

Increasingly southerners and non-Arab groups perceived that they were being deprived of the representation within the organs of the Sudanese state that might have allowed them to stake an effective claim to these resources. Indeed, by the mid-1980s, there was no significant southern representation in northern Sudan, either at the central government level in Khartoum, or at the local level in southern Kordofan. Government attempts to control, and even eliminate, educated Dinka and Nuba were part of a strategy to deprive these groups of representatives or spokesmen.

Successive governments attempted to prop up the highly inequitable political economy. They permitted powerful groups—either through granting legal rights or immunity to prosecution in practice—to exploit natural or human resources through the use of violence (legal or illegal). In addition, the government armed and encouraged the economically marginalized Baggara Arabs to fight the Dinka and the Nuer. The Baggara were allowed to benefit from stolen cattle, access to grazing land and the cheap (or even) free labour of southern Sudanese captives and famine migrants. By dividing and manipulating civil society in this way, government policy greatly exacerbated ethnic and religious tensions.

When the southern rebel Sudan People's Liberation Army (SPLA) was formed in 1983, northern Sudanese labelled the southern and non-Arab population as a whole as 'rebels' and 'infidels', undeserving of the state's protection, and who might be legitimately subjected to extreme exploitation. Civil war justified Khartoum in a strategy of violence in order to maximize its extraction of resources from southerners, with impunity.

This strategy not only led to famine, but also deprived famine victims of relief. Northern merchants played a key role in creating high grain prices by manipulating the supply of grain reaching southern towns. When such 'forced markets' created famine, government officials deprived southern famine victims of aid, arguing that such groups were outside Sudan's political community and therefore undeserving of protection under the law.

The economic benefits of such tactics were threefold. First, by forcing southerners to leave their homes in search of food, the government depopulated resource-rich areas, which facilitated control of such territory, and cleared land for the expansion of mechanized farming. Second, the out-migration of famine victims provided a source of cheap labour, and, in some cases forced or slave labour for Sudanese Arab farmers. Third, both merchants and army officers profited from the high price of travel of the migrants on 'authorized' lorries and other transport.

In addition to their effect in perpetuating violence, the economic and political practices underlying the civil war also undermined the efficacy of emergency aid. Keen concludes that policies will be ineffective in bringing about a successful end to the conflict in Sudan unless the international community recognizes and addresses the rationality of violence. Equally, policies to alleviate suffering during war (like famine relief) must understand these political economy effects or they too will prove ineffectual.

2.7   Uganda

Like Afghanistan and Mozambique, Uganda illustrates the massive socio-economic costs that prolonged civil war can inflict, especially where the violence is geographically pervasive and state failure undermines public entitlements. In Uganda, however, external actors—including governments and NGOs—played a much smaller role than in the former two countries, either in instigating violence or in providing relief.

Matovu and Stewart explore both the economic causes and consequences of Uganda's civil war—giving special attention to the effects of intergroup disparities in provoking violence—as well as examining the consequences of war for macro-performance, meso-spending, and household well-being. They use both qualitative and regression analysis, as well as a household survey of the region worst affected by conflict. It emerges that the costs of war have been particularly heavy in Uganda not only as a result of the direct destruction and death generated by combat, but also from the generalized instability generated by the Amin dictatorship. The lack of alternative institutions to replace collapsed government services compounded the heavy economic and social costs at all levels of the economy.

Colonial policies helped sow the seeds of Uganda's post-independence conflict. In particular, colonial administrators accorded the Buganda of south-central Uganda a privileged position, both politically and economically. Western and northern Ugandans lacked economic opportunities in their own territories, and some moved to Buganda as low-paid labourers. As a result, at the time of independence, horizontal economic and political inequalities reinforced ethnic divisions and, in so doing, helped transform inter-group tensions into violent conflict, particularly during 1966 (the attempted Buganda Secession), 1978–9 (overthrow of Amin), and 1983–5 (defeat of Obote's second regime).

Indiscriminate state-sponsored violence was a primary cause of massive deaths, estimated at around 300,000 people during Amin's era, and 500,000 in Obote's second regime. During these episodes, the authorities carried out numerous arrests, without much differentiation between rebels and civilians. Together with forced disappearances, executions, rapes, and the expulsion of British and Asian economic interests during Amin's economic war, such tactics generated a pervasive climate of instability and fear. Violence took on added ethnic dimensions, as massacres were carried out against rival groups, with Obote, a northerner, persecuting the traditionally privileged Baganda, and Amin, a westerner, targeting northern tribes as well.

The prolonged political instability—including the whole Amin era as well as the war episodes—largely account for the heavy macro-costs generated by conflict in Uganda. The economy experienced particularly large declines in periods corresponding to intense political uncertainty, namely, the 1971–8 period associated with Amin and the 1980–5 period before Museveni took over. Growth dropped significantly during the years of fighting, that is, 1979–80 and 1983–5, and fluctuated at zero during the Amin years of instability. The investment ratio showed a similar pattern and there was a large decline in exports and imports and an acceleration of inflation. Tax revenues dwindled to almost nothing—around 2 per cent of GDP in 1980, recovering a bit during the early years of Obote's second regime, but falling dramatically again between 1984 and 1986. Government expenditure fell correspondingly.

Regression analyses confirm these results, revealing that the prolonged political disturbances actually had a *larger* impact than specific war episodes, although the latter events do, of course, form part of the prolonged disturbance. For example, political instability exhibited a significant and negative impact on all major macro-variables—i.e. investment, savings, tax revenue, government expenditure, exports and imports—and a positive effect on defence spending. In contrast, the specific war episodes had a significant effect on only a few of the same aggregate indicators.

At the mesolevel, private-sector allocation changed according to expectations, with an increase in less transaction-intensive activities. With the disruption in national and international markets and rising transactions costs, subsistence agriculture rose and industrial activities declined. Agricultural production rose as a proportion of GDP from under just half in 1970 to over 70 per cent in the worst war years of 1980 and 1983; manufacturing declined from 7 per cent of GDP in 1975 to 2 per cent in 1981.

Public-sector allocations also shifted in accordance with expectations, defence spending crowding out expenditure on social services as a portion of the already minimal government expenditure over the war period. There was a steady decline in both education and health as a percentage of GDP from the early 1970s, with an especially sharp decline in the war years. By 1987, health expenditures had fallen to almost nothing. Defence expenditure, on the other hand, increased steadily from the 1960s, reaching peaks in 1971, 1981, and 1990.

The combination of declining social expenditure and falling GDP translated into damaging declines for household welfare and income. Most social indicators worsened during the 1970–80 period, including calorie intake per person, primary enrolment, the ratio of doctors to people, and access to safe water.

Yet it is difficult to gauge the effect of war at the household level from national statistics, as data for important indicators such as income poverty do not exist. The authors therefore undertook a retrospective survey of 56 residents of the Luwero district, one of the areas most affected by war from 1981 to 1986. The results of the survey give graphic expression to many of the negative microlevel effects of war identified in the introductory chapter. The displacement of residents, caused by the fighting, and the loss of entitlements to assets like land, had a profound effect on production activities, particularly subsistence farming, which all but ceased to exist in this locality. Compounding this effect was the destruction of functioning markets—itself exacerbated by the frequency of displacement—which led to the collapse of money-generating activities.

Even before the war the provision of health and education services had been poor. With the violent conflict of 1983–5, health centres ceased to exist, with a consequent rise in sickness and mortality. School buildings were destroyed and both students and teachers displaced. Children abandoned education on a massive scale, often joining rebel groups in the area both for a sense of purpose and as a means to survive.

Access to market, public, and even direct entitlements dropped sharply among the respondents, with acute consequences for household incomes and welfare, especially as neither NGOs nor refugee camps provided significant support, in contrast to the situation in Afghanistan.

The effects of displacement had lasting effects, as most respondents reported that it was extremely difficult to resettle after the war given the lack of income-generating activities that could be undertaken by returnees, and the generally deficient facilities. Another problem, common to almost all the conflicts under consideration, was the difficulty of reintegrating young people involved in conflict back into education.

The retrospective survey makes clear that the conflict had comprehensive negative effects at the microlevel in the area where most of the fighting took place. One might expect the country as a whole to have suffered less. Yet the evidence of a large decline in macro-performance for the whole economy, and extreme shifts in private and public allocation at the mesolevel, suggests that Uganda suffered particularly heavy costs compared with other countries at war (see also the comparative evidence in Chapter 4 of this volume).

No strong quasi-official or NGO response arose to counteract the collapse of revenues and reduced government health and education services, as occurred in Afghanistan or Sri Lanka. There were few refugee camps. Moreover, individual survival strategies, appeared to be less extensive and effective than in Mozambique or Sri Lanka. Informal survival strategies did develop, as many studies have documented (see, for example, Green 1981; Meagher 1990), but the range of activities appears to have been more limited, geared towards trade and smuggling rather than production.

Nevertheless, from the view point of inter-group distribution, some positive effects did occur during the war. As a result of both conflict and policy, there was some diminution of the gap between the northern and southern regions, although the south remains relatively privileged. Nevertheless, the narrowing of regional group disparities may partially explain the reduced propensity to conflict in recent years, though war continues in the periphery of the country, much of it related to disputes in neighbouring countries. These peripheral wars are still costly, perpetuating the state of under-development in the areas affected, and involving a large rise in the share of military expenditure in the government budget which is squeezing social and economic expenditures. But the peripheral conflicts have not impeded economic growth for the country as a whole, and have been associated with some aggregate social progress as well.

3 Statistical Overview of Country Experiences

To provide a clearer comparison of the magnitude and direction of the effects in the case-study countries, we briefly review data for the seven countries with respect to the main variables identified in the theoretical framework in Chapter 1. The deficiencies in wartime data are extensive and, consequently, the picture which emerges is incomplete, with gaps for war years plaguing most variables, particularly for Afghanistan and Mozambique. In this comparative section, we rely on international data sources only. The country studies themselves draw on national data sets which are sometimes more complete. Another problem is that many of the conflicts occurred in the context of severe economic vicissitudes such as prior economic recession and the international debt crisis, so that negative developments cannot solely be attributed to war. As a result, the trends identified here only provide a rough indication of the various wartime effects. Still, some interesting comparative findings emerge to complement the individual case studies.

As expected, national income per capita fell during conflict in almost every case, with Afghanistan, Mozambique, and Nicaragua experiencing the greatest declines (Figure 5.1). In Sierra Leone, GNP per capita fell sharply in the 1980s, before war broke out. In contrast to the other cases, Sri Lanka experienced a steady *increase* in its GNP per capita, which nearly doubled over the war years.

Tax revenues as a proportion of GDP did *not* invariably fall during conflict as had been predicted. In Nicaragua and Mozambique, tax receipts actually increased. But

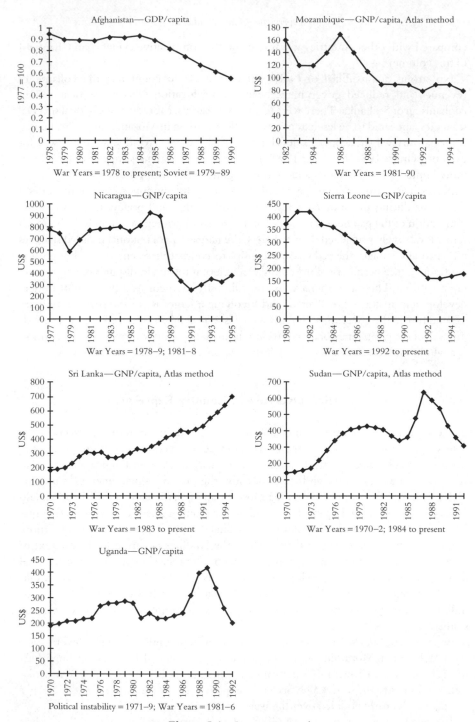

Figure 5.1 Income per capita

Source: World Bank (1997); UNCTAD, *Least Developed Countries*, and own calculations (Afghanistan); World Bank, *World Tables* (1992) (1995 Uganda).

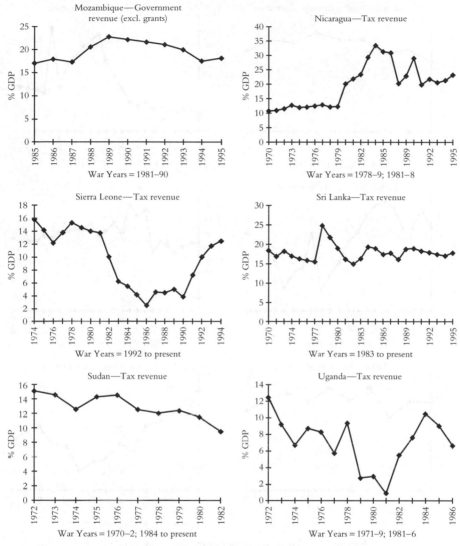

Figure 5.2   Tax revenue (% GDP)

Source: World Bank (1997).

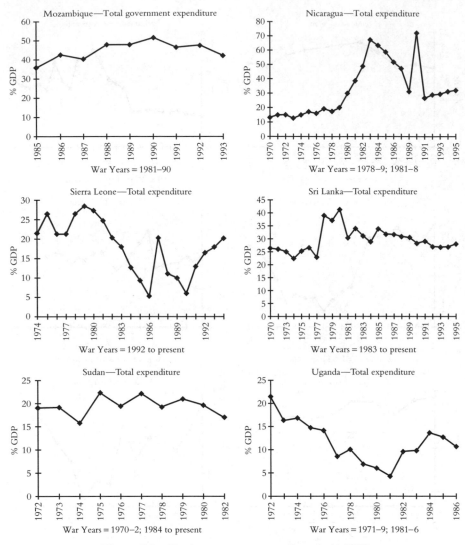

Figure 5.3   Total government expenditure (as % GDP)
Source: World Bank (1997); ADB, *African Development Indicators* (1994–5, 1997).

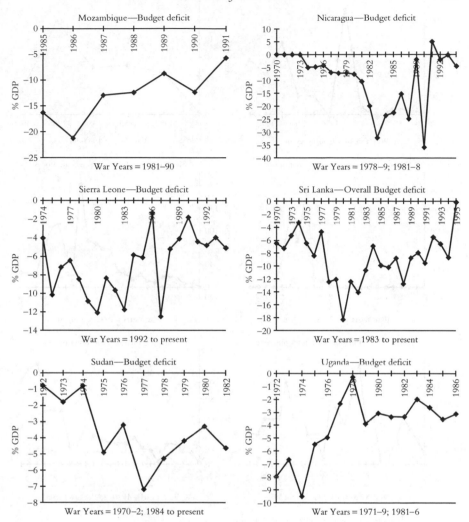

Figure 5.4 Budget deficit (as % GDP)

Source: As Figure 5.3.

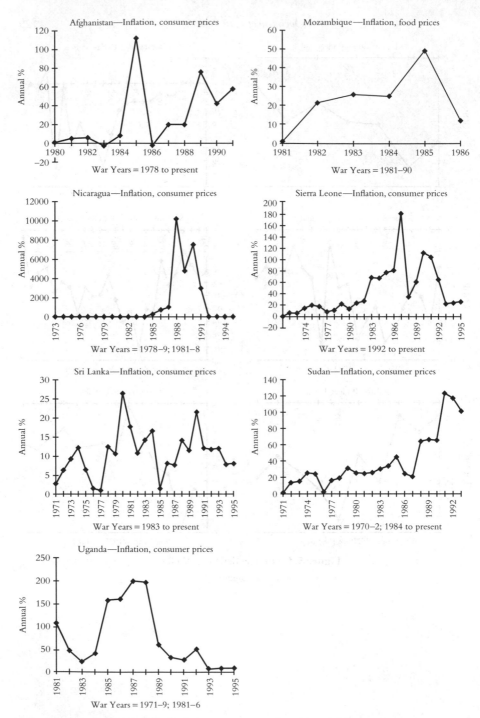

Figure 5.5 Inflation, consumer prices (% annual increase)

Source: As Figure 5.2.

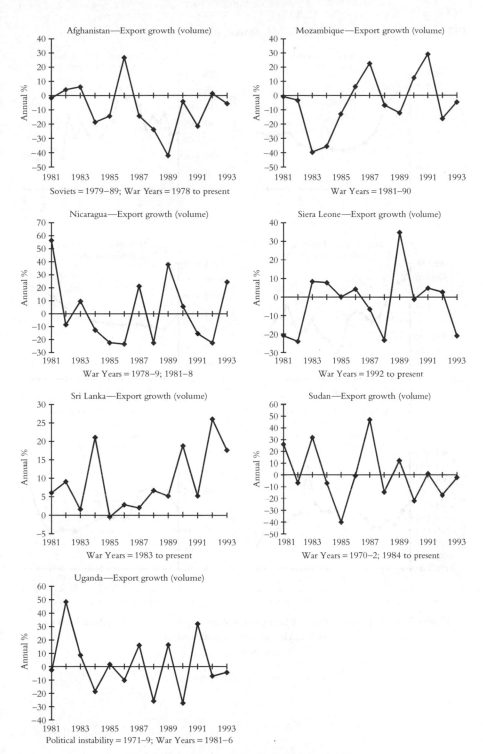

Figure 5.6 Exports growth, volume (annual %)

Source: As Figure 5.2.

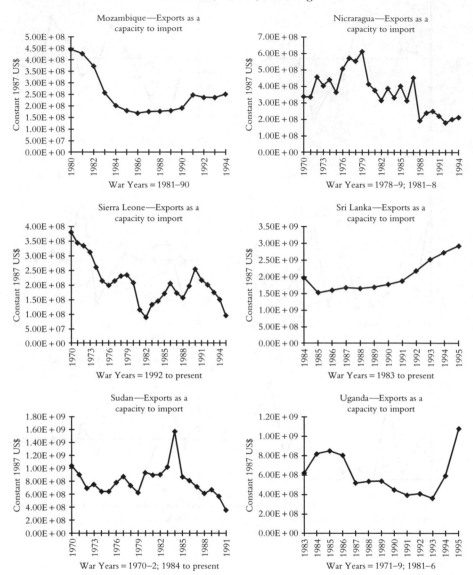

Figure 5.7 Exports as a capacity to import (= current price value of goods and services deflated by the import price index)

Source: As Figure 5.2.

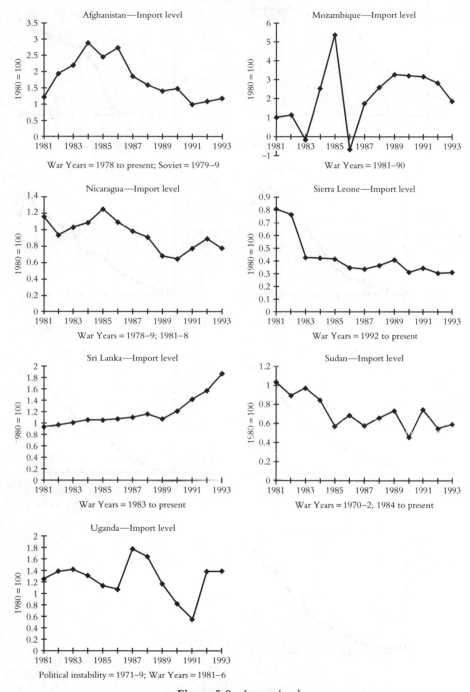

Figure 5.8 Import level

Source: World Bank (1997) and own calculations.

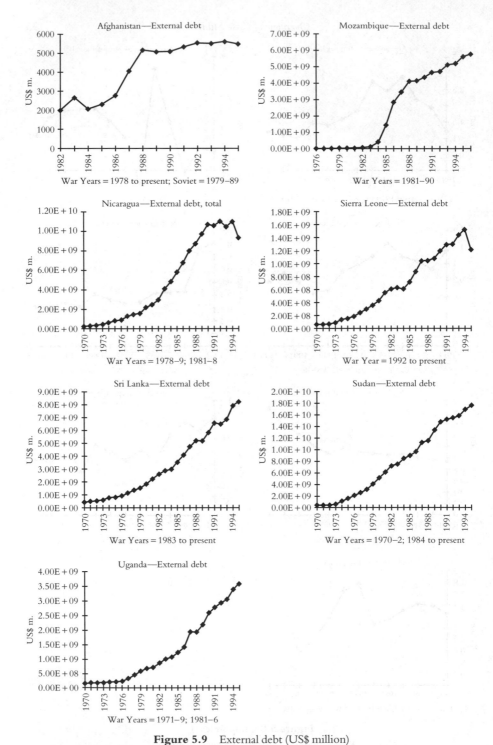

Figure 5.9 External debt (US$ million)

Source: World Bank (1997); ADB, *African Development Indicators* (1992, 1997).

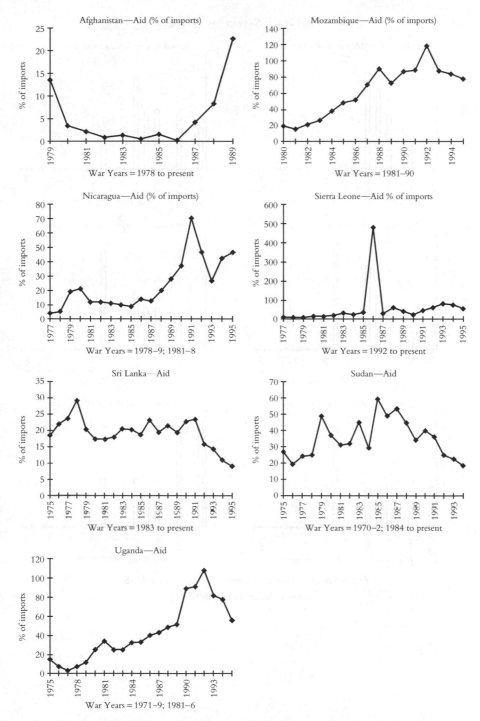

Figure 5.10 Overseas development aid (% of imports of goods and services)
Source: As Figure 5.2.

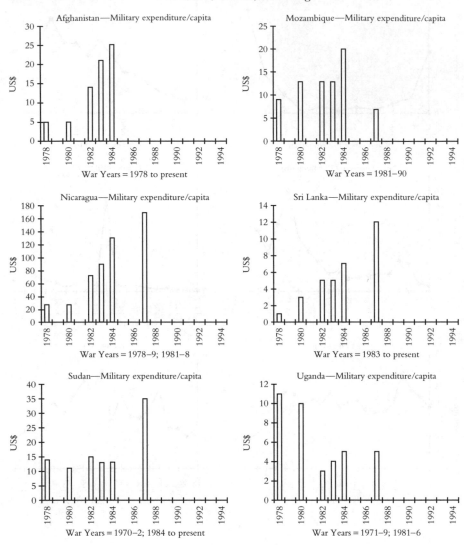

Figure 5.11 Military expenditure per capita (US$)
Source: Sivard (1991, 1996).

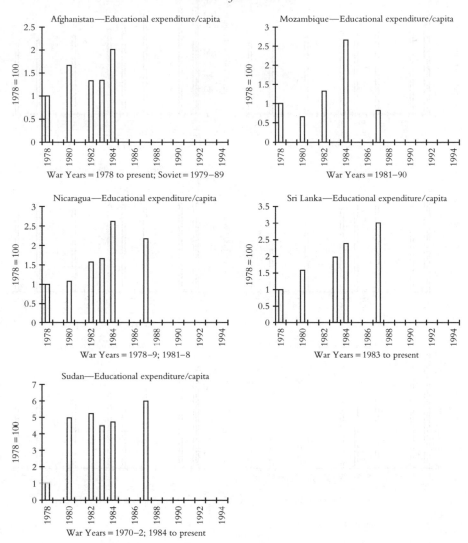

Figure 5.12   Education expenditure per capita (US$)

Source: As Figure 5.11.

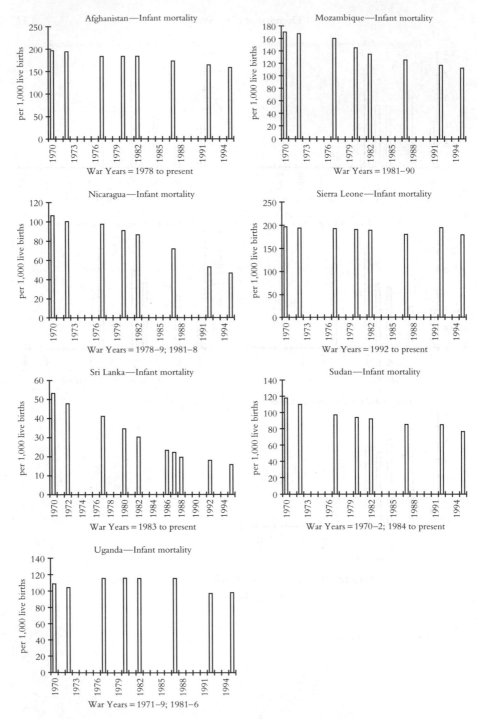

Figure 5.13   Infant mortality (per 1,000 live births)
Source: As Figure 5.2.

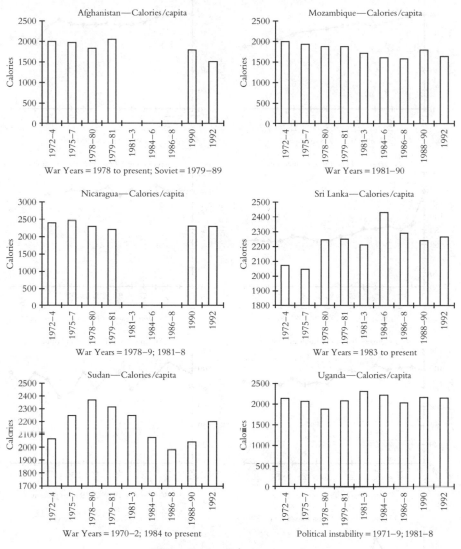

Figure 5.14 Calories per capita

Source: FAO, *Food Production Yearbook* (various years).

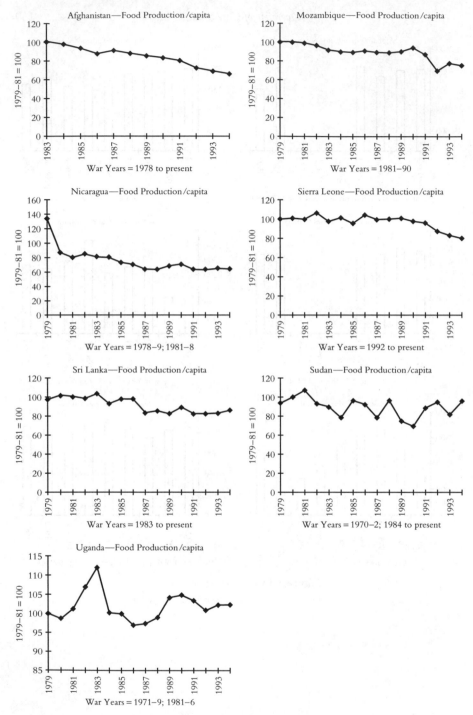

Figure 5.15   Food production/capita

Source: As Figure 5.14.

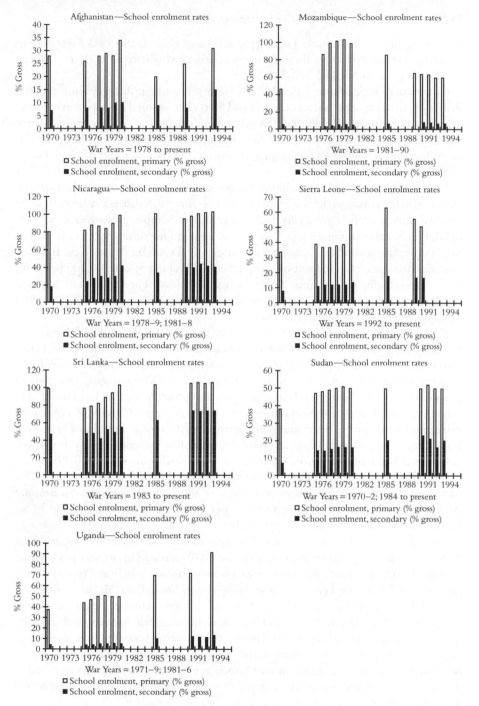

Figure 5.16 School enrolment rates

Source: As Figure 5.2.

there were sharp falls in Sierra Leone (pre-war) and Uganda. Sri Lanka was able to maintain revenue collection throughout its conflict, which stayed fairly constant at roughly 20 per cent of GDP.

Government expenditure varied broadly with revenues: in those countries with a sharp drop in tax receipts, such as Uganda and Sierra Leone, total government expenditure as a portion of GDP also fell sharply, but in others, such as Nicaragua, where tax collection increased, expenditure rose during conflict (Figure 5.3). In Sri Lanka, government expenditure was maintained consistently at the comparatively high rate of 30 per cent of GDP.

Government expenditure was invariably greater than revenue, and budget deficits increased in the course of the war in most countries for which data is available. In some countries, budget deficits were very high, reaching, for example, more than 30 per cent of GDP in Nicaragua (Figure 5.4). Predictably, inflation in consumer prices tended to rise sharply during conflict, although sometimes with a time lag (Figure 5.5). Inflation rates reached dangerous proportions in Nicaragua, peaking at over 10,000 per cent, while high inflation rates of over 100 per cent were recorded in Afghanistan, Uganda, and Sudan. Sri Lanka once again proved the exception, with wartime inflation rates never exceeding 25 per cent per annum.

Exports earnings declined in all countries except for Sri Lanka (Figures 5.6 and 5.7), and quite drastically in Mozambique and Sierra Leone. The decline in foreign exchange earnings led to a drop in imports (Figure 5.8), but mostly not proportional to the fall in export earnings. Some countries, such as Afghanistan and Mozambique, were able to compensate for lost foreign exchange through rising foreign aid and borrowing, displaying increased rates of imports during some of the war years (Figure 5.8). Sri Lanka was again exceptional in maintaining its export capacity and, as a result, its importing power, in the face of declining external aid. External debt increased rapidly in all cases, with the greatest rise in wartime indebtedness occurring in Sudan and Nicaragua (Figure 5.9). Aid as a percentage of imports increased in a few countries, notably Mozambique and Uganda and for some part of the period Nicaragua, Sudan, and Afghanistan, while it remained constant or decreased for most of the period in Sri Lanka, Sudan, and Sierra Leone (Figure 5.10).

Data for mesolevel changes is particularly sparse, but what is available suggests that wartime defence expenditure as a percentage of GDP increased in all countries (also see Chapter 4), while data for Nicaragua shows a massive rise to more than 8 times pre-war rates (Figure 5.11). The data on social spending is very limited; on this basis the picture seems to be a mixed one (Figure 5.12). Educational expenditure per capita rose quite sharply for a time in Mozambique and Nicaragua but then fell; in Sudan it fluctuated, generally on a rising trend; in Sri Lanka it rose throughout the war period; in Afghanistan it appears to have risen in the early Soviet period, but after that there is no data; while there is no data at all for Uganda and Sierra Leone. But the case studies indicate falls in expenditure in the later years in Afghanistan and in Uganda, especially in the Amin years.

Evidence on access to education is more comprehensive (Figure 5.16). Educational access mostly declined during conflict, particularly in Afghanistan and Mozambique where large population displacements occurred. Sudan and Uganda showed periods of worsening during acute conflict. But enrolment rates rose in Nicaragua and Sri Lanka where outlays increased. Given the patchy coverage of most of the wartime data, such trends must be treated with caution, especially as some of the more piecemeal evidence presented in the case studies suggests more drastic effects.

Infant mortality rates were very high in some countries—nearly a fifth of live births in Afghanistan, Mozambique, and Sierra Leone—and showed rises in some periods (Figure 5.13). Sierra Leone and Afghanistan, both with high rates initially, showed almost little improvement over the war period, while Uganda recorded a worsening over the years from 1971 to 1986. But some countries, notably Sri Lanka, Nicaragua, and Mozambique, showed a general decline in infant mortality during conflict, probably due to increases in public expenditure on social services detailed in the case studies. Although information on malnutrition for conflict years is scant, the decline in food production which occurred in most of the cases, together with evidence of declining calorie consumption per head, suggests that the prevalence of malnutrition increased over war years (Figures 5.14 and 5.15). Taking 2,200 as the minimum caloric requirement, Figure 5.14 shows that, on average, nutrition was deficient *all the time* in Afghanistan and Mozambique, and some of the time in Uganda, while the rest of the cases appear to have met the standard average requirement, although the maldistribution of food entitlements in Sudan meant that many in the south were malnourished.

What emerges from this comparison is that although many of the trends predicted by the theoretical framework occurred, the magnitude of such effects varied considerably. At the macrolevel, almost all the countries studied, except for Sri Lanka, experienced a decline in income, revenues and expenditures, budget deficits and inflation, and a collapse of exports and imports. The degree of such effects varied, with Mozambique, Nicaragua, and Uganda experiencing declines of significant magnitude, while the declines in Sudan were less severe. At the meso and household level, while there was also a general decline in indicators, once again Sri Lanka, Nicaragua, and Mozambique experienced less drastic declines in social welfare, and even some improvements, while Afghanistan, Sierra Leone, and Uganda correspond to 'classic' cases where the social costs were significant. In Sudan, average performance was not so poor, but the adverse regional distribution meant that conditions in the south worsened (see the case study and the evidence in Chapter 7 of this book).

In these cases, as with the larger sample of cases reported on in the previous chapter—which, of course, included almost all the present set of countries—the magnitude and sometimes the direction of the economic and social effects of war varied. The concluding section will consider how the case studies explain these differences.

4   Conclusions

Comparing the seven countries on the basis of the case studies and the statistical overview we may classify them broadly according to how heavy the social and economic costs, as shown in Table 5.1.

Table 5.1 A summary of economic and social costs of conflict in sample countries

Country	Economic costs			Social costs			
	Growth of GDP		Growth of exports as capacity to import	IMR		Calorie availability	Enrolments
	Annual war years, per capita	Cumulative as ratio of 1995 GDP		War years	Cumulative as % of 1995 population		
Afghanistan	−ve	na	−ve	Poor	na	−ve	Initial +ve Later −ve
Mozambique	−ve	−2.8	−ve	Some improvement	better than region	−ve	Initial + Later −
Nicaragua	−ve	−13.5	−ve	Improvement	0.7	Mixed	Mainly +
Sierra Leone	−ve	−1.5	−ve	Poor	0.6	na	na
Sri Lanka	+ve	Better than region	Mainly +ve	Large improvement	Better than region	Mixed	+ve
Sudan	Mixed	−1.7	−ve	Some improvement	0.2	−ve	Mixed but mainly −ve
Uganda	Mainly −ve	−0.5	−ve	Worsening	2.0	−ve	Mixed

Notes: 1. The cumulative loss represents the difference between actual growth over the period covering one year before the war started and five years after it finished compared with the regional (excluding war-affected countries) average growth, expressed as ratio of 1995 GDP; 2. Cumulative IMR loss is calculated in same way, and expressed as a ratio of 1995 population. na = not applicable.

Sources: Figures in Chapter 5 and Tables 4.13 and 4.14.

Putting this information together, there are the following types of conflict among our case studies:

1. *Heavy social and economic costs*: Afghanistan; Sierra Leone; Uganda. But we should note that some of the Afghanistan social performance was better than might have been expected; and that Sierra Leone data is very poor. Sierra Leone did extremely poorly on both economic and social development prior to the war.

2. *Mixed performance on both the economic and social aspects*: Sudan. But here there was a strong regional dimension with high social costs (and presumably economic) in the south.

3. *Heavy economic costs but moderate social costs*: Mozambique, Nicaragua. In both cases, the social situation improved markedly initially and then deteriorated, but the net position was quite good.

4. *Good performance on both the economic and social aspects*: Sri Lanka. But again there is a regional dimension. In the war-affected areas neither economic nor social performance was so good.

Of course, there was differentiation within each category of behaviour. For example, Nicaragua's economic performance was particularly weak, and so was Uganda's social performance (as judged by IMR). From these cases, it seems that it is more difficult to sustain economic development during conflict than social progress. Moreover, the fact that in both Nicaragua and Mozambique, which initially did protect the social aspects, performance began to fall off, suggests that it is difficult to sustain good social performance against a background of failure in the economy.

To try and explain these different types of performance we need to turn to (a) the nature of the war; (b) the nature of the economy; and (c) the responsiveness of the key actors: governments, quasi-government, external donors and NGOs, and the people themselves.

First, the nature of warfare conditioned the magnitude of wartime effects, with particular types of combat proving to be more economically damaging. Those conflicts restricted in geographic coverage and with fairly consistent war aims on the part of the participants involved less damage to production and output. In Sri Lanka, for example, conflict was largely confined to the north-east of the country such that the effects of war on the macroeconomy were relatively small. The Sudanese conflict, confined to the south of the economy, has had some negative economic effects but not nearly so great as the more geographically pervasive wars. Similarly, the post-1986 conflicts in Uganda, which have been confined to the periphery of the economy, have taken place against a background of a growing economy, rising investment, savings, exports, and so forth. On the other hand, in those countries (Afghanistan, Mozambique, and Nicaragua) where warfare has been characterized by prolonged, low-intensity, destabilization campaigns, with a variety of conflicting and changing war aims, the economic losses have been relatively large. Growth was reduced in such war economies not only through direct physical destruction of capital and infrastructure, but also the effects of uncertainty, which led to falls in new private investment and increased transactions costs. The social costs involved in conflicts which affected a wide geographic area also proved high, with the massive displacement of populations and resulting disruption of community networks undermining human development.

Second, the state of the economy prior to conflict affected the severity of the economic costs of war. In general, countries such as Uganda and Nicaragua, with economies highly dependent on a single sector (agriculture) for export earnings, were particularly vulnerable to the effects of production disruptions. In these economies, the knock-on effects of lost export earnings from agriculture reduced foreign exchange availability, leading to a shortage of imported inputs and a further fall in output. As mentioned, in the case of Nicaragua, the costs of such indirect 'multiplier' effects from conflict totalled nearly three times Nicaragua's 1992 total output. In contrast, economies with the ability to adapt to wartime shortages, and with flexible manufacturing sectors, such as Sri Lanka, fared better because they were able to substitute for scarce imports and promote the dynamic components of the economy which contributed to economic growth and exports. Afghanistan, for example, was able to reduce the economic costs by resort to poppy production, which generated substantial incomes and exports.

The third important element differentiating these wars was the responsiveness of various actors; these conditioned both economic and social costs. The government itself is the most important actor—whose response may either worsen or ameliorate economic and social costs. This response depends in part on government power, and in part on policy choice. Weak governments, in control of little territory, without revenue-raising capacity or the ability to deliver goods and services, cannot provide macroeconomic policies likely to promote the economy, nor the meso-policies needed to sustain social progress. In our sample, Uganda, Sierra Leone, and Afghanistan after the Soviet period were all extremely limited in their authority, as indicated by the virtual disappearance of revenue-raising capacity. This loss of authority meant that the formal structure of the economy was severely weakened, and that the government could not be relied on to provide essential social support.

Governments were much stronger in the four other countries—Sudan, Sri Lanka, Mozambique, and Nicaragua—although in each case they lost control over a part of the territory. But having power is only part of the story; it is also a matter of how it is exercised. Sri Lanka is the best case from this perspective, following responsible macropolicies, providing the consistency and security to generate economic growth (though foreign investment did fall off at times when the war was particularly acute). The government also delivered social services in the territory it controlled and provided finance for social services elsewhere. Mozambique and Nicaragua were committed to social and economic development, and their social policies were effective both in extending education and health services, and in delivering food to those in need. In both cases, they also facilitated the movement of food to areas they did not control. However, both countries fell down on the economic side. They both failed to keep the budgetary situation under control; and their economic policies tended to discourage private enterprise and discriminate against the peasantry. As noted above, these failures ultimately also threatened their ability to maintain social progress. Both countries adapted their economic policies as the war proceeded, and were making improvements when the wars came to an end.

Sudan contrasts with the others in having quite strong authority, but deliberately using it to deprive large parts of the population of goods and services. In Sudan, actions taken by Khartoum officials created conditions leading to famine and disrupted famine relief efforts. Neither economic nor social policies were well designed from a developmental perspective.

Although a powerful well-intentioned government adopting appropriate economic and social policies is clearly the best mechanism for promoting development and protecting people during conflict, the studies showed other actors could also play an important role, especially on the social side. Quasi-governmental structures were instrumental in delivering food and services in Sri Lanka and Mozambique in rebel-held territory. While rebel governmental structures could not substitute completely for the government on economic policy—when they controlled the territory convincingly and over the medium term, they could provide a secure environment in which economic activity could take place, if not flourish (as in north-east Sri Lanka).

Foreign NGOs could not perform this role, but they could be useful sources of social service delivery: they were almost the sole providers of social services in Afghanistan, and played an important part in food deliveries in Mozambique. Communities and NGOs were also of some significance in Sri Lanka, again especially in the war-affected areas. Refugee camps, financed and sometimes located outside the country, also provided a safety net for large numbers in Afghanistan and Mozambique—albeit with negative effects on production and self-reliance.

The worst cases—from the perspective of access to social services and the provision of food—were those where none of these actors was effective: the government collapsed; quasi-governmental structures failed to emerge; there were very few NGOs or refugee camps. This was the situation in Uganda in the late 1970s and mid-1980s; and in Sierra Leone in the 1990s; and perhaps, in the south of Sudan, although there was some NGO activity there. Somalia (not part of our sample) represents another war situation of this type.

The role of aid agencies was ambiguous. In some cases, such as, Afghanistan, they played an important role in providing relief services and aiding in rehabilitation efforts. But in others, for example, Sudan and Sierra Leone, aid agencies seem to have compounded problems. Not only did aid resources serve to fuel conflict by representing another wartime resource which fighting groups strove to appropriate, but they also distracted attention away from some of the underlying causes of conflict. For example, in Sudan and Sierra Leone, humanitarian agencies largely ignored government abuses, analysing the situations as humanitarian emergencies, rather than appreciating how certain groups profited from violence and would use aid resources for this purpose. In Nicaragua, although aid was not directly misused by warring parties, it contributed to economic mismanagement by permitting the macro disequilibrium to get worse, allowing the government to continue with ineffective economic policies, and disguising their effects. In addition, while external aid helped countries such as Mozambique and Uganda to finance imports, ameliorating the effects of collapsed foreign exchange earnings, it also contributed to the finance of the war effort.

People's entitlements depend in large part on their own activities, even though these are heavily constrained by their environment, especially during war. In most case, people were able to sustain their entitlements better than might have been expected by adapting their behaviour to the war economy and finding new opportunities emerging from the war situation. In Mozambique, this was exemplified by the emergence of a dynamic informal economy in the urban areas which generated incomes and provided a range of goods and services. In Afghanistan, significant coping strategies included smuggling, poppy and arms production, as well as mass migration abroad. In Sierra Leone and Sudan, much informal and non-legal activity occurred, although it seems mainly of a 'zero-sum' type, with thefts, looting, smuggling, but not much productive activity. In Uganda, an informal economy emerged largely consisting of trading, but not during the worst-affected war areas. Additional subsistence production, however, sustained nutrition outside these areas. The studies show clearly that some people can survive and even profit during war by resorting to a variety of activities, some violent, some illegal, and some productive. In addition, family support systems operate in war, as they do at other times, helping people to survive through increasing the participation rates of women and children (including in fighting), remittances, and relocation of family members.

In assessing the net contribution of these household strategies it is important to differentiate those activities which actually add to the economy's income and output from those which are a matter of redistribution from one set of people to another, and among the latter whether the redistribution improves or worsens the position of the weakest in society. In many activities there are elements of both production and redistribution. Some activities clearly do add to production—for example, urban farming; small-scale mining; poppy production; furniture making. Others add to the country's income, if not world output—for example, remittances from abroad. And some consist in a redistribution from one group to another (looting), or from the government to private citizens (theft and sale of government property; smuggling). In our studies, a good deal of the informal activity seems to have been of the redistributive type, apart from additional subsistence production and some of the productive informal activities recorded in Mozambique and Afghanistan.

Which groups benefited and which lost from the redistributive activities is complex and not easy to ascertain. Some previously relatively privileged groups lost (for example, those in the formal sector; urban groups in Afghanistan; the Dinkas in Sudan); the war situation also allowed previously excluded members of societies to gain access to resources. But the beneficiaries were by no means the weakest members of society. New war elites were created, sometimes with international criminal connections.

The better off, and those with more education, were generally in a stronger position to protect themselves and to profit from war than the low-income and uneducated groups. But there was some variation across the cases. For example, in the case of Mozambique, war provided women with new economic opportunities, and partially undermined traditional attitudes; but following the access to power of the Taliban in Afghanistan, women became much worse off in terms of earning capacity and access to social services. The long years of political instability appear to have had some levelling effect in Uganda, where traditionally less privileged regions gained vis-à-vis the more privileged Baganda, partly because war destruction was centred in Buganda. In Afghanistan too, the historically privileged urban groups were particularly hard-hit. Yet better off Afghanis were able to flee, and it was the weakest groups (widows and the old) who suffered most.

The case studies clearly show that there is no single model of a 'war economy', and that some of the ill effects of war, while very difficult to avoid, can be offset in certain circumstances. Some of these circumstances—in particular, the nature of the war itself, and the authority of the government—are not changeable in the short term. But others may be, including government macro- and meso-policies, the actions of NGOs and aid agencies. We shall consider policy lessons—and how they differ according to the nature of the war and of the government—in the final chapter of this book.

6

The Treatment of Children During Conflict

ERIC GREITENS

1   Children and the Effects of War

Armed conflicts in recent decades have been more deadly for civilians in general and children in particular than in many earlier wars. In the American Civil War (1861–5) and World War I (1914–18) it is estimated that 95 per cent of the casualties were soldiers. In World War II, civilian and combatant casualties were roughly equal. In Bosnia, Rwanda, and Somalia it has been estimated that perhaps as many as 95 per cent of casualties were civilians (Black 1996: 5; and Weiss and Collins 1996: 29). A large proportion of these civilian casualties were children, who constitute approximately half the population in many developing countries. Aggregate estimates of child casualties due to conflict, such as those produced by UNICEF in their 'State of the World's Children Report' (1996), are necessarily crude, but indicate that in the decade 1985–95, over 2 million children were killed, 5 million disabled, 12 million made homeless, and over 1 million orphaned or separated from their parents.

In some conflicts children are the specific targets of campaigns of violence and extermination. In Rwanda, *Radio Mille Collines* frequently broadcast the message: 'To kill the big rats, you have to kill the little ones' to the Interhamwe forces engaged in anti-Tutsi genocide, reminding Hutu citizens that Paul Kagame, leader of the Rwandan Patriotic Front (Tutsi Army) was only three years old when he fled with his family to Uganda. In Chechnya, Red Cross workers found that many dead children bore the mark of systematic execution with a bullet through the temple (Cairns 1997: 19).

Despite the evident horror of some of these findings, the impact of conflict on children eludes simple explanation, for it is neither uniform nor arbitrary, but differs in both manner and degree due to age, gender, region, class, and the attributes of individual children. There is, moreover, a great deal that we do not know about the lives and experiences of children affected by combat. These simple facts are often overlooked, or at least under-explained by relief organizations that are driven by a desire to act, to advocate, to fund-raise, *now* and, understandably, have little time and limited resources to disaggregate hastily collected data during rapidly changing conditions. Relief agencies do not attempt to spell out context-related complexities to donors who do not seek nuanced, in-depth information and frequently take a short-term view of emergencies. Even social scientists face a number of obstacles in their attempts to produce

The author would like to thank Jo Boyden for assistance and advice.

reliable data. Their research is difficult to sustain among unstable populations and in situations of poor security where access to children may be difficult, and long-term follow up may be impeded because of ongoing fighting or population movements. In addition, distrust of strangers is likely to be high in situations of conflict. Investigators may be faced with poor cooperation and inaccurate information. Moreover, the purpose of 'research' may well be lost on war-affected populations unless they understand that it will lead to some practical benefit for them (Richman 1993: 1,288). For these reasons and others, social scientists are rarely able to produce data from areas of conflict that are sensitive to the multitude of social and economic variables affecting children's survival and well-being. Attention to these variables, however, is often crucially important to understanding the situation of war-affected children.

There is, for example, evidence that child health and welfare may vary radically by region due to the uneven effect of conflict on basic services such as sanitation and water supply.[1] There is also evidence that age and gender significantly influence children's experience of conflict, yet many studies of war-affected children fail to make these distinctions (World Vision 1996). Research normally highlights the impact of violence or the effects of separation from family members, but often ignores the effects on children of other kinds of experience such as the sometimes devastating consequences of loss of trust or the opportunity to learn adult work roles.

Social scientists tend to focus, moreover, on refugees, unaccompanied children, and child soldiers. While these groups may be especially deserving of attention, they are often affected by conflict in ways that are substantially different from other children. They have been uprooted from their homes, spent time confined in camps, and may have been separated from their kin and engaged in violence themselves. Research with these groups does not always provide data that are applicable to the majority of children affected by conflict. We know very little, for example, about the large populations of children who are displaced and isolated from humanitarian assistance. Many of these children, as Boyden (1993) has pointed out, live clandestinely, or in destitution, working in exploitative jobs as illegal immigrants in bordering countries. Nor is there much known about the large numbers of children who live with families that are not their own. Children are often taken in as an extra hand, or to enable the family to qualify for an extra food ration, and there is some evidence that they are at high risk of abuse or abandonment on repatriation. Even within well-researched population groups, important aspects of children's experience are frequently overlooked. Investigators of child soldiers, for example, rarely pursue or publish data concerning the sexual abuse and rape of boys.

While much research tends to concentrate on children's experiences during periods of violence, circumstances *after* the cessation of violence are often at least as important. Richman (1998) cites a study of Jewish children who were in hiding during the Holocaust which found that decisions taken after the end of the war as to whether the

---

[1] See, for example, Boyden (1993: 35), quoting Smyke on the differences in health among Afghan refugee children living in Pakistan, children still in Afghanistan, and Pakistani nationals.

children should stay with their foster parents or go to relatives or to a children's home, strongly affected their subsequent psychological state.

In addition to the large gaps in existing knowledge about children during wartime, there have also been a number of incisive criticisms of the research that does exist. Dawes (1992), Cairns (1997), and Richman (1993) have all questioned, for example, whether the concept of post-traumatic stress disorder is appropriate for research on war-affected children, and whether the methodology employed in many 'trauma' studies is reliable. Save the Children (SCF) (1996) recalls:

A European psychologist on a UN contract arrived in Mozambique to find out what proportion of the children were traumatized by the civil war. The psychologist spoke no Portuguese, had no experience of epidemiological research and had never previously worked in Africa. Translation of the questionnaires into Portuguese was of questionable quality and the questions were poorly understood by local teachers charged with putting them to the children. No attempt was made to ensure that the questions were valid or translated into local languages.

Results were not shared with local authorities or communities; instead, those who initiated the research merely announced, in melodramatic statements to the media, that a very high proportion of Mozambican children suffered from post-traumatic stress disorder.

Richman (1996) has argued that researchers typically fail to make a distinction between normal distress following adverse circumstances, and mental illness. She writes, 'Most children in conflict zones are showing a normal response to extreme circumstances, and require support rather than psychological treatment. . . . Reports stating that large numbers of children affected by conflict have serious psychological problems because they have high scores on screening questionnaire[s], are valueless if there is no adequate information on reliability and validity.' Dawes (1992) argued that most children exposed to violence, 'do not develop serious forms of psychopathology'. Yet, Cairns and Dawes (1996) noted that a large portion of research concerning children and war still takes place under the rubric of psychopathology. Authors in the field, they noted, had a 'tendency to stress the negative' even when their own results show otherwise. Dawes (1992) concluded that more detailed and rigorous research was needed in this area, 'if we are to move beyond the more common rhetoric on this subject which seems to predict without sufficient care, the return of William Golding's little savages whenever children experience war or civil conflict'.

Mindful of how varied children's experience of conflict can be and of how little we know for certain about many large groups of affected children, it is still possible to sketch some of the impacts of war on children's lives. Whether they are the intended victims of violence, or the random casualties of conflict, war kills and injures large numbers of children, as indicated above. Child casualties are sometimes the direct result of being in the line of fire, but often occur after intensive combat has ceased. The Red Cross, New Zealand (1999) notes that children make up a significant proportion of the 1,200 people maimed, and 800 people killed, throughout the world each month by landmines. During 1998 in the city of Kabul, Afghanistan, roughly 55 per cent of landmine victims and 86 per cent of victims of unexploded ordinances were 18 years old or younger (Dec and Landis 1998: 6). Throughout the world, children are at risk primarily because their economic duties (such as collecting water and scavenging) require them to travel in dangerous areas, and also because they are curious and often see weapons as objects of play. Mines that are manufactured to maim an adult usually kill a child. Children who do survive are frequently disabled and unable to contribute to their families economically, and are thereby forced into begging.

In addition to injuries received as bystanders in conflict, children are also killed and maimed in their military roles as conscripted soldiers, porters, messengers, or voluntary recruits. High levels of active participation in conflict by children are attributable to their availability, expendability, and willingness to carry out orders requiring them to engage in ruthless acts. The precise number of child soldiers and children otherwise participating in war around the world is unknown, and unknowable, although fairly conservative estimates place it at around 200,000.[2]

The great majority of physical damage suffered by children as a result of conflict comes, however, not from weapons, but from the secondary effects of disease and deprivation. Children weakened by malnutrition are susceptible to diarrhoea, malaria, measles, and respiratory infections. Infant and under-5 mortality rates are often substantially higher in countries during or just after conflict compared to countries of similar socio-economic status that are at peace.[3] In Somalia, during 1992, one-half or more of all children under 5 on 1 January were estimated to have died by the end of the year—90 per cent from malnutrition and disease (United Nations Children's Fund 1996). During wars in Angola, Afghanistan, Sierra Leone, and Mozambique, between a quarter and a third of children died before their fifth birthday (Black 1996: 12).

Increases in disease and deprivation are in many cases linked to state failure and the disruption of services, as many conflicts in the developing world take place in debilitated or collapsing states. Because of their symbolic and practical value to the community, health centres and schools are often the targets of violence, and the absence of effective government imperils the delivery, or replacement, of such vital services. Even where governments continue to function during wartime, the transfer of resources from social and economic to defence spending generally affects children disproportionately. A Stockholm International Peace Research Institute study found that in sub-Saharan Africa, defence spending competed directly with socio-economic services, with a major pernicious effect on child health. The direct effects of disruption to services are difficult to gauge, however, as in many poor countries only a small proportion of the population makes use of formal services. Informal systems of healthcare, learning, and childcare are equally likely to be disrupted by conflict, but information on the consequences in terms of child welfare is lacking.

Sexual violence and abuse also tend to increase during wartime and are commonly used to humiliate and degrade, instil terror, and promote social division. Cairns (1997) estimates that as many as 80,000 women and girls were raped in former Yugoslavia.

---

[2] See, for example, Brett and McCallin (1996): for a discussion of approximate numbers of child soldiers active in 1996. Save the Children (1998: 1) estimates that, as of 1998, 'At least 300,000 children under the age of 18 are currently taking part in hostilities around the world.'

[3] For example, the under-5 mortality rate in Afghanistan in the early 1990s was 257, almost two and a half times that of neighbouring India.

In Rwanda, mass and public rape was employed as an instrument of terror—an attempt to destroy the fundamental social fabric and to shatter people's sense of security, self-esteem, and identity. Tutsi women and girls, some as young as 5, were raped in their homes, in the bush, and publicly at roadblocks, with grave physical and psychological consequences. A significant number of these women and girls bore children by the perpetrators and many were shunned by their families and communities (African Rights 1995: 748–9). The increased vulnerability of girls in camp situations means that many may have to trade sexual favours for food, shelter, or physical protection. Prostitution sometimes results, as described in World Vision (1996).

Often, it is difficult to isolate violence as a distinct causal factor in children's suffering, as there are many outcomes of conflict not directly related to physical violence. Boyden (1993) quotes Zwi, Macrae, and Ugalde who note that:

The negative impacts of war on child health and welfare are linked as much to changes in the social environment (the displacement of communities, the breaking up of families and social structures, the weakening of household food production and nutrition security, the loss of access to school, etc.) as to the direct and indirect effects of violence on the health of individuals.

Other studies have highlighted the insidious effect of psychological warfare on children whose exposure to actual violence was not so substantial, observing that children in the midst of war are as much preoccupied by problems associated with material hardship and crime as with political violence (Boyden 1993: 13). In many conflicts marked by widespread civil unrest, entire villages are disrupted and whole communities forcibly moved, so that the social networks upon which children rely for their care and protection are fractured. In 1999, UNHCR served over 22.4 million refugees and displaced persons around the world. More than half of this population are children.

When social networks are disrupted and ways of life altered or shattered, informal and subsistence economic activities increase. In most developing countries, children play a large role in these informal economies as, for example, herders of livestock, gatherers of firewood, and carriers of water.[4] As noted, these activities often place them in danger, the gendering and seasonality of subsistence tasks resulting in differential risks. For example, in northern Iraq, there was an increase in injuries and deaths due to mines among young girls and women during the autumn and early winter, when they collect firewood intensively. Boys were similarly affected in the spring, when snows melt and animals are taken to fresh pastures (Boyden 1994: 264).

In addition, during wartime children are often required to assume greater responsibility, taking on the roles of adults who have been killed, are fighting, or are otherwise absent. Changes in the demographic structure of households can also lead to the collapse of informal mechanisms for shared childcare, deterioration in intra-familial relations, and changes in the age-thresholds for marriage, childbearing, work, and decision-making (Boyden 1994: 259). In refugee camps in Burundi it was found that 55 per cent of girls married earlier than would have been expected outside of the camp situation.

---

[4] Save the Children (1995: 6) notes that in many economies in the developing world 'children routinely contribute between 15 per cent and 40 per cent of family income.'

There is evidence from Somalia and Liberia that some families marry off their daughters at an early age to militia men in order to secure their own protection (World Vision 1996: 19). Family livelihoods can be affected by the loss of a breadwinner or by rising prices in the war economy, requiring children to leave or postpone their education in order to work. In particularly desperate circumstances, when the regular means of livelihood have been destroyed, or seriously impaired, children may be sold or sent away in the hope that they will find work and remit income to the family, or at least fend for themselves.

2   Western Aid, the Media, and the Portrayal of the Vulnerable Child

As some of the statistics above indicate, war can and does have profound effects on children. Often it tears their lives apart. In the light of such evidence, the media, policy-makers, and the Western relief community typically portray children as innocent, vulnerable victims of war, passive beings subject to malevolent forces outside their control. This view, based on a particular Western conception of childhood, dominates relief policy. The relationship between children and violence, is, however, more complex than is usually portrayed. An understanding of children as active survivors of violence, or as significant perpetrators of violence, is often displaced by accounts of 'vulnerable' children.

The prominence of 'innocence' as one of the primary markers of childhood is distinctly modern. An understanding of children as sinful beings in need of (often harsh) discipline, has been a dominant force in European thought. Cunningham (1995) quotes from a German sermon of the 1520s:

just as a cat craves mice, a fox chickens, and a wolf cub sheep, so infant humans are inclined in their hearts to adultery, fornication, impure desires, lewdness, idol worship, belief in magic, hostility, quarreling, passion, anger, strife, dissension, facetiousness, hatred, murder, drunkenness, gluttony, and more.

If this seems preposterous to us today, it is largely because of how the Romantic movement fundamentally altered Western perceptions of childhood. Today, childhood is often understood as a time of innocence, purity, and naturalness, and is frequently juxtaposed against a view of adulthood as a process not only of maturation, but also of engagement with a corrupted society. The roots of this view lie in the thought of philosophers such as Rousseau, poets such as Wordsworth, and the economic changes of the late nineteenth century. Following industrialization, large numbers of children —no longer working in rural environments and many not working in industry— were withdrawn from the labour market and the streets to spend their time in homes and schools. Rather than children contributing to family income, parents invested their surplus income in their children. This economic change corresponded with a demographic shift from a high birth-rate/high child-mortality society, to a low birth-rate and low child-mortality society in Western countries. The overall tendency was towards a view of childhood as a distinct phase in the life cycle, with its own needs and characteristics, and a close association with nature in its untamed state. Wordsworth's *Ode on Intimations of Immortality from Recollections of Early Childhood* is a key text in this Romantic trend,

> Not in entire forgetfulness,
> And not in utter nakedness,
> But trailing clouds of glory do we come
> From God who is our home:
> Heaven lies about us in our infancy!

The *Ode* was part, and reflection of, the trend away from viewing children as sinful, to a belief in a childhood that was flowing in glory, touched by God. The aim of adults was no longer simply to prepare their children for adulthood or to save a child's soul, but to keep the child in themselves alive. Childhood in the Western world came to be understood as a time of innocence and a period of dependency when children's physical and emotional weakness, coupled with their lack of knowledge, make them highly susceptible to conflict. This view was reflected in the words of Mr Cancino, Rapporteur of the Third Committee of the UN General Assembly, who in presenting the 1959 Declaration of the Rights of the Child to the United Nations stated the treaty's point of departure was 'the undisputed principle that the child is weak and therefore requires special care and safeguards' (Kuper 1997: 42).

The innocence and vulnerability of the child is a dominant theme in the Western media coverage of foreign wars and emergencies. There exists a symbiotic relationship between the media and relief agencies, as the latter depend on media coverage to raise the profile of their work, and the media depend on relief-agency staff to 'guide journalists to the most horrific villages or homes struck by famine or violence' (Weiss and Collins 1996: 189). Weiss and Collins (1996) quote a BBC correspondent covering the Somalia famine who remarked:

Relief agencies depend on us for the pictures and we need them to tell us where the stories are. There's an unspoken understanding between us, a sort of code. We try not to ask the question too bluntly, 'Where will we find the most starving babies?' And they never answer explicitly. We get the pictures all the same.

The media, under great pressure to find an engaging story, frequently go to great lengths to find 'traumatized' children, who have lost their parents, been raped, wounded, or fought as child soldiers.[5] In my work with and for humanitarian organizations as a documentary photographer I have observed that the same children are often photographed and interviewed multiple times by various agencies, to the extent that one aid worker described such children as 'media stars'. I have also been told by publicists for relief organizations that my photographs were unusable because they 'did not show disabilities clearly enough'. Media attention and relief publicity that is focused exclusively on the suffering of distressed children can be harmful to the children involved, especially when the pursuit of 'trauma' stories engenders a lack of sensitivity to

---

[5] Personal observation, and see also Richman (1996: 20).

children's needs and a voyeuristic interest in their suffering (Richman 1996: 20). This is an area of concern to some organizations that have begun to draft principles to guide their use of images,[6] yet the exploitation of children continues, at least in part, because of the economic value of images of suffering for fund-raising and brand promotion.

Images of suffering children play against the Western perception of an appropriate childhood. Representations of children who are poor, hungry, working, disabled, sick and suffering, do not conform to the Western ideal, appearing to the general public as 'unnatural'. They elicit unease, sympathy, and horror—and hence make for effective charitable appeals (Burman 1994: 238).

Advertisements for child 'sponsorship' or 'adoption' have generally typified this approach. The use of the images of specific children in 'child sponsorship' appeals suggests that agencies are saving individual children. This invites the belief that political and environmental crises can be resolved by helping single children, with scant regard for the social context in which they live or the complex structural problems affecting their wellbeing. While the image is usually of an individual child, we are told that there are many such children in need of our sponsorship. If this is the case, then surely it is appropriate to question whether there may be systemic problems that are putting children at risk. If so, it is also fitting to ask, how would sponsorship of individual children help address such problems?[7]

In many campaigns, we are given little or no sense that the children portrayed are knowledgeable about or playing an active role in the struggles and forces that surrounded them. Such appeals also suggest that the children have no access to resources other than those the relief community has to offer. There are no adults in the pictures, no communities mentioned in the advertisements. The entire familial and wider social context in which these children live is stripped away, so that what stands between the child and the giver is nothing but a prepaid envelope in which to place a donation.

In this way the weakness and dependency of the child is contrasted with the strength and the agency of the donor. Certain authors have noted that the process at work in relief agency advertising and interventions is not only one of Western adult agency and Southern child dependency, but involves a wider dynamic—one of the 'infantilization' of 'the South'. Entire communities and nations are portrayed as weak and without knowledge—or at least without the strength or knowledge to help their own children. Burman (1994) notes, for example, that the imagery of children works to confirm the failure of the rest of their peoples and cultures to provide for them. Such imagery, it is argued, is part of a neocolonial dynamic in which, once again, Western technology and generosity can be applied to problems in the developing world, thereby aiding the passive citizens of that world. Burman cites the 1994 Concern campaign, 'Angola: A Cry for Help' in which the picture of a child was superimposed on an outline of the

---

[6] See, for example, Interaction PVO Standards (1993) and Save the Children (UK) (1993), both covered briefly by Cate (1996: 24–5).

[7] The first 'child adoption' programmes were initiated by the Save the Children Fund after World War I. Today's 'child-sponsorship' programmes are still prominent. Relationships with individual children are still pursued through the exchange of photographs and letters, though relief agencies increasingly market these programmes as being directed at poor communities in general, rather than at children alone.

country. This, Burman argues, positions 'all Angolans as dependent victims unable to fend for themselves without food from the mother country'.

Robertson (1998) has noted that at the very time that aid workers in Bosnia were working to convince mothers and health workers of the benefits of breastfeeding, an infant formula company in the United Kingdom was running the following advertisement:

This is the real face of Bosnia today . . . how must this mother feel knowing her baby is aching with hunger? She must be desperate for someone to give her food to save him. . . . [images of mothers breastfeeding their babies in camp situation] How can this mother cope knowing she is helpless to protect her daughter from illness and infection? . . . Just 20p a day can provide a life-saving 'baby box' for Bosnia, each one containing over 30 essential items to keep a baby alive and healthy. [image of mother and baby with bottle, indoors] . . . please don't forget the children of Bosnia [logo on screen of a manufacturer of breast milk substitutes].

There was at the time, however, 'no under-nutrition and no nutritional reason why women could not breastfeed'. Robertson writes that:

Large commercial interests were working against the health interests of infants and children and the media was using the angle of 'starving babies'. This made the general public in Europe respond by 'wanting to help'. . . . Inexperienced NGOs wanted to bring infant formula while WHO [World Health Organization] and UNICEF were trying to promote breastfeeding. Eventually, massive amounts of uncontrolled, incorrectly labelled infant formula [was] being distributed during the war in Bosnia.[8]

The International Baby Food Action Network (1996) has noted that 'Charity appeals for funds and food aid often use the "hungry baby" image or transmit the perception of malnourished mothers who cannot breastfeed their babies.' They note that 'after one TV appeal, thousands of tins of BMS [breast milk substitute] were collected for what turned out to be 12 babies in former Yugoslavia.' Their investigations revealed that 'the baby food industry donates large quantities of BMS and publicizes these donations widely in the press.' The companies, they argued, not only received valuable publicity, but sought to open new markets, as 'mothers who received a certain brand of BMS as a gift are likely to favour that brand over other products.'

Industry, the media, and relief agencies, all use images of vulnerable children to sell their products, promote their stories, and enhance the profile of their organization. The children portrayed are usually passive, innocent victims of war, hurt and injured by overwhelming evil forces. This view is sometimes accurate, particularly in the case of infants and very young children, but for older children, adolescents, and youths under 18 (who are classed as 'children' by the United Nations) the picture is often very different. Boyden (1994) cites research which suggests that, 'the experience of being able to exercise some control over events, a sense of personal mastery or competence in stressful situations and the presence of protective and supportive others, all serve to ameliorate distress.'

---

[8] Arana (1998: 12–16) has noted the impact of similar problems during natural disasters in Mexico.

Richman, Punamaki, Dawes, and Cairns have all argued along similar lines. Studies from South Africa and the Gaza Strip have shown that it is precisely children's *political activity* that helps them deal with situations of violence. They have found that 'the more children experience political violence, the stronger their ideological commitment and in turn the less their suffering.' Punamaki, in studying Palestinian children, suggested that: 'Psychologically the most functional way of coping with the military occupation is to fight against it.' In another Palestinian study, children who scored highest on measures of 'national behaviour' and 'national identity' were those who had been exposed to the most political violence. In fact, anxiety-withdrawal symptoms were *negatively* related to national sentiment. This led authors to postulate that national sentiment acts as a buffer against depression and anxiety in the face of a chronically frustrating situation (Richman 1993: 1,289). On their view, it was specifically children's political awareness and engagement with conflict that was a protection from suffering.

There is, however, widespread resistance to the notion that children, 'may actively take part in and design strategies of political struggle, not merely as political puppets but as committed believers in what they are doing' (Boyden 1993: 7). While noting that large numbers of children are forced to fight in wars, and that others 'choose' to fight only because fighting offers them a source of security, research concerning fighting children also noted that many children make a genuine choice to join armed struggles. Goodwin-Gill (1994) has argued that children are usually recruited or attracted to participate because schools that might otherwise occupy their time are destroyed or closed, fields they might otherwise plant are off-limits because of fighting or mines, relatives and neighbours are arbitrarily arrested, abused, or tortured, because 'a gun is a meal-ticket', and because children can be very useful in battle. Goodwin-Gill notes, however, that sometimes children 'are among the first to join; or are the prime movers in the conflict'. 'What moves them lies deep in the roots of conflict, in the social, economic and political issues defining their lives . . . The line between voluntary and coerced participation is fluid and uncertain' (quoted in Stavenhagen 1994: 10). That children might actively *choose* to fight is, however, an idea frequently dismissed in the relief literature. Hammarberg (1994) argued that:

There is a notion that many children actively participate voluntarily in war. This is both an oversimplification and an incorrect assessment. Many children that are believed to participate voluntarily are driven to do so because their environment is not suitable for children. If their rights were fully respected, these children would never have to choose the option of active participation.

Much of the advocacy literature similarly argues that the term 'volunteer' is misleading in so far as 'brutal circumstances leave little room for genuine choice' (Save the Children 1998: 5; Human Rights Watch 1996: 2). Research conducted for the UN by the Quaker UN office in Geneva, however, showed that the majority of children who chose to join armed opposition groups did so as a result of personal experience of ill-treatment of themselves or their families by government troops (Brett and McCallin 1996: 36; Save the Children 1998: 5). Such evidence suggests that children may fight for reasons similar to those of adults—to protect themselves and their families, and to eliminate government oppression. Children fight for other, less political reasons, of course. Muhumuza (1995) concluded that many child soldiers in Uganda joined because they were attracted to the excitement of war and because they admired their peers in the army. There seems to be a chasm, however, between the findings contained in thorough studies on child soldiers that suggest a large degree of agency and choice on the part of children—and here we do well to remember that most 'child' soldiers are actually 15–17-years-old—and the advocacy literature that so often accuses states and armies of 'allowing children to fight the wars of adults' (Save the Children 1998: 8).

Conceptualizing children as the passive victims of conflict may underestimate their active role in armed struggles and their capacity to adapt to and understand the processes of conflict. In places where 14-year-olds are expected to work and assume adult responsibilities, it is not surprising that they are drawn into a community's conflicts. Throughout the world, in areas such Cambodia, Chiapas, and the Gaza Strip, children play significant roles as soldiers, activists, and protesters.

3 Prioritizing the Vulnerable Child

In 1990, UNICEF declared its adherence to the 'principle of first call' in the distribution of relief aid, stating that children should have a first call on societies' concerns and capacities 'at all times and in all circumstances'. 'Children first' policies in wars and emergencies have been prominent in many relief efforts this century. Almost always, the justification for a 'children first' approach lies in the perception of children as innocent, vulnerable, and critically in need of Western assistance. That children should be awarded priority, might seem, to many, the most uncontentious of assertions. Its universal appeal, however, has not gone unquestioned. Last (1994) argues that,

the principle of 'children first', if it includes every child and is to be applied literally in the field, is not only impracticable but unacceptable in many cultures. The *social* value of a particular child's life—or of human life generally —is simply not an absolute, in all circumstances, in all cultures.

Even in practical terms, prioritizing children's safety and welfare is more difficult than might appear. In many developing countries, where banks, police, courts, and welfare agencies are absent or limited in scope, families and communities are the main guarantors of children's security (Last 1994: 201). Under such circumstances, removing children from their families and communities is likely to endanger their safety, and trying to serve children alone, or *first*, is certain to be problematic, and possibly harmful if it isolates children from their caretakers. Campaigns to prioritize children often cite historical precedent as a basis for their appeal. The 'children first' principle, however, as originally conceived and implemented, was never intended to promote the separation of children from their families.

It was Article 3 of the Declaration of Geneva, adopted by the Save the Children International Union in 1923, and unanimously endorsed by the members of the League of Nations in 1924, that first prescribed that the child 'must be the first to receive relief in times of distress'. Eglantyne Jebb (1929), founder of Save the Children (UK) and author of the Declaration, wrote that,

The fundamental principle which underlies the provisions of the Declaration is that every child should have a chance, and by this is meant not a chance of an existence of selfish enjoyment, but a chance of fulfilling, through service to its fellow-men, the object for which the child was born.

In *Save the Child!* Jebb (1929) held that the five-point Declaration was meant to be a practical expression, in succinct form, of the convictions of those who 'have given prolonged thought to the interests of children, and of mankind through its children'. Jebb's belief was that children must be given the means, both material and spiritual, to develop properly, and that, in turn, children should be brought up in the knowledge that their talents must be devoted to service. Others were invited to endorse and support these convictions.

The Declaration is often misleadingly referred to as the 1924 Declaration of the Rights of the Child. The instrument was not legally binding on the members of the League of Nations; it only required that they be guided by its principles. There is no sense in which Jebb was trying to establish a system of 'legally protected entitlements' in the modern sense of the word 'rights'.

Jebb believed that children should be first in one very specific sense—they should be *fed* first. She wrote, 'The duty of the community to the individual may be summed up in the word "food".' Jebb had undertaken relief work in Macedonia during the Balkan wars of 1912–13, and there she had witnessed famine and its impact on young children. After World War I, the Allied blockade of Germany and Austria led to devastating food shortages. Jebb was arrested for handing out a protest leaflet showing a starving Austrian child that read, 'Our Blockade has Caused This'. The Save the Children Fund (SCF) grew out of an organization called the 'Fight the Famine Council' that had been formed to protest against the blockade.

Eglantyne Jebb was not alone in her concerns about child malnutrition, for following World War I, there was much popular interest in the significance of calories, diet, vitamins, and measurements for malnutrition. Archival records from SCF relief efforts in Germany and Austria show that aid staff were intensely concerned to obtain 'statistical reports' on child nutrition and child malnourishment (Jebb: Archive Papers). Nutrition was then a new science, and SCF aimed to be systematic and scientific in its distribution of relief aid. It was clear to the agency that children suffered greatly, arguably more than adults, from food deprivation and that malnutrition early in life could have permanent and lasting consequences for health and growth.

As international concern for children developed in this century, the formal emphasis on the priority of children was removed. The original five-point Declaration of 1924 was amended in 1948 and a new Article 2 established that 'the child must be cared for with due respect for the family as an entity' (Last 1994: 195). By 1959, further revisions had been made, such that Principle 8 of the Declaration read, 'the child shall in all circumstances be *among the first* to receive protection and relief' (italics added) (Kuper 1997: 143; Last 1994: 195). And Principle 7 read, 'the best interests of the child shall be the guiding principle of those responsible for his education and guidance; that responsibility lies in the first place with his parents.' In the UN Convention on the Rights of the Child, completed in 1989, all talk of children as a principle of first call was dropped, the text reading that, 'the best interests of the child shall be a primary consideration' (Last 1994: 195).

Over time, concern for children in international treaties extended beyond the once dominant issue of food, and shifted from a fairly general declaration of intent to a legally binding accord based on the modern notions of 'rights'. During the same period, emphasis was increasingly put on children being treated within families and communities, as *one of*, but not *the*, primary consideration in relief efforts.

In 1990, however, UNICEF returned to the 'principle of first call'—employing it as a general and universal priority with application to all children, in all communities, in all situations, and at all times.[9] The question of central concern here is whether such a policy is appropriate for modern relief efforts in wars in the developing world.

4 The 'Children First' Principle Today

Despite its recent advocacy by UNICEF, there are serious concerns about the aptness and effectiveness of 'children first' policies in the distribution of relief during political emergencies. The most fundamental criticism is that such policies fail to provide sustainable support for children in the long term. We can immunize or feed a child for one day, one week, or one month, but sustained change necessitates supporting the families, communities, and networks in which children live so that they may overcome poverty and other adversities. If support for children is to have a lasting beneficial effect, it is essential that external interventions mesh with local values and practices, and the only way to achieve this is to engage fully with the situations in which children live and are provided for, rather than trying to isolate and aid children alone.

Last (1994) argues that the 'principle of first call' is an obstacle to understanding. He maintains that the principle oversimplifies complex issues in that there is seldom a ready consensus over *what* priority *which* adults should give to *which* children in *what* context. In present day Albania, for example, an aid coordinator intending to apply 'children first' principles would have to identify the children to be prioritized (native Albanians or Kosovan refugees; teenagers or infants; those who had suffered direct violence at the hands of the Serbs; or all children indiscriminately?), the adults to do the prioritizing (aid workers, native Albanians or Kosovan refugees?), and the specific geographic areas, and issues to be prioritized. All of these questions might be answered, but a 'children first' principle does little to provide answers.

An even greater concern is that a 'children first' approach to emergency situations can lead to the inappropriate design of interventions in several ways. First, the idea that children should be first might suggest simple top-down interventions: we imagine a group of people in the developing world waiting to be fed/immunized/educated and

[9] UNICEF argued in the *1990 State of the World's Children Report* that, 'Transcending its detailed provisions, the Convention on the Rights of the Child [1989] embodies a fundamental principle which UNICEF believes should affect the course of political, social, and economic progress in all nations over the next decade and beyond . . . children should have the first call on societies concerns and capacities . . . a commitment at all times and in all circumstances.'

picture the enlightened relief worker treating the children *first*. This denies the agency of children and their communities. Second, the approach suggests that all children are essentially the same, or at least similar in so far as the distribution of aid is concerned. But children differ in terms of abilities, experience, knowledge, and culture—all of which should be considered in the design of effective relief and development policies. Some children, for example, may by virtue of their status as workers, carers or even parents, have culturally recognized roles in providing for other members of their community. To mark such children out as the first recipients of aid is, possibly, to interfere with a community's own methods for dealing with hardship and emergency. Third, children do not have the same social value in different cultures. This is reflected, for example, in the infanticide of the disabled, selective neglect, or underfeeding of girls. These facts of social life complicate the principle of first call as applied to children, and necessitate an approach which recognizes the variation in values that different cultures award children. Grouping all children together as one class of aid recipients under the banner 'children first' may well obscure these important issues. Fourth, the UNICEF declaration distracts us from the fact, discussed earlier, that in many developing countries, children's security depends on families and communities, not the state. In such social groups, the roles of adults are critical to the well-being of the children as Last noted.

There are, usually, fewer adults than children. From the adults come the skills which they pass on to the young, but the adult's task is above all to maintain the well-being of the group, and to ensure it does not fall apart through conflict or lose touch with others. Loss of adults from the household therefore calls into question its viability in a way the loss of a child does not.   (Last 1994: 201)

This is not to argue that parents or other adults should invariably come before children. However, 'children first' policies may not be healthy if they discount the variation among children or neglect the communities children require if they are to flourish.

5   Children-First Policies: Past and Present

Child evacuation from war zones is perhaps the most dramatic example of 'children first' relief policies. Its long history, researched by Ressler (1992), forcefully demonstrates the defects of intervening on behalf of children independently of their communities. During the Spanish Civil War, more than 20,000 children were sent away by their parents on various evacuation schemes. The idea of evacuating children separately from their parents was promoted by parties outside the country who were seeking to help (a trend that continues through to the present day). Even with all the hardships of war, Spanish families did not readily accept the idea, as Ressler wrote:

Organizers were obliged to use a variety of publicity techniques to convince parents to send their children. An assurance that helped persuade parents was that Basque teachers and priests would accompany the children. Even so, few wealthy families reportedly sent their children on these evacuations. The promises of food and good care in the face of harsh family circumstance and great uncertainty influenced parents to send their children . . .[10]

After the children left Spain, their experiences were mixed. Though they arrived in host countries with siblings and friends, most were dispersed, breaking these relationships and destroying the last remaining bond the children had with their families. Moreover, the quality of care delivered to the children varied widely across countries and organizations.

The care provided in England was deemed to be generally unsatisfactory. Many of the children later reported that they had been dealt with in a dehumanizing way upon arrival, and that when they left the hastily prepared and poorly organized reception camps, they were sent to homes which lacked nurturing care. Throughout the world —in Belgium, Mexico, England, France, and the Soviet Union—children were often badly treated and faced public hostility. The costs related to the care of these children also became a contentious issue. As Ressler described:

In England, for example, the Home Office agreed to accept Basque children only if it could be arranged at no cost to the treasury; private funds were to be gathered for the children's education and care. From a private agency perspective, it was easy to raise money for the cause of evacuated children when the children first arrived but as months dragged into years fund raising became increasingly difficult. Many programmes had substantial financial limitations that reflected on the services provided to the children.

In most situations, institutions and private 'humanitarians', no matter how well motivated, were unable to provide for the well-being of children as well as their parents (even in difficult circumstances) would have. Where care was satisfactory, repatriation often became problematic. Children had become part of the families and communities to which they were evacuated and foster families were reluctant to send them back into uncertain situations. Political issues aggravated matters, as some host countries refused to recognize the new Spanish government, and, later, repatriation was made difficult by the Spanish government itself whose Civil Guard mistrusted evacuees. The length of the evacuations surprised everyone. To quote again from Ressler:

When the evacuations were planned and initiated, it was generally assumed that the children would be gone for no more than a few months. Children and their families expected the sojourn to be little more than a pleasant summer holiday. Experience proved quite the opposite. While some of the children returned to their parents during and immediately after the war, many were unable or unwilling to return and did not see their families again for many years, some as long as 20 years.

During World War II, many of the experiences of the Spanish Civil War were repeated—in evacuations from Yugoslavia, Poland, and Germany. The internal British evacuation of children is another much-studied example. Almost 750,000 unaccompanied children were evacuated from cities to the countryside, and one year later, 315,000 of those children were still living in their billeted situations. Several studies were conducted on the social and psychological impact of the British evacuations on the evacuees:

---

[10] See Ressler (1992) for a more in-depth history of the child evacuations summarized here.

Anna Freud and Dorothy Birmingham's careful analysis of the impact of separation of infants from their mothers is particularly important. In an essay on reactions to evacuation they wrote: 'The war acquires comparatively little significance for children so long as it only threatens their lives, disturbs their material comfort or cuts their food rations. It become enormously significant the moment it breaks up family life and uproots the first emotional attachments of the child within the family group. London children, therefore, were much less upset by bombing than by evacuation to the country as a protection against it.'[11]

The International Committee of the Red Cross, reflecting on its experience with evacuations during World War II, concluded in 1945 that except in medical emergencies, children would be better served and remain more secure if helped in their own country rather than sent overseas. It was observed that evacuees were often homesick and found it difficult to readapt to their home countries when repatriated.

Yet evacuations persisted. During the Greek Civil War between 23,000 and 28,000 children were separated from their parents and sent abroad. For a variety of reasons, only one-quarter of these children ever returned. During the Nigerian Civil War, beginning in 1967, the idea of using empty planes to evacuate starving children quickly became an international cause and roughly 4,500 children were evacuated to Gabon. There are other examples—the evacuation of Finnish children to Sweden, of Cuban children to the USA, the Vietnamese airlift of children to the USA, and attempts to evacuate Khmer children from Thailand. In all these cases the issues and problems encountered have been similar. Based, sometimes, on a genuine concern for the security of children, in other cases on personal, political, military, organizational, financial, and ideological motives, relief agencies (most often from outside the country under siege) have implemented such schemes, claiming them to be in the best interests of the children. There are many cases where evacuations clearly saved children's lives, such as when some children were taken out of Nazi Germany, but the strategy is problematic for children, and the effects of evacuation have frequently been more severe than the dangers from which the children were evacuated. Names and identities have been lost, and abuse suffered. Some children, inadequately supervised, have been taken away by what might have been well-intentioned but misdirected individuals, other children have been abducted and sold.[12]

'Children first' policies continue in the present day. Though there is arguably more sensitivity to child evacuations than in the past, other children first policies are still in evidence in many parts of the world. In Goma, Zaire, after over one million refugees from Rwanda crossed the border, outbreaks of cholera and other diseases began ravaging camps which were overcrowded, underfed, and unorganized. In the midst of this terrible human tragedy, during which CNN was broadcasting pictures of unaccompanied children crawling through piles of dead bodies, and hundreds of people were dying everyday, international agencies gave priority consideration to the needs of

---

[11] Ressler 1992: 10–11. Other studies, it should be noted, were less negative as to the effects of evacuation on children's well-being. However, all noted the lack of concentration that was an almost uniform characteristic of evacuated children, varying degrees of neurosis formation and enuresis (lack of bladder control), and that for children with conflictive relationships with parents, evacuation seemed to accentuate the conflict and resulted in the child acting it out.   [12] Ibid. 20.

children, and began supporting the establishment of unaccompanied children's centres and orphanages locally. Large numbers of 'orphanages' sprang up almost overnight, many established by local citizens who could not bear to watch children die. Others were established by desperately overwhelmed international personnel who, sometimes despite their better judgement, felt there was no better way to save children's lives. As the emergency began to stabilize, desperate parents placed their children (temporarily, they believed) in centres where they would be able to receive food, clothing, shelter, and education.

Providing for unaccompanied children helped aid agencies to raise funds. And, in a refugee situation that was greatly complicated by the presence in the camps of the Hutu military, supporting unaccompanied children seemed a neutral and stable way to provide aid. Unfortunately, there was, understandably, little oversight in the centres, and less scrupulous 'directors' are reported to have stolen children from the camps and placed them in their institutions, motivated by the fact that their funding was based on the number of children served.

A pernicious cycle developed. Money poured into those shelters that offered better services, which in turn attracted more parents (who often lived near the shelters) to place their children in care. Several months into the emergency, international relief agencies in Rwanda were reporting that there were nearly 120,000 unaccompanied children in Goma. Yet estimates of the probable number of unaccompanied children in the area, based on past experience of the number of unaccompanied children generally found in refugee populations, suggests there were at most 30,000 (Ressler, Boothby, and Steinbock 1988: 115).[13]

Some organizers of shelters cut back on their services to unaccompanied children in order to make a profit. Some children were 'adopted' or placed with families in the camps even though their own mothers or traditional caretakers were themselves residing in the camps, and expected to take the children back once they could provide for them. Some centres moved location, often by several miles, and, assuming the children in their care to be orphaned, accidentally separated from, or abandoned by their families, failed to inform the parents. When parents began a desperate search for their children, the tracing systems that had been set up by the relief organizations were doubly taxed. These problems were not confined to Goma, but were manifest throughout Rwanda and bordering countries where various 'children first' programmes has been initiated. Save the Children (1996) reported that:

In Rwanda in late 1994, an NGO assisting national family reunification efforts made a decision affecting a group of children at a care centre in a town far from the capital, Kigali. Without prior consultation, and knowing little about these children, the NGO moved them to the capital so as to 'speed up the process of reunification'. But the vast majority were not orphans; in fact, they knew the whereabouts of their parents and relatives. Most had been left at the centre by parents

---

[13] It is estimated that usually 3–5% of all children in refugee situations are 'unaccompanied' and living on their own, due to either involuntary separation (including abduction, becoming lost, orphaned, a runaway, or being removed form the parents as a result of the suspension of parental rights) or voluntary separation (due to abandonment, the child being entrusted to others, being surrendered by the parents, or the child living independently with parental consent).

attempting to secure better material advantages for their children than existed in their communities. It was the aid organization moving them to the capital that caused them to become unaccompanied.

A local NGO in Tanzania, with good intentions but little experience in refugee emergencies, opened a child care centre for orphan children from a camp for Rwandan refugees that attracted media attention and donor interest. It also attracted a large number of alleged orphans, many of whom in fact had parents or relatives in the camp. Quickly outgrowing its capacity to maintain an adequate level of care, the centre became unmanageable for those trying to run it, with negative effects on the children.

A year into the emergency, aid organizations were still dealing with tens of thousands of children living in collective shelters, and with a tremendous problem of reunification. With each passing month, the situation deteriorated as children became more settled in their institutional environments and their memories of parents and family faded. The tide was turned when international agencies led by Food for the Hungry International, with support from UNHCR, began to interview children who asked to be admitted to unaccompanied children's centres more thoroughly. Finding that the great majority of children were not unaccompanied, but sent by caretakers unable to provide for their children, Food for the Hungry began to provide services *directly to families and caretakers* who were in need. They concentrated especially on those families that had attempted to send their children to unaccompanied children's centres or had removed their children from such centres. Meal tickets, blankets, cooking tins, and shelters were provided, follow-up visits made, and educational programmes and services offered to the children.[14]

One of the continuing challenges facing aid organizations that work with children in emergencies is to find ways of redirecting relief away from institutions, to families and community-based initiatives.[15]

6 Conclusion

In an emotionally taxing field in which many practitioners work only briefly, institutional learning is often weak. Organizers of relief aid, confronting difficult and complex situations, frequently concentrate on assisting 'innocent' and 'vulnerable' children without addressing the underlying problems that might lead families and communities to feel they are unable to care for their children.

There are over thirty civil wars currently being fought in the developing world. Millions of children are affected by these conflicts. They are the victims, the perpetrators, the witnesses, and the story-tellers of this violence. They are active survivors as well as sufferers from conflict, and their needs and abilities are varied. For the great

[14] For an additional perspective on the international response to the problem of unaccompanied children in Rwanda see de la Soudière 1995.

[15] Petty *et al.* (1997) provide a valuable perspective on how thinking on this issue was shaped by the tragedy in Rwanda, the efforts made by some in the international community to improve practice after Rwanda, and some of the remaining obstacles to better aid responses for unaccompanied children.

majority of children in the developing world, their chief source of protection lies in their family and community relationships. Relief policies that seek to address children's needs must be designed with the abilities and strengths of children and their communities in mind.

7

Food Aid During Civil War: Conflicting Conclusions Derived From Alternative Approaches

FRANCES STEWART AND EMMA SAMMAN

1 Introduction

Food aid was initially intended as an instrument of development aid. But in recent years it has increasingly been used as part of emergency relief, with many of these emergencies originating from violent conflicts. The emergencies are the outcome of a coincidence of events—civil war, mass human flight and refugee concentrations, and failures of food supply or delivery. While in the 1970s and 1980s, there were only two emergencies per year evoking a concerted international response, by the mid-1990s the number exceeded fifteen in most years (Donini 1996: 11) and in 1998 there were eighteen (DHA 1998). Consequently, official aid devoted to emergency relief, including food aid, grew from US$845 million in 1989 to nearly US$5 billion in 1995 (DHA: 7), though it has fallen somewhat since.[1] The proportion of food aid going towards relief during emergencies also increased. From the late 1970s to the mid-1990s, it rose from 10 per cent to roughly 30 per cent of total food aid (World Food Programme 1996), while the proportion of World Food Programme (WFP) Emergency Operations owing to 'man-made disasters' rose from 35 per cent in 1975 to 90 per cent in 1996.

The role of food aid during civil war raises questions which were not considered in the earlier discussion about the impact of food aid (see, for example, Clay and Singer 1985) where the main topic at issue was the effect of food aid on agricultural incentives. None the less, much of the earlier discussions about food aid for development remain relevant, while some of the new issues associated with food aid during conflict shed light on the operation of old-style food aid. For convenience, we shall term conflict-related food aid, CONFAID, and development-related food aid, DEVFAID.

CONFAID needs to be considered from three perspectives: its 'humanitarian', 'economic', and 'political economy' role. The 'humanitarian' dimensions concern its success in avoiding or alleviating human suffering. Its 'economic' role refers to how it affects the economy at macro-, meso-, and microlevels. The 'political economy' role relates to how political forces influence its use. CONFAID invariably has effects at all

We are grateful for very helpful comments from Nick Stockton on a previous draft of this chapter.

[1] According to DHA (1998) data, from 1994 to 1998 the amount of donor funding for Complex Humanitarian Emergencies fell from US$1.9 to US$1.0 billion while the number of emergencies increased (internet).

three levels. Moreover, the three interact with each other, so that consequences at one level have implications for the others. Serious policy mistakes have been made because of a narrow-minded focus on the humanitarian impact of aid to the exclusion of its other effects, as well as failure to appreciate the complexity of the effects in each role. Appropriate policies can only be devised if there is an understanding of each dimension and of the interactions among them. In an undoubtedly sketchy way, this chapter aims to disentangle some of these relationships. Our assumption is that the humanitarian objective, that is, the reduction of deaths and the relief of suffering, is the major object-ive of CONFAID—indeed this, of course, is how it is presented to the public in developed countries. But it is essential to understand the other dimensions in order to appreciate how to achieve this.

The chapter approaches the issue first by a consideration of the role of CONFAID in three conflict situations—Sudan, Mozambique, and Afghanistan—exploring in each case the impact of CONFAID in humanitarian, political economy, and economic dimensions. It then draws some general lessons, drawing on the three examples, and finally discusses some policy implications stemming from the analysis.

2   The Sudan: 1983–

Sudan received a large amount of food aid during the 1980s and 1990s, adding to domestic cereal supplies by an average of one-fifth each year and to GDP by an annual average of 0.8 per cent. Despite this inflow and the fact that the country's agricultural potential is high, there has been recurrent and horrifying famine in 1984–5, 1988–9, and again in 1998, while food aid reached only a fraction of those in need.

Sudan is potentially capable of producing enough food to feed its population. By the end of the 1970s, it became self-sufficient in the production of basic foodstuffs as well as an exporter of sizeable quantities of sorghum, groundnuts, and cattle. With the onset of the debt crisis in the early 1980s, the government acted to reorient agricultural produc-tion towards cash crops. According to the logic of comparative advantage, exporting cash crops should have yielded a greater surplus with which to import food; however this logic was distorted by government priorities. While Sudan became more reliant on food imports with its self-sufficiency ratio falling from 91 per cent from 1979–81 to 86 per cent from 1988–90 (FAO*a*, internet), the government used much of the foreign exchange earnings to buy arms (Africa Watch 1990, cited in Macrae and Zwi 1994: 13).

Food shortages in the Sudan can be directly traced to the politics of war.[2] Drought notwithstanding,[3] the crises were principally a problem of distribution and government

[2] According to Per Pinstrup-Andersen, Director General of IFPRI (International Food Policy Research Institute), 'Nowhere else on earth is the link between armed violence and hunger as clear as it is right now in Sudan' (IFPRI News release, 3 June 1998).

[3] The increased prevalence of drought is partly attributable to an accelerating rate of desertification, as farmers deplete forests for fuel. The FAO estimates that Sudan lost 11 per cent of its forest between 1980 and 1990 (http://www.fao.org/NEWS/FACTFILE/FF9806-e.htm). This high rate, of course, is also attributable to the war to the extent that less oil is imported and therefore reliance on traditional sources increases.

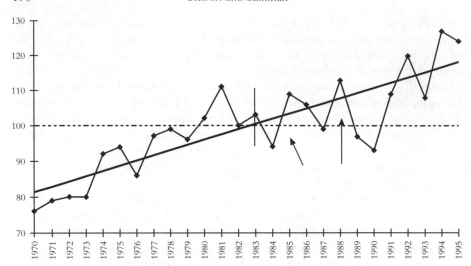

Figure 7.1   Sudan, agricultural production index (1989–91 = 100)

Note: The vertical bar denotes the beginning of the war; arrows denote periods of famine.

Source: World Bank (1997).

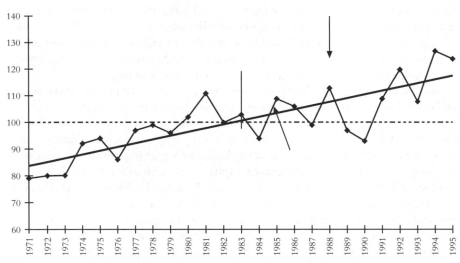

Figure 7.2   Sudan, per capita food production (1989–91 = 100)

Note and *Source*: As Figure 7.1.

intent rather than absolute shortage. Indeed, World Bank data show a steady though uneven rise in both agricultural production and per capita food production from 1978 onwards (see Figs. 7.1 and 7.2), while average per capita caloric consumption has declined only slightly since the late 1970s, from 2,220 in 1979–81 to 2,040 in 1988–90

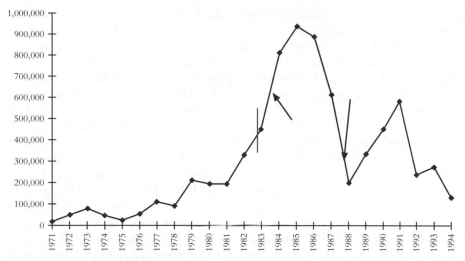

Figure 7.3 Sudan, food aid in cereals (tonnes)

Note and *Source*: As Figure 7.1.

to 2,202 in 1992[4] (FAO*a*, internet and UNDP 1997). Moreover, as shown in the charts, there is no clear correlation between falls in food production and periods of famine.

Both civil wars—1955–72, and 1983 onwards—arose as southern groups rebelled, to assert their economic, political and cultural rights which were being denied by the northern–dominated government, discussed in greater detail in Keen, Chapter 8, Vol. II. The government responded with a destructive military campaign; by enacting policies designed to deprive certain southern groups, notably the Dinka and Nuba, of their livelihood and ability to obtain food; and by exploiting and obstructing relief efforts. The southern insurgents initially coalesced into the Southern People's Liberation Army (SPLA). In 1991, however, the group split into two warring factions, intensifying the conflict. It has been suggested that fighting between these factions may have wrought as much destruction as the northern army (Shalita 1994: 147). Some observers believe that Sudan is on the verge of becoming 'another Afghanistan', in which war degenerates into a series of 'interminable localized conflicts' (CAFOD 1996, internet).

2.1 CONFAID and Humanitarian Effects

Food aid was minimal prior to the beginning of the war in 1983 (see Fig. 7.3). In the decade leading up to 1983, it totalled 1.4 million tonnes of cereals, while in the following decade, it amounted to 5.8 million tonnes, adding an average of 20 per cent to domestic production each year between 1983 and 1994; in 1986, at its peak, it added 57 per cent. Thirty per cent of the total received between 1983 and 1994 was in response to the 1984–5 famine, which occurred mainly in the north largely unrelated to war.

---

[4] According to the FAO and WHO, 2,200 calories are sufficient to meet basic nutritional needs.

Despite the sizeable inflows of CONFAID, severe food shortages occurred in the southern regions of Bahr-el-Ghazal and Equatoria from 1988 onwards. In 1988, an estimated 30,000 people died in camps; the mortality rate of 1 per cent per day in some camps was far higher than any levels recorded before or since for famines in Africa (de Waal 1997: 94). At the peak of the crisis, slightly over 7 per cent of the displaced population died every week in Meiram (Keen 1994*a*: 111). De Waal cites certain camps in northern Bahr-el-Ghazal in which all children died as the worst example of famine deaths in Africa (de Waal 1990, cited in Duffield *et al.* 1995: 106–7). As of mid-1998, the WFP estimated that nearly one-half of the population of southern Sudan faced food shortages, while 171,000 children and expectant mothers were severely malnourished (WFP 1998, internet). In twelve rebel camps, UNICEF found 51 per cent of children to be malnourished, 20 per cent severely so (USAID 1998, internet). Although data are extremely unreliable, the US Committee for Refugees (USCR) recently gave a 'conservative' estimate of the number of deaths resulting from war and war-related famine of 1.9 million, which 'far surpasses the death toll in any current civil war anywhere in the world'. They estimate that at least 70,000 people died in the first six months of 1998 alone (USCR 1998, internet).

The amount of relief actually received by starving communities was small. In 1992, it was estimated that food aid in Sudan reached less than 10 per cent of the potentially reachable population (UNICEF 1992, cited in Karim *et al.* 1996: 15); in 1996, it reached approximately 20 per cent of the population in rebel areas (p. 17).[5] These figures mask considerable regional variation.

One reason for the humanitarian failure of CONFAID was poorly designed procedures. As shown in Figure 7.3, much of the food aid arrived after the worst of the famine in 1984–5 and 1988–9. The most serious problem was the international perception of famine as a situation that followed a nutritional emergency. Accordingly, relief waited until an actual famine was signalled, by which time it was too late to avert starvation (Keen 1994*b*: 182–3). This led to a misreading of key indicators; migration, for example, was seen as an early symptom rather than as a sign of an ongoing famine in an advanced state.[6]

Reactions to the 1984–5 famine illustrate these procedural issues. For example, in northern Darfur and Kordofan, signs of drought were apparent by 1983, while food production was 25 per cent of normal (de Waal 1997: 91). By January 1984, the USAID office in Sudan had received reports of the spontaneous migration of villagers, yet it waited until March to alert its US counterparts of an incipient crisis, and until June to make its first request for emergency relief.[7] Similarly, in the south the migration of hungry villagers in search of food was interpreted as a sign of impending rather than actual crisis. Yet the fact that people were willing to leave their villages in such insecure

---

[5] Karim *et al.* notes that these two years represent low points for Operation Lifeline Sudan.

[6] Similarly, Duffield (1993) notes that for pastoralists, a better indicator of impending crisis is herd condition—in which food-related problems are first manifest—rather than the anthropometric measurement of children—a sign of advanced crisis (p. 146).

[7] At first, they believed that the migrants were nomadic or semi-sedentary people engaged in normal activities (Brown 1987, internet).

conditions indicated desperate circumstances (Keen 1994*b*: 183). Donors tend to wait for clear quantitative evidence of crisis rather than responding to less concrete, qualitative indicators (IDS 1995, internet), so that the belated response meant that relief mostly arrived after starving people had congregated in camps.

Efforts to secure aid in a timely manner were further inhibited by donors' slow and inflexible response. Frequently, long periods separated requests for aid, their approval and the actual arrival of the food. In the 1984–5 famine, this process took as long as 11 months. Often food was requested to cover pre-harvest periods prior to the rainy season; its late arrival meant not only that the worst of the crisis had already passed, but also that transport was impossible into all but easily accessible areas because of the poor state of the roads in the rainy season.

Quantities of food supplied were often too low. In-country missions tended to base their need assessments upon minimal projections of the at-risk population, upon the accessible rather than most in need, and upon what they expected to be approved rather than what was required. Consequently, requests drastically understated the true dimensions of the crises. Even so, donors often sent less aid than was requested; over the course of the 1984–5 operation, for instance, USAID in Washington approved just 65 per cent of the total requests for emergency assistance.

Internally, logistical problems hindered relief efforts. Prior to the first famine, there were no structures in place to disperse food rapidly in an emergency so donors had to institute mechanisms after receiving requests for food relief, including putting together an in-country team, making arrangements with the government, assessing infrastructural needs, and establishing contracts for the delivery of relief. Mistakes were made in targeting the relief. In 1984–5 USAID—who supplied 70 per cent of aid to Darfur and Kordofan—insisted that its food aid be 'monetized' with the result that some of the poorest villages received nothing (African Rights 1997: 58). Further, some regional governments used food aid to pressure certain villages to pay tax arrears; those who did not received no aid. In addition, road transport was contracted to a private trucking company without adequately specifying the areas to which food was to be delivered. Drivers delivered the food to the most easily accessible villages rather than those most in need.

Other policy errors arose from a poor understanding of Sudanese society. For instance, planners tried to target aid by importing Western definitions of concepts such as 'households', 'female-headed households' and 'widows' which had limited meaning in Sudan (Karim *et al.* 1996: 172). They did not appreciate normal seasonal variations in levels of nutrition, the role livestock played in society, the complexity (and insecurity) of certain land tenure arrangements, nor types and stages of various coping mechanisms. Evaluation and monitoring was weak or non-existent: 'No evaluations of the effectiveness of food aid programmes or their impact have been carried out nor has there been any systematic monitoring of inputs. Estimated needs are rarely reconciled with deliveries. Consequently little is known about what people actually receive' (Karim *et al.* 1996: 7, 124, 126, 172).

However, although such procedural issues certainly played a role in both famines, the political economy of the way food and hunger was manipulated—in particular through the actions of the Sudanese government with the complicity of the international community—is undoubtedly primarily responsible for the gross failures of CONFAID from a humanitarian perspective.

2.2   Political Economy of Food, War, and CONFAID

Famine in the south of Sudan had its origins in government strategy during the civil war. Government forces sought to destroy southern infrastructure, marketing networks and input delivery mechanisms and to displace the population from their lands (FAO 1998, internet). To bolster its political base, and further its policy of 'islamicization', the government divided potential opposition by forming and arming opposition groups, usually on the basis of ethnicity, encouraging them to raid villages thought sympathetic to the SPLA. A principal target was the Dinka people of the South, a relatively wealthy group whose economy was based upon livestock. A combination of raids on their cattle and scorched-earth tactics deprived them of their livelihood and the assets that normally protected them against famine. Selling of these assets, at low prices, became necessary to buy food at prices that were often manipulated by speculators.[8]

The government also engineered the food crises through non-military means: by disrupting the channels which had allowed for the movement of grain from the north to the south; exporting the strategic grain reserve in years of shortage[9]; and putting Islamic Banks, known for speculative hoarding, in charge of the grain reserve. For instance, the Faisal Islamic Bank (FIB) bought an estimated 30 per cent of the 1983–4 sorghum crop in Kordofan, which it stored and later sold at inflated prices (Gurdon 1986: 56). Such behaviour continued in later years.[10] When grain prices spiralled in 1990 and panic buying occurred, the government had no grain to release onto the market, as it had all been exported. That year, to safeguard incoming food for the benefit of the capital, the government banned its internal movement under penalty of death (de Waal 1997: 103),[11] imposed other administrative constraints on the movement of cereals and introduced heavy local and road taxes, amounting to 43 per cent of consumer prices in some areas (USAID 1996, internet). In May 1998, despite the prospect of wide-scale famine in the south, the government announced it would donate 5,000 tons of sorghum to Niger (Interpress Service 1998, internet).

[8]   For instance, Keen (1994*a*) recounts that in July and August of 1987, terms of trade for cattle buyers were 27 times more favourable in the famine town of Abyei in southern Kordofan than in the market town of El Obeid in northern Kordofan (p. 114).

[9]   Data on Sudanese exports are difficult to obtain, but according to a 1991 *Observer* article, EC customs forms reveal that Sudan exported 97,000 tonnes of sorghum for use as animal feed that year (Shalita 1994: 144). According to de Waal (1997), 500,000 tonnes of grain were sold to the EC and Saudi Arabia for use as animal feed in 1990, leaving 9,500 tonnes of mostly inedible grain as the strategic reserve (p. 100).

[10]   In the summer of 1995, Islamic Banks played a role shaping market conditions in certain areas in which the average price of a sack of sorghum rose 28-fold from S10 (US\$7.70) to S280 (US\$215); the price of a sheep fell from S150 to S3; and a camel, from S250–300 to about S50 (Gurdon 1986: 56).

[11]   De Waal (1997) notes that this is the first instance in which US pressure wrought a positive change in policy: the US told the Sudanese government it would not release 35,000 tonnes of grain from its warehouses unless it could distribute it as it saw fit. The government complied, removing the bar on internal movement (p. 103).

A key element of the government military campaign was the displacement of civilians and their relocation in camps. People deprived of land fled or were forcibly relocated to camps, only to endure further deprivation. In the case of Nuba villages, for instance, civilians were forcibly relocated; men were sent to labour camps for large commercial farms, while women and children were forced to become unpaid domestic servants. The ethnic 'cleansing' of Khartoum in the mid-1980s led to the forcible removal of 500,000 people to desert camps, where, according to a UN official, 'not even a locust can survive' (Shalita 1994: 146). To date, it is estimated that 4 million people, more than 80 per cent of southern Sudan's population, has been internally displaced at some time since 1983 (USCR 1998, internet).

Within the camps, restrictions on movement inhibited not only agriculture and trade but also coping mechanisms—such as foraging for wild berries and other so-called 'famine foods'[12] and migration—preventing the hungry from providing for themselves. Such prohibitions constituted 'a sentence of death by starvation' (African Rights 1997: 95). Once they had sold any physical assets and exhausted help from familial relations, the dispossessed became a cheap source of labour. Karim *et al.* (1996) suggest that the creation of a labour reserve of migrants to the north, working for subsistence wages or sharecropping, has been one of the governments' war aims which donor agencies have unwittingly supported through their allocation of relief.[13] Indeed, slavery re-emerged as southerners were taken as captives to the north, a practice which the government condemned officially but overlooked in practice.

For most of the war, bilateral donors and the UN have deferred to government dictates. In so doing, they permitted the worst famine in the African continent to proceed untrammelled, and shaped and prolonged the course of the war. According to de Waal (1997), relief efforts masked a total lack of engagement with the political processes that had caused famine, and consequently, with those which might lead to its resolution (p. 158). By confining themselves to a consideration of 'technical aspects' of food security, policy-makers divorced these aspects from underlying social and political causes (Karim *et al.* 1996: 126).

Government policy was designed to prevent any relief from reaching the south—a goal in which it was initially joined by the SPLA. When, owing to international pressure, this was no longer feasible, it sought to use aid to supply its soldiers and garrisons. Before 1989, donors acted in concert with the government to isolate the south. NGOs active in the south were the only critics of such policy, but their appeals were unheeded. According to Keen (1994*b*), 'until the end of 1988, the lobbying power of the Dinka within donor organisations was scarcely greater than their lobbying power within the Sudanese government' (pp. 173–4). Donors entirely ignored the causes of war and population displacement. By hingeing their strategy on food relief through camps,

[12] 'Famine foods' were those high in caloric value but difficult to obtain and normally undesirable; examples include grain infested by termites, peanut shells made into flour paste, seeds of a poisonous plant soaked to remove toxins and boiled; dried watermelon seeds and shells; dry grass, roots and tree bark, and palm seeds and leaves of the tebeldi tree (Brown *et al.* 1987, internet).

[13] They write, 'wage labour—once a seasonal activity in the subsistence rural economy—has become a survival strategy for people forcibly displaced . . . The Review believes the UN has worked uncritically within the policy framework established by the (government) towards the displaced' (p. 10).

donors encouraged further dislocation, and became complicit in the military strategy of displacement. They failed to link the provision of aid to progress on peace or humanitarian access.

Such policies allowed the government to stipulate the quantity and destination of relief, and how it would be delivered. Donor governments accepted government prohibitions on entering rebel areas. There was little criticism when the government expelled the UN special representative in 1986 and four NGOs in 1987–8[14] for activities in the south. Donors entrusted the government—and in certain instances, the military—with delivering aid. They ceded responsibility for monitoring relief to NGOs, but refused to support NGO appeals for diplomatic support to enter rebel territory or to acknowledge government abuses of aid shipments.[15] Soldiers plundered much of the aid. For instance, in May 1987, the government promised that food would be delivered to the south on trains, with an estimated 324 wagons of relief a month. In fact, only 32 wagons left between March 1986 and March 1988 (Keen 1994*a*: 113). The army was heavily involved in the grain trade, and had a powerful incentive to restrict supplies. It insisted upon accompanying relief convoys, ostensibly to provide protection; in reality, it was more likely either to transport military supplies or consumer goods to sell at a premium in areas of scarcity.

Apart from scattered NGO activity, no significant relief reached southern areas during the second famine until after the worst food shortages had passed. International media exposure in 1989 prompted major donors to reconsider their stance, and the United States and UN informed the Sudanese government that they would provide aid directly to the SPLA unless the government cooperated in relief efforts. Operation Lifeline Sudan (OLS) was founded as an umbrella group to coordinate the activities of humanitarian agencies in the country. The policy was to negotiate with both sides to allow relief into needy areas of the north and south.

For several months, OLS successfully provided relief to both government and rebel areas. A temporary ceasefire allowed unescorted relief convoys to travel along neutral relief corridors, accompanied by numerous monitors to reduce diversion. Relief provided greatly increased. In the first six months of 1989, 13,500 tonnes of aid were delivered to Bahr-el-Ghazal, compared to a total of roughly 7,300 tonnes altogether between 1986 and 1988 (Keen 1994*b*: 130), although the allocation of relief tended to favour government areas. After a few months, Sudan faded from the international media spotlight. The military government that came to power in June 1989 once again curtailed the provision of aid, simply by blocking relief flights.[16] The army bombed OLS planes and humanitarian targets, and on occasion attacked relief personnel. The SPLA also obstructed relief and attacked aid workers, but to a lesser degree.

---

[14] The NGOs expelled included World Vision, the primary conduit for US aid to the south.

[15] One consequence was that aid requests were never adjusted to include expected 'leakage'.

[16] On several occasions all flights to afflicted areas have been prohibited. In October 1995, the government banned the use of the C130 cargo planes, the principal aircraft used to deliver relief, to Bahr-el-Ghazal, there over 500,000 people faced starvation. In April 1996, it banned all scheduled OLS flights. In February 1998, all flights were again suspended, with exceptions to be made on a case by case basis; this was the largest suspension since OLS began in 1989. The blockade was lifted in April 1998.

After 1989, the army concentrated on diverting relief to its own benefit. Relief favoured government towns over rebel garrisons, and certain areas such as Equatoria over Bahr-el-Ghazal because fewer Dinka lived there. In 1995, Bahr-el-Ghazal received 19 per cent of its needs and Equatoria, 118 per cent[17] (Karim *et al.* 1996: 144). Within garrison towns, the government advocated the differential provisioning of relief according to ethnicity.[18] Aid allowed the government to sustain certain garrison towns, notably Juba, which would almost certainly have fallen otherwise. In the Nuba mountains, the government stipulated that UN aid should be delivered not to SPLA areas but instead to government 'peace camps', which served to facilitate and legitimate 'the near-genocidal campaign against the Nuba' (de Waal 1997: 148).

In 1998, a similar pattern emerged. Again, donors were largely indifferent to conditions in the south until the media began to broadcast news of widespread hunger. In February and March, the government blocked all relief flights to the south with the exception of three aircraft which could only meet about a quarter of relief needs (SCF 1998, internet). Only in April did the UN exert sufficient pressure on the government to lift this blockade, but the government still needed to approve all relief shipments. In July, the SPLA announced a three-month ceasefire in Bahr-el-Ghazal while the government agreed to a one-month truce to permit the delivery of relief (*The Economist* 18 July 1998: 65).

While over time, OLS has been able to secure a degree of operational autonomy in rebel areas in the south, the government retains close involvement in determining needs and overseeing distribution in war-affected areas in the north. In fact, 'an implicit understanding has emerged that OLS, as a neutral UN-coordinated operation, is confined to those non-government areas that the (Sudanese government) is willing to concede are temporarily beyond its control' (Karim *et al.* 1996: 2).

Politically, then, the government's manipulation of CONFAID contributed greatly to the fulfilment of its war aims by preventing food reaching its enemies and encouraging desired population movements, including the flow of southerners to the north and into camps.

2.3 Economic Effects

Sudan has been the recipient of huge amounts of aid, with financial flows considerably exceeding food aid. Total ODA amounted to 8 per cent of GDP between 1983 and 1991, and to 59 per cent of government revenue in 1982, the last year for which official data are available. In 1988–9 aid from Western donors provided roughly half of recurrent government expenditure (Keen 1994b: 175), almost as much as the value of export earnings and about one-quarter of the budget deficit. Food aid constituted about one-tenth of the total, at about 1 per cent of GDP annually on average between 1983

---

[17] That same year, Khartoum received 176 per cent of its needs and southern Kordofan, 812 per cent.

[18] In Wau, southern Sudan, Fertit people were encouraged to steal grain at the expense of Dinka communities. Food aid in Meiram was diverted to Baggara herdsmen for use as fodder despite the presence of severely undernourished Dinka (Keen 1991, cited in Macrae and Zwi 1994: 20).

and 1992 (ranging between 0.3 and 1.4 per cent). Food aid amounted to 20 per cent of domestic production between 1983 and 1994, with a peak of 57 per cent in 1986.

From a macro-perspective, food aid contributed substantially to foreign exchange and government revenue. It was particularly important from 1990 onwards when ODA fell sharply. It probably acted to moderate food price inflation, which fluctuated between 23 per cent in 1987 and 124 per cent in 1991. Inflation reached 47 per cent in the first famine and 63 per cent in the second, although there was considerable regional variation. The food aid may have released some foreign exchange from food imports for other types of import (economic as well as military), while the monetization of the aid contributed to government revenue. The additional external resources throughout the conflict may have helped prevent negative growth—GDP grew by just 0.6 per cent between 1980 and 1990, but much faster at an estimated 6.8 per cent between 1990 and 1995. In the war context of Sudan the disincentive effect of food aid on domestic production as a result of an adverse movement in the terms of trade was probably insignificant because of general food scarcity. However the massive movement of migrants into camps, encouraged by food aid, prevented people carrying out their normal economic activities, including notably farming.

Food aid supported government expenditure directly through revenue from sales, including expenditure on arms. However, despite a sharp increase in defence expenditure, the share of GDP going to education and health was broadly maintained at 0.2 per cent of GDP in 1986 and 0.3 per cent in 1992 for health, 4.3 per cent in 1982 and 4.8 per cent in 1992 for education. Indirectly, the large inflows of aid may have also contributed to this.

On aggregate, both social service availability and human indicators improved over the war period, partly due to the role of both financial and food aid. But inequalities worsened with the situation in the south deteriorating absolutely as well as relatively to the north. Disparities between the north and south had been large to begin with; for instance, in 1983 life expectancy was 36 years for the south compared to 48 for the country as a whole (House 1989: 203; UNICEF 1985). In 1984, there were 98 doctors per 100,000, but in Bahr-el-Ghazal and Upper Nile the ratios were 0.8 and 0.7 per 100,000. From 1983 to 1988, the number of hospitals in the south declined from 34 to 15 (Twose and Pogrund 1988: 37). While 500 new wells were dug in Kordofan between 1983 and 1987 in the north, in Bahr-el-Ghazal, about 300 were lost over the same period (p. 49). Very few schools remained in operation in the south by the mid-1990s; the majority had either been destroyed or turned into military barracks. National literacy rates were 43 per cent for men and 12 per cent for women in 1988, but 20 per cent and 10 per cent respectively in the south. A 1996 Oxfam study suggests literacy in some southern areas may have fallen to 15 per cent for men and 1 per cent for women (Peters 1996: 37). One observer commented in 1988, 'although north Sudan [is] not exactly [a model] of development, the cities and towns and villages in the South have deteriorated to the point where they are practically unsuitable for human habitation' (Twose and Pogrund 1988: 9). In 1988, per capita GDP in the south was estimated at US$150 compared to US$320 for the country as a whole. Thus while the massive inflow of food aid and associated support for government revenue did sustain public entitlements in the aggregate, for political reasons it failed to do so in the war-affected areas where it was needed the most.

2.4   Conclusion on the Effects of CONFAID in Sudan

Despite needs being apparent from 1983 onwards, major quantities of grain were only delivered after shortages had developed into famines. Moreover, those most in need failed to get access to the CONFAID. Logistical and procedural problems were only a small part of the story. Humanitarian solace was denied because the Sudanese government controlled the aid and used it to prosecute the war. The economic effects of the substantial food aid helped sustain the economy and contributed to government revenue, which financed large military expenditures as well as sustaining social expenditure. However, inequality in social service provision increased and southern Sudanese living standards fell. Thus, we can conclude that in Sudan, the political economy dimension of CONFAID defeated its economic and humanitarian aims.

3   Mozambique: 1975–92

In Mozambique, food aid was substantially greater relative to GDP than in Sudan, contributing an average of 4 per cent to GDP each year between 1976 and 1991, and an annual average of 67 per cent to domestic cereal production. Although it failed to avert famine in 1983–4, 1987, and 1992, CONFAID was important in mitigating shortages.

Conflict in Mozambique arose from circumstances directly following independence in 1975. It pitted Frelimo, a merger of pro-independence forces who formed the newly constituted government, against Renamo, founded by Portuguese special forces units who had fled to Southern Rhodesia. Several characteristics of the war conditioned its impact. It lasted 16 years, fuelled by heavy external involvement not only in providing financial and strategic support to both sides, but also in the actual fighting. Fighting was widespread geographically rather than confined to a particular ethnic group or region of the country. The state was unable to reach more than a military stalemate against its opponents.

The tactics employed by the conflicting groups meant that emergency relief operations had to contend not only with the initially precarious food production situation—at independence Mozambique was one of the poorest countries in the world—but also with the scale of population displaced by conflict (an estimated 6 million, or one-third of the population), and the huge amount of food needed—in certain years, 90 per cent of the country's cereal requirements. At independence over 80 per cent of the labour force worked in agriculture. But agricultural production was beset by the abandonment of plantations by settlers as well as Frelimo's plans for agricultural collectivization, control of all local trading, and forced recruitment of labour for its farms. Investment bypassed the peasant majority in favour of mechanizing costly and inefficient state farms. In addition, Mozambique suffered from adverse climatic conditions which culminated in the 1992 drought, the worst the country had faced in a century.

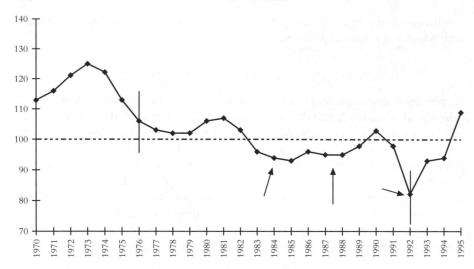

Figure 7.4 Mozambique, agricultural production index (1989–91 = 100)

Note: The vertical bars denote the beginning and end of the war; arrows denote periods of famine.

Source: As Figure 7.1.

The war had an extremely detrimental effect on food production with an estimated fall in agricultural production of over 40 per cent between 1973 and 1992, while per capita food production was about halved over the same period[19] (see Figs. 7.4 and 7.5). Between 1981 and 1983 food production fell by over one-fifth. The marketed production of maize and rice fell from 150,000–230,000 tonnes per year between 1970 and 1975 to just 40,000–75,000 tonnes per year from 1985 to 1988, during which time the population grew by 30 per cent. These statistics, however, neglect the parallel market and probably also underestimate a retreat into subsistence production. But other data also show a dramatic deterioration in agriculture. The proportion of land under cultivation fell from 10 per cent in 1983 to 4 per cent in 1989. In 1975 there were an estimated 1.4 million head of cattle in Mozambique, but by 1988, only 490,000 remained. By 1986, the harvest of some major crops stood at roughly 10 per cent of 1981 levels. The sharp falls in production are reflected in average per capita caloric consumption which fell from 1,978 in 1974–6 to 1,881 in 1979–81 to 1,680 in 1992 (FAO, various), levels well below estimated requirements.

During the war, food marketing systems virtually collapsed; food was almost unobtainable on the official market. By 1991, no more than 10 per cent of marketed food in Mozambique was domestically produced. When available, it was sold at inflated prices on the parallel market. The collapse of rural trading networks discouraged peasants from producing a food surplus as there was almost nothing for them to buy (Africa Watch 1992: 110).

---

[19] Corresponding figures in 1991 (before the drought) were 37 per cent for agricultural production and 96 per cent for per capita food production.

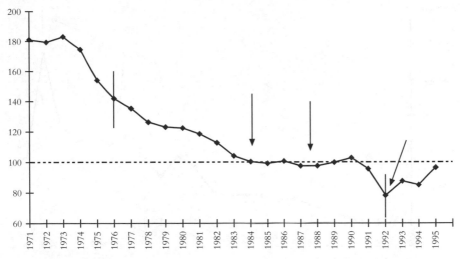

Figure 7.5 Mozambique, per capita food production (1989–91 = 100)
Note and *Source*: As Figure 7.4.

3.1 Humanitarian Effects

As the fighting was widespread, with the conflict waged for maximum territorial control, it encompassed virtually the whole of the population. The location of the most vulnerable, therefore, varied with shifts in the fighting. The worst affected were the displaced, especially those in camps, the hungry in Renamo areas who were unable to get to camps, and those cut off from any sort of market. An estimated 6 million people —out of a population of 15 million—were displaced from their farms over the course of the war. About 4.2 million people crowded into the protected Beira and Limpopo transport corridors, while 1.7 million went to refugee camps in Malawi, Zambia, Zimbabwe, and Tanzania.

Aid arrived late. Food aid was not forthcoming until 1984 and large amounts of aid began to arrive only after 1987, at the height of the conflict. The amounts of food aid delivered rose sharply in the years of worst famine mortality (see Fig. 7.6). Between 1980 and 1992, a total of US$7.6 billion of food aid was granted, including 5.2 million tonnes of cereals (nearly 65 per cent of the total domestic cereals production). In 1989, almost 20 per cent of the population relied solely on food aid. Logistical hurdles again impeded the timely delivery of aid. Until late 1991, bureaucratic obstacles at airports delayed some incoming aid. Poor infrastructure further impeded its disbursal. In the early 1990s, only 10 per cent of roads were judged to be in good working order. In 1993, the government admitted that food aid was rotting in the ports owing to a lack of transport facilities (Vincent 1994: 92). Of the government-owned fleet of 400 trucks intended to convey aid, less than two-thirds were judged operational in 1992. Because

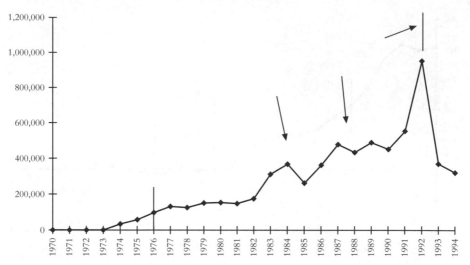

Figure 7.6   Mozambique, food aid in cereals (tonnes)

Note and *Source*: As Figure 7.4.

the fleet contained about six different types of vehicles, all given by different donors, it was difficult to maintain spare parts necessary to keep them in working order.

Widespread poverty and a near collapse of the trading system meant that most of the population lived in a state of 'chronic emergency'. In September 1991, it was reported that 60 per cent of the population lived in absolute poverty, spending more than 80 per cent of their income on food. In November 1991, USAID ranked Mozambique as the 'hungriest' of 91 nations around the world. In Mozambique the urban population which had risen from 13 per cent of the population in 1970 to 35 per cent by 1995, was vulnerable as well as the rural. With the collapse of state farms and marketing channels in the 1980s, urban food supplies were sharply reduced, rendering the whole popula-tion almost wholly reliant on international aid.

These precarious circumstances descended into acute food shortages in 1983–4, 1987, and 1992. In 1983 and in 1992, drought was a primary contributor, but the 1987 famine conditions were solely a product of war (Africa Watch 1992: 102). However, only in 1983–4 did the situation lead to mass deaths when an estimated 100,000 people starved to death (de Waal 1994: 26). For the rest of the time, shortages induced chronic hunger and rising malnutrition rather than mass starvation. For most of the period, observed rates of malnutrition among the population at large were not significantly higher than everywhere else in non-war affected Africa in either urban or rural areas (albeit based on deficient data). But worse conditions were found among the displaced and refugees. A survey of displaced people carried out in 1983 found a death rate of 96 per thousand per year, about five times the norm. In 1986, an estimated 50 per cent of children under 5 among Mozambican refugees in Malawi were chronically mal-nourished. A 1989 survey of camps in the Lugela district of Mozambique found that deaths among children under 4 during 1988 year were equivalent to 18 per cent of the under-4 population. Malnutrition in urban areas also rose: between 1982 and 1990, the number of children admitted to Maputo Central Hospital with acute malnutrition tripled (African Watch 1992: 110–12).

The fact that there were mass deaths from lack of food only in 1984 indicates that the humanitarian objectives of CONFAID were partially fulfilled. The main reason for this, in contrast to Sudan lay in the different political economy prevailing.

3.2 Political Economy Dimensions

As in the Sudan, the manipulation of food and hunger was a deliberate weapon of war. Both sides used landmines[20] and scorched-earth tactics. The strategy of Renamo in particular was predicated upon destroying the country's economic and social infrastructure,[21] including villages, markets and transport routes. This disrupted most market transactions and jeopardized subsistence production. In 1983, an estimated 25 per cent of normally marketed grain was lost to Renamo action in some provinces. Moreover, in the areas under Renamo control, there was an onerous form of taxation with civilians made responsible for providing a certain amount of food and/or labour to soldiers. Along with high levels of violence, including systematic sexual abuse, this policy contributed to widespread population flight to government areas. Government forces were also accused of violence but of a less systematic nature.

Frelimo actively sought to depopulate areas of Renamo support, engendering the 'massive depopulation' of central Mozambique. Its policy of forced removal ('recuperation') of rural people to government relief camps was facilitated by the supply of CONFAID. However only in one province, Zambezia, the 'breadbasket' of the country, is there evidence that in 1990 the government used the mass destruction of crops as a weapon against Renamo. Nevertheless, the herding of people away from their sources of livelihood and into camps (466 camps were established between 1986 and 1988 alone), rendered them dependent on external supplies and more vulnerable to illness leading to famine conditions (Vines 1992: 2).

De Waal (1994) suggests that the camps induced famine by denying people their own economic strategies, which were key to their survival. As in Sudan, coping strategies included restricting food consumption, labour migration, gathering wild food, accumulating debt, and as a last resort, selling such assets as livestock, jewellery, and grain reserves. Keen and Wilson (1994) note, 'the greatest mortality in Mozambique was in places where the pursuit of livelihoods was curtailed or impossible' (p. 214).

As in Sudan, the dispersal of aid was closely aligned with the government. When large amounts of aid began to arrive after 1987, control of most of the relief allowed the government to make great inroads into Renamo territory. However, Renamo also

[20] An estimated 10,000 to 15,000 people, mainly civilians, were killed by landmines. A 1995 British Medical Journal article stated that without mines, agricultural production could increase nearly 4 per cent (cited in War Child Landmine Project, internet).

[21] More than 70 per cent of all schools and 50 per cent of all clinics were destroyed, forcing teachers and medical personnel to flee the rural areas (Donini 1996a: 57). Between 1982 and 1986 alone, over 40 per cent of all health centres were destroyed (UNICEF 1996: 11).

attempted to align itself with relief so as to gain the support of the population; in 1991, after the ICRC had set up clinics in Renamo-dominated zones, Renamo established its own control centres close to them, which gave it protection against air raids, access to ICRC supplies, and allowed it to demonstrate to the peasantry symbolically that it could also attract international relief (Vines 1992: 16). Because relief efforts were primarily associated with the government, much of Renamo territory was inaccessible. An aid worker reported that 'need assessment appears to be based on "what can be delivered" rather than "who is in need of help"' (Gnocchi 1991: 6). Renamo blocked attempts to send aid, even though by June 1991 it was estimated that over twenty people a day were dying from starvation in its territory. It was not until July 1992, three months prior to the Peace Agreement, that Renamo and the government agreed to allow unarmed relief vehicles safe passage into their respective areas.[22]

Theft and diversion of aid led to cancellations of some shipments, and reduced the amount available for the most vulnerable. Soldiers on both sides were responsible for stealing food aid, mostly to feed themselves or sell, though incidents were reported of Renamo destroying food simply as a display of strength. Estimates of theft vary. In certain provinces, losses of up to one-half of initial supplies were recorded. The EU estimates that some 10 per cent of its relief was lost to Renamo attacks. Frelimo soldiers dispatched to protect convoys would also loot; in December 1991, for instance, out of an emergency train shipment of 1,000 tonnes of food, only 140 arrived intact. In 1992, an NGO mission reported losses of up to 80 per cent in the delivery of food from some provincial to district centres.

Since the aims of the government and of donors were broadly in concert over the question of humanitarian aid, Frelimo did not act to thwart relief efforts, although on occasion the army did. Although the government controlled the aid, the bulk of it was channelled through NGOs who became the chief providers of public welfare. The UN too ceded to donor pressure to use NGOs. Donors preferred to give money through NGOs due to policy disagreements with Frelimo, fear of corruption, and because they believed this would ensure relief reached its intended beneficiaries. NGOs, which numbered 7 in 1970 and had grown to 250 by 1994, actively fought to increase their 'share' of relief effort. According to Donini (1996a: 61), 'the extensive and deliberate use of external NGOs by donors as an alternative to government structures had greatly weakened such structures and, more generally, the indigenous capacity to cope with emergencies' (p. 61)[23] and the creation of parallel structures contributed to the weakening of the welfare-oriented parts of the state (de Waal 1994; Donini 1996a).

3.3 Economic Effects

By 1993, Mozambique was the most aid-dependent nation in the world (Vincent 1994: 89). Between 1980 and 1992, it received a total of US\$7.6 billion in overseas aid.

---

[22] This was the result of negotiations conducted by UNCERO, formed in 1987 to coordinate humanitarian aid and represented the group's only tangible accomplishment.

[23] For instance, NGOs were able to attract the most competent civil servants to their cause by offering higher and dependable salaries (Donini 1996a: 73).

Foreign aid accounted for an average of 40 per cent of GDP over the period climbing from 8 per cent in 1980 to 115 per cent of GDP in 1992. This covered 237 per cent of export earnings and most if not all government spending (it was three times government spending in 1988, the last year for which such data were available).[24]

A total of 5.7 million tonnes of cereals were shipped to Mozambique over the course of the war; relative to national production, the proportion veered between 13 per cent in 1976 and 401 per cent in 1992, and averaged 67 per cent per year. Food aid between 1976 and 1992 amounted to a total of US$810m. From 1981, food aid ranged from 1.2 per cent of GDP (1981) to 10.7 per cent (1992), averaging 3.7 per cent. Until September 1991, the government levied a tax of US$150 for every tonne of food arriving in its airports, through which it earned additional revenue and foreign exchange.

The macroeconomic effects of food aid clearly contributed substantially to GDP, government revenue and spending and foreign exchange. On the basis of the limited data, it seems that the food aid played a major role in containing prices. Food price data available for 1981 to 1986 shows an average inflation rate of 20 per cent per year. Data for consumer prices, available for 1988 to 1992, show an average annual increase of 40 per cent per year. Most food aid was intended to stabilize the food market by subsidized sale through parastatals. However much of this food—estimates range from 55 per cent to 75 per cent—was diverted to the parallel market where it was sold at twice its subsidized price.[25] The major beneficiaries were a class of merchants and government middlemen who used their gains—estimated at US$100 million—to import luxury goods and to invest overseas. None the less, the increase in supply would have played a role in moderating food prices.

Although food aid made a sizeable contribution to the economy, this was easily outweighed by the negative effects of the war, especially on agricultural production, and per capita income is estimated to have fallen sharply (see Chapter 1, Vol. II). This made it difficult to sustain government expenditure levels, even though it appears taxation rose as a share of GDP as did the budgetary deficit. The limited data suggest that the government began the post-independence period with progressive plans for human development, particularly in education and health, but these were increasingly set aside owing to military exigencies. In the first six years after independence primary school enrolment doubled; secondary school enrolment increased nearly sevenfold; the literacy rate increased 15 per cent; 90 per cent of children were immunized and the infant mortality rate fell 20 per cent (Waterhouse 1996: 10 and 51). But during the war years much social infrastructure was destroyed. Defence spending, meanwhile averaged 10 per cent of GDP. In 1985 and 1988, the two years for which spending data are available, defence consumed 42 per cent and 38 per cent of government spending respectively (IISS, various), among the highest rates in the world. About 70 per cent of this sum was used to finance defence imports (Vincent 1994: 91); this was a crucial loss of foreign exchange which could have been used to purchase inputs for productive activities. Social expenditure per capita is estimated to have fallen by about a fifth during the

[24] Most fiscal data are not available for the war years.
[25] The 1995 devaluation of the currency reduced the differential between the parallel and official exchange rates from 2,100 per cent in 1989 to 3.6 per cent (FAO 1997a, internet).

1980s; the ratio of doctors to population worsened, school enrolments worsened from 1980 to 1987, and infant mortality rates also rose in the early 1980s (World Bank, *World Development Reports*, various). It seems likely that one way or another much of the resources provided by the taxation of food aid were devoted to defence expenditure.

3.4   Conclusions on the Impact of CONFAID in Mozambique

The impact of CONFAID on Mozambique was mixed. At times it provided for an estimated 90 per cent of the country's cereal consumption and, thus, undoubtedly helped to prevent a large proportion of the population from starving. However, it also probably helped to prolong the war by feeding the estimated one-third of the population who became refugees. A principal impact was on the economy. At a macrolevel, it injected huge sums into a desperate economy; at a mesolevel, it allowed for very high defence spending and may have helped sustain social expenditures beyond what they otherwise would have been; and at a microlevel, the effects were mixed depending upon the dispersal mechanisms and projects. The main difference from Sudan was that it was disbursed under the supervision of a mainly well-intentioned government that wished to reach the whole population and emphasized spending on human development. Consequently, the political economy distortions observed in Sudan were low. However, the close association of relief efforts with the government prevented donors from providing full relief to Renamo areas, while the development of parallel structures to provide services appeared to weaken the state's ability to do so itself.

4   Afghanistan: 1979–

Food aid to Afghanistan was relatively insignificant quantitatively, accounting for an annual average of 0.6 per cent to GDP and adding just 3.6 per cent each year to domestic cereal production. But it had some impact at the microlevel. Moreover, food aid was important in encouraging a huge outflow of people from Afghanistan by sustaining those in refugee camps in Pakistan and Iran, with implications for the course of the war. The value of food aid received by Pakistan is estimated at US$850 million between 1980 and 1995 (more than Afghanistan received over roughly the same years). Conflict did not induce famine in Afghanistan; the majority of the population retreated into subsistence production or left the country. But malnutrition increased, particularly in the cities.

Conflict in Afghanistan arose from a combination of internal political changes and shifts in the international context. Within the country, a modernizing elite, many espousing radical change, arose to challenge the traditional Pashtun elite who dominated the government. The internal schism was made worse by the actions of outside powers. With the rise in oil prices in 1973, Afghanistan assumed a prominent role in Cold War politics mainly owing to its proximity to the Persian Gulf. The Soviets trained the army that launched a successful coup in 1978 under Najibullah. Directly after the coup, US and USSR aid to the country increased as much as fiftyfold (Rubin 1998: 14).

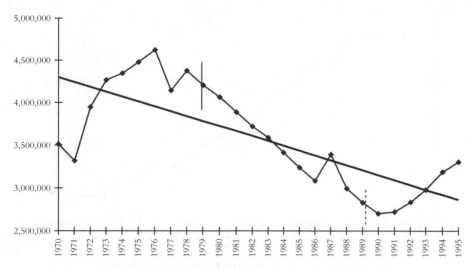

Figure 7.7   Afghanistan, cereal production (tonnes)

Note: The solid vertical bar denotes the beginning of the war; the dashed bar denotes
the end of the Soviet period.

Source: As Figure 7.1.

War began with the Soviet invasion of December 1979 to prop up the faltering
regime against rural Mujahedin insurgents. After prolonged guerrilla warfare against
the Soviet-backed regime, the Soviet army began to withdraw in 1988. The weak
Najibullah government remained in power another three years owing to internal divisions. When the regime fell in 1992, conflict fragmented as rival militias fought to take
over the state. Afghanistan had become the most armed country in the world, marked
by a proliferation of local warlords[26] and severe factional fighting. In September 1996,
the Moslem fundamentalist Taliban militia assumed control of Kabul and two-thirds of
the country. By the end of the 1990s, it was estimated that 90 per cent of the country
was free from war, though Kabul and the North continued to suffer sporadic fighting.

Afghanistan's pre-war economy was primarily agricultural. In the 1960s and 1970s,
the government introduced green revolution technology in wheat production and
promoted the development of small-scale farming by making inputs available heavily
subsidized or on credit. World Bank data shows a sharp rise in cereal production over
the course of the 1970s (see Fig. 7.7). By 1978, Afghanistan was self-sufficient in
food production with a limited network of local markets. Rubin (1997) estimates that
the average daily caloric intake of 2,025 was slightly higher than India and lower than
Pakistan, but contained more protein than both. The economy was predominantly one
of subsistence agriculture and pastoralism, together comprising 60 per cent of domestic

---

[26] Identity was primarily defined on the basis of kinship, clan, and tribe; national identities were still
nascent.

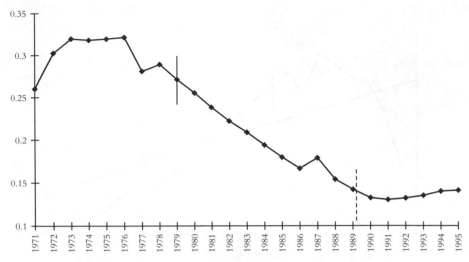

Figure 7.8   Afghanistan, per capita cereal production (tonnes)
Note and *Source*: As Figure 7.7.

production, employing about two-thirds of the labour force. The cash economy
was estimated to account for about half of GDP in 1972. According to impressionistic
evidence, this lack of market penetration was associated with a high degree of equality,
where a system of pre-capitalist social relations provided for the relatively deprived.

During the war, production fell substantially owing to population flight and military
destruction. Five million Afghans, between one-third and one-quarter of the population,[27] fled to Iran or Pakistan, and another estimated three million were displaced internally (Rubin 1997). Between 1978 and 1986, at least one-third of previously cultivated
land was abandoned (ibid). Interviews with refugee farmers indicate considerable
destruction of villages, irrigation facilities and livestock. For instance, in one study of
farm families, over half reported the bombing of their villages in 1985 alone (Swedish
Committee for Agriculture 1988). Roughly ten million landmines were buried. Marketing networks were disrupted in most places. The government put pressure on
farmers to grow cash crops to be sold to government factories, rather than subsistence
crops that would contribute to rural autonomy (Rubin 1997). Mujahedin commanders,
in turn, expected farmers to stop producing for the market and to store surplus in case
of shortage.

Between 1979 and 1995 per capita cereal production fell by half (see Fig. 7.8). In
1997 production was estimated at 63 per cent of 1979 levels. Most observers believe
that agricultural production fell throughout the 1980s, and picked up slightly in the
1990s (see SCA 1988; UNDP 1993; UNCTAD various editions), owing to reduced
military activity and the shift to the cities. This is reflected in changes in the average per

---

[27] There has never been a complete census of Afghanistan; the first attempt was made in 1979, but
interrupted by the war. As a result, all population data is estimated.

capita calorie supply. Estimated at 2,025 in 1978, it was measured at 1,770 in 1988–90, 1,523 in 1992, and 1,670 in 1996 (FAO, various)—well below adequacy. The country became largely dependent on imports, sold mainly in cities. In the 1980s, the bulk of imports came from the USSR. In the 1990s, around 30 per cent of the food supply was imported, mainly from Pakistan and Iran (FAO 1997*b*, internet).

Over the 1990s, a large share of the population saw their entitlements shrink. Massive unemployment, coupled with inflation, resulted in low incomes which severely limited access to food, especially in the urban areas (FAO 1997*b*). From the late 1980s, hyperinflation became a severe problem, as the government began to print money in 1987 to sustain arms imports after the Soviet withdrawal. Much anecdotal evidence suggests inflation continued to increase sharply, although no official data is available. According to a FAO survey (1997*b*), a clerk's salary, when paid, was US$15 per month, while bread and tea alone for a family of six cost US$37 per month.

Coping mechanisms particular to Afghanistan developed. In general, the population used a strategy of dispersal in which families would split with some members in Kabul, some working on the land and others outside the country (Marsden 1998: 14). When possible, villagers would commute from refugee camps or from mountain hideaways to plant crops on their land. A pre-capitalist form of social relations prevailed in many instances with the destitute relying upon charity or 'borrowing' from family or neighbours. A widespread coping measure, particularly in later years, was the cultivation of poppies to produce heroin. Poppy production increased twelvefold from the early 1980s, and quadrupled between 1989 and 1996. By 1996, Afghanistan was responsible for 40 per cent of the world's total production (Donini *et al.* 1996*b*: 2).

Malnutrition appears to have increased in the aggregate, and also to have shifted from the rural to the urban population. In the early 1980s, malnutrition affected 15 to 20 per cent of children under 5 with considerable regional variation (D'Souza 1984: 26), while a 1994 CARE study found growth stunting (a key indicator of chronic malnutrition) in nearly half the children under 5 and a 1997 UNICEF survey showed malnutrition (wasting) affecting 35 per cent of children under 5. A 1997 International Committee of the Red Cross (ICRC) survey of Kabul found that about 80 per cent of the population sampled suffered from some form of malnutrition (EIU 1997: 60). Most of the rural population were somewhat protected from the breakdown of markets by the fact that they could retreat into subsistence production. Before the war, the average farm produced three times subsistence needs; however, in food-deficit areas, such as the mountainous north-east, local production met only half of needs during the war and only one-third as of 1998 (Johnson 1997: 10). In such areas, the breakdown of markets could have severe repercussions. People living in the north-east, who were also principal targets of Soviet aggression, and those in the mountainous central areas, who relied primarily on rainfed agriculture, were the most prone to famine (D'Souza 1984).

4.1 Humanitarian Aspects of CONFAID

Although acute food shortages did occur—as well as the high prevalence of malnutrition —there has been no widespread famine to date. CONFAID played an important role in achieving this. Prior to 1992, migration to Iran and Pakistan acted as a safety valve to Mujahedin supporters, while Soviet aid in its areas of influence prevented the emergence of famine. Food was always available to supporters of both sides in either Kabul, Iran, or Pakistan. Before 1992, Soviet supporters were granted food in a system which was also a means of social control (Rubin 1997). People who worked for the government in some capacity were given ration books to use for food supplied by the USSR; by 1992, over 500,000 people used these coupons. Since each coupon-holder was estimated to support nine people, the majority of those in government areas would have had access to these subsidies. In the early 1980s, the Soviets supplied 100,000 tonnes of wheat per year at subsidized prices, equal to 7.5 per cent of the country's pre-war production. By the late 1980s, they were supplying 250,000 tonnes per year, more than the entire consumption needs of the capital.

In contrast to our other cases, the eight million refugees who fled Afghanistan do not appear to have been the most vulnerable segments of the population. Micro studies (SCA 1998; BAAG 1996*a*, *b*, 1997*a*, *b*) suggest that it was the better off who were able to leave, and the most destitute who remained, particularly in the cities. The most vulnerable strata of society included widows, orphans, the disabled, the elderly, and the unemployed as well as those in isolated rural areas—particularly women and children.[28] The fact that refugee camps in adjacent countries were run by sympathetic hosts, bolstered by huge amounts of western aid, ensured that refugees were well looked after. In camps in Pakistan, they were provided with rations of wheat, tea, and cooking oil. In Iran they were encouraged to find accommodation and work to provide for themselves, but provided with free health and education, and food subsidies on the same basis as Iranian citizens.

Between 1992 and 1998 the majority of refugees—nearly four million—returned and began to rebuild their communities. Through the UNHCR repatriation programme, returning families were given wheat, cash, and a tarpaulin.[29] Refugees returning from Iran said that this aid was sufficient to maintain their families while they planted their first crops (BAAG 1997*b*). In certain villages, NGOs took over the role of the state in assisting with inputs for agricultural development—namely flood-protection structures, irrigation systems, and water pumps—though their capacity was obviously far smaller. In some areas, production has returned to pre-war levels (see BAAG 1996*a* and 1997*b*).

An estimated 2.6 million refugees remained outside the country in camps in 1998, 1.4 million in Iran, and 1.2 million in Pakistan (UN 1998, internet). With political changes and continuing insecurity, new groups of people have become refugees. However, assistance provided diminished considerably. In Pakistan rations were phased out between 1992 and 1995. The Iranian government began to impose restrictions on migration and employment in view of an economic downturn. Nevertheless, very few

---

[28] Estimated to be around 1.75 million people in 1998.
[29] Refugees returning from Iran were given US$25 and 50 g. of wheat, while those coming from Pakistan received US$100 and 300 g.

people returned from Iran, and others continued to migrate in search of employment.[30] Approximately three million Afghans were displaced internally during the conflict. Free food was available in camps until l996, when it was replaced by activities to promote self-reliance. From 1992, the UNHCR played an active role in voluntary repatriation, offering returning refugees food rations and cash incentives. But many returning refugees moved to cities rather than returning to their villages, placing an additional burden on the urban food supply.

More than half the population fled Kabul when it became a war zone in 1992. Donors shifted their relief programmes towards the cities. In 1996, 80 per cent of Kabul's population was dependent on some form of external assistance (UN 1996, internet). The primary problem was a lack of purchasing power especially among widows, orphans, the disabled, and the unemployed. The bulk of aid was targeted at these vulnerable groups. A l995/6 UN survey identified over 100,000 in need of support.

Insecurity aside, the main logistical problem impeding the provision of aid was the mountainous and inhospitable terrain. Moreover, the condition of roads was extremely poor owing to war and neglect, and the country's one railway line reached only from Kabul to its suburbs. Observers reported extensive corruption, particularly with respect to food aid; one report suggests, 'less than half of the overall assistance is believed to have got through to the intended recipients' (Rubin 1997: 42), but this is difficult to substantiate.

4.2 Political Economy Effects

The strong political divide between the government and the Mujahedin was echoed in the activities of aid groups, apart from the UN and ICRC. The activities of most NGOs were constrained by which side they supported. Before 1988, Western NGOs, including groups which sought to provide relief to Mujahedin-controlled areas, were based in Pakistan and their actions were subject to the approval of the Pakistani authorities. The Pakistani officials often decided who the beneficiaries would be, in essence placing the NGO under the auspices of a party or military commander (Donini 1996a: 41). Moreover, Mujahedin parties based themselves in refugee camps where they exercised a high degree of control over the distribution of rations and influenced the activities of NGOs through representation in their staffing (Marsden 1998: 12).

Political distortions in the distribution of food arose from the interaction of local level commanders with donors. At the beginning, the separation between military assistance and humanitarian aid was not clear. Before 1992, NGOs had to rely upon Mujahedin parties to distribute relief within Afghanistan. In this way, much aid was disbursed

---

[30] In villages in the adjoining Farah province, up to 90 per cent of young men sought work in Iran due to food shortages in their villages. If discovered, they had to pay bribes to Iranian officials, or face imprisonment. As a result of high transaction costs, and low wages in Iran, remittances were not an important source of income for villages. Moreover, agricultural development proceeded at a slower pace due to the absence of a young labour force (in turn, eliminating the possibility of increased production that would allow them to stay).

through military commanders who were not held strictly accountable for its use. In addition, donor aid was often linked to covert military operations. At the provincial level local warlords used their power to command the attention of NGO groups. Parties carrying aid had to use bribes to distribute aid to certain areas (Marsden 1998: 13). From 1992 onwards, NGO access improved and their dependence on Mujahedin elements lessened. With the end of the Cold War, working 'on both sides' became the norm.

In the 1992 period, donors were so strong relative to the state that, by and large, they were able to enact their own agenda at the national level. In fact the first act of UNOCHA, the coordinating body for UN activity, was to persuade the government and resistance to allow UN staff free movement into all areas of the country in a 'humanitarian consensus'. However, local level commanders continued to use their power to garner the attention of donors. As conflict became increasingly fragmented, NGOs, including many indigenous ones, became relatively more important as they were better suited to undertake local-level activity.

When the Taliban came to power in 1996, national political effects became more pronounced. The Taliban have sought to use hunger as a weapon of war, prohibiting donor agencies from entering areas controlled by their enemies. Following fighting in 1997, the Taliban instituted a land and air blockade on delivery of humanitarian aid to central Afghanistan. In spite of reports of deaths from starvation, and WFP estimates that 10,000 tonnes of food would be needed to avert 160,000 deaths, the Taliban rarely permitted relief and stipulated the amounts that could be provided. For instance, in May 1998 the UN was only permitted to transport 1,000 tonnes of wheat into the region.[31] The Taliban maintained its uncompromising stand in spite of two severe earthquakes that hit the region in the first half of 1998.[32] The UN and NGOs frequently had to withdraw staff from certain regions due to insecurity including looting of their offices. In March 1998, for example, UN agencies suspended operations in south-west Afghanistan complaining that they had been subject to government interference and staff harassment. In July 1998, the Taliban ordered all relief agencies in Kabul to move to a derelict building, and closed the office of 35 NGOs that refused. The UN and ICRC remained.

4.3   Economic Effects

The effects of food aid on the macroeconomy are difficult to quantify, owing to a paucity of statistics and the fact that amounts of food received include substantial amounts of Soviet aid-in-kind—notably US$600 million in 1992—which was not methodically accounted for. However, according to the limited data available, it seems likely that official aid was an important source of revenue and food aid less so. GDP data from 1980 onwards are not always credible; the most reliable figures suggest an annual contraction during the 1980s of nearly 2 per cent a year and of 7.4 per cent between

---

[31] The WPF had to agree to a compromise in which 200 tonnes would be delivered to Taliban areas and the remaining 800 tonnes to areas previously blocked.

[32] The first of which left 15,000 people homeless, while the second is believed to have affected 100,000 people (*The Economist*, 6 June 1998: 23).

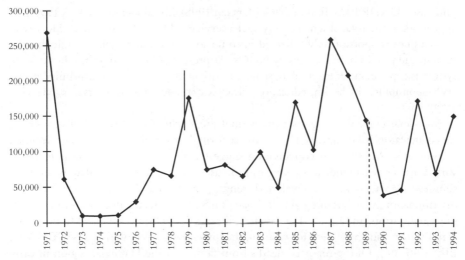

Figure 7.9   Afghanistan, food aid in cereals (tonnes)

Note and *Source*: As Figure 7.7.

1990 and 1994, with significant growth in 1995, when much of the country was stable. Further contraction accompanied resumed military activity.[33]

Foreign aid, especially in the 1980s, played a key role in allowing the Soviets to retain control of the cities and develop the necessary infrastructure to permit the sale and transport of natural gas to the USSR. By 1990, Afghanistan's public debt was estimated at US$5 billion, most of which was owed to the Soviets and was granted on highly concessionary terms. ODA, which does not include Soviet contributions, fluctuated between 0.2 and 19 per cent of GDP between 1980 and 1994, averaging 4.3 per cent per year.

Afghanistan received 283 million tonnes of cereals between 1979 and 1994 (see Fig. 7.9), which represented just 3.6 per cent of domestic production, much less than in either Sudan or Mozambique. As a percentage of GDP food aid was small, less than 1 per cent a year between 1979 and 1994. However, these estimates exclude the very large flows of food aid delivered to the third of the population living in refugee camps outside the country. Moreover, in the urban areas in Afghanistan, aid was proportionately more important. Indeed, during the Soviet era, most of the population received some food aid, directly or indirectly, while in 1997, half of the population of Kabul benefited from externally funded relief (UN 1998, internet).

At the mesolevel, defence spending was high, estimated by IISS at 9 per cent of GDP in 1985 and 7 per cent in 1989. This proportion probably increased after 1992 as indirect evidence suggests that the Taliban devoted virtually all its resources to arms

[33] The analysis relies upon GDP figures derived from the UNCTAD and UNSYB growth estimates. Both UNDP (1993) and IISS estimates for GDP are higher in the 1980s. But their estimates seem inconsistent with the scale of quantifiable damage.

purchases (UNDP 1993; Rubin 1997; Marsden 1998). Social spending fell. A 1998 UN appeal notes 'the total absence of any social services' (UN 1998, internet). However, this was not proportionately reflected in some social indicators, which indicated the widespread provision of services by NGOs. At present, 70 per cent of the health-care system is dependent on external assistance. In urban areas, NGOs have assumed primary responsibility for health, education, clean water, and sanitation services (Marsden 1998: 13).

Anecdotal evidence suggests that in rural areas where NGOs are active, certain social indicators have improved, while in other rural areas and cities, they have declined considerably. Marsden, in conversation suggested that the pattern appears to be so varied that aggregate indicators were of little use. Indeed, those compiled by different sources vary widely in both levels and trends.[34] Women and children face particular discrimination, which is integral to Taliban policy, and reflected in barriers to employment, education, and health. For instance, literacy in 1995 was reported to be 47 per cent for men and 15 per cent for women, the lowest rate in the world (UNICEF 1998; EIU 1997: 66). Of the reported deaths from famine in the Hazarajat region in early 1988, most were women and children. Food aid has not contributed towards maintaining public entitlements, nor to offsetting such discrimination.

At the microlevel, by and large, the effect of food aid has been positive; in some areas it has supplied the most disadvantaged groups, who often had no other means of access. Certainly, the manner in which food aid was provided conditioned its impact. One example is a WFP project which provided flour to selected bakeries in five urban areas in order to make bread available at subsidized prices to vulnerable urban groups, who were issued with coupons for its purchase (Donini *et al.* 1996*b*: 38). An estimated 800,000 Afghans benefited from this service in 1997. Over 30 per cent of the bakeries were home-based to ensure the availability of bread to widows, who numbered nearly 30,000 (UN 1998). While this was effective in targeting the neediest groups, it also served to drive local commercial bakeries out of business because they were unable to compete, thus undermining their productive capacity. Since in the cities, the main problem seems to be a lack of purchasing power rather than food, providing cash rather than food might offer a better solution.

4.4   Conclusions on CONFAID in Afghanistan

On the whole, CONFAID has effectively provided relief to refugees seeking security and the more recently impoverished, especially in cities. Political economy effects changed with changes in the political situation. Under Soviet influence, supporters and their opponents received aid from either the Soviet government or the West; from 1992 to 1996, the state was too weak to affect the provision of aid, rather the political power and intentions of local commanders determined its distribution; and more recently the Taliban has acted in a very obstructive manner. Food aid has had a negligible impact at

---

[34] For example, UNDP (1993) concludes that infant and child mortality rose sharply between 1980 and 1990 while UNICEF (various) finds that the opposite is true.

the macro- and mesolevels within Afghanistan as it was not large in total, but has had more pronounced effects in some areas at a microlevel. It is also likely to have affected the economies of Iran and Pakistan.

5 Some General Findings

5.1 Failed Humanitarian Effects

The declared intention of those providing CONFAID is to reduce suffering by reaching those in danger of starving as a result of food shortages. Yet, in actual cases this intention is often not achieved. Moreover, even when it does help prevent starvation in the short term, it can prolong suffering over many years by contributing to the financing of the war and diverting people from their normal economic activities.

The aid frequently arrives too late and, even after its arrival, many die in the camps, while there are often signal failures to deliver the aid to those in need when the government is made responsible for deliveries or is able to regulate donor access. Examples of such failures include the events described in Sudan; Tigray, Ethiopia, 1983–5; and Somalia in the early 1990s (see for example, de Waal 1989, 1994, and 1997; Keen 1994b; Hendrie 1994). In Sudan and Ethiopia, it is estimated that only 10 per cent of the food requirements of people living in camps were met (de Waal and Africa Watch, cited in Duffield 1993: 144). Food relief in Tigray in 1985–6 provided about 5 per cent of the diet of the hungry rural population, 20 per cent of the diet of townspeople and 100 per cent of the diet of militiamen (de Waal 1994: 136). In Somalia, only 12 per cent of food aid reached the civilian population for whom it was destined (Askin 1987, cited in Macrae and Zwi 1994: 19).

Moreover, in the medium term CONFAID tends to undermine domestic food production, not so much because of the negative effects on incentives, but more because it encourages people to move to camps where the food is provided—this was the case in each of the three cases discussed above. In Mozambique and Afghanistan, there was a massive and long-lived movement of people away from farming areas leading to prolonged agricultural stagnation. While there are usually other reasons for people to move—including the obvious search for security—delivery of food to camps provides a powerful additional reason and one which often outlasts the initial security motive. With people away from the fields, domestic food shortages are inevitably prolonged, perpetuating the crisis.

Once in camps, people's normal coping mechanisms are undermined, while disease frequently escalates leading to mass deaths. In his study of relief operations in Darfur and Kordofan, de Waal (1989) found no correlation between mortality rates and socio-economic status and noted that despite the ready availability of food, mortality was highest in 'famine camps'. De Waal concluded that 'the chief reason for famine deaths was a deteriorating public health environment rather than under-nutrition. Mass migration, unclean water and the rapid spread of communicable disease could alone account for the raised death rates' (African Rights 1997: 57). The appropriate policy response, he suggested, would be to focus upon providing health services and clean water with a focus on the population aged 1 to 5, the most susceptible to disease (de Waal 1989: p. ii). Evidence from southern Sudan reinforces this point: 'all available assessments report the major causes of morbidity to be malaria, diarrhoea, respiratory tract infections and measles' (Karim *et al.* 1996: 123).

Complex coping strategies by those affected also need to be taken into account. Such strategies include displacement, labour migration, foraging for wild foods, the sale of assets such as livestock, land, jewellery, grain reserves, and farm implements, and reliance on extended families and members of the community to lend or donate relief. These strategies are often undermined by CONFAID policy, most obviously when people are forced to move away from their own communities. But even when this is not the case, market interventions such as helping to sustain cattle prices, for example, may be more effective in maintaining food consumption than providing grain directly. Similarly, loans or grants to prevent asset stripping may encourage long-term food security (IDS 1995, internet). However it is also important that policy-makers distinguish coping strategies—which are temporary in nature and do not undermine long-term food security—from 'crisis' strategies which involve unsustainable asset depletion (Duffield *et al.* 1995: 112).

The failure of CONFAID is also due to a lack of understanding of its economic and political economy effects. Unless the workings of the economy at war are understood, short-term food aid may fail to prevent an ongoing deterioration in conditions, while political economy effects may prevent food aid from reaching those in need. Indeed, as we have seen, especially in the case of Sudan, unless countered, such effects may mean that CONFAID becomes a weapon in a continued war leading to a worsening humanitarian situation.

5.2   *The Economic Effects of CONFAID and the Impact on Entitlements*

Entitlement failure is the proximate cause of starvation, according to Sen's (1981) theory of famines. Entitlement failure occurs during war for a variety of reasons: because people's subsistence activities are directly attacked, they leave their farms for fear of violence and hence lose their direct entitlements; because employment and wages fall as a result of the various disruptions (including notably foreign exchange shortage) caused by the conflict; because of an escalation of food prices resulting from war-induced deficit financing, or because markets no longer work to deliver food as transport is disrupted; or because declines in food production cause food-price rises. Finally, legal entitlements may be destroyed by theft.

Effective aid should aim to address the cause of the entitlement failure, or at the very least, not make it worse. Yet it rarely does so directly. In so far as the problem is escalating food prices owing to a decline in food availability, food aid does make a direct contribution. But it fails to deal with the other problems—as noted above it generally induces a further and more permanent move away from farming areas, perpetuating the decline in direct entitlements and in domestic food supplies; it normally does nothing to create employment and makes no contribution to real wage decline, except possibly by moderating food-price inflation; it does not contribute to the resuscitation of markets and transport links. While food aid itself is a form of food entitlement which compensates recipients for their lost entitlements and permits them to survive, its failure to address the causes of the initial entitlement loss means that it perpetuates dependence. This was clearly illustrated in the case of Afghanistan where much of the food aid was delivered outside the country, and entirely failed to address the political and economic problems inside the country which led to the entitlement loss. Moreover, CONFAID's effectiveness as a short-term palliative is heavily dependent on how good the targeting is; for both administrative and, to a greater extent, political reasons, targeting may be very poor, as we saw in the case of Sudan.

While CONFAID is generally not designed to regenerate entitlements, where it is sizeable it does have macro- and mesoeconomic effects which can in fact contribute to this end. The economic effects of CONFAID have to be understood in the context of the workings of the war economy, which vary according to the nature of the conflict and its duration, as well as to the character of the economy subject to conflict, as discussed in Chapter 1.

If CONFAID contributes significant resources—say, around 1 per cent or more of GDP—the effects on the macroeconomy and on market and social entitlements may be sizeable. CONFAID can provide foreign exchange indirectly (by releasing foreign exchange that would otherwise be used for imports). Resources for government expenditure may arise from the sale (or taxation) of food aid, or, if not sold but distributed free, by allowing the government to run a larger deficit without generating massive inflation. Moreover, if used in 'food for work' programmes, CONFAID can sustain employment and contribute to infrastructural development. Potentially then, when large the macro effects of CONFAID may be significant and positive, sustaining imports and output levels, and government expenditure, and it may also help maintain social expenditures. But clearly these positive effects depend on how CONFAID is used. If the additional resources are used for military imports and other military expenditures, it will not help the productive sector nor sustain social entitlements.

In our examples, the macro effects were significant in Sudan and Mozambique. In both countries much of the additional resources went to military expenditure. However, indirectly the large flow of resources may have contributed to sustaining social expenditure. In both countries the food aid appeared to help moderate food price inflation, and thus, helped many people indirectly, beyond the direct recipients. In Afghanistan, the macro effects of CONFAID inside the country were not significant, although financial aid was large and did have macro implications. Massive CONFAID (and other aid) outside the country contributed significantly to the resources of Iran and Pakistan, and to their ability to host Afghan refugees.

CONFAID undoubtedly facilitated the massive movement of people into camps in all three countries. Once in camps, health frequently worsened dramatically most notably in Sudan in 1988. The result of this huge movement of people was to undermine the economy of each of the countries, as the productive activities of a large proportion of the work force effectively ceased—approximately one-fourth to one-third of the population was displaced in each of the three cases. Movement into camps had highly negative consequences from the perspective of outputs, entitlements, and health and well-being. To some extent such movement was a direct consequence of the war—enforced by the government of Sudan, encouraged by the government of Mozambique, and provoked by fighting in Afghanistan. But the movement was certainly greater and lasted longer because of the existence of substantial quantities of CONFAID.

5.3   Political Economy Effects

Politics are never more important than during conflict. Actors in conflict—including the government and outside agencies—have particular aims that often do not encompass either the 'national' interest, or the prevention of mass deaths. War aims vary with the conflict and the group and over time. Most groups want to defeat their enemies (their tactics may include inducing mass starvation), and to sustain their own livelihood (which may require taking food and other resources away from other groups for their own use). Success in taking food from enemy groups may be thought to contribute to their defeat.

Food is very often an important weapon of war in civil conflict, with the ability to secure it being essential to sustain a particular group and the loyalty of its 'supporters'. Conversely, preventing 'enemy' groups getting access to food will help secure their defeat or even elimination. Restricting enemy groups' access to food may include forcing farmers to leave their land, mining, destroying or stealing other sources of food entitlement, for example, as well as preventing food aid reaching the target population, as amply illustrated in the case of Sudan. Conflict reduces the relevance of legal entitlements, since systematic theft (that is, extra-legal entitlements) becomes a normal and accepted aspect of behaviour. Some groups become economic 'winners' during conflict. Their livelihoods are sustained—and indeed improved—by the war, since it creates economic opportunities, including from theft and black market activities, profiting from shortages (see Rangasami 1985, ch. 3; Duffield 1993; Keen 1994*b*). For the economy as a whole, the magnitude of economic loss due to war almost always exceeds the gains, as indicated by the finding of a negative change in GDP per capita in conflict-affected countries (see Chapter 4). However, particular groups may gain sufficiently so that they are motivated to prolong the conflict in order to sustain and enlarge their gains. CONFAID is a war-related resource which provides an additional economic motive—for both the government and particular groups who succeed in profiting from it—for prolonging conflict.

Since CONFAID is often channelled via the government, its overall effect largely depends on the strength and nature of the government. This determines whether the aims of humanitarian policy and those of the government coincide. In our examples, CONFAID was channelled through the government in both Sudan and Mozambique. In the first case, the effect was that it failed to reach those in need and helped sustain a repressive government; but in the second, the Mozambican government did try to reach as much of the population as possible, and many people survived as a result of aid. CONFAID generally appears to reinforce pre-existing governmental tendencies towards the distribution of resources rather than establish new ones (see de Waal 1994). The presence of CONFAID may 'buy' political support for the regime (as well as generating revenue), while the entrance of external actors—such as aid agencies—during times of crisis helps to shift blame for the famines from the government to the agencies themselves (African Rights 1997: 52). However, where the government is bypassed in the distribution of CONFAID, it may be weakened.

CONFAID is provided virtually entirely by official international donors. Hence the motivation and performance of donors as well as governments largely determine its effectiveness. The motivation of CONFAID donors inevitably contains political as well as humanitarian elements. The supply of food aid constitutes an important source of support for the government in the midst of a civil war, enabling it to prosecute the war, to use the food aid as a source of finance and to feed the troops, and to prevent it getting to opposition groups and strengthening them. This was the case in Sudan. Conversely, where the government is bypassed and CONFAID goes to camps in neighbouring countries and/or is distributed via NGOs to opposition areas, it also constitutes a political act, weakening the government and strengthening non-government and opposition elements—as in Afghanistan. Though the international community may regard CONFAID as essentially humanitarian, it is more realistically viewed as essentially political. In some areas, the political decision of donors about how to distribute the CONFAID may actually defeat its humanitarian objective—as occurred in Sudan.

Donors' motivation is, therefore, a critical element in determining the impact of CONFAID. For bilateral donors especially, a major determinant is donor perception of the geopolitical significance of the outcome of the civil war. Support for the Sudanese government was regarded by the USA as important in the context of both Middle Eastern and Cold War stability—hence the massive aid flowing via the government prior to OLS. Conversely, the West wanted to undermine the Soviet-backed regime in Afghanistan and therefore channelled CONFAID to camps in Pakistan and Iran, and via NGOs in Afghanistan, while the USSR supplied food aid to the Kabul government it backed. The Mozambique case is more surprising from this perspective, as the government received massive food aid (albeit mainly distributed through NGOs) despite its unpopularity with the USA who had been providing military support to the opposition forces. However, the Mozambique CONFAID was mostly supplied via the UN, which may explain this apparent contradiction. As the Mozambique government itself did not systematically deprive opposition areas of food aid, the humanitarian objective prevailed.

It is thus clear that the political economy aspects of conflict have serious implications for the analysis of CONFAID, often undermining the conclusions derived from economic analysis as well as humanitarian objectives. The reasons for this, are, in summary:

• The economic analysis presented above is focused on understanding the creation and distribution of legal entitlements. Extra-legal entitlements acquired by forcible theft and the removal of legal entitlements through the same process can help sustain some groups and undermine others, reducing the relevance of the analysis of legal entitlements. Economic analysis might suggest, for example, that one group has adequate entitlements and is not in need of support—for example, a cattle-owning group. But fighting groups can deliberately distort trading conditions and deprive the people of most of their assets, leaving them without means of support, as happened to the Dinka in Sudan.

• The war aims of different groups, including aid donors and governments, may be such that any CONFAID is deliberately diverted away from the humanitarian 'target'. CONFAID is not delivered, purportedly for logistical reasons. Donors deliver the aid late, and fail to monitor it, apparently for administrative reasons. But in reality these events are best explained by the political economy of the situation: governments do not want to meet the food needs of particular groups, while aid donors may not wish to undermine the government for political or economic reasons.

• The CONFAID may sustain war gains for some groups at a time when the country's food production is being deliberately undermined through war. It may also shape the course of the war allowing some groups to secure the allegiance of parts of the population by virtue of the food they can supply. Far from feeding those targeted for humanitarian aid, CONFAID may be directed away from those most in need, with adverse humanitarian consequences. Even where it does meet the short-term needs of vulnerable groups, it can reduce their medium-term ability to meet their own needs and prolong the war, so that the humanitarian balance remains uncertain.

6   Conclusions

The three country studies presented an overview of the effects of CONFAID: Afghanistan, Mozambique, and Sudan. These cases were chosen because they illustrate different facets bearing on the success of CONFAID at each of the levels. The Sudanese case illustrated how CONFAID may be used politically to sustain the government and prolong the war, while being deliberately withheld from those most in need. In the case of Mozambique, CONFAID seems to have prevented mass deaths and to have contributed to the maintenance of social and food entitlements. Nevertheless, it helped finance the war while its administration via NGOs served to weaken the government. In Afghanistan, CONFAID's main contribution was outside the country, leading to mass exodus and a consequent decline in production within the country. However, CONFAID in Iran and Pakistan protected the food entitlements of refugees and provided them with health and education services.

As with DEVFAID, it is essential to understand the workings of each economy, to ensure, even in principle, that CONFAID reaches those in need. Moreover, again like DEVFAID, additional food is not necessarily what those threatened with death actually need, or need most. The economy of a country at war is more complex and *sui generis* even than the typical poor developing country in normal times, as are the coping strategies of those affected. Consequently, in-depth study of the particular situation is essential. Time tends to be at a premium in these situations, but early monitoring, and study of previous situations, can give important clues to appropriate action.

The need to understand a particular situation becomes especially critical when political economy considerations are incorporated. To prevent the misuse of CONFAID, it may be necessary to avoid government channels and deliver CONFAID directly to rebel groups,[35] or circumstances permitting, to forge a genuine 'humanitarian consensus' with strong international backing to force the government to promote appropriate distribution. However, the record of such attempts (for example, via OLS) are not good, with only temporary compliance when the government is strongly opposed. Moreover, aid donors, and even the UN and NGOs, are part of the political economy story and one cannot assume that they would invariably support such a strategy.

From the perspective of its economic effects, whether extra food supplies from CONFAID will help protect entitlements depends on the particular constraints the economy is facing, as well as the nature of the war. If, for example, the main problem is a lack of foreign exchange, leading to output decline and consequently unemployment and entitlement failure, food aid should be used to release foreign exchange previously used for food imports for productive inputs. Or if the problem is accelerating inflation due to a rising budget deficit, food aid would best contribute if it were sold, thereby bolstering the government's budgetary position. The issue of incentives for food production arises with CONFAID, like DEVAID, but in this context the diversion of manpower to camps is generally more important in leading to a decline in output than the effect on the domestic terms of trade. Where entitlement failure is due to loss in employment as a result of economic contraction which cannot be reversed in the short run, CONFAID supporting employment (food for work) is appropriate—particularly if the work can be designed to help the reconstruction of infrastructure. For many of these ends, financial aid (and/or debt cancellation) would be more effective than food aid. Even where production has severely declined owing to war conditions, cash can be used to import food from neighbouring countries, normally ensuring a speedier response than the delivery of CONFAID.

For the most part, actual CONFAID makes little contribution to the macro requirements of recipient economies—and indeed such requirements are not considered when it is planned. It tends to undermine local food production, not so much because of the terms of trade effect but because it is usually delivered to camps, encouraging people to abandon their farms. The appropriate action to avoid adverse effects on farming varies with the context. Where people can stay in place as regards their physical safety, but lack food or money to buy it, food aid, or increased purchasing power (via work schemes or in some other way), needs to be delivered to the farming area. The choice between cash or food depends on whether the problem is a genuine lack of food in the area, or a deficiency of incomes. The situation is similar to that of DEVFAID except that during conflict, transport disruptions and general insecurity may mean that cash may fail to attract food supplies. But generally, local people are much better than aid agencies (or governments) at transporting goods across war zones, so cash reaching the needy in a war zone may be sufficient with any food aid sold centrally, thereby avoiding

---

[35] De Waal (1994) describes how the ICRS/SRCS successfully did so in Somalia, while official efforts were unsuccessful.

an inflationary impact. Where a conflict is raging (as in Uganda, for example, in the Luwero triangle in 1983–5), continued farming may be impossible and people have to move, but even then, the worst scenario is their movement into camps where they cannot farm or conduct most other survival activities so that dependence and reduced production become inevitable.

At the mesolevel, what is usually needed is additional government resources for the social sectors and other forms of human support. Assistance for the health sector would often be more effective from the perspective of saving lives than food aid. CONFAID may make a contribution if sold, with receipts going to the government, but this is unusual as the sale of the food appears to conflict with its humanitarian objectives. Moreover, the contribution of CONFAID depends on the government spending the proceeds of food sales on social and economic development, rather than the military, and distributing services equitably. As we have seen, during war the rise in military expenditure tends to absorb any resources released by CONFAID, but none the less it does permit higher government expenditure in total, so the additional resources may permit some increase in levels of social expenditure. But such expenditure still may not go to those in need, as in the case of Sudan.

The main policy conclusions from the economic analysis are:

- that it is essential first to identify the economic constraints which are causing entitlement failures;
- CONFAID should be designed to relax these constraints. In the majority of cases, it is likely that this would imply a radically different use of aid resources; and
- in many cases, financial aid may be more appropriate to achieve these ends than CONFAID.

Considering the complex issues raised by this multidimensional approach, it is not surprising that there are so few successful examples of mass delivery of CONFAID. Although failure to analyse the economic effects of CONFAID is an important reason why it fails to meet its humanitarian objectives, the political economy features discussed earlier often provide more powerful reasons.

To correct this dismal story, the first requirement is that the humanitarian objective be given explicit priority at an international level. It must be recognized that in the midst of war CONFAID will inevitably form part of a political equation. Neutral international monitors, whose mandate is humanitarian while taking cognizance of the economic aspects discussed above, should monitor the distribution of all CONFAID, identifying mechanisms by which CONFAID can be distributed to those most in need. Mechanisms would include distribution via the government where it has a record of directing resources to those in need in rebel as well as government-controlled areas; or via NGOs or directly to rebel authorities where the government fails to reach those in need. Careful, speedy and well-publicized monitoring, making use of independent NGOs on the ground, is essential.

In the absence of such a system, CONFAID may be counter-productive from a humanitarian perspective, bolstering regimes which are responsible for deprivation. Even with such a system in place, CONFAID may help prolong wars, and contribute to worsening medium-term food security. Its use should be restricted to clear food-supply emergencies. In general, financial aid is likely to be preferable, as it can more easily be moulded to fit needs and has fewer adverse side effects. But financial aid can also be readily abused, especially in the middle of a war.

8

The International Political Economy of Conflict in Poor Countries

VALPY FITZGERALD

1 Introduction

For the last quarter of the twentieth century, armed conflict continued to be an endemic condition in the poorer countries of the globe, despite the ending of geopolitical confrontation between the superpowers and the virtual completion of the decolonization process. These conflicts are widely regarded as both originating in and contributing to the condition of underdevelopment or 'economic regress'[1]; but to the extent that these societies are integrated into the world economy, global economic conditions must have some effect on the progress of these conflicts and on the human hardship they cause. None the less, scholarly research and policy analysis has tended to focus on the local causes and effects of war, taking the international context as given.

During the Cold War, the nuclear threat had the ironic consequence that war between major powers was prevented by the balance of terror of mass extinction. None the less, war was prosecuted by proxy in developing countries undergoing varied processes of popular struggle against colonial domination or autocratic rule. However, by the late 1970s it seemed reasonable to expect a decline in the frequency and intensity of armed conflict in developing countries. Firstly, the acquisition of constitutional independence by almost all developing states would eliminate 'national liberation' as a major cause of conflict in developing countries. Secondly, the effective end of the Cold War meant that the great powers would no longer need to support opposition movements in each others' sphere of influence (or to support repressive regimes in their own) for geostrategic reasons.

In the words of the Carnegie Commission on the Prevention of Deadly Conflict (1997):

After the unparalleled horrors of the first half of the twentieth century, and the unprecedented risks of annihilation during the Cold War, it was reasonable to assume (wishfully) that mass killing would go away by the close of the century. Policymakers of good will and human decency were confounded and often paralysed by the rush of murderous events in the 1990s. Deep perplexity led to hesitation.

The 'perplexity' appears to relate as much to the way in which the 'international community' should intervene in such cases, rather than the way in which the international

---

[1] See Sen (1994) for a discussion of the concept of economic regress.

system itself affects the conflict process. Again, the OECD development ministers and agency heads have reported:

Violent conflict in developing countries engages the basic values and interests of our societies. Together with others in the international community, our countries are committed to finding better ways to help such conflicts at their roots—before the toll of human and material destruction spirals and before an international response becomes vastly more difficult and costly. . . . Wars have set back development in many countries, including some of the poorest; excessive military expenditures have too often taken priority over more productive public investments and responses to complex emergencies have come to represent a major claim on development-cooperation budgets.   (DAC 1998: 5)

The intra-state and inter-state conflicts which spread in the 1980s and 1990s involved not only attempts by governments to repress particular groups from above, and by these groups to overthrow oppressive regimes from below by gaining control of the central government ('vertical' conflicts); but also attempts by particular groups defined by geographical areas or ethnic identities to break away to form new nation states and attempts by the central government to prevent this ('horizontal' conflicts). Both types of conflict inevitably become 'internationalized' because the warring parties resorted to friendly states for material resources and political support.[2] Such support might be forthcoming from major powers for traditional reasons of strategic interest, or because of social activism by pressure groups within them. The involvement of neighbouring states in such internal conflicts, and the frequency of conflicts between contiguous states over border disputes (involving supposed ethnic affinities and control over natural resources) have also become increasingly common.

Even though armed conflicts in developing countries have not generally been directly conducted by developed states since the early 1980s, they have been strongly influenced by these states because both sides require hard currency to support their military activities and supply the population on whom they rely for support. Thus the relationship with the world economy affects the intensity of the conflict and often its duration, through trade, finance, or aid with one or more of the contending parties.

In Section 2, the changing nature of the world economy itself, and in particular the independence of economic actors from nation states, is related to the provision of economic resources required to sustain conflict. The impact of trade, finance and aid on the process of conflict itself are discussed in more depth in Section 3. In Section 4 the consequences of the particular form of insertion into the global economy that conflict economies experience is related to the prolongation of war and the extent of human hardship on the one hand, and to the international political economy of intervention on the other. Finally, in Section 5, the policy consequences are derived for both international economic institutions and individual donor governments, suggesting that ability to wage war—and thus the human cost of conflict—might be reduced by changing the way in which the global economy is regulated.

---

[2] Conflicts *between* developed and developing nations (such as the UK–Argentina, US–Iraq, Israel–Palestine, or NATO–Yugoslavia conflicts) fall outside the remit of this volume.

2   Economic Globalization and Armed Conflict

2.1   Globalization and the Outbreak of Conflict

A number of changes in the global economy itself over the past quarter-century have a significant bearing on the way that conflicts can and do take place in developing countries, and in consequence for their economic and human costs.

The international financial agencies claim that there is a positive relationship between integration into the world economy and the reduction of conflict.[3] This is attributed to two developments expected to arise out of the process of structural adjustment by which a country becomes integrated into the world economy: an increase in economic growth which will generate more remunerative employment and permit greater expenditure on social services in the long run, on the one hand; and a process of privatization which reduces the discretionary powers of the state and strengthens civil society, on the other. Moreover, it is argued that this 'virtuous circle' should be reinforced by the refocusing of welfare programmes on the poor through the targeting of limited public expenditure. Conflict is thus seen as arising from 'state failure' associated with corruption, rent-seeking behaviour, neglect of small-scale agriculture, government control over the economy, and financial repression. In other words the problem is domestic and political in origin, although aid donors can use conditionality appropriately in order to make the state more efficient and democratic.

This contrasts sharply with the view of other UN agencies[4] to the effect that rapid integration into the world economy can actually reduce social cohesion and intensify conflict. The mechanisms identified are the creation of open unemployment as firms attempt to recover competitiveness by shedding labour, and governments reduce the civil service in order to service debt, on the one hand; and the reduction of social services coverage generally and especially of marginal social groups or rural regions as the state is scaled back, on the other. The process of privatization can actually worsen this situation as state managers become private entrepreneurs. Moreover, income distribution has tended to worsen as the result of globalization and there is a weakening of solidarity within communities and neighbourhoods (see for example, Cornia 1999; Hurrell and Woods 1999). In some circumstances, effective and legitimized government becomes almost impossible as the state becomes increasingly less relevant to the satisfaction of everyday needs. Duffield (1999: 1) goes further to argue that, '[R]ather than promoting stability, globalization has helped illiberal and quasi-feudal forms of political economy to expand.' What is clear is that poor and economically vulnerable countries appear to be prone to armed conflicts which aggravate poverty and make sustainable economic development difficult to attain. Because these countries form an integral part of the global economy, and are subject to dominant forces within that economy, the actions of major actors in the global economy must have considerable effects on the course of conflict. Limiting international concern to the issue of how

---

[3]   See in particular World Bank (1996) and the IMF (1997).
[4]   Such as the UNRISD (1995) and the UNCTAD (1996).

aid agencies can bring conflicts to an end begs the question as to the role of the global markets themselves.

FitzGerald (2000) explores a number of potential transmission mechanisms running from global economic developments to the *outbreak* of conflict, in order to test these hypotheses. Both positive (conflict-preventing) and negative (conflict-promoting) linkages can be found not only in the effects of the globalization process itself, such as trade liberalization, commodity price trends and capital mobility, but also in the process of international development cooperation designed to ameliorate the consequences, such as aid programmes, debt overhang and adjustment policies. However, it is not possible to identify a simple and direct connection between the economic globalization, increases in poverty, and armed confrontation—in part because most of the statistical indicators measuring economic vulnerability imply that conflict and non-conflict countries suffer from similar problems.

Three main economic factors appear to contribute to the outbreak of conflict, and by extension to its continuance. These are all potentially related to global economic changes. These factors are:

(1) The widening of disparities in income or wealth within a society, which can arise from both the impoverishment of some groups or the enrichment of others. The disparities can be vertical (between social classes) leading to what is sometimes termed 'class conflict' or horizontal (between territorial, ethnic, or religious groups) which frequently leads to 'regional conflict'. In both cases the creation of a collective sense of injustice and resentment on the part of prejudiced groups undermines the legitimacy of existing institutions, and makes violence appear as the only solution; but vertical tensions usually lead attempts to overthrow the government while horizontal tensions frequently lead to attempts at secession and the creation of an independent state.

(2) An increase in uncertainty as to the economic prospects of dominant or subordinate groups (or both), in terms of real incomes and asset ownership (including access to common resources), which generates collective insecurity. This sense of insecurity may be subjective, but is none the less perceived as real, and increases the tendency towards aggressive behaviour in wealth accumulation (that is *de facto* or *de jure* theft) and 'self defence' which challenges the legitimacy of the state monopoly over military force. Again, this can lead towards either a collapse of central authority or the constitution of separate territorial entities; but it can also lead to suppressed conflict under an increasingly authoritarian state.

(3) The weakening of the economic capacity of the state to provide public goods, which undermines the legitimacy of the existing administrative system. Lack of financial resources can mean that the government no longer provides all social and territorial groups with acceptable access to social services and economic infrastructure, nor mediates between 'winners' and 'losers' in the economic development process (particularly during major economic reforms) by appropriate resource transfers, nor even maintains law and order. In consequence, the 'social contract' between state and society no longer receives wide support, and allegiance is transferred to those actors (ranging from security companies to warlords) who can offer security and incomes, albeit only to limited social groups or geographical areas.

It should be stressed that it is the *interaction* between these three factors, in economies *which are already vulnerable*, which brings about armed conflict. A weak state in an economy without sudden changes in equity or security can survive for long periods without conflict—as was the case in Rwanda or Cambodia after independence; in contrast, a strong state perceived as broadly 'fair' by the majority of the population (and by the poor in particular) can survive considerable shocks and group insecurity as has been the case in Tanzania, or even attempts at secession such as in Sri Lanka; while in other cases legitimate states with low inequality can be effectively destabilized by external intervention which increases insecurity—as in the case of Mozambique or Nicaragua.

2.2   The Changing International Private Sector

The global process of trade liberalization and deregulation of capital flows itself involves the creation of trans-border markets which are independent of any one nation state, and are not subject to a system of international public or private law. Meanwhile, the global network of large transnational corporations is being consolidated.[5] These firms are generally careful to ensure that their behaviour in developing countries is strictly legal: this is often due more to the oversight exercised by regulatory authorities in the country where the firm is headquartered rather than the local judiciary, which can come under pressure not to offend foreign investors in peacetime and is often inoperative in wartime. In the last resort, pressure from consumers in developed countries on multinational firms' activities in developing countries have become an effective sanction— although this pressure has mainly been applied to environmental and labour concerns rather than to the activities of such firms in conflict situations.[6]

In contrast, multinational firms are less able to rely on decisive intervention by their 'home' country on their behalf in order to protect their assets in conflict situations. This is due in great part to the declining willingness of major powers to intervene militarily to protect 'their' investors—the counterpart being the increasing pressure to intervene for humanitarian reasons.[7] The fact that many large global corporations are of non-US origin while the UK and France have lost their geostrategic capacity also limits this form of protection. Some protection is offered by the Bretton Woods institutions, explicitly through formal insurance provisions against expropriation and war damage, and implicitly through the conditioning of financial support on pro-business policies in general and liberal foreign investment policies in particular. However, multinational corporations in poor countries have increasingly found it necessary to come to their own understanding with the local power structure.

---

[5] See UNCTAD (1999) for this process and its relationship to economic development in general.

[6] An interesting exception is the decision of a number of US multinationals not to withdraw from Nicaragua during the 1980s, despite pressure from Washington to do so and a trade embargo. The reason appears to have been in part the policy of the Sandinista government not to expropriate their assets, and the experience of the negative publicity after the activities of ITT under the Allende administration in Chile (Austin and Ickis 1986).

[7] Although the Gulf War can be interpreted as a conflict to protect a key oil source rather than to protect Kuwaiti sovereignty—let alone the defence of human rights or democracy.

These multinational corporations are often established investors in conflict economies. They are frequently key sources of fiscal income and foreign exchange for the state, especially when other sources of revenue and exports have been undermined by the process of conflict itself. Moreover, multinational firms' production and transport facilities require adequate physical security for their operations and reasonably predictable contract arrangements. In consequence, their relationship with the state and local society will inevitably be complex and potentially confrontational. On the one hand the state needs the revenue from these firms to survive, which gives firms considerable capacity to influence national economic policy or even the composition of government itself. On the other hand, opposition groups often establish direct relationships with multinational corporations already operating in a particular region, and the foreign firm itself may encourage the relationship in order to ensure local security and, perhaps, influence with a possible future government. Although additional investment is less likely under conflict than in peacetime, the multinational company may thus play a key role in how the conflict develops. However, it is essential to distinguish between multinational firms operating in the primary sector on the one hand, and those in the secondary and tertiary sectors on the other.

Investors in mining and energy, and to some extent in 'enclave' export agriculture such as bananas, are attracted to a country by specific natural resources, which are located in specific regions. They are generally responsible for infrastructure provision and labour training as well as management and technology. In consequence, so long as physical security can be assured and an attractive royalties deal can be struck, profitable production can be achieved. Further, the competition among multinational companies for access to natural resources makes the taking of substantial financial risks inevitable in such projects. In consequence, the acquisition of natural resource concessions, considerable exploration expenditure and even the construction of transport facilities may become profitable for such firms, as well as the maintenance of existing production facilities and their potential expansion. Indeed, operating in conflict situations could be said to be an integral part of corporate culture of natural resource firms.[8] In view of the location of existing facilities or potential investments in remote areas where the armed opposition operates or may even rule, negotiation with non-governmental forces can become inevitable—and even attractive.

In contrast, multinational firms in industry and services face a different situation. They are dependent on stable and growing domestic markets in the case of most manufacturing and all banking in poor economies, on a skilled labour supply and good transport facilities in the case of manufactured exports, and above all on civil order and the absence of violence in the case of tourism. Thus existing activities of firms in these sectors are likely to be constrained in times of conflict—although there may be exceptions, such as hotels catering to journalists or import-substituting manufacturing. The importance of such firms as a revenue base for the government derives not so much from the profits generated as from their role in activities subject to excise duties, such as air transport, fuel distribution, tobacco and beverages, or luxury tourism. New

---

[8] And inspiring at least one outstanding contribution to literary culture—Conrad's *Nostromo*.

investment is extremely unlikely in war conditions, although the maintenance of operations can be seen as an 'option' on future investments and the prevention of market access to competitors.

On a smaller but increasingly important scale, foreign entrepreneurs (often from neighbouring countries) are attracted to conflict economies due to the opportunities for the predatory exploitation of 'projects' such as gems mining or logging which do not require large infrastructural investment. These investors generally operate outside the law—indeed may set up private 'armies' of their own—and their disintegrative effect on both state and civil society is probably much greater than that of large multinational firms which have longer-term objectives and an international reputation to protect. While the individual *power* of these predatory foreign investors is less, their *opportunities* are greater as they do not bear any of the external costs arising from their activities —in other words, they are not subject to any home government sanction nor to consumer pressure. These may be combined with the management of cross-border operations by both non-resident and resident nationals who enjoy considerable capital mobility; such efforts tend to be concentrated on low-risk activities such as 'rest and recreation' facilities and the distribution of imported products. These entrepreneurial groups can exercise considerable influence on both the government and opposition groups through their knowledge of and access to international trading and financial networks.

The effects of such activities is that there is a real sense in which there has come into being an 'international informal sector' that is not subject to any set of rules other than short-term profit. This international informal economy has emerged as the result of new global networks (such as the narcotics trade or the Chinese diaspora) and offshore centres established for tax and legal evasion purposes. These networks and centres create new opportunities for financing conflict because they can supply arms or foreign exchange to get them; and they can market smuggled goods, particularly those with a high unit value such as narcotics, timber, and gems.

2.3 The New International Public Sector

Poor economies, despite their increased integration into world economy, remain highly dependent upon 'aid' in the sense of non-market resource flows from abroad. These account for over one-half of both the total import bill and of government budgetary resources in the least developed countries (UNCTAD 1998). The way in which this aid is organized has also changed considerably with the end of the Cold War. No longer subjected to clear geostrategic priorities, aid has become increasingly dispersed between agencies for two reasons: first, because of the decline in the relative importance of the great powers (particularly the USA and the USSR) as a source of aid; and second, because of the proliferation of non-governmental organizations as channels for aid.

The decline of military assistance within aid programmes with the end of the Cold War has meant that in general the conflicts in the developing world are no longer mainly *directly* financed by the governments of industrial countries. However, the subsidization of arms exports by industrial countries sales, which mainly benefits established middle-income developing states, strengthens their capacity for internal repression or for threatening weaker neighbours. The arguments given for continuing this practice are various: that only defensive weapons are sold (overlooking the fact that most can be used for more than one purpose); that the subsidies are essential in order to maintain defence jobs and technological capacity (although this could equally be applied to, say, automotive exports); and that other 'less scrupulous' suppliers would fill the gap (ignoring the potential for international cooperation). It is also true that the stock of infantry equipment and ammunition—the main *military* requirement for conflict in developing countries[9]—already 'on the market' is very large, and that a considerable number of developing countries (ranging from Brazil to China) are major arms exporters. None the less, the official support by OECD countries of arms industries and military exports is undoubtedly a contributory factor to conflicts in poor countries.[10] Many of the sales of small arms go to countries already in conflict—for example, it is estimated that 20 per cent of UK export licences for small arms, light weapons, and ammunition go to countries in conflict, including Sri Lanka, Zimbabwe, and Colombia (the *Guardian*, 4 Nov. 1999).

The role of the international financial institutions (principally the International Monetary Fund and the World Bank, supported by the relevant regional development bank) in conflict economies is an ambiguous one. The general approach of these IFIs to war economies appears to be that normal development lending is suspended while hostilities continue, and that their main task is in post-war reconstruction. However, a number of pressures lead to intervention in some cases. First, the combination of rising debt burdens, default on repayment schedules, exhaustion of reserves, and need for urgent balance of payments support makes a comprehensive approach to the debt necessary. Interestingly, the main creditors in this exercise are often the IFIs themselves, because commercial debtors write off their losses in such countries (or transfer them to their home governments) and bilateral donors are willing to tolerate delays or to roll over debt much more easily. Second, aid agencies concerned by mounting inflation, collapse of public administration, black markets, and rising levels of poverty —which tend to undermine their own projects and programmes—turn to the IFIs in order to 'straighten out the economic situation'. Third, the government itself— possibly out of desperation at its own inability to resolve the situation—may call in the IFIs in order to determine the economic reforms required to renew access to foreign funds.

Aid donors—whose declared interest is that of alleviating the lot of the poor and promoting a rapid reconciliation of the warring parties—have generally ceded their considerable power of policy conditionality to the international financial institutions in relation to macroeconomic stabilization. The constitutional missions of the Fund and the Bank are to establish currency convertibility, debt repayment, and fiscal solvency on

---

[9] Indeed, 'neither non-state warfare nor warfare between poor states would trouble the world's conscience or threaten its security were it not for the ready availability of cheap weapons' (Keegan 1998: 68).

[10] This issue is not addressed in OECD documents on conflict and development; although the case for banning the production, trade, and use of landmines is recognized (DAC 1998: 96).

the one hand, and promote integration into the world market, and foreign private investment on the other. External debt can be renegotiated under a policy conditionality constructed from the Fund and Bank programmes, and some degree of debt cancellation may even be granted by bilateral donors. What is unclear is how the policy conditionality would protect the most vulnerable victims of war, provide incentives for the ending of hostilities or restore the country's capacity to repay debt while the war continues or reconstruction is undertaken. The application of standard monetary stabilization or structural adjustment policies are likely to have negative consequences.[11]

Development aid and humanitarian assistance—particularly the latter—is being increasingly channelled through non-governmental organizations (NGOs) for a number of reasons, including the desire to reduce state activities and increased activism in the civil societies of industrial nations (Edwards 1999), as well as the running down of traditional diplomatic representation in countries without a large market potential. In conflict situations where the capacity of the domestic government to provide social services in particular regions (or indeed outside the main cities) is often undermined NGOs may become the only effective form of public provisioning to the poor. When significant populations are forced to migrate, either within the country or across borders, NGOs and other humanitarian organizations such as the UN become the main suppliers of refugee camps. They thus become an integral part of the conflict (de Waal 1997).

3   The Impact of the Global Economy on the Process of Conflict

3.1   Foreign Trade

Foreign trade is pivotal to poor economies, particularly to the sustainability of the state itself and the viability of urban areas. The process of conflict itself has direct consequences for both traditional exports and imports.[12] On the export side, output is likely to fall under conflict conditions—depending upon the location of natural resource projects relative to war zones and the strategy of the warring parties—as is the quality of the product, so the export revenues fall as both volumes and unit values decline. In consequence, traditional export markets may be lost even without any application of trade sanctions by other countries. As Table 8.1 indicates, the real purchasing power of conflict economies appears to have declined during the 1980s, although there seems to have been some recovery subsequently. Chapter 4 above indicates a similar pattern.

The combination of declining traditional export revenues and the breakdown of established systems of civilian control over trade channels (including frontier controls and trans-border transport) on the one hand, and increasing shortages of foreign exchange (and thus its black market value) on the other inevitably lead to a rise in export smuggling. When the products involved are locally produced small-farmer export crops

---

[11] See the discussion in Chapter 2.   [12] See Chapter 2 for an extensive discussion.

Table 8.1   Trends in the purchasing power of vulnerable economies' exports

	Annual change in income terms of trade (%)	
	1980–90	1990–3
All LLDCs	0.1	4.8
Conflict LLDCs	−1.3	1.5
Non-conflict LLDCs	8.9	0.7
All developing countries	1.8	8.0

Source: Appendix.

(such as maize or coffee) in trans-border trade, the change represents little more than a geographical reorganization of trade, and forms part of the coping strategies of the rural populations involved. However, export smuggling also has a darker side when the export of rare timber, precious stones, or narcotic drugs is involved. These 'new' products involve the criminalization of trade, new relationships with international distribution networks, and usually the involvement of military forces on both sides of the border which is required in order to secure the trade channels.

In other words, conflict conditions both promote, and are promoted by, the shift from formal to informal channels of trade. On the one hand, the reduction in the flow of and quality of traditional export products reduces participation in formal channels of international commodity trade. On the other hand, the attractions of informal and illegal trade channels are increased, as is the ability of organized crime to form alliances with the warring parties. The generation of foreign exchange in this way is one of the key determinants of both sides to continue operations.

On the import side, access to formal markets remains possible unless trade sanctions are applied, but the lack of bank credit makes suppliers who can offer trade credit—albeit at higher prices—more attractive. To these economic factors must be added changes in military economies. War is increasingly becoming an activity of poor rather than rich states, and waged with limited resources. Expensive weapons such as submarines are of little practical use in the developing world; while the mass-produced assault rifles are cheap, robust, and deadly even in the hands of children.[13] Further, armies in the field in developing countries need few supplies beyond diesel fuel, light vehicles, rudimentary telecommunications, and basic foodstuffs—they can thus 'live off the land' (including humanitarian aid stocks) for considerable periods and supply themselves indefinitely through normal commercial import channels if they have access to foreign exchange.

---

[13] Although the concept of 'childhood' itself may differ between Western aid agencies and local society —see Chapter 6 in this volume.

Table 8.2   Import volumes of vulnerable economies

	Conflict LLDCs	Non-conflict LLDCs	All LLDCs	All developing countries
Imports/GDP (1994) %	25.0	45.3	34.9	16.0
Import volume growth				
1980–90	0.3	3.0	1.6	0.3
1990–4	9.6	2.2	6.0	4.5

Source: Appendix.

Simultaneously, the end of the Cold War itself led to an abrupt reduction in the demand for light infantry weaponry by the governments of developed countries as they reduced their own armed forces. Arms producers have found new markets in developing countries, which have also been offered existing military stocks at reduced prices. In consequence, the supply of weaponry has become not only more abundant and affordable, but it is now unconditioned by strategic priorities, depending only on the ability to pay.

As Table 8.2 shows, poor conflict economies appear to suffer from 'import compression', in the sense of having lower import to GDP ratios than other less-developed economies. Import volume growth was slower in the former than the latter group in the 1980s, but faster in the 1990s; possibly reflecting the reversal of the income terms of trade noted above, and the changing pattern of external aid after the end of the Cold War. In fact, Table 8.4 implies that almost all registered imports in conflict economies are funded by ODA, implying that export revenue is mainly used for debt service and 'unregistered' imports not passing through customs—in other words, smuggled luxuries and military supplies.

3.2   Foreign Investment

Poor economies rely on two sources of foreign finance: private and public. Private finance is likely to dry up rapidly in conflict situations. Long-term international bank finance and bond issues for the domestic government and firms will be unavailable due to the risks involved, and commercial credit limited to very short-term facilities at high interest rates secured against traded commodities. Multinational firms, as discussed above, cease new investment projects in manufacturing and services—even if they are prepared to continue operations. Their concern is to protect their existing assets, and to establish profitable relationships with the eventual victors in the conflict. In contrast, large multinational firms in energy and mining will continue to negotiate for natural resource concessions; while new private 'informal' finance may become available for arms supplies and illegal exports.

New financial groups emerge, often based on the extraordinary profits available from wartime trading and are typically connected with armed groups. They may even receive tacit support from the government, if only because they create employment and the only alternative to their current mode of operation may simply be that flight capital remains abroad. However, once consolidated and in potential receipt of a peace dividend, they may well be powerful supporting factors for a settlement.

The experience of Africa in particular gives cause for concern in this context. Aid to Liberia declined sharply in the 1980s and both sides in the civil war obtained finance from logging concerns, rubber companies, and iron ore extraction; while in Sierra Leone control over gem resources was a focus of armed conflict itself, leading to the contracting of foreign mercenaries financed by forward diamond sales.[14] During the Nigerian civil war, Shell agreed to pay royalties to the Biafran separatist administration rather than the central government, thus making secession possible, while Rothschild's acquired exclusive concessions on Biafran niobium, uranium, coal, tin, and gold. During the civil war in the Congo, Kabila's forces were financed initially by gold-mining, and in the latter stages by US mining firms (Fairhead 2000).

Perhaps the most extreme case is that of Angola, where the UNITA insurgents relied on international diamond sales after direct funding from the USA and South Africa was cut off; although this new source of funding was also severely reduced after UN sanctions forced major diamond buyers' corporations to withdraw; meanwhile, however, the government (unable to come to an agreement with the IMF for 'normal' loans) was able to obtain large up-front payments from oil drilling licences, raise international loans by mortgaging future oil production, and even to involve military equipment suppliers in equity stakes in drilling blocs in order to finance its rearmament programme (UN/OCHA 1999).

3.3 Foreign Debt and Foreign Aid

The status of the outstanding debt in conflict situations is ambiguous: international banks, bilateral donors and multilateral institutions take different positions when faced with conflict economies unable to service debt. Private bank lenders are usually prepared to suspend payments of principal and accept interest payments alone, or even write off debt in the face of inability to fulfil service obligations. At best they can expect Paris Club terms in exchange for restructuring debt for later payment—hopefully after the conflict is over—and at worst expect to write off losses against tax liabilities. Similarly, bilateral donors are likely to suspend service requirements de facto, if necessary by rolling them over with new aid commitments. Where diplomatic relations are broken off or economic sanctions applied, new lending ceases but no determined effort is likely to recover existing debt. In consequence, as Table 8.3 indicates, conflict LLDCs appear to have somewhat lower debt levels than their non-conflict equivalents, although the level rises over time. Similarly, debt-service ratios are higher as lenders attempt to recover their assets.

---

[14] Reno (2000), who argues that in these circumstances 'warlords base their political power on control over production and exchange rather than mobilizing populations through effective state institutions.'

Table 8.3   Debt in vulnerable economies

	Conflict LLDCs	Non-conflict LLDCs	All LLDCs
Debt/GDP (%)			
1983	70.3	78.0	74.2
1993	110.1	128.0	114.2
Debt service/exports (%)			
1983	23.8	20.0	21.9
1993	15.8	15.4	15.6

Source: Appendix.

In marked contrast to bilateral official lenders, multilateral lenders (that is, the Bretton Woods institutions and the regional development banks) do not restructure—let alone suspend or cancel—debt for countries in conflict. Indeed, if multilateral debt is not serviced on time, further lending is suspended and the whole principal becomes payable. In consequence, bilateral aid is often diverted to maintaining multilateral debt service rather than alleviating the economic burden of conflict on vulnerable groups. This problem reflects a more general one in that debt renegotiation in conflict situations is an ad hoc process in response to short-term liquidity problems rather than part of a comprehensive approach to peace building or the protection of vulnerable groups. In particular, the 'highly indebted poor countries' (HIPC) initiative is not related to conflict resolution or the protection of vulnerable groups at all. The first HIPC qualification conditions involved such a long period of macroeconomic probity that a conflict economy could not qualify, while the conditions became even more stringent in the enhanced HIPC framework.

Finally, at the household level, capital movements also intensify in wartime. On the one hand, capital flight from richer households increases as wealth-holders move their assets abroad in order to avoid their destruction or sequestration, or to provide for subsequent emigration. To the extent that these transfers are usually not registered with the central bank or the tax authority, they also represent a considerable resource loss to the country as a whole. The internationalization of finance has made such transfers easier, and non-residents can usually avoid tax in the country of destination, particularly if an offshore centre is used. On the other hand, poorer households can become a source of capital *inflows* due to the emigration of some members and the subsequent generation of remittances in order to support family members left behind. Economic emigration of this kind inevitably intensifies under conflict conditions, and the remittances can become a key element of the survival strategies of vulnerable groups, and even for the economy as a whole.

As Table 8.4 demonstrates, poor conflict economies receive lower levels of aid than their more peaceful counterparts in terms of per capita receipts or as a share of GDP. None the less, such aid seems to be more important to conflict LLDCs in terms of import finance; while as might be expected, the grant element is higher.

Table 8.4 Aid to vulnerable economies

Aid ratios in LLDCs, 1988–94	Conflict LLDCs	Non-conflict LLDCs	All LLDCs
ODA per capita (US$)	119.7	159.0	97.5
ODA/GDP (%)	16.4	32.8	24.6
ODA/investment (%)	104.9	117.1	111.2
ODA/imports (%)	90.1	78.9	84.6
Bilateral/total ODA (%)	57.6	63.5	60.6
ODA Grant Element (%):			
Bilateral	53.0	60.0	56.5
Multilateral	25.0	18.6	22.7

Source: Appendix.

4   The International Response to Conflict and the Burden on Vulnerable Groups

4.1   *International Economic Sanctions*

As the previous section of this chapter has suggested, the patterns of external trade shift fundamentally during conflict. On the one hand, foreign exchange becomes scarce as exports fall and import requirements rise; and on the other hand, the pattern of trade itself moves from 'formal' to 'informal' channels, while the product mix itself can alter towards illegal transactions. As Chapter 2 has argued, the effect of foreign-exchange shortages is particularly felt in those sectors reliant upon imported inputs, affecting employment there, and also upon urban areas where basic public services such as transport, power, and water deteriorate or even break down. In contrast, those rural sectors where production is not greatly affected by fighting, or where the population has not been forced to migrate, may be much less affected. In consequence, the effect on vulnerable groups of changes in external trade will be differentiated. Moreover, the measures taken by the government to distribute imports—and whether parallel markets are allowed to emerge—will also have an important effect on outcome for vulnerable groups.

These effects are clearly intensified if the major powers apply economic sanctions to states in conflict: indeed this is the intention of such measures. Such sanctions have come to be seen as a substitute for direct military intervention, with the aim of preventing states from attacking others or of oppressing domestic groups. There is little evidence that this type of measure does have the desired effect, particularly since the very process of globalization and 'informalization' of international trade means that the affected country can continue to trade (unless a blockade is imposed, which is very rare) but at more disadvantageous terms. Whatever efforts the affected government may make to protect vulnerable groups, shortages of essentials supplies and forced unemployment are likely to affect them heavily.[15]

---

[15] For the case of Iraq, for example, see Alnasrawi (2000).

Moreover, the process of globalization has been accompanied by a gradual strengthening of the multilateral rules enforcing the principles of free trade. By reducing the scope for individual countries to apply protectionist measures unilaterally, the GATT and the WTO also limit the ability of states to apply trade embargoes against each other. Although national security considerations are usually included in trade treaties as a justification for denying market access, the criterion of national security cannot be invoked unless a real threat can be demonstrated. In consequence, the US trade embargo on Nicaragua in 1990 was ruled illegal under international law by both the GATT (FitzGerald 1987) and the International Court of Justice (ICJ 1986). Further, attempts by a government to prevent firms in its jurisdiction from trading with a particular country (such as the US Helms–Burton Act) are very difficult to apply in practice because multinational groups can of course use affiliates domiciled elsewhere. However, the major powers (above all the USA) continue to apply economic sanctions wherever they feel that such actions are geopolitically justified or where the pressure from the electorate is strong enough.

The arms trade is still mainly conducted under licence from the governments of the main producer countries. Export licences can be used in a discretionary manner to control the access of conflict states to modern weaponry, although supplier states seem not to have used this instrument with great wisdom and by definition they do not affect non-state belligerents. In fact, because only access to new modern weapons systems is affected, as light infantry supplies can easily be obtained on the open market, arms-supply licences are at best an indirect means of influence. Only if there were comprehensive international regulation of arms trade would these sanctions become effective.

4.2   Conditional Development Assistance

Denial of access to international finance is more frequently used than trade sanctions in order to put pressure on belligerent states. This relates mainly to public funds because although private flows are regulated for prudential reasons (and increasingly to monitor criminal activities) commitments to freedom of capital flows and existence of offshore centres make private credits to conflict states almost impossible to restrict if the investor is determined to extend them. Official bilateral credits—mainly export credit guarantee facilities—can be and are used to place pressure on the governments in conflict economies, as are longer-term development loans. The larger powers can also affect the loan programmes of multilateral financial institutions: the USA in particular has used this instrument extensively.

There is, however, no evidence that this has affected the level of conflict in practice, while as in the case of trade it is reasonable to suppose that the economic cost of financial restrictions is likely to affect vulnerable groups disproportionately unless the debtor government makes special provision to protect them—in which case it is far from clear why such sanctions should be imposed in the first place—unless, of course, the objective is to affect the decision-making elite and achieve a policy change that will be to the advantage of the poor. If development finance cancellation was properly designed in the first place—in other words it followed DAC criteria and was clearly targeted at poverty reduction, particularly in wartime[16]—then financial sanctions would logically affect vulnerable groups disproportionately.

The shift towards humanitarian assistance in conflict situations does not just reflect conditions in the developing world. It also reflects the growth of the human rights culture in industrial societies, which has the effect of privileging interventions to protect citizens against the state. Increasing international media exposure of abusive state power and ethnic conflict in many parts of the world has placed strong electoral pressure on the governments of rich countries to intervene in order to protect vulnerable groups even where vital economic or strategic interests are not involved. In addition, situations of state collapse involving refugee spillovers into neighbouring countries may threaten regional peace and security. This strengthens the case for international humanitarian intervention designed to protect vulnerable groups from the consequences of conflict in the first instance, and subsequently to bring the conflict itself to an end (DAC 1998).

In consequence, NGOs have become more engaged in conflict conditions than before (Edwards 1999; Willets 1996). Their declared intention is to alleviate human suffering by their activities in conflict situations; particularly by providing water, food, shelter, and basic medical services to vulnerable groups in the short run, and helping these groups to reconstruct their livelihoods or resettle elsewhere in the longer run. NGOs rarely supply warring parties directly, but can do so indirectly—principally by provisioning the population groups upon which these parties rely for support. Moreover, because the supplies needed by light infantry (particularly food and medicines) are very similar to those required by the civilian population, it is very difficult for NGOs to be entirely sure who the 'end-user' actually is. Even if troops are not users, their families may well be while any increase of supplies in a shortage situation makes it easier for quartermasters to supply themselves on local markets.

This problem is complicated by the fact that in any one situation NGOs may be found operating on both sides and forced to enter into arrangements with the warring parties. There may be insufficient coordination among NGOs to exercise effective leverage on either of the parties to conflict to ensure that the level of human hardship is minimized. There is a marked contrast with the tradition of humanitarian intervention in Europe during the two World Wars, when Red Cross access to military prisoners and civilian refugees was recognized under international law (Moorehead 1998).

The fact that vulnerable groups become reliant on aid agencies if the conflict continues leads to the question: does humanitarian aid prolong suffering? While it may be the case that aid provides resources indirectly to the belligerents, wars in developing countries appear to end by political exhaustion and loss of support for armed forces rather than by conquest as such, let alone formal surrender by the vanquished army. Loss of control over population groups or territory is as much a matter of security provision as of standards of living.

---

[16] See DAC (1998), especially chapter 3.A.

4.3   International Humanitarian Intervention

The last resort of world powers is professed to be direct intervention in order to protect vulnerable groups. Intervention on humanitarian grounds is profoundly at odds with the traditional concept of order and relationships between states. Indeed the UN Charter in Article 2 (7) upholds the primacy of the domestic jurisdiction of a state unless its domestic policies threaten international peace and security. Strictly, Chapter 7 of the Charter only authorizes coercive measures (including economic sanctions as well as military intervention) in order to repel external aggression. In consequence, advocates of intervention on humanitarian grounds have sought to reinterpret the legal and political grounds for intervention.

There is no explicit provision for humanitarian intervention which would involve a state's domestic affairs. However, in 1977 an arms embargo was imposed on South Africa under Chapter 7; and the exclusive state jurisdiction provided by Article 2(7) was steadily weakened by UN adoption during the 1980s and 1990s of a wide range of declarations and covenants upholding human rights and outlawing genocide, torture, and racial discrimination. These have arguably become part of customary international law (Brownlie 1990).

None the less, during the 1980s the Security Council extended the concept of threats to peace considerably, often without General Assembly consent: 'peace enforcement' strategy has been undertaken in Somalia, Haiti, Rwanda, and Bosnia and Yugoslavia without the direct appeal to a vital security interest by the intervening states. Indeed, it is now becoming very difficult for governments to argue that where no vital interest is involved, combatants in civil wars should be left to fight it out until a victor emerges and a degree of order restored so that the resulting state can be recognized de facto in the traditional manner.

Military interventions for 'prudential' reasons are supposed to be governed by clear criteria, such as clear and limited political objectives; willingness to commit the resources (including casualties) necessary; and an unambiguous exit strategy. The problem of intervention for humanitarian reasons is thus all the greater because the objective is not for a delinquent state to desist from some action, or even to overthrow a particular regime, but rather to transform the political system in line with western 'values' of human rights and democratic government. The UN interventions in both Somalia and Bosnia started as humanitarian relief operations; which then became open-ended as coercive disarmament of combatants was attempted. In the Haiti case the government was too weak to resist intervention; but in that of Rwanda the potential for failure was an important factor in preventing intervention.

The benefits to vulnerable groups of humanitarian interventions vary widely, and although the immediate relief effect of establishing population sanctuaries and relieving starvation are usually positive, the longer-term economic effect is far from clear. This is because the scale of intervention in relation to the local economy is large: local employment and trading patterns are distorted, prices of building material are driven up, and new consumption habits created. As Chapter 7 has shown, the impact of food aid on vulnerable groups and on the course of war itself vary widely with the particular context.

Finally, the expenditures by aid agency offices and personnel can have a considerable impact on poor war-torn economies because the scale of expenditure can be very large compared to local incomes. Local expenditure on offices, housing, counterpart staff, and so on can generate a substantial flow of foreign exchange into the informal sector and serve to drive up some non-traded prices—particularly housing and construction. The recruitment of counterpart staff in a small market for skilled labour may well also undermine key public sector activities such as health, which the aid programmes are designed to supplement. Under these circumstances, the scale of aid agency activity can have a determinate effect not only on the supply of basic goods and services to vulnerable groups, but also on the level of macroeconomic activity and the rate of inflation. However, bilateral agencies and NGOs do not usually enter into a policy dialogue with the domestic government on macroeconomic policy, which may well mean that their expenditure does not have the intended effect on the welfare of vulnerable groups. Moreover, when such operations cease, the ability of vulnerable groups to re-establish sources of income and social support in a sustainable local economy may not exist—as the experience of Cambodia suggests (FitzGerald 1994).

5 Policy Implications

It is difficult to draw specific policy conclusions from such a broad survey of the issues, particularly because international economic policy intervention necessarily implies a judgement as to the relative merits of the objectives of the contending parties in the conflict. There seems to be some official consensus on the actions to be taken by international agencies *within* the conflict country:

In organized violent conflict and confrontation, preventive diplomacy and military measures are generally utilized for moderating conflict, ending hostilities and starting peace negotiations. Humanitarian aid and, where possible, continued development activities should support these efforts. In some circumstances this may require collaboration to implement cease-fires so that humanitarian assistance for war victims and displaced persons can be provided. The delivery of humanitarian assistance in such conditions presupposes assent and cooperation of the parties involved in the conflict. Negotiation with warring parties regarding the deployment of peace-keepers and the organization of humanitarian aid itself can simultaneously open the way for other diplomatic initiatives aimed at ending the conflict. These initiatives require close coordination among security policy, diplomacy, humanitarian aid and development cooperation organizations.   (DAC 1998: 23)

However, there is no reference in this consensus as to what regulatory actions might be undertaken in the *international* economy—despite the fact that this greatly influences the intensity, extent and duration of the conflict. Some appropriate policy measures stemming from the argument in this chapter include:

- The suspension of official bilateral and multilateral debt payments for the duration of the conflict; the resources released thereby to be allocated to the provision of health and education services to all vulnerable groups without discrimination.

- The maintenance of access to normal trade and banking channels by conflict economies in order to avoid recourse to clandestine markets; avoiding the use of embargoes as being largely ineffective in reducing conflict and usually prejudicing the vulnerable.
- A closer regulation of international trade in those commodities which tend to be involved in illegal exports and military funding in conflict economies—such as oil, gems, and timber—by importing countries and multilateral organizations.
- The establishment of a 'code of conduct' for multinational companies operating in or negotiating with countries at war, especially in relation to their use of private armies, and contracts undertaken which provide war finance in exchange for concessions.
- A commitment by developed countries to ensure that their interventions in developing countries in pursuit of their own national security (including the interdiction of narcotics supply and transit) do not provoke or prolong local conflicts.
- A multilateral commitment to address the issue of arms supplies to belligerents—actual and potential—building on the success of the campaign to reduce the use of anti-personnel landmines and involving developing-country arms exporters.
- Revision of the lending criteria of the Bretton Woods institutions and the regional development banks to ensure that their loan or debt conditionality does not aggravate or prolong conflict.

These policy implications may appear somewhat ambitious, but they do indicate where concerted action is needed if the severity, extent and duration of conflicts in poor countries are to be reduced. They would add considerably to the present commitments to humanitarian emergency aid, diplomatic peace-making efforts, and potential military intervention.

International legislation and enforcement are not on the horizon. A first practical step would be effective monitoring of these economic activities and international disclosure of the results. At present this role is only partially carried out by UN agencies, increasingly complemented by the less systematic—but often more effective—efforts of NGOs.[17] The impact on large multinational corporations can be considerable as it affects their image among consumers. A second step would be the establishment of clear codes of conduct for foreign firms operating in conflict countries, which could be enforced by making receipt of official support—ranging from export credit guarantees to supply contracts to aid agencies—conditional on adherence to such a code. A third would be to charge the Bretton Woods institutions themselves—who have shepherded poor economies into greater integration with global markets and claim to lead other aid agencies in economic coordination—with the production of regular reports on trade and investment activities in conflict economies. Greater transparency as to who in the international economy is benefiting from conflict and suffering in conflict countries could only have a salutary effect.

---

[17] The effectiveness of NGO monitoring is illustrated by De Beers announcement in October 1999 that it would no longer buy diamonds from the Angolan rebels, and it was reviewing its operations in Guinea and the Democratic Republic of Congo, under pressure from Global Witness (reported in the *Financial Times*, 11 Oct. 1999).

STATISTICAL APPENDIX

Of the 48 'least developed countries' (LLDCs) defined as such by the United Nations[18] 24 have undergone serious conflicts during the past three decades. Some middle-income countries are also conflictive—such as Colombia, Peru, Guatemala, Lebanon, Iraq, Iran, and Yugoslavia; but the main grouping of conflict-prone countries is clearly among poor economies.

Tables 8A.1 and 8A.2 report the main results of the statistical exercise on the LLDC countries listed in UNCTAD (1996). In the tables 'Conflict 1990–6' refers to those countries experiencing conflicts between 1990 and 1996 (see list below) and 'Conflict

Table 8A.1   Income and trade

Variable	Conflict 1990–6	Conflict 1970–89	All conflict	No conflict	All LLDCs	All LDCs	T-stat	F-stat
GDP per capita level ($)								
1980	346	417	373	588	488	828	−1.33	0.16
1994	256	401	304	486	395	984	−1.76	0.66
GDP per capita (% change p.a.)								
1980–9	−1.3	0.8	−0.5	−0.1	−0.2	1.2	−0.57	0.30
1990–4	−3.3	0.5	−1.8	0.2	−0.7	1.8	−1.27	2.38
Export purchasing power (% change p.a.)								
1980–9	−3.0	1.8	−1.3	1.5	0.1	1.8	−1.40	0.54
1990–4	9.7	7.6	8.9	0.7	4.8	8.0	−0.87	1.96
Export structure (% of total exports)								
Food	34.8	34.3	34.6	44.1	39.3	11.0	−1.00	0.75
Agricultural raw materials	16.4	28.2	20.3	14.7	17.5	2.8	0.88	1.22
Fuels	15.8	4.1	11.9	3.0	7.4	22.5	0.52	1.23
Ores	12.5	1.2	8.7	12.5	10.6	3.6	−0.58	0.39
Manufacturing	18.9	30.0	22.6	21.0	21.8	59.0	0.21	0.75
Imports								
Imports/income 1994 (%)	26.4	22.6	25.0	45.3	34.9	26.0	−0.44	1.05
Vol. 1980–9 (% change p.a.)	−2.3	5.1	0.3	3.0	1.6	3.9	−0.74	1.83
Vol 1990–4 (% change p.a.)	6.1	16.1	9.6	2.2	6.0	11.7	−0.69	0.78
Import structure (% of total imports)								
Food	25.4	16.2	22.2	23.6	22.9	8.6	−0.41	1.27
Agricultural raw materials	6.6	4.3	5.8	2.0	3.8	2.7	1.62	6.74
Fuels	12.3	9.3	11.2	12.2	11.7	7.9	−0.56	3.28
Ores	0.5	0.7	0.5	1.0	0.7	2.6	0.19	1.07
Manufacturing	52.1	64.6	56.2	58.1	57.1	75.8	−0.34	2.84

Sources: UNCTAD, *Least Developed Countries Reports* (various years); Geneva: United Nations Conference on Trade and Development.

[18] Afghanistan★★, Angola★★, Bangladesh★, Benin★, Bhutan, Burkina Faso, Burundi★★, Cambodia★★, Cape Verde, Central African Republic★, Chad★, Comoros★, Djibouti, Equatorial Guinea, Eritrea★★, Ethiopia★★, Gambia, Guinea, Guinea-Bissau, Haiti★★, Kiribati, Lao PDR★, Lesotho, Liberia★★, Madagascar, Malawi, Maldives, Mali, Mauritania, Mozambique★★, Myanmar★, Nepal, Niger, Rwanda★★, Samoa, Sao Tome, Sierra Leone★★, Solomons, Somalia★★, Sudan★★, Togo★★, Tuvalu, Uganda★, Tanzania, Vanuatu, Yemen★★, Zaire★★, Zambia. Source UNCTAD *Least Developed Countries Report 1996* (Geneva 1996); asterisk (★) indicates serious conflict since 1970, double asterisk (★★) since 1990.

Table 8A.2   Debt and aid

Variable	Conflict 1990–6	Conflict 1970–90	All conflict	No conflict	All LLDCs	T-stat	F-stat
Debt/GDP							
1983	70.7	69.6	70.3	78.0	74.2	−0.51	0.57
1993	130.4	72.1	110.1	128.0	114.2	0.12	1.08
Debt-service exports							
1983	25.0	21.5	23.8	20.0	21.9	0.85	1.92
1993	14.2	19.0	15.8	15.4	15.6	−0.92	0.66
ODA per capita ($)							
1981–7	22.7	27.7	24.4	119.7	73.1	−3.96	0.07
1988–94	33.1	42.0	36.0	159.0	97.5	−3.70	0.24
ODA/GDP							
1981–7	10.9	13.7	11.9	30.1	21.2	−3.70	0.24
1988–94	17.3	14.8	16.4	32.8	24.6	−2.56	1.16
ODA/Investment							
1981–7	67.9	111.9	83.9	125.0	105.3	−0.42	1.86
1988–94	94.2	123.8	104.9	117.1	111.2	−0.68	1.06
ODA/Imports							
1981–7	74.8	84.0	78.0	61.3	69.8	0.53	2.51
1988–94	94.5	81.9	90.1	78.9	84.6	0.81	1.33
% of ODA 1988–94							
Bilateral	59.5	53.8	57.6	63.5	60.6	−1.90	1.00
Multilateral	40.5	46.1	42.4	36.5	39.4	1.90	1.52
Grant/ODA 1988–94							
Bilateral	55.8	47.4	53.0	60.0	56.5	−1.95	0.94
Multilateral	28.2	19.0	25.0	18.6	22.7	2.61	1.96

Sources: As Table 8A.1.

1970–89' refers to those experiencing conflict between 1970 and 1989. 'All conflict' is the group made up of the previous two sub-groups. 'No conflict' is the rest of the LLDC group, while 'All LDCs' refers to the universe of developing countries as a whole.

Standard statistical tests to see if the 'conflict' and 'non-conflict' samples are significantly different are also shown: the Student's T-test to see if the sample means are significantly different, and the F-test to check for significant differences in variance. For these sample sizes the 95 per cent confidence interval for the T-test is 1.68, and the 90 per cent interval is 1.31; while the 95 per cent interval for the F-test is 2.10. As can be seen from Tables A.1 and A.2, the two samples do not generally appear to have clearly significant differences in their means or variances—except in the cases of income, export, and aid levels. This problem is extensively discussed in FitzGerald (2000).

9

The Costs of War in Poor Countries:
Conclusions and Policy Recommendations

FRANCES STEWART AND VALPY FITZGERALD

Quand les riches se font la guerre ce sont les pauvres qui meurent.

Jean-Paul Sartre, *Le Diable et le bon Dieu* (1951)

1 Understanding the War Economy as a Precondition for Policy Design

1.1 The Neglect of War

Many of the poorest economies have been seriously affected by armed conflict during the past three decades, as shown in this book. In such economies, the human costs of conflict are not only the result of direct violence—casualties from fighting between combatants, the undisciplined behaviour of troops, deliberate terrorizing of civilians, and the sowing of landmines—but also arise from hunger, forced migration, and the collapse of public services stemming from the wider effects of prolonged conflict on the economic and administrative structure of the country as a whole. The indirect consequences of conflict—including raised deaths from hunger and disease—generally far outweigh direct destruction and battle deaths.

Hence the question of how best to approach the problem of conflict-affected economies, and particularly how to ameliorate the human costs, is an immediate and ongoing one. No serious attempt to eradicate world poverty can afford to neglect this subject. Yet, for the most part economies in conflict are put to one side by the donor community in their poverty-focused policies. Where such economies are considered, the main policy advocated—reasonably enough at first sight—is to bring the conflict to an end. We, of course, support this objective and would continue to give it priority. However, these wars appear to last for many years despite the efforts of the international community; so it is essential to devise policies that may help reduce human costs while war is ongoing. Moreover, post-war reconstruction takes many years too—over a decade in most cases—and is heavily conditioned by economic events that took place during the conflict itself.

Our aim here and in the companion volume of case studies has been to further understanding of economies at war in order to contribute to the identification of appropriate policies to reduce human hardship, even though the heterogeneity and complexity of war-affected economies make simple generalization extremely difficult. Appropriate policies must be sensitive to the conditions in the particular economy, the nature of the conflict, and the political situation, in ways that we develop below. This type of sensitivity is always difficult for international donors, who prefer simple formulas whether they are dealing with monetary or exchange-rate policy, or emergency aid. Moreover, the urgency of war seems to prevent research or careful analysis. Yet, the many major mistakes that the international community have made in recent years are a convincing demonstration of the need for deeper analysis, for thought before action.[1]

There is a combination of reasons for such errors. One is the neglect of economic analysis of countries at war, either because it is implicitly assumed that there is no economy when a country is at war so there's no particular economic policy that is appropriate; or because the assumption is that economies at war are just like any other economy subject to an exogenous negative shock so that similar policies are relevant to those applied peacetime. Both positions are fundamentally incorrect. The former, because economic transactions still go on, people still have to make a living in order to survive; the latter, because economies at war *are* different from non-war economies in important respects—the objectives of policy and the responses to it differ, so that outside assistance or policy advice can misdirect resources unless the mechanics of the economy at war are understood. A second reason for the mistakes is the failure to understand the political economy of the countries at war, so that assistance is used by warring parties as an instrument of war rather than, as intended, to support the livelihoods of the poor and thus reduce human costs. A third reason is the political economy of the donor community itself: political and economic objectives and constraints of donors often outweigh humanitarian objectives—this appears to have been an important factor in each of the cases where external intervention failed.

1.2   Policy Design in Wartime

Improved understanding of economies in conflict should help correct the first error. Design of policies so as to work with rather than against the domestic forces of political economy, as far as possible, should help correct the second. However, to the extent that the main problem with donor actions lies with the misguided objectives of the donor community itself, we cannot speak of a policy *error* as such. The error may lie in our assumption that the overriding objective of donors is humanitarian and development-oriented.

The international community clearly plays a key role in many conflict situations—not least because of the financial resources it controls.[2] None the less domestic actors are far more important. Government policy can ameliorate or accentuate human costs:

---

[1] From Cambodia, through Somalia and the Sudan, to Rwanda international action has all too often failed to alleviate human costs, and has often contributed to the prolongation or deepening of the war. See Keen (1994b), Macrae and Zwi (1994), and de Waal (1997); as well as Kevin Toolis, 'The Famine Business', the *Guardian*, 22 August 1998; Jimmy Burns and Frances Williams, 'Refugee agency lost in wilderness of bungling and waste', the *Financial Times*, 20 July 1998.

[2] On average, one-half of imports and government budgets in the least developed countries are financed through official development assistance (UNDP 1998).

this is only partly a technical matter—it is also a political issue. Where, however, the government itself aims to impoverish, or even eradicate, a section of the population in order to benefit another section, offering the government policy advice on how to reduce human costs is totally dysfunctional, and other means must be found for protecting the population. In contrast where the government wants to promote widespread access to basic needs by the population as a whole, then advice on how to do so, as well as financial support, may be highly productive. The situation is thus extremely complex, requiring a simultaneous understanding of economic behaviour and the political economy of local actors, including the government as well as international actors— hence the dangers of over-simplification and generalization. Yet even a small improvement in understanding could greatly improve the situation, so the effort is worth making.

This concluding chapter thus draws on the analysis presented in this volume in order to focus on the policy implications for governments and donors. The political economy considerations emerging from the preceding chapters are summed up in Section 2, illustrating the domestic and international forces that contribute to policy formation in war. Section 3 then reviews our findings as to economic behaviour in war-affected countries and the resulting social costs, suggesting that the economic policy adopted can have a considerable effect on the welfare outcome for vulnerable groups. Section 4 turns to the design of national policies aimed at reducing the costs of conflict. The local policies we recommend to both governments and donors focus on the maintenance of the entitlements of vulnerable groups and the reduction of horizontal inequality between groups. Section 5 follows with a discussion of the international policies needed, suggesting a focus on the regulation of international trade and finance in such a way as to reduce the material incentives for conflict. We conclude the book by outlining the constraints on and the scope for policy formation in wartime in Section 6.

2   The Political Economy of War and Poverty

2.1   Groups in Conflict

There is no doubt that civil war has been a major cause of poverty among some significant parts of the population of economies at war, a conclusion that is powerfully supported by the empirical evidence in this book. Yet, as was pointed out in Chapter 3, there is a rationality about most of these 'modern' conflicts,[3] which generally have an underlying economic rationale, as well as political dimensions. On the one hand, groups aim to enhance or protect their economic position through the armed struggle; on the other hand, while welfare losses are widespread, some private individuals[4] can gain greatly from the war economy itself in ways that they cannot in normal times, and for this reason these groups may wish to continue the conflict. So in order to help

---

[3] Termed 'new' wars by Kaldor (1999).
[4] Including those seeking private gain *within* the state, of course.

reduce the human costs of war and to bring the conflict to an end it is essential to address these political economy motivations.

The conflicts with which we are concerned are *organized group* conflicts: that is to say they are not exclusively a matter of individuals randomly committing violence against others. Since *group mobilization* is involved, to understand the causes of conflict and possible approaches to a solution we need also to understand the underlying motivation for such mobilization. Differences in individuals' circumstances—cultural, geographic, or economic—provide the potential for the construction of group identity as a source of political mobilization. Political leaders, in government or outside, may use this potential in their competition for power and resources, in the course of which they enhance group identification by reconstructing history around symbols such as linguistic or religious differences. However, cultural distinctions alone are not sufficient to bring about violent group mobilization.[5] Real or perceived economic and political differentiation among groups is of fundamental importance to group mobilization during civil war: what we have termed *horizontal inequality* in Chapter 1. Persistent and widening horizontal inequality is a major source of conflict, and no solution to a conflict is likely to be endured unless it narrows such inequality both in its political and economic dimensions.

Policies, therefore, need to be assessed for their impact on horizontal inequality as well as for the implications for reducing economic and social costs. Most policies directly aimed at reducing the social costs of conflict might reduce horizontal inequality, to the extent that they target vulnerable groups, and would be unlikely to enhance it. For example, in the case of Sudan were the south to be targeted for additional entitlements on poverty alleviation grounds this would contribute to a reduction of horizontal 'ethnic' inequality and thus ameliorate the conflict. Similarly, in Sri Lanka it appears that some of the policies to reduce social costs would especially favour the relatively deprived Northeast and thus contain the secessionist movement. In contrast, broader economic policies designed to revitalize the export economy can widen horizontal inequality and create conflict conditions—as in the case of NAFTA and the Zapatista movement in Mexico. Again, the increased sense of inter-group deprivation arising from fiscal austerity measures after the Indonesian financial collapse probably contributed to armed repression of East Timor and the subsequent international intervention.

The implication of horizontal equity considerations, therefore, is that the redistribution of economic or political power between groups needs to be considered explicitly in policy formation by both domestic governments and international agencies. Further, this means ensuring that the distribution of entitlements of all types is *inclusive*: incorporating all major groups in society and reducing inequalities between and within groups over time.

---

[5] 'Men may and do certainly joke about or ridicule the strange and bizarre customs of men from other ethnic groups, because these customs are different from their own. But they do not fight over such differences alone. When men *do*, on the other hand, fight across ethnic lines it is nearly always the case that they fight over some fundamental issues concerning the distribution and exercise of power, whether economic, political, or both' (Cohen 1974: 94).

2.2   The Functionality of Conflict

Our study challenges both the conventional approaches of conflict in developing countries, which might be termed the 'irrational' and the 'bureaucratic' models. In the first model, war is depicted as irrational, mindless, and chaotic.[6] However, our research shows that war can serve important functions for the actors involved, thereby explaining its prolongation despite the heavy costs incurred. In many developing countries, the pursuit of individual or group objectives is not impeded by—and indeed may be assisted by—the state of civil war. In the second model (Contamine (1980); Davis (1970); Marwick *et al.* (1990)), the origin of war is 'rational' (that is, it has economic or political purposes), but the dominant logic is military with the state and the armed opposition being the only significant actors. Civilians are involved only as collateral casualties, while individual or group objectives are subjected to the broader interest of defending or overthrowing the state. This model can be applied to major international wars, but in civil wars it is clear that war is shaped by—and in turn shapes—political and economic processes already at work within a society, with 'civilians' as both explicit targets and active participants.

As well as factors leading to group mobilization, the motivation of individual actors needs to be understood and addressed. While there are many losers from war, there are also gainers. The gainers include those who orchestrate the violence, who acquire power and resources; and some of those carrying out the violence who may secure an occupation when previously they had been unemployed, and are able to loot and rape without recrimination. In addition there are the indirect beneficiaries—such as the arms manufacturers, the speculators and traders who gain from shortages, and smugglers. The war may not have started because of these gains, but once started these groups all have a motive for continuing war.

The economic *functions* of war for particular individuals and groups thus help explain its origin and continuation. For example, war may serve to perpetuate or even enhance the economic and political power of certain people (warlords), through protection rackets and monopolies. Acquisition of effective control over natural resources in unstable regions permits lucrative deals to be struck with foreign investors. Military mobilization raises the income of military personnel who might otherwise be unemployed and generates profitable supply contracts. People who are marginalized in peace may gain more from the possibilities of banditry in war than they lose from loss of security. Equally, war can facilitate the exploitation of labour and even permit the re-emergence of slavery. Particular groups can gain control over resources such as land, relief supplies, and state funds. Finally civil war can also serve international functions by helping regional or global powers to secure or maintain a distribution of influence that serves their strategic interests.

In practice, of course, different types of wars inevitably serve distinct functions. A key variable is the degree to which violence is controlled through bureaucratic hierarchies.

---

[6] See for instance Scheff (1994). This is essentially a Hobbesian view except while Hobbes saw conflict as intrinsic to humankind, the irrationality model seems to imply that it is a characteristic of 'primitive' or 'backward' developing countries alone.

Groups have economic strategies during conflict, as they do in peacetime, but during conflict they are obliged to change these strategies rapidly and adapt to new conditions simply in order to ensure survival. New strategies for the accumulation of wealth also emerge. Some of these strategies can be exploitative, depending on removing resources from others (for example, by withholding food) or using the labour of others with minimal rewards (as with slavery). Some strategies may be destructive of long-term development, such as stripping forests or consuming seed. However, other strategies— such as new health or educational services in 'liberated zones'—may contribute to public welfare. The key issue is thus to identify what type of strategy is adopted, and how more constructive strategies may be encouraged.

3   Economic Behaviour in Wartime

3.1   *Some General Lessons about Economic Behaviour in War*

Most of this study has been devoted to identifying economic behaviour in war-affected countries. Despite serious methodological problems about identifying precise effects, which were discussed in Chapter 1, the statistical analysis in Chapter 4 and case studies summarized in Chapter 5 point to some general findings about economic behaviour during civil war.

First, *economic growth* is almost always negatively affected, sometimes dramatically so, such as in Mozambique and Nicaragua; but aggregate output is least affected where the conflict is confined to one geographic region and export decline can be contained, as in the case of Sri Lanka or in the recent conflicts in Uganda. The *agricultural sector* is usually particularly badly hit in civil wars in developing countries, as people are forced to move in the course of the conflict, as a result of fighting, landmines, or to camps to secure food. Agricultural output plummeted in Afghanistan, Mozambique, Cambodia, Uganda, and Nicaragua during the worst war periods. However, it held up in Sri Lanka and did not fall so dramatically in Sudan—cases where the conflict was more confined geographically.

Second, *exports* are also invariably negatively affected. This partly stems from the general fall in production; partly from a shift towards domestic markets in order to sustain domestic consumption in the face of falling production; and partly from disruptions in international markets. Contrary to what might be expected at first sight, *import capacity* usually holds up—often growing even though exports often fall. This is due to the availability of aid, and foreign debt which spiralled in every country at war studied, leaving a huge post-conflict debt burden. None the less, foreign exchange tends to be diverted towards military expenditure and essential consumption goods[7] leading to a shortage of foreign exchange for economic inputs. In some cases—notably Nicaragua —this import compression was one of the main causes of a collapse in production.

Third, there is a *sectoral shift* from tradable to non-tradable sectors, as a consequence of market disruptions, including undermining of formal organizations, such as banks,

---

[7] In fact a considerable portion of the imports often take the form of food aid.

reduced trust, and failures of the transport system.[8] One aspect of this—a major consequence of conflict—is a switch to subsistence and informal activities, including simple production (even arms) and trading (particularly smuggling); Mozambique illustrates the development of the urban informal sector most graphically. The ability to retreat to subsistence agriculture also helps protect nutritional standards—it did so, for example, during the Amin era in Uganda.

Fourth, *consumption* per head inevitably falls with per capita GDP, even though domestic savings decline due both to attempts to maintain consumption levels and to uncertainty as to asset values. Attempts by households to maintain consumption and by the government to protect current expenditure lead to foreign borrowing and increased aid dependence—in other words 'foreign savings' replace 'domestic savings'.

Fifth, as expected, government capital formation and large-scale foreign and private *investment* generally falls quite sharply, due to budgetary restrictions and increased uncertainty respectively. In the case of Sri Lanka, reduction in foreign and private investment due to war-induced uncertainty appeared to be the main cost of war at a macrolevel. None the less, in general aggregate investment does not appear to fall by as much as domestic savings, possibly due to small-scale investment as the informal sector expands, and aid-funded projects—as was the case in Mozambique and Nicaragua.

Sixth, contrary to a priori expectations, government *revenue* as a share of GDP does not invariably fall among countries in conflict. In many cases, such as Nicaragua and Mozambique, it rose quite sharply, while in some others government revenue-raising ability was totally undermined—for example in Uganda and in Sierra Leone. This difference was important in determining whether the government could sustain public entitlements. In all cases government *expenditure* rose more than revenue and budget deficits widened, financed by a combination of foreign and domestic borrowing and increased money supply. But despite the rising budget deficit, *inflation* was quite moderate in the majority of cases, and hyperinflation was rare.

Seventh, the share of government expenditure allocated to *military* items invariably increases, making it difficult to sustain social and economic expenditure, and in almost all cases the share of social expenditure falls, sometimes severely. In those cases where government revenue collapsed there was a dramatic decline in public entitlements: this was true of both Uganda and Afghanistan. However, both Nicaragua and Mozambique gave increased priority to social expenditure compared with the pre-war situation and thereby succeeded in increasing public entitlements, but this was exceptional. Public entitlements fell in most cases, although some governments did attempt to sustain health services and food rations throughout the country, even in rebel-held areas: the governments of both Sri Lanka and Mozambique aimed to do so.

Eighth, in some places *civic entitlements* compensated to some extent for lost public entitlements, for example, through NGO efforts to provide services in parts of Afghanistan, and to deliver food and other services in Mozambique. NGOs, community organizations, and rebel administration provided services in the north of Sri Lanka.

[8] The expansion of subsistence, illegal, and informal activities in wartime in developing countries means that official statistics can greatly understate production, so that the aggregate costs of conflict may not be as great as they appear from official data. In addition, of course, statistical services themselves deteriorate.

None the less, in the worst affected areas of Uganda, southern Sudan, and Sierra Leone, communities disintegrated as people fled, and NGOs were able to do little.

Ninth, as a result of falling entitlements, *heavy human costs* were experienced in most countries, over and above the deaths and injuries from the war itself, with worse infant mortality rates than would have occurred in the absence of war, and deteriorating nutrition, health, and educational standards. In the worst case—of Ethiopia—estimated additional infant mortality compared with what the country would have experienced if rates had changed as in the region as a whole from 1965–94 amounted to nearly 5 per cent of the 1994 population (Chapter 4). Communities disintegrated in the worst-affected areas, and there was massive forced migration. As much as one-third of the population left Afghanistan, for example. There were also massive deaths from war-induced famines, notably in the Sudan.

Tenth, every study indicated *heavy development costs* as every type of capital was subject to destruction or weakening (including physical plant, land, human resources, social, and organizational capital), and new investment in each was reduced. Yet new forms of capital did emerge, including social and organizational (with new informal systems of banking and quasi-government structures being constructed in rebel-held areas, for example), though the extent varied considerably.

These findings represent broad conclusions drawn from a large range of war-torn countries. Of course, many poor countries have had similar economic experience without the additional shock of open war and therefore caution is needed before attributing all observed effects to the conflicts,[9] but our comparisons show that on many counts the experience of the conflict-affected countries was worse than regional performance or neighbouring countries not at war.

3.2   Distributional Effects

Although it proved difficult (often impossible) to get sound statistical data on income distribution—either vertical or horizontal—all our case studies indicate unequal distribution of the costs and benefits of conflict, with some groups gaining and others losing severely. In the Sudan, aggregate economic performance was reasonable in view of the civil war, but the southerners were severely and deliberately deprived, while particular northern groups—especially the army itself—gained from the war. In Sierra Leone war gangs on both sides gained from looting at the expense of the majority of the population. In Uganda, the Baganda suffered the main costs of the 1983–5 war, while more recently northerners have borne the main costs.

Women and men experience war differently. Men and boys are more likely to be involved in actual fighting; and to suffer more from lost formal-sector employment opportunities. For women and girls, new roles and opportunities sometimes open up during war, as heads of household and chief providers, but they suffer heavily from lost household entitlements, especially worsening food situation and health facilities. They are often the target of mass rape. Our evidence showed that boys suffered more

---

[9] As is shown in FitzGerald (2000).

than girls from reduced schooling during conflict, as might be expected, but females suffered more from raised mortality rates, perhaps because of the reduced availability of maternity services and because families may give priority to feeding boys when resources are very scarce. In general we did not find that women's relative employment situation changed radically during war, contrary to the findings for the industrialized countries.

3.3   Variations in Behaviour during War

While there were some changes which were widely shared by countries at war, an important finding was that there were also considerable variations, with some much more able to protect themselves against the costs of war than others. This variation is important because it suggests that policies might be able to reduce some of the costs. Variations were due to differences in the economy, in the nature of the war, and in the strength of responses by governments and other actors, including the people themselves.

In economies with a large subsistence sector, for example, people were able to protect their basic nutrition by retreating into subsistence, but only where the war was not too extensive there. For example, many people retreated into subsistence in Uganda during the Amin era, but in the war of the mid-1980s, this was impossible for many farming areas because their territory came under systematic attack. Countries, or people, heavily dependent on exchange for their food were more vulnerable to trade disruptions, like the southern Sudanese and Iraq. The formal sector was especially vulnerable to a shortage of foreign exchange, and where this was relatively large and inflexible the loss in output and employment was greatest, as in Nicaragua.

The nature of the war affected the extent of the costs: costs were less when the war was confined to one part of the country, while the worst destruction of entitlements occurred when a large proportion of the rural areas were under attack leading to massive movements of population. Targeted bombing of major infrastructural facilities, such as occurred in Mozambique, was particularly disruptive of the formal economy.

Variations in costs were also due to the nature of the government: government collapse led to the heaviest economic and social costs as government could sustain neither personal security, nor public entitlements. In these situations of near anarchy, human survival was extremely difficult. Where the governments retained a certain amount of strength—represented by their revenue-raising capacity—and used this strength, at least in part, to serve the whole population, then they could moderate the costs, by sustaining public entitlements including ensuring adequate food supplies. In our case studies Nicaragua, Mozambique, and Sri Lanka represented examples of governments which were reasonably effective and benign even in war. This represents one case in each continent and three out of the eight cases we studied: not such a rarity as might be imagined.

However, strong government did not improve the situation where the government itself was determined to destroy the livelihoods or even the existence of certain sections of the population. The Sudanese government policy towards the Dinka, aimed at undermining their economic survival, is one example; while a more extreme version is represented by the Hutu attacks on the Tutsi in Rwanda; Amin's, and subsequently Obote's, policies in Uganda also came close to genocide. In some cases quasi-governments emerged in rebel-held areas, which were quite effective in upholding security within the area and administering services. The part of Sri Lanka controlled by the Tamils was the most notable example.

International actions also contributed to variations in costs. For example, the large supplies of food aid in Mozambique undoubtedly reduced death rates, while in Sudan food aid was too little, too late, and its delivery and use were distorted by government policy. In Afghanistan, massive support for the refugees in Iran and Pakistan greatly lessened the human costs, while within the country the activities of NGOs in providing services did likewise. The international community did little to offset costs in Sierra Leone and the USA in particular did its best to increase the burden of civil war for vulnerable groups in Nicaragua by trade and aid embargoes.

People's own actions moderated the human and economic costs. In almost all cases, people found new economic possibilities—many created by the war—which enabled them to survive. The burgeoning of the informal sector in Mozambique was one example; the massive growth of poppy production and exports in Afghanistan is another. People also protected themselves by fleeing the war, leaving the country in huge numbers in Afghanistan, or relocating within the country in Mozambique. People were rarely totally passive victims, but in the worst situations, there was little they could do to protect themselves.

4   National Policies Aimed at Reducing the Costs of Conflict

4.1   Economic Behaviour and Policy Design

The exploration of economic behaviour during war, and especially the variations in behaviour and outcomes, suggests that economic and social policies of both governments and donors can be designed to reduce the economic and human costs of conflict, *even during the conflict*. Government policies should be constructed so as to lessen the human and development costs of war, while aid donors should not wait until the conflict is over before resuming development aid. In both cases, the design of policy clearly needs to be different from peacetime in order to take into account the special circumstances of war.

Understanding the functions of war also sheds new light on policy design. Some well-intentioned policies may actually contribute to the functionality of war, but others may counter it. War-related aid (food aid and finance), for example, gives rise to the potential for private gains through trade or theft—every country study of food-aid makes some reference to these gains. Controlling exchange rates may drive a wedge between parallel rates and the official rate creating opportunities for profiteering. Yet spiralling depreciation/inflation—which may be the alternative—also offers large gains to illicit traders. Import controls, food rations, and subsidies may also generate opportunities for black-market gains. However, if policies are introduced which are effective in maintaining output, employment, and entitlements, they offer alternative livelihoods to exploiting the war and reduce the incentive to rely on the war economy. Without such policies, war profiteering may represent the only survival mechanism.

The design of policies must take into account the administrative capacity of the government, which varies among countries according to the general level of development and also to the impact of war itself on this capacity. In our sample of countries there were important differences—for example, the administrative capacity of Nicaragua and Sri Lanka was sustained throughout the war, but in other cases—such as Uganda under Amin and Sierra Leone—governments lacked the capacity to carry out many of the policies which might otherwise be desirable.

4.2 Relief versus Development?

The objective of policies in conflict situations goes beyond immediate relief, and should include the prevention and reversal of the destruction of the capacity of poor households to meet their own needs and of a poor economy to sustain itself. In other words, the objective is not simply to sustain livelihoods in the short term, but to reduce medium-term vulnerability and dependence by creating conditions in which households (and society) can become self-sustaining. This double requirement is imperative because policies which simply bring short-term relief (for example, via feeding schemes in camps) essentially prolong dependence, and are often associated with rising death rates from disease. None the less, policies aimed at reducing longer-term vulnerability and contributing to a self-sustaining economy (and households within it), will clearly fail if they do not also meet acute short-term needs.

Although the ultimate aim is to protect people at a microeconomic level—to help sustain their capacity and entitlements—relevant policies are mainly at macro- and mesolevels, because adverse developments at these levels as a consequence of conflict are largely responsible for hardship at the level of the household. Hence the appropriateness of macro- and meso-policies need to be measured in terms of their success in contributing to the objective of reducing household vulnerability.

Our approach contrasts sharply with the views represented by the so-called 'relief–development continuum', where policies directed towards immediate short-term relief alone are held to be relevant in wartime, while only after peace has been reached can a smooth transition be made towards longer-term development. It is often suggested that economic development aid should be suspended until the conflict is over as efforts are likely to be wasted, and all aid should be diverted to 'relief'. For example, 'efforts to begin reconstruction now would be a waste of effort and resources'.[10] Both relief (offsetting acute deprivation in the short term) and development (contributing to a self-sustaining position for households and economies) should be central aspects of the aims of policy in conflict-affected countries: first, because one would be a failure without the other—acute deprivation will simply recur if policies don't contribute to

---

[10] Lancaster (1990: 40), referring to the Horn of Africa.

a self-sustaining solution, while relief may not be possible unless some development-related activity takes place (for example roads are reconstructed); in many cases, reconstruction of important elements of economic infrastructure and of agriculture and export capacity is essential to reduce the ongoing human costs of conflict; second, the weakening and death of human beings through short-term deprivation constitute a serious development cost; and third, particular policies almost always have implications for both relief and development and rarely fit neatly into just one end of the 'continuum'. From our perspective—that of aiming to reduce medium-term vulnerability—policies which are only valid at one end of the spectrum are nearly always suboptimal.

4.3   *Maintaining Macroeconomic Stability*[11]

The aim of macroeconomic policy during conflict should be to avoid large reductions in output and employment, on the one hand, and an escalation in inflation, on the other. Each can lead to sharp changes in income distribution and the destruction of market entitlements for significant sections of the population. As shown in Chapter 2, these reductions in output are the outcome of a great number of adverse developments associated with war—including physical destruction as well as economic disarticulation. Increased transaction costs and loss of productive capacity, and shortage of foreign exchange, arising from falling exports and diversion to military expenditures are the central features.

In the short term macro-policies thus need to focus on the development of a credible framework of market rules and institutions and the maintenance of transport links in order to contain transaction costs. In order to counter the distortions caused by foreign-exchange shortages which are unavoidable in a war context, policies should aim to ensure that the foreign exchange that is available goes to priority use—including basic inputs for industry and agriculture, essential medicines, and food. Import controls are usually required for the allocation of foreign exchange in wartime as the market would allocate foreign exchange to the consumption of war profiteers, not capacity-creating essentials. These should be backed up by capital controls to moderate the inevitable capital flight; which should be supported by appropriate regulatory action on the part of aid donors. Of course, whether the government has the administrative capacity to undertake these policies effectively must also be considered.

Balance-of-payments management under conditions of uncertain export income and aid commitments is extremely difficult. The most obvious requirement is for adequate foreign-exchange reserves, which may require international cooperation to sustain, as well as the protection of import rationing and capital controls. Exchange-rate policy should be designed to maintain a competitive real exchange rate in order to avoid disincentives to exports, but it is important to maintain control over the nominal exchange rate in the inevitable macroeconomic disequilibrium of war. Otherwise, the spiral of currency depreciation and cost of living inflation will affect entitlements adversely.

---

[11] See Chapter 2 for a more extended discussion.

Inflation control is a fundamental priority as it is a major source of uncertainty and speculation in the private sector, makes public budgetary and financial control difficult if not impossible, and can cause acute hardship as it impacts on household purchasing power. Inflation control requires adequate supply and demand management and is not simply a matter of money supply. None the less, there needs to be some restraint on budget deficits. Specific policies are needed to prevent excessive food-price inflation given the damaging effects on human well-being: these are discussed below.

A critical requirement, from the perspective of controlling budget deficits as well as that of maintaining public entitlements, is to strengthen revenue raising. The relative decline of the formal sector, the fall in exports and imports, both typically sources of revenue, the increasing share of undeclared war profits, illegal activities, and subsistence production, all tend to undermine revenue raising. The government needs to compensate by devising taxes on war-related activities. The sale of food aid can be one important source of revenue; as can be compulsory savings bonds, high taxes on non-basic consumption such as tobacco, alcohol, bottled drinks, and petrol, combined with high margins on services such as telephones and electricity. As noted above, a sharp decline in revenue is not an inevitable concomitant of war: Sudan, Nicaragua, and Sri Lanka succeeded in sustaining revenue as a share of GDP.

Macroeconomic management is extremely difficult during conflict in poor countries, partly because the resources devoted to it are liable to be limited in both quantity and quality. Hence rather simple rules are desirable, among which the most important appear to be:

1. sustaining tax revenue as a proportion of GDP;
2. containing the budget deficit to a level consistent with sustainable debt;
3. maintaining a restrictive monetary policy and a competitive real exchange rate and
4. allocating scarce foreign exchange to essential imports.

4.4 Preventing Entitlement Failure

Both social and economic policies need to be directed at sustaining the share of aggregate output going to maintaining entitlements of the vulnerable. On the social side, meso-policies need to be devised with the objective of sustaining public entitlements on basic health and education; and ensuring everyone has access to adequate food. Preventive health measures, notably immunization, are particularly vital in war when unusual movement of people causes infections to spread rapidly.

Clearly, maintaining fiscal revenue is essential so that there are resources available for public expenditure on these items. With sufficient total levels of expenditure, public entitlements to health and education can be sustained even with a substantial increase in military expenditure—which is normally unavoidable. Moreover, basic health and education (that is primary health and education) account for only a fraction of social expenditure, so that strong prioritization of these services can ensure their maintenance even if the total is being cut. Yet the problem is not only one of money. Teachers and doctors may flee in a war context, and health and education facilities can be destroyed. A flexible approach—involving, for example, mobile clinics and classrooms, the training and use of basic health workers and primary school teachers, and periodic popular campaigns for immunization and sanitation—is needed. There are examples of such flexibility: Mozambique experimented with mobile clinics and classrooms when Renamo was targeting health and education buildings; both sides in El Salvador called a successful halt to hostilities on three separate days so that infants and children could be immunized during the war.

Ensuring adequate access to food is one of the most fundamental aims of policy during conflict. Subsidies and rationing may be needed to prevent excessive economic and social costs—these are all policies which advanced countries have adopted during war.[12] Food security during conflict requires that food prices are monitored and escalating prices prevented, through some combination of releasing supplies, controlling prices, and rationing. Sudden price changes can cause destitution or starvation.[13] Thus it is *not* appropriate to move towards a deregulated food market during conflict. A variety of policy instruments may contribute to food security—the most appropriate depending on the context. Food aid can be sold commercially in the urban areas (thereby moderating prices), with the proceeds used to support the budget, including the food-support schemes discussed below. If urban food prices escalate, food rations at subsidized prices may be effective for urban populations, and relatively easy to administer.

For the rural population, a combination of ensuring adequate agricultural support (seeds, fertilizer, and so on, whose supply is often interrupted in war), employment schemes, and the provision of food in schools and clinics, can achieve wide food access without encouraging movement into camps. Unless there is an acute problem of food supply in the rural areas—which may occur when there is drought as well as war—it is better to support rural population with loans, supplies of inputs or paid work—than directly with food. This avoids the misallocation of food, logistical problems about its delivery, and disincentives to local farmers. There are occasions when war causes a complete disruption of food production—for example, when there is massive flight, or very intensive fighting, or troops purloin the food available—but this is normally confined to particular areas of the country so that if purchasing power is supported, food will be supplied commercially from other areas or neighbouring countries.

The worst type of food policy consists in emergency supplies delivered to refugee camps. This encourages people to move to the camps, leaving their normal economic activity and spreading infectious diseases; it also disrupts the normal channels of food supply, reducing farm and traders' incomes and thereby creating entitlement problems. In most circumstances, it is preferable to release food for sale via market channels so long as prices can be stabilized. Entitlements can best be assured by work programmes, with direct support only for the very young and the very old. Food deliveries via schools may also help in promoting attendance and reducing the economic incentive for children to

---

[12] See Hancock and Gowing 1949; Hurtsfield 1953; Milward 1979, for British economic policy; see US Strategic Bombing Survey 1945; Milward 1965, for German policy; and Vatter 1985, for US policy during World War II.   [13] This was the cause of the Bengal famine according to Sen (1981).

become soldiers or thieves to ensure food supplies. Food relief via camps is normally only necessary because action is delayed long after early warning signs have been observed, when the other policies discussed here would have been effective. Sometimes this policy is adopted because it fulfils other war-related policy objectives, as appears to have been the case in each of the conflicts where camps played an important role—Afghanistan, Sudan, and Mozambique. The delay may itself be manipulated by those who want certain sections of society to move into camps.

On the economic side, meso-policies should be designed to support the market entitlements of the vulnerable by employment creation and assistance for agricultural production; and in support of macro-policies aimed at reducing transaction costs and maintaining production, by allocating resources to essential investments. Such policies include the repair of energy facilities, export capacity, transport links, and food stores; reducing vulnerability where possible by constructing small-scale decentralized projects and supporting production activities with credit facilities and productive inputs. The fundamental objective should be to protect essential entitlements where people live, with the appropriate combination of policies varying according to the circumstances. This requires early action, before an acute entitlement failure develops, and implies effective, regular, and geographically comprehensive monitoring of human well-being, with speedy communication of results to relevant policy-makers. Such monitoring need not rely on official data collection alone: it can be drawn from the coordinated efforts of communities and NGOs.

Taking into account private motivations for war may modify the policies described earlier—but they should not reverse them because they are essential to reduce social and economic costs, and offer alternative mechanisms of survival. The following modifications may be appropriate: first, even stronger emphasis on employment creation, via public works, to provide alternative occupations for those who live by war; second, aiming to ensure supply and demand are such that black-market opportunities are minimized; and third, when peace negotiations eventually start, extending cash incentives and land grants for soldiers to abandon violence, and for their leaders, loan finance for civil enterprise or even government jobs.

5 International Policies to Reduce the Costs of Conflict

5.1 *Global Regulation and the Human Costs of Conflict*

The ability to wage war—and thus the human cost of conflict—can be reduced by changing the way in which the global economy is regulated. To the extent that globalization involves the creation of trans-border markets which are independent of any one nation state, and are not subject to a system of international public or private law, it creates new opportunities for financing conflict. Unregulated and largely extra-legal markets supply arms or foreign exchange to buy them and thus efforts should be made to prevent these 'parallel markets' emerging by strict regulation of illegal exports from the demand side, and of illegal imports from the supply side. Possible measures include the international regulation of international trade and investment in 'sensitive' commodities such as arms, oil, gems, and timber with a view to minimizing the destabilizing effects of these activities in conflict countries. This could be achieved within existing multilateral trade agreements and the multilateral investment arrangements currently under negotiation, by creating specific conditions for conflict countries. In addition, donors should take the lead in systematic monitoring of the activities of multinationals in countries at war, especially in relation to their use of private armies, and contracts offered, for example, in providing war finance in exchange for concessions.

The arms trade is still mainly conducted under licence from the governments of the main producer countries. Comprehensive international regulation of the arms trade should be taken more seriously than at present—particularly by OECD members with a professed commitment to international humanitarian objectives. While multinational firms cannot be prevented from stopping new investment in conflict situations and protecting existing assets, they should be dissuaded from negotiating new contracts with military leaders or from employing international military security firms, both of which are liable to fuel the conflict. In addition, care should be taken that the destabilizing effects of donors' parallel interventions in poor countries (in fields such as the interdiction of narcotics supply and transit) do not undermine the positive effect of humanitarian assistance.

Multilateral lenders (that is, the Bretton Woods institutions and the regional development banks) should suspend principal payments on their debt for countries in conflict, so as to avoid bilateral aid being diverted to maintaining multilateral debt service rather than alleviating the economic burden of conflict on vulnerable groups. In addition, the 'highly indebted poor countries' (HIPC) initiative should contain special provisions for countries in conflict, relating requirements to conflict resolution and the protection of vulnerable groups rather than to long periods of macroeconomic probity that conflict economies cannot fulfil. This might be achieved by the suspension of debt payments against commitments to maintain health and education without discrimination; or possibly payment of debt service into accounts for aid agencies to dispense.

The threatened withdrawal of official bilateral credits, longer-term development loans, and multilateral investment funds to put pressure on the governments in conflict economies should be applied with great care. If the development finance to be cancelled was properly designed in the first place—in other words it was clearly targeted at poverty reduction—then aid sanctions would affect vulnerable groups disproportionately. Even if untargeted, reduced finance is likely to contribute to further hardship.

5.2   Donor Agency Activities in Countries in Conflict

The international community veers between the judgement that the standard adjustment package should be introduced and the view that adjustment should be postponed until the war is ended. Neither view is correct. On the one hand, economies do function during war, and appropriate macro- and meso-policies are needed, designed to maintain macro-stability and sustain entitlements; on the other, conventional conditionality packages are generally not appropriate during a major conflict, as the price system functions poorly, and the inevitable wartime disequilibria can have devastating consequences for entitlements. Therefore administrative allocation of foreign exchange, intervention in food markets, and rising tax pressure should be accepted by donors even if they are inconsistent with the usual 'Bretton Woods style' adjustment package. Thus donor conditionality needs to be altered during war—as Chapter 2 shows.

A key requirement at a macrolevel is to sustain import capacity, usually under threat as a result of falling export earnings, so as to moderate the negative effects on GDP. From this perspective, the international community should avoid the use of trade and financial embargoes which are typically ineffective in reducing conflict and usually hit the vulnerable worst; maintain access to normal trade and banking channels by conflict economies in order to avoid recourse to clandestine markets; and suspend bilateral and multilateral debt payments for the duration of the conflict, the resources released thereby to be allocated to the provision of health and education services to all vulnerable groups without discrimination.

In addition to macro-requirements, wartime policy conditionality needs to relate to the two overriding wartime distributional objectives: to sustain public health entitlements and food entitlements for the *whole* population, and to correct substantial horizontal inequalities.

With regard to social costs, donors should support governments and others in their efforts to sustain public entitlements and food access. This involves: supporting revenue-raising efforts with technical assistance; the sale of food aid; devoting aid to primary health and education expenditure as well as using conditionality to help secure adequate government support for these sectors; supporting government efforts to ensure adequate entitlements to food by contributing to agricultural support and employment schemes; providing food aid, where no other sources are available, but avoiding supplying food aid to camps as far as possible. Aid policy should also contribute to the strengthening of the capacity of the state to deliver the public goods of health, education, and security to all citizens. The specific policies that are most appropriate will vary according to the situation. What is needed is first, to make the sustaining of access to food and basic health services an overriding priority; secondly, to identify where these are under threat; thirdly, to support government efforts to ensure universal access, with resources and technical support; and fifthly, where the government is either refusing or failing to ensure adequate access, to provide resources directly or through NGOs.

International actors should support (and possibly organize) the real-time *monitoring* of social and economic conditions during conflict, so that there is early warning of impending entitlement collapse. As we have seen, official monitoring efforts tend to disintegrate during war not only because of a general weakening of the administrative machinery but also for political reasons. Local NGOs, supported by foreign NGOs, are often best placed to monitor conditions, but some central coordination is needed to make this systematic and country-wide. Quick and comprehensive monitoring of changes in human and economic conditions during conflict is probably the most important contribution the NGO community could make to alleviating costs.

Explicit reorientation of development assistance towards reducing horizontal inequality, that is, inter-group and inter-regional inequality, should be incorporated into the design of humanitarian aid in response to conflict-related emergencies. Close co-ordination between donors is needed in order to ensure that the large part of imports that they finance directly does in fact bring about poverty alleviation and reasonable inter-group fairness as condition for further support.

5.3   International Actions to Prevent Conflict

At present humanitarian relief is usually mobilized *after* conflict has broken out, and thus often has to face collapsed administrative, production, and transport systems as well as large population movements leading to health and nutrition emergencies. It is widely agreed that such intervention would be better used in preventing such emergencies from occurring in the first place. Appropriate international economic measures would have to be applied to *all* vulnerable countries as it is not meaningful to attempt to fore-cast conflict situations in individual countries with adequate precision sufficiently far ahead to take corrective action. In other words, the various 'early warning' systems can only identify upcoming conflicts when conditions have deteriorated to such a point that they are almost irreversible.

There are two separate tasks here for the international community: on the one hand, to reduce the economic vulnerability of poor economies (that is, to remove them from the 'conflict-prone' group); and on the other, to ensure that those countries remaining in the vulnerable group do not slide into conflict. The first task might seem to be merely that of 'development policy' in the conventionally accepted sense of market orienta-tion, macroeconomic stability, investment in human capital, and so on. While these may well make up a sufficient strategy for the middle-income countries, it is far from clear that this is the best course for the low-income economies without sufficient assets or institutions to enter the international market directly. Moreover, in conflict-prone countries, especial attention has to be given to reducing horizontal inequalities.

International regulation of international trade and investment in 'sensitive' com-modities such as arms, oil, gems, and timber is required with a view to minimizing the destabilizing effects of these activities in vulnerable countries. A first step in this direction could be the monitoring of international trade in these commodities by UN agencies, revealing the identities of both buyers and sellers to international scrutiny.

Structural adjustment assistance to low-income vulnerable economies should focus on strengthening export capacity, before import liberalization; and the securing of long-term credit for investment before reforming the financial sector. This should stabilize incomes and jobs for vulnerable groups in the short term, while reassuring the population as a whole as to benefits of integration into the world economy in the longer term, both of which should reduce the potential for conflict. Establishment of external solvency by cancelling all outstanding official debt would support this integration, with the condition that the fiscal resources released from debt service be used only for the reduction of monetized deficits and net additions to the provision of public health and education.

The explicit reorientation of coordinated international development assistance towards reducing inter-group and inter-regional inequality, and towards strengthening the capacity of the state to deliver the public goods of health, education and security to all citizens, would imply the adoption of the reduction of conflict potential (and by extension, the reduction of vulnerability) as the key priority in development cooperation with poor countries, rather than broader notions of 'economic development' which can disguise redistribution of income and assets between social or regional groups which increase conflict potential.

6 The Problem of Policy Formation during War

We have stressed the problems of policy formation during war throughout this book. In the first place, government war aims may be to ensure the destruction of entitlements, not to protect them. Many governments give priority to military expenditure over social. Moreover, governments may have no control over events in rebel areas, and may also have very limited resources to do anything at all. Similarly, international agents—especially bilateral donors—often allow foreign policy considerations to override humanitarian ones. Multilateral development agencies are subject to similar political considerations as the major powers under whose influence they come; moreover, they are generally unwilling to modify their policies, whatever the costs, because of the dangers of 'backsliding' towards market-unfriendly policies and prefer to wait to support such economies until after the conflict. Finally, NGOs may be as concerned with their own access to resources and employment security as with the welfare of the people they deal with (see de Waal 1997).

If heavy human costs are to be avoided, it is essential that economic and social policies aimed at protecting entitlements are effective not just in government-held areas, but throughout the country including in rebel-held areas. In some contexts, the government itself may be prepared to deliver services to rebel-held areas. For example, this was the case in Sri Lanka and Mozambique—from an ideological perspective both governments were committed to reaching all the people, and also, presumably saw political benefits from so doing. In strong contrast, however, the Sudanese government systematically deprived the south of most services. Alternative mechanisms of authority may then be needed to alleviate human hardship. Rebel authorities in 'liberated zones' may have to be supported in their efforts to raise revenue in areas under their control and take responsibility for public entitlements, employment, and food policies —as they did in Tamil-held areas of Sri Lanka for many years. Renamo also made some contribution to feeding schemes in their area of control, as did some of the local commanders in Afghanistan.

The problem is made worse where the government has very limited resources, or lacks authority, or refuses to adopt policies that support popular entitlements, *and* there are no stable and powerful alternative sources of authority. Afghanistan, Sierra Leone, and Somalia all became examples of countries with governments that had inadequate control or resources during the course of the conflict. In such cases, neither the government nor rebel authorities are in a position to carry out the policies recommended here. In these cases, the burden of carrying out the policies rests heavily on foreign humanitarian organizations, working with local NGOs and communities. These are the cases where the human costs of conflict are likely to be very high although foreign and local NGOs were fairly effective, it seems, if in a somewhat uneven way, in Afghanistan. The other particularly difficult case is represented by cases such as the Sudan which refused to adopt policies to support basic entitlements, yet there was no clear alternative source of authority. The operational need to channel aid through rebel authorities or NGOs independently of the country's government requires the subordination of national sovereignty to humanitarian criteria. This may well require the de facto international recognition of belligerents on humanitarian rather than political grounds—in the way that the Red Cross has traditionally done in the wars between industrial countries.

For donors, war presents political problems which are rarely confronted in normal times, raising morally and politically complex issues. On the one hand, from the perspective of reducing economic and social costs of war, donors should channel aid and support trade through governments during conflict so long as they believe that the aid will contribute to the required economic reconstruction or social services, even if they regard the governments in question as politically undesirable. However, where the government lacks authority or the will to reach rebel areas, then donors also need to channel support to those in authority in these areas and NGOs active there—which may conflict with donors' declared intention of 'not taking sides'. Avoiding political authority altogether and using NGOs alone as an aid channel[14] is not a solution because NGO activities tend to be uneven and temporary, and it is governments (whether recognized or not) which form the only authority which can ultimately ensure security.

A further issue is whether the external support is used directly or indirectly to finance the war and, if so, whether the long-term effect on human suffering of this is not greater than the relief provided. In each of the three cases of food aid examined in Chapter 7, it is arguable that this may have been the case. In the Sudan, food and other aid clearly contributed greatly to government revenue and food for government troops, probably permitted prolongation of the war and the periodic famines and horrendous human hardship that resulted. In Mozambique, the food did reach those in need, but it allowed massive population movement into camps and contributed to war finance. In Afghanistan, support for refugees outside the country allowed a third of the population to leave, while the remainder were able to finance their fighting from external finance (much of it military).

Additional resources from outside will inevitably partly go to war finance; the issue is to what extent and this has to be decided on a case-by-case basis. If donors refuse military aid and insist that economic and social aid is directed to creating self-sustaining capacity, this may reduce the war-finance element. Keeping out altogether does not seem a viable alternative: on the one hand, the private sector, NGOs and politically motivated donors will continue to intervene where it seems in their interest to do so. On the other, there is not much evidence to substantiate the claim that stopping

---

[14] This often occurs because of the tendency of donor governments to withdraw diplomatic missions from war-torn countries and effectively delegate their representation to their NGO aid agencies.

assistance brings conflict to an end—many conflicts, for example in Sierra Leone or in Somalia—have continued without significant external resources, while trade embargoes have not generally been successful in securing political ends.

In general, moreover, the collapse of government appears to be the worst possible outcome for both economic development and human welfare. Hence external (official and NGO) policies should normally support government authority and government revenue-collection efforts. Leverage may be presented by the need for foreign finance; war conditionality would include ensuring the government gives priority to social programmes and promotes food security throughout the country.[15] Yet even this assumes 'benign' donors. Some donors come close to this position and our discussion is particularly addressed to them. Roughly, these are the small bilateral donors, and parts of the United Nations such as UNICEF who have least vested interests.[16] A major task for these 'independent' donors may well be to monitor other agencies and bilateral donors to ensure that their own policies/projects are supporting development and not war.

Human suffering during civil war is so great that in our view every effort should be made to encourage governments and donors to follow policies that moderate these costs for ordinary people, even if such policies are bound to be controversial and imperfect.

[15] Boyce (1995) suggests the use of war conditionality, somewhat on these lines.

[16] Even this is not strictly so—UNICEF has been criticized for its policy in Sudan. Inevitably active policies in a war arena lead to some co-option by the major actors— this is exemplified by the recent criticisms of UNHCR's actions in Rwanda, see the *Financial Times*, 29 July 1998; 7 August 1998.

REFERENCES

Africa Watch (1991), *Evil Days: 30 Years of War and Famine in Ethiopia*, New York; London: Human Rights Watch.

—— (1992), 'Famine and Food as Tools of War', in *Conspicuous Destruction: War, Famine and the Reform Process in Mozambique*, New York: Human Rights Watch.

African Development Bank (ADB) (various editions), *African Development Indicators*, Abidjan: World Bank.

African Rights (1994), *Rwanda: Death, Despair and Defiance*, London: African Rights.

—— (1995), *Rwanda: Death, Despair, and Defiance*, 2nd edn., London: African Rights.

—— (1997), *Food Policy and Power in Sudan: A Critique of Humanitarianism*, London: African Rights.

Ahlstron, C. (1991), *Casualties of Conflict*, Uppsala University, Sweden: Department of Peace and Conflict Research.

Albala-Bertrand, J. M. (1993), *The Political Economy of Large Natural Disasters with Special Reference to Developing Countries*, Oxford: Clarendon Press.

al-Khafaji, I. (1994), 'State Terror and the Degradation of Politics', in F. Hazelton (ed.), *Iraq Since the Gulf War: Prospects for Democracy*, London and New Jersey: Zed Books and Committee Against Repression and for Democratic Rights in Iraq.

Alnasrawi, A. (2000), 'Iraq: Economic Embargo and Predatory Rules', in E. W. Nafziger, F. Stewart, and R. Väyrynen (eds.), *The Origins of Humanitarian Emergencies: War and Displacement in Developing Countries*, Oxford: Oxford University Press.

Arana, M. (1998), 'Inappropriate Donations of Baby Milk/Food as Aid', in *Report of the International Meeting on Infant Feeding in Emergency Situations*, Split, Croatia, 22–4 (Oct.), 12–16.

Austin, J. E. and Ickis, J. C. (1986), 'Managing after the Revolutionaries Have Won', *Harvard Business Review*, May–June.

Auvinen, J. and Nafziger, E. W. (1999), 'The Sources of Humanitarian Emergencies', *Journal of Conflict Resolution*, 43/3: 267–82.

Barry, T. (1987), *Roots of Rebellion: Land and Hunger in Central America*, Boston: South End Press.

Bartov, O. (1985), *The Eastern Front 1941–45: German Troops and the Barbarisation of Warfare*, London: Macmillan.

Benoit, E. (1978), 'Growth and Defense in Developing Countries', *Economic Development and Cultural Change*, 26/2 (Jan.), 271–80.

Bhaduri, A. and Skarstein, R. (1996), 'Short-period Macroeconomic Aspects of Foreign Aid', *Cambridge Journal of Economics*, 20/2: 195–206.

Black, M. (1996), 'Children in War: Report and Summary', Reading: Children's Aid Direct.

Boyce, J. K. (1995), 'External Assistance and the Peace Process in El Salvador', *World Development*, 23/12: 2,101–16.

Boyden, J. (1993), 'Children and War: A Survey of Surveys', Stockholm Radda Barnen.

—— (1994), 'Children's Experience of Conflict-Related Emergencies', *Disasters*, 18/3 (Sept.).

Bradbury, M. (1993), 'The Somali Conflict: Prospects for Peace', Oxfam Research Paper no. 9, Oxford.

Brett, R. and McCallin, M. (1996), *Children: The Invisible Soldiers*, Stockholm: Radda Barnen.

British Agencies Afghanistan Group (BAAG) (1996a), *Exile and Return: Report on a Study on Coping Strategies among Afghan Refugees in Iran and Returnees to Afghanistan*, London: The Refugee Council.

—— (1996b), *Living in Exile: Report on a Study of Economic Coping Strategies among Afghan Refugees in Pakistan*, London: The Refugee Council.

—— (1997a), *A Population on the Move: A Study of the Socio-economic Manifestations of Displacement in relation to Kabul, Afghanistan*, London: The Refugee Council.

—— (1997b), *Return and Reconstruction: Report on a Study of Economic Coping Strategies among Farmers in Farah Province, Afghanistan*, London: The Refugee Council.

Brown, V. et al. (1987), *An Evaluation of the African Emergency Food Assistance Program in the Sudan, 1984–5*, AID Evaluation Special Study no. 50 (http://gopher.info.gov/HORN/sudan/sudan/sudan_a.html).

Browning, C. (1995), *The Path to Genocide: Essays on Launching the Final Solution*, Cambridge: Cambridge University Press.

Brownlie, I. (1990), *Public International Law*, 4th edn., Oxford: Clarendon Press.

Brück, T. (1996), 'The Economics of War', M.Phil diss., University of Oxford.

Burman, E. (1994), 'Innocents Abroad: Western Fantasies of Childhood and the Iconography of Emergencies', *Disasters*, 18/3 (Sept.).

Cairns, E. (1997), *A Safer Future: Reducing the Human Cost of War*, Oxford: Oxfam.

—— and Dawes, A. (1996), 'Children: Ethnic and Political Violence—a Commentary', *Child Development*, 67: 129–39.

Callwell, C. E. (1990) (first pub. 1896), *Small Wars: A Tactical Textbook for Imperial Soldiers*, London: Greenhill Books; Novato, Calif.: Presidio Press.

Carnegie Commission (1997), *Preventing Deadly Conflict (Final Report)*, New York: Carnegie Corporation.

Cate, F. H. (1996), 'Communications, Policy-Making, and Humanitarian Crises', in R. I. Rotberg and T. G. Weiss (eds.), *From Massacres to Genocide: The Media, Public Policy, and Humanitarian Crises*, Harrisonburg, Va.: R. R. Donnelley.

Catholic Fund for Overseas Development (CAFOD) (1996), *The Civil War in Sudan: A Threat to International Security* (http://www.cafod.org.uk/sudan.htm).

Chingono, M. (1994), 'War, Social Change and Development in Mozambique: Catastrophe or Creation of a New Society?', Ph.D. thesis, University of Cambridge.

Clay, E. J. and Singer, H. (1985), 'Food Aid and Development: Issues and Evidence, A Survey of the Literature since 1977 on the Role and Impact of Food Aid in Developing Countries', Occasional Paper 3, Rome: World Food Programme.

Cobban, A. (1965, 1957), *A History of Modern France*, i. *1715–1799*, London: Penguin.

Cohen, A. (1974), *Two-Dimensional Man, An Essay on the Anthropology of Power and Symbolism in Complex Society*, Berkeley: University of California Press.

Collier, P. (1995), 'Civil War and the Economics of the Peace Dividend', CSAE Working Paper Series, 95–8, Oxford.

—— and Gunning, J. W. (1995), 'War, Peace and Private Portfolios', *World Development*, 23: 233–41.

—— —— (1999), 'The IMF's Role in Structural Adjustment', CSAE Working Paper Series, WPS-99-18, Oxford.

Contamine, P. (1980), *War in the Middle Ages*, Cambridge, Mass. and Oxford: Blackwell.

Cornia, G. A. (1999), 'Liberalisation, Globalisation and Income Distribution', Working paper no. 157, Helsinki: WIDER.

Cornia, G. A., Jolly, R., and Stewart, F. (1987), *Adjustment with a Human Face*, Oxford: Oxford University Press.

Cranna, M. (1994) (ed.), *The True Cost of Conflict*, London: Earthscan Publications.

Cunningham, H. (1991), *The Children of the Poor: Representations of Childhood since the Seventeenth Century*, Oxford: Blackwell.

—— (1995), *Children and Childhood in Western Society since 1500*, London: Longman.

D'Souza, F. (1984), *The Threat of Famine in Afghanistan: A Report on Current Economic and Nutritional Conditions*, London: Afghan Aid Committee.

DAC (1998), *Guidelines on Conflict, Peace and Development Cooperation*, Paris: OECD Development Assistance Committee.

Davis, R. H. C. (1970, 1957), *A History of Modern Europe: From Constantine to Saint Louis*, London: Longman.

Dawes, A. (1992a), 'Moral Learning in Contexts of Political Conflict', Paper given at Conference on 'The Mental Health of Refugee Children Exposed to Violent Environments', University of Oxford, January (mimeo), p. 26.

—— (1992b), 'The Management of Children Exposed to Political Violence: The Problem of Large Numbers and Limited Resources', Psychology Department, University of Cape Town, Rondebosch, South Africa (mimeo).

de la Soudière, M. (1995), 'Case Study: Tracing and Family Reunification for Rwandan Refugee Children in Goma, Eastern Zaire 1994–95, a Diversified and Decentralised Approach', in M. Brown *et al.* (eds.), *Children Separated by War: Family Tracing and Reunification*, London: Save the Children.

de Waal, A. (1989), *Famine that Kills, Darfur, Sudan, 1984–5*, Oxford: Clarendon Press.

—— (1994), 'Dangerous Precedents? Famine Relief in Somalia 1991–93', in J. Macrae and A. Zwi (eds.), *War and Hunger: Rethinking International Responses to Complex Emergencies*, London: Zed Books.

—— (1997), *Famine Crimes: Politics and the Disaster Relief Industry in Africa*, Oxford: James Currey.

Dec, J. and Landis, L. (1998), *Children in Crisis*, London: Save the Children.

Di Addario, S. (1997), 'Estimating the Economic Costs of Conflict: An Examination of the Two-gap Estimation Model for the Case of Nicaragua', *Oxford Development Studies*, 25: 123–41.

Dixit, A. K. and Pindyck, R. S. (1994), *Investment under Uncertainty*, Princeton: Princeton University Press.

Donini, A. (1996a), 'The Policies of Mercy: UN Coordination in Afghanistan, Mozambique, and Rwanda', Occasional paper no. 22., Providence, RI: Thomas J. Watson Jr. Institute for International Studies.

—— *et al.* (1996b), *Afghanistan: Coordination in a Fragmented State*, New York: United Nations, Department of Humanitarian Affairs.

Drèze, J. and Gazdar, H. (1991), 'Hunger and Poverty in Iraq, 1991', *World Development*, 20/7: 921–46.

—— and Sen, A. (1989), *Hunger and Public Action*, Oxford: Clarendon Press and WIDER.

Duffield, M. (1992), 'Notes on the Parallel Economy, Conflict and Relief in the Post Cold War Era', in C. Petty *et al.* (eds.), *Conflict and Relief in Contemporary African Famines*, London: Save the Children Fund and the London School of Hygiene and Tropical Medicine.

—— (1993), 'Disaster Relief and Asset Transfer in the Horn', *Development and Change*, 24/1: 133–57.

—— (1994a), 'The Political Economy of Internal War: Asset Transfer, Complex Emergencies and International Aid', in J. Macrae and A. Zwi (eds.), *War and Hunger: Rethinking International Responses to Complex Emergencies*, London: Zed Books.

—— (1994b), 'Complex Emergencies and the Crisis of Developmentalism', *IDS Bulletin, Linking Relief and Development*, 25/3 (Oct.), 37–45.

—— *et al.* (1995), 'Sudan Emergency Operations Consortium: A Review', University of Birmingham Department of Public Policy (mimeo).

—— (1999), 'Globalization and War Economies: Promoting Order or the Return of History', University of Birmingham, International Development Programme (mimeo).

Economist Intelligence Unit (EIU) (1997), *Afghanistan Country Profile 1997–98*, London: EIU.

Edwards, M. (1999), *Future Positive: International Cooperation in the 21ˢᵗ Century*, London: Earthscan.

Ellis, F. (1993), *Peasant Economics*, 2nd edn, Cambridge: Cambridge University Press.

Enzensberger, H. M. (1994), *Civil War*, London: Granta.

Fairhead, J. (2000), 'The Conflict over Natural and Environmental Resources', in E. W. Nafziger, F. Stewart, and R. Väyrynen (eds.), *The Origins of Humanitarian Emergencies: War and Displacement in Developing Countries*, Oxford: Oxford University Press.

FitzGerald, E. V. K. (1987), 'The Evaluation of the Economic Costs to Nicaragua of US Aggression: 1980–84', in R. J. Spalding (ed.), *The Political Economy of Revolutionary Nicaragua*, London: Allen & Unwin, 195–216.

—— (1993), *The Macroeconomics of Development Finance*, London: Macmillan.

—— (1994), 'The Economic Dimension of the Social Development and Peace Process in Cambodia', in P. Utting (ed.), *Between Hope and Insecurity: the Social Consequences of the Cambodian Peace Process,* Geneva: UNRISD.

—— (2000), 'Global Linkages, Vulnerable Economies and the Outbreak of Conflict', in E. W. Nafziger and R. Väyrynen (eds.), *War and Destitution: The Prevention of Humanitarian Emergencies*, London: Macmillan.

Food and Agriculture Organisation (FAO) (1997a), *State of Food and Agriculture* (http://www.fao.org/WAICENT/FAOINFO/ECONOMIC/esa/sofa/sofa97e/w5800e07.htm#E37E25).

—— (1997b), *Afghanistan* (http://www.fao.org/WAICENT/FAOINFO/ECONOMIC/giews/english/alertes/srafg897.htm).

—— (1998), *Sudan Special Alert, no. 282* (http://www.fao.org/waicent/faoinfo/economic/giews/english/alertes/1998/sa282sud.htm).

—— (1990), *Food Self-sufficiency Ratios in Sudan* (http://www.fao.org/relief/sudan/sufood.htm).

—— (various years), *Food Production Yearbook*, Rome: FAO.

Foucault, M. (1988), *Power/Knowledge: Selected Interviews and Other Writings 1972–1977*, ed. and trans. C. Gordon, London: Harvester Press.

Freud, A. and Birmingham, D. (1944), *Reactions to Evacuation: War and Children*. New York: International Universities Press.

Gantzel, K. J. (1994), 'War in the Post World War II World: Empirical Trends, Theoretical Approaches and Problems on the Concept of "Ethnic War"', Paper presented to Symposium on Ethnicity and War, San Marino Centre for Interdisciplinary Research on Stress.

Gersovitz, M. (1983), 'Savings and Nutrition at Low Incomes', *Journal of Political Economy*, 91: 841–55.

Glomm, G. and Palumbo, M. G. (1993), 'Optimal Intertemporal Consumption Decisions under Threat of Starvation', *Journal of Development Economics*, 42: 271–91.

Gnocchi, M. (1991), 'Duty Travel Report to Mozambique, 8–18 September 1991', New York, WFP (mimeo).

Goodwin-Gill, G. (1994), 'Conclusions and Recommendations from the Henry Dunant Institute Study, "Child Soldiers" ', in *Child Soldiers: Report from a Seminar by Radda Barnen and the Swedish Red Cross* (Feb.), 12–13, Stockholm: Radda Barnen.

Green, R. (1981), 'Magendo in the Political Economy of Uganda: Pathology, Parallel System or Dominant Sub-mode of Production', IDS Discussion Paper, no. 164.

—— (1992), 'Conflict, Food and Famine, Reflections on Sub-Saharan Africa', in C. Petty *et al.* (eds.), *Conflict and Relief in Contemporary African Famines*, London: Save the Children Fund and London School of Hygiene and Tropical Medicine.

Greitens, E. (1994), 'Care, Protection and Reunification for Unaccompanied Children in and from Former Yugoslavia,' in *Refugee Reports*, US Committee for Refugees, Washington (July).

Gurdon, C. (1986), *Sudan in Transition: A Political Risk Analysis*, London: EIU.

Halevi, K. (2000), 'The Political Sources of Humanitarian Disasters', in E. W. Nafziger, F. Stewart and R. Väyrynen (eds.), *The Origin of Humanitarian Emergencies: War and Displacement in Developing Countries*, Oxford: Oxford University Press.

Hammarberg, T. (1994), 'What Can Non-governmental Organizations Do to Stop the Recruitment of Child Soldiers?', in *Child Soldiers: Report from a Seminar by Radda Barnen and the Swedish Red Cross, 12–13 February*, Stockholm: Radda Barnen.

Hancock, G. (1992) (first pub. 1989), *Lords of Poverty: the Power, Prestige, and Corruption of the International Aid Business*, New York: Atlantic Monthly Press.

Hancock, K. and Gowing, M. (1949), *British War Economy*, London: HMSO.

Hanlon, J. (1991), *Mozambique: Who Calls the Shots?*, Oxford: James Currey and Indiana University Press.

Hazelton, F. (1994) (ed.), *Iraq since the Gulf War: Prospects for Democracy*, London and New Jersey: Zed Books and Committee Against Repression and for Democratic Rights in Iraq.

Heller, P. (1975), 'A Model of Public Fiscal Behaviour in Developing Countries: Aid, Investment and Taxation', *American Economic Review*, 65: 313–27.

Hendrie, B. (1994), 'Relief Aid Behind the Lines: The Cross-border Operation in Tigray', in: J. Macrae and A. Zwi (eds.), *War and Hunger: Rethinking International Responses to Complex Emergencies*, London: Zed Books.

Hicks, N. (1990), 'Expenditure Reductions in Developing Countries Revisited', *Journal of International Development*, 3: 29–38.

Holt, P. M. and Daly, M. W. (1988), *A History of the Sudan: From the Coming of Islam to the Present Day*, London and New York: Longman.

House, W. J. (1989), 'Population, Poverty and Underdevelopment in Southern Sudan', *Journal of Modern African Studies*, 27/2: 201–33.

Human Rights Watch (1996), 'Children in Combat', *Human Rights Watch Children's Rights Project*, 8/1 (Jan.).

Hurrell, A. and Woods, N. (1999) (eds.), *Inequality, Globalization and World Politics*, Oxford: Oxford University Press.

Hurtsfield, J. (1953), *The Control of Raw Materials*, London: HMSO.

International Court of Justice (ICJ) (1986), *Nicaragua versus The United States of America: Judgement of The International Court of Justice*, The Hague: International Court of Justice.

IMF (1997), *World Economic Outlook, May 1997*, Washington: International Monetary Fund.

Institute of Development Studies (IDS) (1995), 'Confronting Famine in Africa', IDS Briefs, 3 April (http://www.ids.susx.ac.uk/ids/publicat/briefs/brief3.html).

International Baby Food Action Network (1996), *Crucial Aspects of Infant Feeding in Emergency and Relief Situations*, Germany: International Baby Food Action Network.

International Federation of Red Cross and Red Crescent Societies (1997), *World Disasters Report*, Oxford: Oxford University Press.

International Institute for Strategic Studies (IISS) (various editions), *The Military Balance*, London: IISS.

Interpress Service (1998), *Politics: Sudan Donates Food to Niger amid Famine in the South* (http://www.oneworld.org/ips2/may98/17_50_081.html).

Jebb, E. (1929), *Save the Child*, London: The Weardale Press.

—— (Archive Papers), Early Records of Save the Children's Work and Institutional Development, London: Save the Children Archives.

Johnson, C. (1997), *Afghanistan: A Land in Shadow*, Oxford: Oxfam.

Kaldor, M. (1999), *New and Old Wars*, London: Polity Press.

Kaplan, R. (1994), 'The Coming Anarchy', *Atlantic Monthly* (Feb.).

Karim, A. *et al.* (1996), 'Operation Lifeline Sudan: A Review', July (mimeo).

Keegan, J. (1998), *War and Our World: The Reith Lectures*, London: Hutchinson.

Keen, D. (1993), *The Kurds in Iraq: How Safe is their Haven Now?*, London: Save the Children Fund.

—— (1994*a*), 'The Functions of Famine in Southwestern Sudan: Implications for Relief', in J. Macrae and A. Zwi (eds.), *War and Hunger: Rethinking International Responses to Complex Emergencies*, London: Zed Books.

—— (1994*b*), *The Benefits of Famine: A Political Economy of Famine and Relief in Southwestern Sudan 1983–1989*, Princeton: Princeton University Press.

—— and Wilson, K. (1994), 'Engaging with Violence: A Reassessment of Relief in Wartime', in J. Macrae and A. Zwi (eds.), *War and Hunger: Rethinking International Responses to Complex Emergencies*, London: Zed Books.

Keilson, H. (1992), *Sequential Traumatization in Children*, Jerusalem: Magnes Press.

Keynes, J. M. (1939), 'Paying for the War', *The Times*, 14 and 15 Nov., repr. in D. Moggridge (1978) (ed.), *The Collected Writings of John Maynard Keynes*, xxii, London: Macmillan.

Killick, T. (1995), *The Flexible Economy: Cause and Consequences of the Adaptability of National Economies*, London: Routledge.

Kuper, J. (1997), *International Law Concerning Child Civilians in Armed Conflict*, Oxford: Clarendon Press.

Lancaster, C. (1990), 'The Horn of Africa', in A. Lake *et al.*, *After the Wars*, Washington: Overseas Development Council.

Last, M. (1994), 'Putting Children First', *Disasters*, 18/3 (Sept.).

Lee-Wright, P. (1990), *Child Slaves*, London: Earthscan.

Machel, G. (1996), *Promotion and Protection of the Rights of Children: Impact of Armed Conflict on Children*, United Nations: Internet Publication (August).

Macrae, J. and Zwi, A. (1994) (eds.), *War and Hunger: Rethinking International Responses to Complex Emergencies*, London: Zed Books.

Marsden, P. (1998), 'Afghan Episodes', *New Routes*, 3/1: 11–14.

Marwick, A., Waites, B., Elmsley, C., and Golby, J. (1990), *War and Change in Twentieth-Century Europe*, Milton Keynes: Open University.

Maxwell, S. and Singer, H. (1979), 'Food Aid to Developing Countries: A Survey' *World Development*, 7: 225–47.

McCallin, M. (1991) (ed.), *The Psychological Well-Being of Refugee Children: Research, Practice, and Policy Issues*, Ankara, Turkey: International Catholic Child Bureau.

Meagher, K. (1990), 'The Hidden Economy: Informal and Parallel Trade in Northwestern Uganda', *Review of African Political Economy*, 47 (Spring), 64–83.

Milward, A. (1979), *War, Economy and Society, 1939–45*, London: Allen & Unwin.

—— (1965), *The German Economy at War*, London: Athlone Press.

Moon, B. E. (1991), *The Political Economy of Basic Human Needs*, Ithaca and London: Cornell University Press.

Moorehead, C. (1998), *Dunant's Dream: War, Switzerland and the History of the Red Cross*, London: HarperCollins.

Mosley, P. and Weeks, J. (1993), 'Has Recovery Begun: "Africa's Adjustment in the 1980s" Revisited', *World Development*, 21: 1,583–606.

Muhumuza, R. (1995), *A Case Study on Reintegration of Demobilized Child Soldiers in Uganda*, Uganda: World Vision.

Mysliwiec, E. (1988), *Punishing the Poor: The International Isolation of Kampuchea*, Oxford: Oxfam.

Nafziger, E. W., Stewart, F., and Väyrynen, R. (2000) (eds.), *Weak States and Vulnerable Economies: Humanitarian Emergencies in Developing Countries*, Oxford: Oxford University Press.

Norman, A. V. B. (1971), *The Medieval Soldier*, New York: Barnes and Noble.

O'Sullivan, M. (1997), 'Household Entitlements during Wartime: The Experience of Sri Lanka', *Oxford Development Studies*, 25/1: 95–122.

Padley, R. and Cole, M. (1940) (eds.), *Evacuation Survey: A Report to the Fabian Society*, London: Routledge.

Peters, C. (1996), *Sudan: A Nation in the Balance*, Oxford: Oxfam.

Petty, C. *et al.* (1997) (eds.), *Keeping Children with Families in Emergencies, Meeting Report*, London: Save the Children.

Pinstrup-Andersen, P., Jaramillo, P. M., and Stewart, F. (1987), 'The Impact on Government Expenditure', in G. Cornia, R. Jolly, and F. Stewart (eds.), *Adjustment with a Human Face*, Oxford: Oxford University Press.

Ramsbotham, O. and Woodhouse, T. (1996), *Humanitarian Intervention in Contemporary Conflict: A Reconceptualization*, Cambridge: Polity Press.

Rangasami, A. (1985), 'Failure of Exchange Entitlements Theory of Famine: A Response', *Economic and Political Weekly*, 20/41 (12 and 19 Oct.), 1,747–53.

Ravallion, M. (1985), *Markets and Famines*, Oxford: Clarendon Press.

Red Cross, New Zealand (1999), 'Landmines', Red Cross New Zealand: 21 September (www.redcross.org.nz/ccue_lmv.html).

Reno, W. (2000), 'Liberia and Sierra Leone: the Competition for Patronage in Resource-Rich Economies', in E. W. Nafziger, F. Stewart, and R. Väyrynen (eds.), *The Origins of Humanitarian Emergencies: War and Displacememt in Developing Countries*, Oxford: Oxford University Press.

Ressler, E. (1992), *Evacuation of Children from Conflict Areas*, UNHCR and UNICEF.

—— Tortorici, J. M., and Marcelino, A. (1993), *Children in War: A Guide to the Provision of Services*, New York: UNICEF.

—— Boothby, N., and Steinbock, D. J. (1988), *Unaccompanied Children: Care and Protection in Wars, Natural Disasters, and Refugee Movements*, Oxford: Oxford University Press.

Richman, N. (1993), 'Annotation: Children in Situations of Political Violence', *Journal of Child Psychology and Psychiatry*, 34/8: 1,288.

—— (1996), 'Principles of Help for Children Involved in Organised Violence', Save the Children Working Paper no. 13, London: Save the Children.

—— (1998), *In the Midst of the Whirlwind: a Manual for Helping Refugee Children*, Stoke-on-Trent: Trentham Books.

Robertson, A. (1998), 'The Impact of Infant Feeding Practices: From Relief to Sustainable Development', in *Report of the International Meeting on Infant Feeding in Emergency Situations, Split, Croatia, 22–4 October*.

Roemer, M. (1989), 'The Macroeconomics of Counterpart Funds Revisited', *World Development*, 17: 795–807.

Rubin, B. (1997), 'Afghanistan: The Last Cold War Conflict, the First Post-Cold War Conflict', Paper prepared for WIDER study of Complex Human Emergencies, Helsinki: WIDER.

Russell, B. (1961), *The Principles of Social Reconstruction*, London: Unwin.

Russell, C. (1971), *The Crisis of Parliaments: English History, 1509–1660*, Oxford: Oxford University Press.

Saith, A. (1985), 'Primitive Accumulation, Agrarian Reform and Socialist Transitions: an Argument', in A. Saith (ed.), *The Agrarian Question in Socialist Transitions*, London: Cass.

Save the Children (1995), *Towards a Children's Agenda: New Challenges for Social Development*, London: Save the Children.

—— (1996), 'Promoting Psychosocial Well-Being Among Children Affected by Armed Conflict and Displacement: Principles and Approaches', Save the Children Working Paper no. 1, London.

—— (1998), *Stop Using Child Soldiers!* London: Save the Children, 8.

Save the Children Fund (SCF) (1998), *Briefing: Sudan Emergency* (http://www.oneworld.org/scf/updates/sudan.htm).

Scheff, T. J. (1994), *Bloody Revenge: Emotions, Nationalism and War*, Boulder: Westview Press.

Sen, A. K. (1981), *Poverty and Famines: An Essay on Entitlement and Deprivation*, Oxford: Clarendon Press.

—— (1991), 'Wars and Famines: On Divisions and Incentives', STICERD, Discussion Paper 33, London: LSE.

—— (1994), 'Economic Regress: Concepts and Features', *Proceedings of the World Bank Annual Conference on Development Economics*, Washington: World Bank.

Shalita, N. (1994), 'The Sudan Conflict', in M. Cranna (ed.), *The True Cost of Conflict*, London: Earthscan Publications.

Shawcross, W. (1984), *The Quality of Mercy: Cambodia, Holocaust and Modern Conscience*, London: Deutsch.

Shindo, E. (1985), 'Hunger and Weapons: The Entropy of Militarisation', in *Review of African Political Economy (War and Famine)*, 33 (August).

Sivard, R. (1991, 1996), *World Military and Social Expenditure 1991, 1996*, Washington: World Priorities.

Small, M. and Singer, J. D. (1982), *Resort to Arms: International and Civil War, 1816–1980*, Beverley Hills and London: Sage Publications.

Snow, D. M. (1993), *Distant Thunder: Third World Conflict and the New International Order*, New York: St. Martin's Press.

Stavenhagen, R. (1994), *Double Jeopardy: The Children of Ethnic Minorities*, Innocenti Occasional Papers, Child Rights Series, no. 10, Florence: UNICEF, International Child Development Center.

Stewart, F. (1985), *Basic Needs in Developing Countries*, Baltimore: Johns Hopkins University Press.

—— (1993), 'War and Underdevelopment: Can Economic Analysis Help Reduce the Costs?', *Journal of International Development*, 5/4: 357–80.

—— (1995), *Adjustment and Poverty: Options and Choices*, London: Routledge.

—— (1998), 'The Root Causes of Conflict: An Overview', in E. W. Nafziger, F. Stewart, and R. Väyryhen (eds.), *The Origins of Humanitarian Emergencies: War and Displacement in Developing Countries*, Oxford: Oxford University Press.

—— and FitzGerald, E. V. K. (eds.) (2000), *War and Underdevelopment: Country Experience*, Oxford: Oxford University Press.

Swedish Committee for Agriculture (SCA) (1988), *The Agricultural Survey of Afghanistan*, Stockholm: SIDA.

Thaxton, R. (1982), 'Mao Zedong, Red Miserables, and the Moral Economy of Peasant Rebellion in Modern China', in R. P. Weller and S. E. Guggenheim (eds.), *Power and Protest in the Countryside: Studies of Rural Unrest in Asia, Europe, and Latin America*, Durham: Duke Press Policy Studies, Duke University Press.

Theweleit, K. (1987), *Male Fantasies*, Cambridge: Polity.

Thomas, C. (1987), *In Search of Security: The Third World in International Relations*. Boulder, Colo.: Lynne Reiner.

Tilly, C. (1982), 'Routine Conflicts and Peasant Rebellions in Seventeenth-Century France', in R. P. Weller and S. E. Guggenheim (eds.), *Power and Protest in the Countryside: Studies of Rural Unrest in Asia, Europe, and Latin America*, Durham: Duke Press Policy Studies, Duke University Press.

Tuchman, B. (1989), *A Distant Mirror: The Calamitous Fourteenth Century*, London: Macmillan (first pub., A. A. Knopf, 1978).

Twose, N. and Pogrund, B. (1988), *War Wounds: Developmental Costs of Conflict in Southern Sudan*, London: The Panos Institute.

UNOCHA (1999), 'Angola: Government Mortgages Oil Sales for Military Equipment', New York: UN Office for the Coordination of Humanitarian Affairs (IRIN-SA).

UNCTAD (1997), *The Least Developed Countries Report 1997*, Geneva: UN Conference on Trade and Development.

—— (1998), *The Least Developed Countries Report 1998*, Geneva: UN Conference on Trade and Development.

—— (1999), *World Investment Report*, Geneva: UN Conference on Trade and Development.

—— (various editions), *The Least Developed Countries*, Geneva, UNCTAD.

UNDP (1993), *Afghanistan Rehabilitation Strategy: Action Plan for Immediate Rehabilitation*, i–vi, Kabul: UNDP.

—— (various editions), *Human Development Report*, New York: UNDP.

UNICEF (1990), *State of Women and Children in Cambodia*, Phnom Penh: UNICEF.

—— (various editions), *State of the World's Children*, New York: UNICEF.

United Nations (1996), 'Consolidated Inter-Agency Appeal Emergency for Afghanistan, Supplement', New York, UN Department of Humanitarian Affairs (http://www.reliefweb.int).

—— (1997), *Statistical Yearbook*, New York: United Nations.

—— (1998), '1998 Consolidated Inter-Agency Appeal Emergency for Afghanistan', New York, UN Department of Humanitarian Affairs (http://www.reliefweb.int).

United Nations Children's Fund (1990), *State of the World's Children, 1990*, Oxford: Oxford University Press.

—— (1996), *State of the World's Children, 1996*, Oxford: Oxford University Press.

United Nations Department of Humanitarian Affairs (DHA) (1998), *Finance Database Southwestern Sudan, 1983–1989*, Princeton: Princeton University Press.

United Nations High Commissioner for Refugees (1996), *Refugee Children: Guidelines on Protection and Care*, New York: United Nations High Commissioner for Refugees.

—— (1999), 'Home Page', United Nations High Commissioner for Refugees, June (www.unhcr.org).

United States Agency for International Development (USAID) (1996), *North Kordofan Food Insecurity Aggravated by Barriers to Internal Trade*, FEWS Bulletin, Washington (http://gaia.info.usaid.gov/fews/fb960724/hr960724.htm#Kordofan).

—— (1998), *Sudan-Complex Emergency, Situation Report*, no. 2 Washington (http://www.info.usaid/gov/hum_response/ofda/sud071398sr.htm).

United States (1945), *The United States Strategic Bombing Survey*, Washington: US Government Printing Office.

United States Committee for Refugees (USCR) (1998), (www. refugees.org.).

UNRISD (1995), *States of Disarray: The Social Effects of Globalization*, Geneva: UNRISD.

Utting, P. (1987), 'Domestic Supply and Food Shortages', in R. Spalding (ed.), *The Political Economy of Revolutionary Nicaragua*, London: Allen & Unwin.

Van Bruinessen, M. (1992), *Agha, Shaikh and State: The Social and Political Structures of Kurdistan*, London: Zed Books.

Vatter, H. G. (1985), *The US Economy in World War Two*, New York: Columbia University Press.

Väyrynen, R. (1996), 'The Age of Humanitarian Emergencies', WIDER Research for Action 25, Helsinki: WIDER.

Vincent, S. (1994), 'The Mozambique Conflict', in M. Cranna (ed.), *The True Cost of Conflict*, London: Earthscan Publications.

Vines, A. (1992), *Hunger that Kills: Food Security and the Mozambique Peace Process*, University of York: Centre for South African Studies Research Seminar Series, 1991–2.

Wallensteen, P. and Sollenberg, M. (1995), 'After the Cold War: Emerging Patterns of Armed Conflict 1989–1994', *Journal of Peace Research*, 32: 345–60.

—— —— (1996), 'The End of International War? Armed Conflict 1989–1995', *Journal of Peace Research*, 33: 353–70.

War Child Landmine Project (1999), *Social Cost of Landmines in Bosnia, Afghanistan, Cambodia and Mozambique* (http://www.warchild.org/projects/mines.html).

War Child Landmine Project (1999), 'The Landmine Project', War Child, June (www.warchild.org/projects/mines.html).

Waterhouse, R. (1996), *Mozambique: Rising from the Ashes*, Oxford: Oxfam.

Weiss, T. G. and Collins, C. (1996), *Humanitarian Challenges and Intervention: World Politics and the Dilemmas of Help*, Boulder, Colo.: Westview.

White, H. (1992), 'The Macroeconomics of Aid: A Critical Survey', *Journal of Development Studies*, 28: 163–240.

Willets, P. (1996), *The Conscience of the World: The Influence of NGOs in the UN System*, London: Hurst.

World Bank (various editions), *World Development Report*, Washington: World Bank.

—— (1998), *Poverty Reduction and the World Bank, Progress in Fiscal 1996 and 1997*, Washington: World Bank.

—— (1997, 1999), *World Development Indicators*, Washington: World Bank.

World Food Programme (1996), *Tackling Hunger in a World Full of Food: Tasks Ahead for Food Aid* (http://www.wfp.org/info/POLICY/HUNGER).

—— (1998), *Emergency Food Assistance to War and Drought Affected Populations* (http://www.wfp.org/op/countries/sudan/emop 582601. Htm).

World Vision (1996), 'The Effects of Armed Conflict on Girls: A Discussion Paper for the UN Study on the Impact of Armed Conflict on Children', World Vision International Staff Working Paper, no. 23, July.

Wuyts, M. (1991), 'Mozambique: Economic Management and Adjustment Policies', in D. Ghai (ed.), *The IMF and the South: The Social Impact of Crisis and Adjustment*, London: Zed Books, 209–35.

INDEX

entitlements (*cont.*):
  in Sri Lanka   117, 119
  see also market entitlements; public entitlements
Enzensberger, Hans Magnus   42
Eritrea   2, 49, 56
Ethiopia   2, 4, 49
  deaths from war in   74
  food aid   195
  GDP loss due to war in   96, 97
  government expenditure in   84, 85, 86, 87, 88, 89
  human costs of war in   90, 91, 94
  infant mortality rates in   92, 98, 232
  macroeconomic effects of war in   80, 81, 82
Europe
  deaths from war in   69, 70, 71, 72
  macroeconomic effects of war in   76, 77
evacuation of children   162–4
exports
  arms trade   65, 211, 214, 218, 240
  as a capacity to import   132
  effects of war on   10, 11, 18, 22, 23, 25, 32, 76, 79, 81, 101, 102, 230
  and the global economy   209, 212–13, 223
  growth   141
  Sri Lanka   118, 142
external debt *see* foreign debt
extra-legal entitlements   6, 7, 10, 46–7

Fairhead, J.   215
Faisil Islamic Bank (FIB)   174
family life, and violence   60
family support systems   147
famine
  Bengal famine (1940s)   14
  and the nature of war   40, 43
  in Sudan   122, 146, 169, 171–4, 232
FIB (Faisil Islamic Bank)   174
firms
  multinational   208–10, 214, 222
  responses to conflict conditions   26–8, 37, 38
FitzGerald, E.V.K.   2, 12, 27, 112, 207, 218, 224
'flexible' economies in wartime   9
food aid   19, 32, 168–203, 234, 244
  in camps   175–6, 181, 183, 197–8, 202, 235, 239
  DEVFAID (development-related food aid)   168, 200, 201
  and emergency relief   168
  sale of   237
  see also CONFAID (conflict-related food aid)
food policies   238–9
food prices
  controls on   31
  effects of war on   14, 56
food production
  Afghanistan   140, 187–9
  effects of conflict on   76, 78, 79, 101, 102

Mozambique   109, 140, 179–81
  per capita   140
  Sudan   140, 169–71
food rationing   18, 28–9, 31, 34, 90, 238
food supplies, effects of war on   26
foreign aid *see* international credit/aid
foreign debt   134, 211, 215–16, 224
  Afghanistan   106
  effects of war on   80, 81, 102, 142
  renegotiation of   212, 221
foreign exchange, and the war economy   25, 26, 27–8, 36, 217
foreign trade *see* trade
'foreign wars', benefit of   64–5
Foucault, Michel   44
France
  banditry in   61
  French Revolution and the Vendée revolt (1793)   53
  and World War I   56
Freud, Anna   164

Gantzel, K. J.   39
Gazdar, H.   45–6, 90
GDP (gross domestic product)
  and food aid
    in Mozambique   179, 185
    in Sudan   178
  government expenditure as a percentage of   86, 142
  government revenue as a share of   231, 237
  losses due to war   94, 95–8, 101–2, 102–3, 144
    Afghanistan   106
    Uganda   124
  per capita, effects of war on   12, 18, 73, 75–6, 79, 89, 125–6, 231
  tax revenue as percentage of   127, 142, 237
gender
  impact of war by   47, 232–4
  see also women
Geneva Convention   50–1
Geneva, Declaration of   159–60
Germany, and World War II   46, 54–5
Gersovitz, M.   28
global economy   204–24
  and conditional development assistance   218–19
  and economic sanctions   217–18
  impact on the conflict process   212–17
  and international policies to reduce the costs of conflict   239–43
  private sector   208–10
  public sector   210–12
  regulatory actions in the   221–2
Gnocchi, M.   184
GNP (gross national product)
  per capita   88
  share of government expenditure in   88